Writings of
Thomas E. Peck

Volume 2

Writings of
Thomas E. Peck

Selected and Arranged
by
T. C. Johnson

Volume 2

THE BANNER OF TRUTH TRUST

THE BANNER OF TRUTH TRUST
3 Murrayfield Road, Edinburgh EH12 6EL
P. O. Box 621, Carlisle, Pennsylvania 17013, USA

*

First published by the Presbyterian Committee of Publication, Richmond, Virginia, 1895–7, as *Miscellanies of Rev. Thomas E. Peck*

First Banner of Truth Edition 1999
ISBN 0 85151 770 6 for the set
of three volumes

Volume 2: 0 85151 768 4

*

Printed and bound
in Great Britain by
Redwood Books,
Trowbridge,
Wiltshire

CONTENTS.

MISCELLANIES

OF THE LATE

THOMAS E. PECK, D. D., LL. D.

PROBATION AFTER DEATH.[1]

"MANKIND believe in hell." It is not a doctrine purely of revelation that the wicked are punished in another world. The belief in such a doom is as universal as the belief in God and in the immortality of the soul. Philosophers who aspire to reach the summits of intelligence, and poets who aspire to sound the depths of the human soul, alike recognize the fearful reality; and the power of both lies in their ability to give expression to what all men think and feel. The philosopher and the poet, as has been well said, are more men than other men; they see more clearly and feel more profoundly than other men; they have greater power of expression; and hence homage is done to them as the hierophants of those mysteries which are enshrined in the recesses of every human soul. This explains the difference, so eloquently expounded by De Quincey, in duration and destiny between what he calls the literature of mere knowledge and the literature of power. "It is the grandeur of all truth which *can* occupy a very high place in human interests that it is never absolutely novel to the meanest of minds; it exists eternally by way of germ or latent principle in the lowest as in the highest, needing to be developed, but never to be planted. . . . It is in relation to the great *moral* capacities of men that the literature of power, as contra-distin-

[1] This article was published first in the *Presbyterian Quarterly*, October, 1889.—Ed.

guished from that of knowledge, lives and has its field of action." The "moral capacities" of mankind are the same in all and the same from age to age, like the appetites of hunger and thirst in the human body; and the literature which deals with them, if it springs from genius, is destined to be permanent. The *Principia* of Newton has already been antiquated: *Macbeth* is "triumphant forever, as long as the languages exist in which it speaks or can be taught to speak." The great subject of Macbeth is penal retribution for sin, and its tremendous power lies in the human conscience, which responds to its awful representations. Shakspere was no theologian, but who can read this tragedy and not feel that there is a hell, or, if there is not, that there ought to be? Plato, Homer, Virgil, Dante, Shakspere, Milton, when they present this dreadful topic, only voice the sentiments of the human soul. Mankind believe in hell.

But they do not believe in it as they do in some other things, because it is their pleasure to do so, because the wish is father to the thought. Not at all; they are compelled to believe in it by the operation of the same power which compels them to believe in God, the power of conscience. The fool who says in his heart "no God," of course will also say "no hell." But as God will not allow his being to be disowned, so he will not allow his moral government, his righteous purpose to punish sin, to be disowned. Either of these convictions may be resisted and even suppressed for a time, but only for a time. Men may deny that there is a God, or that they have souls, or that there is a world external to themselves. The zeal and persistency with which they endeavor to prove that there is no hell is no argument against the reality of it; rather the contrary. "What man," says Dr. Shedd, "would seriously construct an argument to demonstrate that there is no such being as Jupiter Ammon, or such an animal as the centaur? The very denial of endless retribution evinces by its spasmodic eagerness and effort to disprove the tenet, the firmness with which it is entrenched in man's moral constitution."

There are many methods of assault upon the doctrine. One is to admit that the Bible teaches it clearly, and then to make this fact a proof against the Bible's inspiration and authority, the doctrine itself being too absurd and monstrous to be believed. Another is to admit the inspiration and authority of the Bible, and upon this ground to argue that it cannot teach the doctrine, and that the places which seem to teach it must receive some other interpretation. These two methods are the same in principle. In both the reason of man is made the judge as to what a revelation from God ought to contain. A third method, near akin to the last, if it can be called a method, feeling rather than logic being judge, is simply to take one's stand on the *goodness* of God, and say it cannot be. This seems to have been John Foster's position, and was probably Origen's. Thousands have passed through just such a struggle as Adolphe Monod describes in his own case, though not always with the same result. "There was a time," says he, "when I was unwilling to believe in endless punishment either for any man or even for the devil; and when I wrote these foolish words, 'If one single creature of God must be eternally unhappy there is no happiness possible for me.' But as I believed at the same time that the Bible was the word of God, and that consequently I could not in peace reject the endlessness of punishment so long as I found it taught in the Bible, I endeavored to persuade myself that it was not taught there. For this purpose I read, I meditated, I commented—attenuating the places which seemed to favor the doctrine—hunting up, exaggerating, forcing those which I hoped to find contrary to it. I did all I could not to find endless punishment in God's word, but I did not succeed. I was convinced by the irresistible evidence of the testimony of the Scriptures. . . . I yielded, I bowed my head, I put my hand on my mouth; I believed in endless punishment with a conviction all the more profound that I had long fought against it."

These good men knew, of course, that there was an incalculable amount of suffering in this world, and not only suffering, but *penal* suffering. They believed that all this suffering was consistent with God's *infinite* goodness; but they could not believe that such goodness could consist with *endless* suffering. Hence, perhaps, the origin of the notion of a probation after death. Such a notion was a sort of flanking of a doctrine which could not be successfully attacked in front. There can be little doubt that this notion is practically Universalism. It is taken for granted that every man who dies in his sins will avail himself of his chance in the next world, and so no man's punishment will be endless, but all will be saved. The fear of future punishment will practically cease to operate. "The spirit of man," says Monod, "being immortal, is so made that that which must have an end cannot appear to him long. A child who had heard it said that the abode of the wicked in hell should be only a thousand years, being threatened for some bad conduct with hell, answered, 'What care I for hell? I shall stay there only a thousand years.' This word was profound as it was artless, and by the mouth of that little child spoke the whole human race." A very striking confirmation of this is seen in the effect of the pagan and papal doctrine of purgatory. Purgatory, according to the Roman doctors, is not a place of *discipline*, but of true and proper *punishment*, to all intents and purposes a temporary hell. Yet how many thousands and millions prefer the prospect of it to the pains and self-denials of a life of repentance and holiness here!

The notion of a probation after death is, therefore, virtually Universalism; and it is the most dangerous form of that deadly heresy, for the reasons already suggested. It is more dangerous because it is more respectable; more reverent towards God, because it recognizes his moral character and his moral government, and "concedes the force of the biblical and rational arguments respecting the guilt of sin and its intrinsic desert of everlasting punishment"; and more reverent towards man, because it respects and does not outrage the judgments and instincts of his moral constitution. It is further respectable in that it concedes that there is no other way of salvation than through the work of Jesus Christ and the work of the Holy Ghost. At any point in the history of the sinner, whether in this world or the next, if he obtains salvation it must be through regeneration, faith, and repentance. It is true that some who hold to probation after death, perhaps the majority of those who so hold, would object to the statement just made, of their concessions to "orthodoxy." Their idea of probation *here* is such as to imply a "self-determining power of the will," or at least a synergistic operation of the will in turning to God; and they have the same idea of probation after death. One great inducement to accept the theory of a *post-mortem* probation is the fact that the evidence then will be too overwhelming to be resisted, and that multitudes whose will was proof against all the appeals of the law or the gospel here, will break down under the light of eternity. They are of the same opinion with Dives in the "parable," that the main reason why men do not repent is that they have not evidence enough, or evidence of the right kind.

While it is the purpose of this essay to discuss the question of fact whether there is a probation after death, in the sense simply of the possibility of a change from a state of sin to a state of salvation, without reference to the *rationale* of that change, yet it may not be amiss to say a few words upon the Pelagian or semi-Pelagian view of the subject.

According to this view, the change from a state of sin to a state of salvation is brought about by "moral suasion." Man was not killed by the fall in Adam. The Pelagian says he was not even hurt; the Low Arminian that he was stunned and seriously hurt; the High Arminian that he was as good as dead, as Eutychus was after he had fallen from the third story; but that, in consequence of the embrace of God's love, his life was still in him, was not allowed to become extinct, or was immediately restored, as in the case of Eutychus in the embrace of Paul. No direct, quickening agency of the Spirit, therefore, is necessary to make him alive. He is to be persuaded by argument, expostulation, remonstrance, entreaty, to stir his torpid, slumbering life into activity and to decide for God. To help him in doing this, the most awful pictures of hell and the judgment are presented to him. If he remains undecided in this life, then we may hope that he may be persuaded by the vision and experience of the reality after death.

Now all this speculation falls to the ground at once, if it be true, as the Scriptures teach, that the sinner is "dead in trespasses and sins," that he needs to be "quickened," "raised from the dead," "new created" by him "who quickeneth the dead, and calleth the things that are not, as though they were." The sinner in this world *will* not turn to God; *will* not come to the Saviour that he may have life. The very *gravamen* of the difficulty is in his *will;* he is incurably averse to God, hates God, and no power of logic or eloquence can change his mind. A clearer revelation of God is only a clearer revelation of what the sinner hates; and if there is to be a clearer revelation of God in the other world, what other effect can it have than to drive the sinner further off from God? Besides, sin is prevented here from developing itself fully by the kindly restraints of domestic and social life, by public opinion and by human law. There is no reason to believe that those restraints will continue to exist in the future world. The dead soul is, as it were, embalmed in this world with the sweet spices of charity and compassion; in the other world the natural process of putrefaction will take its course. These considerations harmonize exactly with the "parable" of the Rich Man and Lazarus. Dives makes no prayer for repentance for himself. He does not pray even for deliverance from his torments, but only for a slight alleviation of them. He does not pray for repentance to be *given* to his brethren. He only thinks of repentance in an external way, as a condition of escaping torment, not as a hearty turning away from sin unto God. Moreover, he expresses his belief that repentance would be the result of the going to them of one from the dead. But as he himself already has the evidence which he desires for them, and yet does not repent, why should he think that *they* would repent? The only reason is that he knows them to be still in a state of probation and his own probation to be ended. There is a possibility of repentance for them, as they are still living, but there is none for him, even if he desired it, and of such desire there is no trace.

Even on the Pelagian and Arminian view, the probability that a man who has all his life resisted the commands and invitations of the gospel will in the other world be more inclined to faith and repentance is exceedingly small. Do not these men know, and do they not teach sinners, that the longer the offers of salvation are resisted the less likely it is that they will ever be accepted? Why, then, annul the force of their exhortations to speedy, to immediate repentance, by teaching that repentance may be postponed to a time even beyond death, and yet be obtained at last?

Let us return now to the question of fact. Is there any proof of a probation after death? It is conceded that the proofs must be obtained from the Scriptures, if there are any proofs at all.

One of the passages—it may be said the fundamental passage, the *locus classicus*—is that of 1 Peter iii. 18–20. This passage is relied on even by such a man as Professor Godet to prove that "the gospel shall be preached to every human soul before the judgment, either in this life or in the next."[1]

[1] See his Commentary on Romans ii. 7, 8, Funk & Wagnall's edition, p. 119, with Dr. Talbot W. Chambers' very clear and able criticism in the Appendix, pp. 517 ff.

On this passage it may be remarked, first, that the Bible proof of a probation after death must be very scant, when the advocates of that view are compelled to appeal to it for support. Everybody knows that it is one of the most obscure places in the New Testament, and that the ablest interpreters are divided in their views about it. In regard particularly to the act or work of Christ there described interpreters differ. *When* was that work done? In the days of Noah, or in the interval between Christ's death and his resurrection? *What* was the work? Agreed that it was a preaching or making a proclamation; agreed, also, that it was a proclamation concerning the work of redemption which he had just achieved upon the cross, the question still remains, For what purpose was the proclamation made? For the purpose of affording to the "spirits in prison" another opportunity of salvation, or for the purpose merely of announcing and celebrating in that dark abode the victory of the Redeemer over the powers of darkness? It is contended by Professor Godet, and those who agree with him, that the time was the interval between the death and the resurrection of Christ, and that the purpose of the proclamation was to offer salvation. It is contended by others that the time was the time of Noah, and the proclamation was the offer of salvation. It is contended by others still, as by Dr. Chambers, that the time was the interval between Christ's death and his resurrection; but that the proclamation was *not* the offer of salvation, or at least that such a purpose is not expressed in the passage, is not necessarily implied in the fact of preaching, and is forbidden by the tenor of Bible teaching. The writer of this paper thinks that the second of the views just mentioned harmonizes best with the scope of the passage and with the reference to Noah and the antediluvian generation, and prefers it for these reasons, while acknowledging the grammatical objections to it. But it is not necessary to arbitrate among these different views. The point here made is that such a passage is too precarious a support for such a notion as that of probation after death, especially as that notion is conceded to be not in harmony with the faith of the church or with the seeming tenor of Bible teaching.[1]

Dr. Chambers, in the criticism above referred to, has another thought of much weight. It is this: "Even admitting (which is not admitted) that the words do mean or may mean that the Lord proclaimed a gospel to the spirits in prison, this proves nothing in respect to the case of others before or since the time of the proclamation in question, for the simple reason that there the circumstances were peculiar and extraordinary; and what is done on momentous occasions is no precedent for ordinary days. Because the conduits run wine instead of water when the king receives his crown, we are not to expect that they will do the same when the coronation is over."[2]

Another text is 1 Peter iv. 6, upon which it is needless to dwell. If it proves a probation after death, it proves also the salvation of *all* the dead; and the boldest Universalism is the result. The apostle evidently refers to what took place in the lifetime of the dead. The gospel was preached to them when they were living, so that they might indeed be condemned by their fellows in "the fiery trial" (verse 12); "but nevertheless their spirits enjoyed immortal life with God" (see Chambers, as above).

Once more, the advocates of a *post-mortem* probation urge the passage in Matt. xii. 32, which seems to imply that some sins may be forgiven in the world to come. Dr. Dorner goes

---

[1] Let it be noted that Professor Godet, and others who contend for a probation after death only for those who never had the offer of salvation in this life, have no right to this passage in support of their view. The antediluvian sinners *had* the offer of salvation. Noah was a preacher of righteousness to them (2 Peter ii. 5), and the Spirit of grace strove with them (Genesis vi. 3) while the ark was preparing.

[2] Page 520.

so far as to say[1] that the sin against the Holy Ghost is "the only sin which is not forgiven either in this world or in the next." All other sins are punishable, but this only will be punished. But of this more in the sequel. Meantime, the point here is that the form of the expression implies that there are sins which if not forgiven in this world may be in the next. The answer is, as Dr. Chambers remarks, that this is turning rhetoric into logic. The thirty-second verse is merely a rhetorical repetition of the thirty-first. Our Lord was considering not the *time* of forgiveness, but the question whether there was forgiveness at all in the case of a certain sin. In order to make the negation as vivid as possible, and to show that the sin he is speaking of shall never be forgiven, he combines the two periods, this world and the world to come. The same meaning is expressed in the parallel passage in Mark iii. 29: "Whosoever shall blaspheme against the Holy Ghost hath never forgiveness, but is guilty of an eternal sin" (thus in the Revised Version).

So much for the scriptural arguments in favor of probation after death. Whatever force they might seem to have, considered by themselves, and this has been shown to be very small, entirely vanishes in the presence of the scriptural arguments on the other side. Let us look at them:

First, The Bible is profoundly silent about any "intermediate place" in which the people dwell who are still, after death, in a state of probation. It speaks of a Sheol or Hades in the sense of the grave or in the sense of the unseen world, or of the state of the dead; but in this sense *all* the dead are there. It speaks of a Hades in the sense of a place of torment, not distinguishable in effect from Gehenna; but this would not be a proper place for the confinement of those who are not yet condemned, and who *may* be justified. It speaks of a "Gehenna of fire," but this is not for those who are still

---

[1] *Christian Doctrine*, § 83 c, p. 72, of Vol. III., T. & T. Clark's Translation, Edinburgh, 1882.

on trial, but for those who are finally and irrevocably condemned. It speaks of heaven, but this is the residence of those whose probation is past, and who have entered into eternal life. Papists are sagacious enough to find some traces of a purgatory there; but if there were such a place, it would be, according to those heretics, the abode of *pious* people who have died in the communion of the church, and who are to pay the remnant of the penalty left unpaid by the Redeemer. It would be no place for the wicked, whose final destiny is still undecided. Some find another place, called, they say, a "ward" or "place of safe-keeping," as Bishop Horsley renders the word for "prison" in 1 Peter iii. 19; but this is a place almost the same as the *limbus* of the Papists, a place in which *pious* people are kept, without suffering, in expectation of their future blessedness. It has been shown, however, that this view has no foundation in that text; but even if there were such a place, it would not be suitable for the wicked on probation. There is, then, no place provided for such a class in the next world, and the inference is natural, if not inevitable, that there is no such class.

Again, in that awful passage, the story of the rich man and Lazarus, which was first spoken by our Lord and then recorded for the purpose of revealing something concerning the state of the dead, and which contains the clearest and fullest view of the fate of the wicked, there are only two places mentioned. It matters not whether or not Abraham's bosom be identified with heaven and Hades with Gehenna, the point is that there are only two places, one a place of "comfort" and the other a place of "torment." It is to be noted, also, that the entrance into either place follows immediately upon the article of death, and that there is a great gulf fixed between them, so that there can be no passing from one to the other. Further, let it be remembered, what has already been noted, that the rich man seeks no repentance for himself, evidently neither expects nor desires it, and asks for no deliverance from his doom. The conclusion from this passage against a probation after death is so clear and certain that it cannot possibly be evaded, except by a method of interpretation which would reduce the Bible, as a rule of faith, to an utter nullity.

In other passages death is spoken of as the event which fixes and determines the destiny of the wicked. For example, Prov. xiv. 32: "The wicked is driven away in his wickedness; but the righteous hath hope in his death." This implies that the wicked hath no hope in his death. Prov. xi. 7: "When a wicked man dieth, his expectations shall perish." Heb. ix. 27: "It is appointed unto men once to die, but after this judgment," or, as the revision has it, "cometh judgment." The word "judgment" is without the article, and the reference is rather to the sentence which immediately follows death than to "the day of judgment." The text teaches that prior to death man's destiny is not decided, he being not yet sentenced; but after death his destiny is settled. When he dies, the private judgment, that is, the immediate personal consciousness either of penitence or impenitence, occurs. . . . The article of death is an event in human existence which strips off all disguises, and shows the person what he really is in moral character. He "knows as he is known," and in this flashing light passes a sentence upon himself that is accurate[1]. In 2 Cor. v. 10, the reference is clear to the final or general judgment, and the teaching is that the sentence which shall be then received will be determined by what was done *in the body*, implying that when the soul left the body the account was closed. If the probation extended beyond the residence in the body, the apostle could not have used this form of speech. Again, our Saviour (Jno. viii.) says more than once to the Pharisees, "If ye believe not that I am he, ye shall die in your sins." To die in their sins can mean nothing else than to die in the state of condemnation

[1] Shedd's *Theology*, II., p. 694.

and pollution in which they had been living in consequence of their rejection of their Messiah and Redeemer; and if the mention of their death in such a connection does not signify the decisive crisis beyond which there is no hope of salvation, it is impossible to devise a rational meaning for it. If our Saviour knew that his hearers would have after death another and a better opportunity to weigh his claims, it would have been more natural to say, "If ye believe not now that I am he, ye will no doubt (or probably) believe when death shall have given you more evidence." At all events, if his hearers had known or believed that their probation would be continued beyond death, they would have laughed at his threatening as a mere *brutum fulmen*. And the same would have been the consequence of all the threatenings of the New Testament, of John the Baptist, of his Master, Christ, and of the apostles[1].

As to Christ, who says more about the destiny of the wicked in the next world than all of his apostles put together, as we might have anticipated he would from his superior compassion, we must either suppose him to have been ignorant of the fact that there was probation after death, or, if he knew the fact, that he deliberately, for his own private ends, used language which implied the contrary, as some preachers who have turned out to be arrant hypocrites and knaves were accustomed to preach the hell and damnation in which they did not themselves believe in order to gratify their lust of gold and of power. But what Christian does not recoil with horror from either supposition as to his divine and immaculate Redeemer.

There are scores of other places in Scripture which would be emptied of their force and meaning by the supposition of a probation after death. There is no space in the limits assigned to this essay for full citations. Some of them may

[1] See this point well stated and illustrated by Dr. Chambers in the criticism on Godet, above quoted.

be found in Gen. vi. 3; Ps. xcix. 12; Prov. i. 24, 28; Eccl. ix. 10; Luke xiii. 24, 25; Matt. xxiv. 42, 50; 2 Cor. vi. 2; Heb. iii. 7; x. 26; Rev. xxii. 11, 12[1].

The discussion thus far has been one concerning probation after death, without limitation as to any particular class of sinners dying in impenitency. But there are many who are willing to concede that the argument is a good and valid one against a general *post-mortem* probation, and yet hold that there are rational and ethical grounds for believing that a probation will be given to all human beings who have not had the offer of salvation made to them in this life. This is just now the most popular and plausible form in which the doctrine is proposed and defended. It is the form in which it is advocated by the professors of the "New Theology" in New England, and, what is of much greater consequence, by Prof. Dorner and by Julius Müller. It is reported in the public prints that Dorner's *Theology* has been adopted as a text-book in one of the theological schools of Presbyterian Scotland instead of the system of Dr. Chas. Hodge (which is very like substituting darkness for light, as Dr. Dorner was, in point of style, one of the obscurest writers on this planet, and Dr. Hodge was one of the clearest); and if this is the fact, it furnishes a clew to the kind of changes which the would-be revisers of the Westminster Confession in that country propose to make. Dr. Müller is a sounder thinker on the whole subject of sin than Dr. Dorner, which makes it the more to be deplored that he should give his countenance to so grave an error. The soteriology of both these learned men is inconsistent, in this particular, with their hamartialogy, as Dr. Shedd says; but the inconsistency is more glaring in the case of Müller, on account of his profounder treatment of the subject of sin.

The fundamental position of Dorner is that, beside the generic character of sinner which belongs to every man by

[1] See Shedd, *Dogmatic Theology*, II., pp. 698 ff.

virtue of his connection with Adam, or, in other words, beside original sin and the actual transgressions which flow from it, something more is necessary to make him damnable, worthy of being damned. "The good must be placed before his eyes, not merely as the voice of conscience or as 'the letter,' but in its most lucid and attractive form, as personal love, in order that decision for or against truth may have decisive significance. This for the condition on the objective side. On the subjective side there must be full freedom of decision from the innermost personality. For good and definitive decision the possibility of evil must still stand open, otherwise it would not be free, so that the knowledge of good cannot yet be absolutely determining for the same. On the other hand, evil decision can only make ripe for the final judgment if it is in nowise naturally necessitated—for example, by generic sin—but if the subject is somehow put into the position to freely strike the decision of himself, and therefore himself to incur the guilt of decided rejection of personal love, which is only possible by means of self-incurred infatuation and falsehood. Now this subjective and objective possibility of free decision is given by God through Christianity as the absolute religion, and therefore Christianity is also the religion of freedom. The manifestation of Christ urges, therefore, irresistibly to decision for or against him, and at the same time, in spite of original sin, makes free decision possible[1]."

The sum of all this is, that "no one will be damned merely on account of the common sin and guilt; but every one is definitely brought to guilty personal decision only through the gospel." No man can be considered a full person or fully a free agent until he is confronted with Christ (a new version, by the way, of Christ's words, "the Son shall make you free"). It is only then that the sin against the Holy Ghost becomes possible; and this sin, says Dorner, is "the

[1] *Theology*, III., pp. 69 ff. of T. & T. Clark's Translation.

only sin that is not forgiven either in this world or in the next." "This is an entirely new position," says Dr. Shedd[1], "not to be found in the past history of eschatology, and invented apparently to furnish a basis for the doctrine of a future offer of redemption." No such absurdity is found in Müller. He founds his hope on Matt. xii. 32. He denies and combats Dorner's position that sin against the gospel is the only damning sin.[2]

Now, if it be true, as Dorner affirms, that prior to Christ, "the incarnate personal love," there was no precise and decided personal character, whether good or evil, no freedom in such a sense as to imply damnable guilt, no "definitive unbelief," and no definitive faith; if this be true, then the larger portion of the Bible is a mass of nonsense and falsehood. One feels the same kind of difficulty in arguing with a man who can hold such a view as he would feel (to borrow an illustration from Henry Rogers) in arguing with an inhabitant of the planet Saturn, where, according to Voltaire's *Micromegas*, a crime of enormous turpitude inspires absolute envy, and the three angles of a triangle are *not* equal to two right angles. One feels that he has no common ground on which he stands with Dr. Dorner, no principles accepted on both sides by which any question can be decided. The only possible method of argument is to appeal from Dorner drunk to Dorner sober, to show that he contradicts and stultifies himself. One of the best discussions in his *Theology* is that on the necessity of Christ's satisfaction to divine justice. He holds that this satisfaction was necessary for the pardon of any man's sins, Jew or Gentile; yet he holds that the only thing which exposes a man to the damnation of hell is the fact that such a satisfaction has been rendered! The penalty would never have been inflicted if Christ had not satisfied God for it When we are reading Dorner on "Christ's Priestly Office," we cannot help wondering whether

[1] *Theology*, II., p. 701.

[2] See Shedd, *ut supra*.

it is the same man who wrote the section on "Personal Free Decision" in the same volume. Here (on the Priestly Office, III., p. 425) he defines the "wrath of God" (Rom. i. 18) to be his holy *justice, which punishes moral evil*, and then adds: "This justice is not merely directed against the sin of definitive unbelief (the sin against the Holy Ghost), as Ritschl thinks, as if all antecedent guilt and sin needed no expiation. God's wrath is directed against *all* iniquity." (Rom. i. 18.) He also quotes John iii. 36, and says: "The wrath of God abides on sinners even before they despise the gospel." Here he either takes back the pernicious nonsense he had written on "Personal Free Decision," or he must mean that the wrath of God abides upon the sinner because salvation is intended for him and God foresees that he will despise it.

The heathen, according to the great theologian of Germany, are in no danger of eternal death unless they should chance to hear the gospel, and God is obliged to give them the gospel either in this world or in the next. So thought not David: "The wicked shall be turned into Sheol, and all the nations that forget God." (Psa. ix. 17.) So thought not Jeremiah: "Pour out thy fury upon the heathen that know thee not, and upon the families that call not on thy name." (Jer. x. 25.) So thought not Paul: "They that have sinned without law, shall perish without law" (Rom. ii. 12); and read Rom. i. 18 32, an appalling description of those who, according to Dr. Dorner, have not attained to their majority or full personal freedom, people who have discourse of reason and yet insult their Creator by likening him to corruptible man, to birds and four-footed beasts, and creeping things. Dr. Dorner says they are not worthy of death, that is (as he defines death, III., p. 425), the "destruction of the soul, misery, all evil." Paul says: "Who knowing the judgment of God, that they which commit such things are worthy of death, not only do the same, but have pleasure in them that do them." Paul says, again (iii. 19), that every mouth is to be stopped, and the whole world to become guilty before

God; and this statement is based upon another appalling description of Dr. Dorner's sinners in their "minority." By no process of "criticism," experts as the Germans are acknowledged to be in all the varieties of that fine art, can the modern professor be reconciled with the ancient apostle. One or the other must be abandoned.

It is very evident that, if Dorner's doctrine be true, the benevolent impulse which has prompted and sustained missions to the heathen is a blind and fatal impulse. There might be other reasons for foreign missions, but there could be no benevolence. "If no man can be lost," says Dr. Shedd, "without the knowledge of Christ, then none of the past heathen world who died without this knowledge incurred perdition for the 'deeds done in the body,' and none of the existing heathen world who are destitute of this knowledge are liable to perdition from this cause. In this case, it is matter of rejoicing that the past generations of pagans never heard of the Redeemer, and it should be an earnest endeavor of the church to prevent all of the present generation of pagans from hearing of him."[1]

It may be noted, in conclusion, how completely the advocates of after-death probation reverse the positions of Scripture in regard to the justice and mercy of God. These positions are, that while justice and mercy are both of them necessary attributes of God, yet there is this difference between them, that God is always just to all, is unjust to none, but he is not merciful to all. "He has mercy on whom he will have mercy." Mercy, in its exercise, is sovereign; justice is not. The after-death probationists deny that this is so, or ought to be so. Like the Universalists, they insist upon God's treating all men alike. It is natural, therefore, in Dorner to avow expressly the opposition of his doctrine to that of Luther and Calvin; that is, the doctrine of predestination. He is right. If his position is the true one, Calvinism is out and out false, and *tremendously* false.

---

[1] *Dogmatic Theology*, II., p. 702, note.

SCIENCE AND REVELATION.[1]

I. SCIENCE is here used in the sense of the methodical knowledge of "nature," of the universe and of man, so far as that knowledge is derived from the study of nature by the human mind, unaided by the light which comes from the Bible. It has nature for its object, and the "light of nature" for its instrument.[2] It embodies the results of the interpretation of nature by man's unaided reason. "*Homo minister et interpres naturae*" says Bacon. It gives us the knowledge of the *works* of God obtained apart from the informations of his *word.*

II. If the universe and the Bible come from the same author, they can never contradict each other—the author being a God whose understanding is infinite and whose veracity is perfect. The notion of a "dualism of truth," as held by some of the schoolmen, is both absurd and wicked. What is demonstrated to be true in science must be true always; and what God testifies in his word must be true always. Any other position is dishonoring to God and fatal to the activity of the human mind. The interpretation of nature must not contradict the interpretation of the word. If a contradiction emerges, it is manifest that one or the other interpretation (the science or the theology) must be wrong. Bear in mind that the question here is not about the *facts*, but about the interpretation of the facts. Facts, phenomena, constitute the basis and starting point of science, but they are not science. One fact or group of facts cannot possibly

[1] Prepared about 1886 or 1887, apparently to relieve the perplexities of certain students as to the church's treatment of Dr. Woodrow.—ED.

[2] See Psa. xix. 1–6, and the contrast with "the law of the Lord" in v. 7 ff, and 1 Kings iv. 33.

contradict another fact or group of facts. Theories may contradict one another (*e. g.*, in astronomy the Ptolemaic and the Copernican). A theory (αεωρια) is a mode of contemplating or looking at facts—an exposition of their meaning—an explanation of the thought of God as expressed in them or by them. A true scientific theory is a true expression of God's thought; a false or inadequate theory is a false or inadequate expression. So we find scientific theories contradict one another.

It must be borne in mind further, that a contradiction can emerge only when the theories aim to express the same aspects or relations of the facts. There can be no contradiction between a theory of astronomy and a theory of chemistry. While the same substance (matter) may be questioned by the astronomer and the chemist, the point and object of the questions are different—concern, phenomena, and qualities wholly different. The astronomer deals with mechanical forces and large masses of matter; the chemist with chemical forces and molecules. The one uses the telescope; the other the spectroscope and microscope.

It follows from this, that it is one thing to say that the Bible contradicts a certain theory or conclusion of science, and a wholly different thing to say that the Bible contradicts the facts which science undertakes to explain. It is a common error of infidel geologists (for example) to confound these two things.

Once more, suppose we take the ground that the Bible and science occupy entirely different spheres, as different as the spheres of astronomy and chemistry, then we may hold that no contradiction can take place between them any more than between those two sciences. The chemist might, as such, undertake to astronomize, and an apparent contradiction might emerge, but it would be the result of an illegitimate process of the mind. So the theologian or the exegete might forsake his proper domain and invade that of the man of science, and *vice versa.* In either case it would not be strange if either should contradict the other. Suppose that the position be taken, a position taken not only by divines[1] but by great names in science,[2] that the investigation of the *origin* of things does not belong to the sphere of science, then true science *cannot* contradict the "Origines" of Moses. Any so-called scientific dictum about origines which contradicts him is *eo ipso* proved to be no scientific dictum.

III. This brings us to another question: When there is an apparent discrepancy in the two interpretations of the *same* facts, which is to control, science or the Bible? In answer, observe (1), That it will not do to take the broad ground that the Bible must always control. Sound theologians (*e. g.*, Turretin, sec. 1, Q. 10; Thornwell, III., pp. 183 ff; Hodge, I., pp. 51 ff) have always admitted the rights of reason and a "judgment of contradiction" as belonging to it. As revelation presents itself with its *credentials* to the human reason, it cannot be otherwise. There is a revelation of God in and to the human soul prior to the revelation made through prophets and apostles, and it is a principle assumed in the Bible itself (*e. g.*, Deut. xiii. 1 ff) that the prior revelation is to regulate our judgment in regard to the posterior. And the same principle is taken for granted by all who admit that there is "internal evidence" of the divine origin of the Bible. That internal evidence is the response which the Bible makes to the rational and ethical judgments and instincts of the human soul. If it contradicted these instincts it would be self-convicted of imposture. No amount of external evidence could, in this case, authenticate it as a revelation from God.[3] It would be simply *impossible* to believe it.

---

[1] See Taylor Lewis in the Introduction to the Commentary on Genesis in Schaff's Lange's *Commentary.*

[2] Dr. Carpenter in Inaug. Brit. Association.

[3] See Thornwell, III., pp. 191 ff; Hodge, I., pp. 52 ff.

So, also, that which contradicts the evidence of the senses, aided by experiment and instruments, cannot be believed. If the Bible taught such contradictions it would be self-convicted of imposture. If, for example, it taught the Papal doctrine of transubstantiation, it could not be received as God's word by any sound understanding; or, having been received as God's word upon satisfactory evidence, the interpretation which makes "this is my body" mean transubstantiation is convicted of falsehood by the testimony of the senses, by the laws of matter, and by the necessary laws of thought. The principle is exactly the same in its application to both questions—"Is the Bible the word of God?" and "Is this the meaning of the Bible?" The infidel (Bolingbroke) who says "the Bible teaches Calvinism, therefore it is not divine," and the theologian (Wesley) who says "the Bible is divine, therefore it cannot teach Calvinism," argue in exactly the same way and upon the same assumption, to-wit: that Calvinism contradicts fundamental truths of the human reason, and if this assumption could be established it would be fatal to the Calvinistic construction of the Bible's teaching, and, we believe, fatal to the claim of the Bible to be God's word. So again, if the theories of the geologists in regard to the age of the world were established as impregnably as the Copernican or Newtonian theory of the starry heavens, and no interpretation of the Bible could be made to harmonize with it, we should be compelled either to resign our faith in the divine origin and authority of the Bible, or to recast and reform our view of inspiration.

We observe next, that in arbitrating between the conflicting claims of science and revelation as to controlling interpretation, the following rule will be as just as any, to-wit: in matters which constitute the distinctive character of revelation, its authority must be supreme; and human reason, which by the terms of the supposition knows and can know nothing concerning these except by revelation, has no other office than simply to accept the testimony, however much that testimony may falsify all inferences and conclusions from analogy. In other matters, what the human reason knows independently of revelation may modify and even control the interpretation. I may illustrate the first part of these rules thus: The origin of the world is from the nature of the case, and, as we have seen, by the concessions of eminent men of science, a matter lying beyond the range of science and of human history. The Creator of it is the only competent witness. Now his testimony, as the church believes, was given through and recorded by Moses; and this testimony must override, control, annul or correct all conclusions and inferences from analogy whatsoever, (*a*), because in all such inferences the only guide of the reason is analogy. It is a maxim universally admitted that "like causes will produce like effects." This maxim makes science a prophet—it can *predict;* and the fulfilment of its predictions establish its claim to be science. But the converse of the maxim, that "like effects must have been produced by like causes" is not equally valid. If it were, science would be a historian as well as a prophet, which it is not. The causes or conditions of wine are well known; and anybody may confidently predict that where these conditions are fulfilled there will be wine. But he who should have argued that the last wine brought in at the marriage in Cana of Galilee must have had the same causes as the other wine, would have been very wide of the truth. Even within the sphere of physical or material causation the disputes constantly arising among men of science about the causes of phenomena are a confession that science is not as confident of its history as it is of its prophecy. It cannot affirm that all the individuals of any genus of plants or minerals had a like origin. The utmost it is competent to say is that it has a right to believe this, until the contrary has been proved. It cannot affirm that all the phenomena of the rocks are the effects of the same causes, operating with the same intensity as we see them now. The uttermost they can demand is that the contrary should be proved. Geology, we may remark by the way, is in the unfortunate predicament of being neither prophet nor historian. The proof to the contrary is the testimony of God by Moses, to say nothing of the rational proof derived from the absurdity of an infinite regress. The general conclusion, therefore, is that authentic testimony must set aside all inferences as to causes drawn from analogy. This is the principle laid down by our Lord in his argument with the Sadducees. (Matt. xx. 29–32.) It is the principle recognized by human law in allowing the testimony of witnesses to override "circumstantial evidence[1]."

The application of the first part of the above rule to the distinctive features of the plan of salvation is too obvious to need argument. The only resort of Socinians, Pelagians, Arminians, &c., is to what they allege to be fundamental truths of the reason, rational and ethical. But the appeal is vain.

As to the second part of the rule (see above), to-wit: "What the human reason knows independently of revelation may modify and even control the interpretation of Scripture," some illustrations may be added to those already given. 1. As to the mode of "mediate or secondary" creation, some assert that science *may* discover that mode, yea, has discovered it in some instances. This is the position of the theistic evolutionists (the "nebular hypothesis," "the origin of species," "the origin of man's body," &c.). Moses seems to teach that the universe, the heavens and the earth and all that in them is, was created within six days (144 hours). Gen. i. and ii. 1–3; Exod. xx. 11. In this last passage, however, let it be noted, the word "create" does not appear, though it does occur in Gen. i. 21, 27, as well as in Gen. i. 1. Compare Gen. ii. 2, 3. Now the formation of the stars in

---

[1] See Dabney's *Theology*, p. 260.

six days is clearly incompatible with the nebular hypothesis; such immense masses of fire, mist and other incandescent matter as the hypothesis supposes, could not be cooled and condensed in the space of three or four (see Gen. i. 16) or even six days. So the hypothesis of evolution as applied to animals and the body of man implies the lapse of a great length of time, certainly of more than forty-eight hours (Gen. i. 20–23), or even 144 hours. If these theories could be established and verified (which I confess I cannot conceive to be possible), some other than the traditional interpretation of the "days" in Genesis would have to be found, or our view of the nature and scope of revelation would, as I have already hinted, have to be recast and amended, or the divine origin of the Bible wholly surrendered.

Again, as to the special point of the origin of man's body, if it be explained according to the hypothesis of evolution as held and expounded by naturalists, it is beset, as already suggested, with the same difficulties; and, in addition, with that of implying that what we call the spirit or soul of man was evolved out of a germ existing in the brute, thus denying the uniform teaching of Scripture as to the constitution of man. Such a doctrine may by courtesy be called "theistic" evolution; but it certainly could not, with any show of reason, be called "biblical."

If the origin of man's body be explained in such a way as to imply that by a process of evolution it had reached its present form and structure (anatomically and physiologically considered), and that God simply put an immortal spirit into it, then we should have the same difficulty about the time, and besides, the difficulty that it would not be the formation of man (Adam, *ανδρωπος*, *homo*—the species), but only the formation or creation of a spirit, suited to an existing anatomy and physiology. Thus formed, Adam would have been surrounded by numerous quadrumanous poor relations, poor indeed, as being destitute of "an intellectual being and thoughts that wander througn eternity." How could such a theory be reconciled with such language as Gen. i. 27; Heb. x. 5?

If, again, it be held that God may have taken some living animal body and reconstructed it so as to make out of it the body of a man, changing its anatomy and physiology so as to make it the fit servitor and instrument of the soul he intended to create, this might be allowed to be a harmless theory. If it can be harmonized with the expression "dust of the ground" (and no great ingenuity is required to do this), then the only difference between this and the traditional view would be, that according to the latter, God used inorganic matter, and according to the former, organic. As to the question of "the dignity of our nature," it would seem that there was less indignity in being made out of organic stuff; for it is agreed on all hands that we rise in the scale when we pass from the inorganic to the organic. A mountain is a bigger thing than a mouse; but a mouse is higher in the scale of created things than a mountain. Given men enough and time enough, men could make a mountain; but all the wisdom and power of mankind could not make a mouse. Grant that the theory is harmless, of what use is it? Its apologetic use is stark naught. It does not help us at all with the infidel. He would say, "This is not *our* evolution, not the evolution which naturalists contend for. It is a hybrid, a cross between nature and a miracle, and we don't believe in miracles; why not go the whole in this case and hold that God formed the whole species out and out, body and soul, at the same time? You are vainly attempting to harmonize revelation and science by a theory which is altogether unscientific. We infidels need no *Deus ex machina* to carry out the drama. Nature is sufficient for all—

> 'Neuters in their middle way of steering
> Are neither flesh, nor fish; nor good red herring;
> Nor Whigs nor Tories they; nor this, nor that;
> Nor birds, nor beasts; but just a kind of bat.'"[1]

[1] Dryden's *Epilogue to the Duke of Guise.*

The theory is indeed a hybrid, and for that reason we may hope will not be prolific.

But while the theory may be in itself harmless, it must be said, as the last Assembly (Augusta, 1886) said, that the method of interpretating Scripture demanded by the theory is dangerous. It runs to meet the infidel with a tone of apology before he makes the assault; it offers to abandon the received interpretation of Scripture in concession to an "improved hypothesis," and a hypothesis which it would seem is incapable of proof. It is ridiculous to demand that the ancient faith of the people of God should be reformed according to the terms of a mere hypothesis.

On the other hand, the distinguished man who has been made to represent this theory of the origin of man's body in our church ought to be fairly and charitably dealt with. His professions of faith in the divine inspiration of the Scriptures and in the doctrinal standards of his church ought to be accepted without hesitation as sincere. The alleged "logical consequences" of his views, while they may be legitimately urged in argument against his views, ought not to be charged against him if he rejects them. He has been righteously acquitted by his Presbytery of the charge of "heresy." How can that be heresy which does not plainly contradict the teaching of Scripture or of our standards? or which does not "strike at the vitals of religion"?[1] Nor can it be said that his error has been "industriously spread." He did not, he tells us, teach evolution in the seminary; the agitation did not begin with him; and his whole course has been one of self-defence—defence of his legal rights as a professor and as a minister in the Presbyterian Church. You have already seen that I have no sympathy with his views in regard to the possible or probable origin of Adam's body. But I am sure he has not been fairly dealt with. The constitution of the seminary and the constitution of the church have both been

[1] Rules of Discipline, Chap. VIII., Art. 5.

violated in persecuting him; and I am also sure that the church will acknowledge it in the end.

His view of "non-contradiction" ought to be carefully discriminated from his view concerning the origin of man's body, though in condemning him the two have often been confounded. The view of "non-contradiction" is the view upon which the church has always acted. There are probably very many of our ministers who hold that the universe was not created in one hundred and forty-four hours, or rather, there are probably few who hold that it was so created; and their good and regular standing is not impaired. Yet there is more apparent contradiction in this view of the teaching of Scripture and our Confession of Faith than in Dr. Woodrow's doctrine. He holds both, but is censured only for one. Why is this? He is reported to hold that the deluge did not cover the whole earth, or at least that the words of Scripture do not necessitate us to believe that the deluge was universal. Other men deemed to be orthodox have held this view. The theories of creationism and traducianism have divided the theologians of orthodox creeds; have divided the theologians of our own church. The traducianists have denounced creationism as derogatory to the honor of God and fatal to the unity of the race of Adam. Creationists, in turn, have denounced traducianism as involving the heresy of materialism. The church has tolerated both. To some minds Dr. Woodrow's doctrine seems less dangerous than that of traducianism. Why should such differences of opinion as to the origin of the souls of Adam's posterity be charitably tolerated, while differences as to the origin of Adam's body are supposed to be incompatible with dwelling together in peace? Turretin's doctrine of "concursus" seemed to my immediate predecessor in this chair in Union Seminary (and I agree with him) to be fatal to the holiness of God and to the free agency of man or of any intelligent creature. Yet Turretin was used as a text-book, and many Reformed theologians who held the same doctrine were recommended to the students as safe guides. Now, why this action of the church? Because it was judged that the Scriptures were silent on these subjects, and therefore the church had no authority to censure one or the other side. The Confession of Faith does not say that Adam's body was created *immediately* from the dust of the ground; it says nothing about the creation of his body. (Chap. IV.) The Larger Catechism (Q. 17) simply copies a part of Genesis ii. 7. The Shorter Catechism (Q. 10) is as silent as the Confession of Faith about man's body. We know very well what the divines of the Westminister Assembly thought of the origin of man's body; but the point is—they did not put those thoughts into a Confession of *Faith*. They judged that such a document should contain nothing which could not be sustained by Scripture. It was a confession of faith, not of *opinion*, and our last Assembly (1886) in its act on the subject of the origin of man's body modestly says: "The church *remains at this time* sincerely convinced,"[1] etc. Would it have used such language if the error in question had been the denial of Christ's expiatory sacrifice, or even the fact of the creation of man, as a being of spirit and body?

[1] The passage referred to is, more fully, as follows: "The church remains at this time sincerely convinced that the Scriptures, as truly and authoritatively expounded in our Confession of Faith and Catechisms, teach that Adam and Eve were created, body and soul, by immediate acts of almighty power, thereby preserving a perfect race unity; that Adam's body was directly fashioned by Almighty God, without any natural animal parentage of any kind, out of matter previously created from nothing." See *Minutes of General Assembly*, 1886, p. 10.—ED.

GOD IN CHRIST.[1]

TALLEYRAND is reported to have said that "language was invented not to convey, but to conceal, thought." This celebrated dictum of the wily diplomatist must yield in intensity, if not in pomp of paradox, to the theory of language propounded by Mr. Bushnell in his Preliminary Dissertation. Both seem to hold that language was an invention, and not an original endowment of man; both are agreed that it does not *convey* thought; and if the doctrines of these "Discourses" be not what the church of Jesus Christ has, in all the periods of its history, pronounced to be damnable heresy, the effect of language, whatever we may say of the design and tendency, is certainly, in the opinion of both, to *conceal* thought. Dr. Bushnell, however, goes one step further than the brilliant but unprincipled Frenchman, and asserts not merely that language was invented not to convey, but that it *cannot* convey thought, however honest the intention of those who employ it. It is afflicted with a constitutional debility, which will always insure its breaking down under the burden of the lightest spiritual idea. In order to illustrate his theory, he entertains us with a hypothetical account of the powers of language-making, which, so far as the objects of the material universe are concerned in it, does not differ much from the descriptions of other fanciful philologists who have contributed to aggravate the curse of Babel. Nor does he differ very widely from other dreamers of the same school, in his history of the process by which the names

[1] Review of a work by Horace Bushnell, D. D. *God in Christ*, Three Discourses, delivered at New Haven, Cambridge, and Andover, with a Preliminary Dissertation on Language. Hartford: Brown & Parsons. 1849. Appeared in the *Southern Presbyterian Review*, April, 1851.—Ed.

of external and material objects were, in the course of time, transferred to the department of spirit, and employed to express the informations of consciousness and reflection. But he contends that the earthly, material dregs of their original associations still cleave to the words, even after they have been promoted to the higher sphere and the nobler functions of the spiritual world. Like Plato's ghosts of wicked men, they were so long submerged in material things that, even when disembodied, they are not free from the admixture of earthy particles, and the law of gravity is still in force against them. This circumstance creates a sad necessity for men—that of always being mistaken in their notions of the meaning of words, when those words stand for spiritual objects or conceptions. There is nothing material in spiritual ideas; but alas for us, the terms which we employ to denote them contain, from the necessity of the case, material elements; the problem we have to solve is not only perplexed and complicated by the presence of unknown quantities, but vitiated by the intrusion of quantities positively false. The very term spirit now smacks of the laboratory. It denotes a substance which the chemist uses to heat his retorts; and in its original and higher acceptation it stands for a more ethereal substance, which profane science has demonstrated to be composed chiefly of so vulgar an element as carbonic acid gas. What, then, are we to do with such dangerous instruments of thought? Is there no remedy? Must we abandon ourselves to a fatal necessity of error in that department of investigation, in the results of which we are most deeply and lastingly interested? Dr. Bushnell shall answer these questions for us (p. 55):

"Since all words, but such as relate to necessary truths, are inexact representations of thought, mere types or analogies, or, where the types are lost beyond recovery, only proximate expressions of the thoughts named, it follows that language will be ever trying to mend its own deficiencies, by multiplying its forms of representation. As, too, the words made use of generally carry something false with them, as well as something true, associating form with the truths represented, when really there is no form, it will also be necessary, on this account, to multiply words or figures, and thus to present the subject on opposite sides or many sides. Thus, as form battles form, and one form neutralizes another, all the insufficiencies of words are filled out, the contrarieties liquidated, and the mind settles into a full and just apprehension of the pure spiritual truth. Accordingly, we never come so near to a truly well-rounded view of any truth, as when it is offered paradoxically; that is, under contradictions; that is, under two or more dictions, which, taken as dictions, are contrary one to the other. Hence the marvellous vivacity and power of that famous representation of Pascal: 'What a chimera, then, is man! what a novelty! what a chaos! what a subject of contradiction! A judge of every thing, and yet a feeble worm of the earth; the depository of truth, and yet a mere heap of uncertainty; the glory and the outcast of the universe. If he boasts, I humble him; if he humbles himself, I boast of him, and always contradict him, till he is brought to comprehend that he is an incomprehensible monster.' "

Now, this is all very fine; but the question will arise, in the mind of every thinking man, what has it to do with Mr. Bushnell's theory? If we were asked why are we bound by the law of God, would it be proper to answer, "the three angles of a triangle are equal to two right angles"? The noble passage from Pascal, and the still nobler passage from Paul (2 Cor. vi. 8, 10), are examples of highly-wrought rhetorical descriptions of human nature and human life. But what have they do with Dr. Bushnell's theory of language? We ask him a question in metaphysics, and he answers us by a lecture on antithesis, illustrated by examples. The *essential* deceptiveness of words is one thing; the propensity of employing antithesis, in an address to the *imagination*, is quite another thing. As to the logical understanding's acquiring more accurate knowledge of ideas and relations by antithesis than by simple, unadorned propositions, we had always supposed that sober men, in imparting instruction, abstained from the use of that and other highly rhetorical methods of *impressing* truth, till they were satisfied that the truth was *logically apprehended*. How common is it, in the use of such figures, to sacrifice truth to point? If taken as a didatic statement, in which light Dr. Bushnell would seem to have us regard it, the fine paragraph from Pascal cannot be exonerated from this charge, or, at least, from the charge of exaggeration. But taken as it was intended to be taken by the splendid genius who conceived it, it is faultless.

The truth is, that this theory of contradiction is framed to serve a turn[1]. The author tells us that it will afford "the true conception of the Incarnation and the Trinity." The precious doctrines of the Bible are to be converted into

[1] The following extract from the Preliminary Dissertation will show that the author's "contra-dictions" are not merely opposite "dictions" in spiritual equilibrium, but what plain people would call *contradictions* in the old-fashioned sense: "So far from suffering even the least consciousness of constraint, or oppression, under any creed, I have been readier to accept as great a number as fell in my way; for, when they are subjected to the deepest chemistry of thought, that which descends to the point of relationship between the power of the truth and its interior formless nature, they become, thereupon, so elastic, and run so freely into each other, that one seldom need have any difficulty in accepting as many as are offered him. He may regard them only as a kind of battle-door of words, blow answering to blow, while the reality of the play, viz., *exercise*, is the same, whichever side of the room is taken, and whether the stroke is given by the right hand or the left." (P. 82.) Truly, we may say of this doctor of divinity, as has been said of those who can believe the contradictory formularies of the Church of England, that he must be blessed with extraordinary powers of digestion, if he escapes dyspepsia after so miscellaneous a feast. The pompous inanities of German Transcendentalism have been profanely compared with the speech of the clown in *Twelfth Night* (A. 4, 8, 2): "As the old hermit of Prague, that never saw pen and ink, very wittily said to a niece of King Gorboduc, 'That, that is, is; so I, being master parson, am master parson; for what is that, but that?—and is, but is?'" But Dr. Bushnell, in prosecuting the brilliant career of discovery on which he has entered, has advanced one step beyond the old hermit, and ascertained that is, is not—is, and that is not—that: the das Ich is das nicht—Ich. In his understanding, truth and falsehood embrace and kiss each other; nay, the twain become one flesh. This is a "higher unity" with a vengeance! This "chemistry of thought" is a wonderful science; it has accomplished for thought what the old alchymists, after all their laborious experiments, could never do for matter. But, seriously, is it not almost incredible, even with the evidence before our eyes, that the understanding of a grown man can be capable of such drivelling folly?

figures of speech, and hence this laborious attempt to confound things that differ. But of this more hereafter.

The juxta-position of Dr. Bushnell's principles and examples may be accounted for by his possession of a faculty of "poetic insight" (as he calls it), which relieves him of the burden imposed upon ordinary mortals—the burden of logical thinking. He stands upon an eminence, which, though it may appear to us, toiling in the vale below, to be surrounded with clouds and mists, is really far above the floating vapors which shade our mundane atmosphere; and from that eminence he has an intuitive perception of eternal and necessary realities. We are very much disposed to envy him the possession of this singular felicity; but, as we are, unfortunately, without it, we are often compelled to employ the humble faculty of *deduction*, and to grope our way back to intuitive principles and fundamental laws of belief by very long and tortuous threads. We think it hard, however, in an author, that, instead of bearing his honors meekly, and commiserating our unhappy condition, he should rail as he does against logic. He has no use for it, it is true; but we have. A man with sound legs will not abuse crutches simply because he has, personally, no use for them. There *are* lame men, and they ought not to be too severely censured if they attempt to achieve locomotion in the best way they can. He will not acknowledge that God can teach *him* anything;[1] but we are

[1] "What, then, it may be asked, is the real and legitimate use of words when applied to moral subjects? For we cannot dispense with them, and it is uncomfortable to hold them in universal skepticism, as being only instruments of error. Words, then, I answer, are legitimately used as the signs of thought to be expressed. They do not literally convey, or pass over, a thought out of one mind into another, as we commonly speak of doing. They are only hints, or images held up before the mind of another, to put *him* on generating or reproducing the same thought; which *he can do only as he has the same personal contents, or the generative power out of which to bring the thought required.*" (Pp. 45, 46.) This is, substantially, the doctrine defended by Mr. Morell and others, that it is impossible for God himself to give us a logical revelation, or, to use their own term, a "theology."

disposed more and more every day to acknowledge the ignorance of poor human nature, and to admire that Socratic modesty which prompts a man to confess that he knows nothing. The "*ουχ οιδα σαφως*" of the Athenian philosopher will be sought in vain in the oracular utterances of the German school. They are gods; it is only in their minds that God comes to a consciousness of his personality; they are able

It is very much like the doctrine of the Meno of Plato, that all our knowledge is "*reminiscence*" merely. God presents us with words, but they are only hints, which awaken the dormant contents of the reason; he "stirs up our pure minds by way of remembrance," but imparts no new knowledge. Is it not marvellous that these men have not perceived the difference between *ideas* and *relations?* It is, no doubt, true that the use of names, in the intercourse of mind with mind, implies that the ideas exist, in a greater or less degree of clearness, both in him who communicates and in him who receives. But the knowledge mainly consists in the *relations* of the persons, things, or ideas denoted by the terms. The ancients had an idea of a Supreme Being, of the material universe, of creation. But the relations among these ideas, expressed in the proposition, "God created the heavens and the earth," they never recognized except to deny, the general principle being "*ex nihilo nil fit.*" Our philosophers neglect to discriminate between truths which are simply expressive of existence and truths which express relations among existing objects. They also confound the perception of "concrete realities" by the "intuitional consciousness" (the process being analogous to that of external perception by the senses) with the apprehension of what are called necessary or universal truths, by the same faculty. According to the first view, it would be as absurd to attempt to give a man an idea of God, who had not the idea already, as it would be to attempt to give a man born blind an idea of color. . . . . Dr. Bushnell does, indeed, admit that there is such a thing as inspiration, but it seems to be very much like Mr. Morell's, and both have probably obtained it from the German masters. He tells us (p. 350 *et seq.*) that it is a great mistake to suppose that inspiration has ceased, and leaves us to infer that, while the tripod continues in Hartford, it will be unreasonable to attach any peculiar importance to the inspiration of Paul or Peter. Truly, any mortal who will thread his way through the sinuosities of this book will be satisfied that, if we have not the inspiration, we have, at least, the contortions, of the sybil. Note, that we have used the term *idea*, in the above remarks, sometimes as equivalent to *object*. In one acceptation of the term, a relation is an *idea*. See some excellent observations on this subject in Mill's *System of Logic*, Book I., chapter ii.

to make a universe out of their own brains, as a spider spins its web from its own bowels. But we confess that we are men, and have not such powers as this; that it is necessary for us to compare, to analyze, to arrange, to deduce, to dig for truth as for hid treasure, and, after we have obtained the precious ore, to smelt it, to separate the pure metal from the earthy admixture; in short, that we are groping our way in a dark world, and are anxious to hear the voice of God amid the gloom, saying unto us, "This is the way; walk ye in it." And we hope Dr. Bushnell and other *illuminati* will pardon us for saying that it is unkind in them, it betrays a want of magnanimity, to laugh at or to abuse us because we are destitute—and that, too, without any fault of our own—of that lofty instrument of knowledge which they possess, and are compelled, in the absence of it, to employ such an antiquated utensil as logic. Let them enjoy to the utmost the distinction of free access into the inner sanctuary of the "pure reason," or "poetic insight," or "intuitional consciousness"; but let them not insult the less happy destiny of those who are doomed to tread the court of the Gentiles, "the logical understanding."[1]

It will be readily imagined by our readers, from the preceding remarks, that it is not our purpose to attempt a review of the "Discourses" themselves. The Preliminary Dissertation has so awed us, that we cannot go further without trembling. If such be the portico, what must the temple be? We shall not invade the retirement of the seer, where he gazes, in solitary rapture, on the unconditioned, the absolute and the infinite. In truth, we do not know that we understand him; we have only learned the language of men, and know nothing of the dialect of those who dwell amidst the clouds which hang around the summit of Olympus.

[1] This image is borrowed from an article on Morell, in the *Westminster Review* for April, 1847, in which the writer handles the nonsense of our Teutonic brethren with very little politeness.

So that there is no danger of our misrepresenting him. To us, the first discourse, seems an odd mixture of Sabellianism and Pantheism; but, perhaps, if cast into the alembic which our author has furnished, and subjected to the powerful agencies of the "chemistry of thought," it may turn out, after all, to be a doctrine with which Spinosa would feel no sympathy, and which can look the damnatory clauses of the Athanasian creed calmly in the face. To us, the second discourse appears to be a sweeping besom of destruction to all the hopes of man, founded upon the atonement of Jesus Christ—an utter impudent mockery of the cries of agony which burst from a world groaning under the curse of the Almighty—taking away from us the precious *work* of our Lord and Saviour, as his first discourse does his *person*. He speaks of a *subjective* atonement; but, as we have not been endowed with the faculty of "poetic insight," we must acknowledge our inability to comprehend any such thing, unless, done into English, it means the effect of the atonement in the hearts of men. His *objective* atonement is not a sacrifice—no! no! It is not exactly a myth—for the death was a real death—but a something which might embody and realize our subjectivity; just as the brilliant creations of the poet's fancy have obtained, though airy nothings, a local habitation and a name, by the pencil of the painter and the chisel of the sculptor. We say that a painting is *beautiful*, but we all know that beauty is not an attribute of the painting, but of the percipient mind; but it gratifies our importunate appetite for objectivity to refer the quality to the painting, instead of regarding it as an affection of ourselves. So the atonement is *in us;* but we speak of it as being in the history of Christ—we refer to something objective. Most people who read the Bible suppose that Christ came into the world *in order* to make a sacrifice for sin—was born *in order* that he might die. But this is their ignorance. The death of Christ was only an incident which occurred in the discharge of his commission, as the death of Alexander, in the full tide of successful war, was. He did not go to Asia for the purpose of dying; neither did Christ come into the world for that purpose; it was a misfortune, which happened to them in prosecuting their benevolent designs, just as a monk of St. Bernard might perish among the snows of the Alps, in searching for the benighted travellers, who were the objects of his kindly solicitude.[1] He denies the *penal* character of the sufferings and death of Jesus; and, this being denied, we care not what he asserts concerning the atonement. If Christ did not die under the curse, all our hopes are vain. We are yet in our sins, and the majesty of the law must be vindicated in our own persons; the gospel is a mockery, and the preachers of it worse than fools.[2]

But we must check ourselves. Perhaps our author means just the contrary of all this, for he tells us that language cannot convey thought. It may be the purest orthodoxy of the Westminster Confession. Some of our readers may be able to judge what his views of the atonement really are, from the fact that they furnished a platform (as he tells us[3]) on which Protestants, philosophers and papists can stand amicably together! We have heard of authors who could "bespeak all reverence for that fancy of Justin and others, that the 'ass and the colt' for which Christ sent his disciples are to be interpreted severally of the 'Jewish and Gentile believers,' and *also* attach much weight to that of Origen, who *rather* expounds them of 'the Old and the New Testa-

[1] See pp. 201, *et seq.*

[2] A distinguished New England scholar is reported to have said, when he abandoned the ministry for other pursuits, that "preaching was a small business." We cordially agree with him. Upon *his* principle (he was a Unitarian), preaching the New Testament *is* the smallest and meanest of all businesses in which an *honest* man can engage.

[3] See pp. 268, *et seq.* The philosophers to whom he chiefly refers are the Unitarians, whom he seems much more anxious to conciliate than any other class.

ments.'" But Dr. Bushnell is determined to let none be before him in the race of absurdity.

The third and last discourse in this extraordinary collection is on "Dogma and Spirit." In the language of men, we should say that this "Discourse" is a very earnest assault on creeds and confessions—a very pathetic plea for the glorious liberty of thinking and believing one thing to-day and another to-morrow, and for the associated privilege of writing one thing on one page and contradicting it on the next. The objection is not to *creeds*, but to a *creed*, as will be seen from a citation in a preceding note. Provided there are more than one, the author's *cacoethes credendi* is agreeably soothed, though we suppose it can never be satisfied but by a universal syntagma, or rather *congeries confessionum.* "He has been readier," he tell us, "to accept as many creeds as fell in his way." The only damning sin is to believe anything *in particular.*

And here we close our notice of the book as such; for we suspect that our readers are as weary as ourselves. The author is a man of great power, unquestionably. There are many eloquent sentences in his book; he uses, with great point and force, the phraseology of spiritual religion. We will add that we have no reason to suspect his *sincerity;* his mind seems to have been in great distress through doubt, and he thinks that in the theories of these "Discourses" he has found rest and peace. He is very naturally anxious that others, who have been in the same afflictions, should share in his consolations, and, therefore, presents them with this "*ductor dubitantium.*" But we are amazed beyond our power to express, that a man in his sense should regard such stuff as affording an adequate foundation of hope to dying men; that he can have the hardihood to say, while acknowledging, in form, the divine authority of the Scriptures, that Paul does not reason in his epistles, or, if he does intend to reason, his reasoning is inconclusive, that the illative particles which occur so frequently in his writings are only the remnants of the discipline of Gamaliel, which he had not been able to throw off,[1] and many other things as outrageously absurd, and yet imagine that he is a sort of Star of Bethlehem, whose only office and design is to lead men to the Saviour of the world. We must say that we have never met with an instance of stranger hallucination in the annals of Christian literature, unless it be the case of the madman, in the time of Tertullian, who imagined himself to be the Holy Ghost.

---

[1] "True, there is a power of reasoning or argumentation about him (Paul), and he abounds in illatives, piling 'for' upon 'for' in constant succession. But, if he is narrowly watched, it will be seen that this is only a dialectic form that had settled on his language, under his old theologic discipline, previous to his conversion; for every man gets a language constructed early in life, which nothing can change afterwards. . . . Besides, it will be clear, on examination, that his illatives often miscarry, when taken as mere instruments or terms of logic, while, if we conceive him rushing on through so many 'fors' and parentheses, which belong to his old Pharisaic culture, and serve as a continuous warp of connections to his speech—now become the vehicle or channel, not for the modes of Rabbi Gamaliel, but for a stream of Christian fire—what before seemed to wear a look of inconsequence assumes a post of amazing energy, and he becomes the fullest, heartiest and most irresistible of all the inspired writers of the Christian Scriptures." (Pp. 75–'6.)

We had thought of commending to the perusal and study of our author the celebrated chapter in Dr. Campbell's *Rhetoric*, in which the question, "How a man may write nonsense without knowing it," is ingeniously discussed and answered. But we fear that it would be far more suitable to recommend to him the concluding chapter of the first part of Hume's *Treatise on Human Nature*, in which the subtle philosopher describes the state of mind into which his speculations had brought him, a description which we were scarcely able to read without tears. A melancholy example of the danger of trifling with the truth and of abusing those faculties which God has given us for its investigation! It is not at all strange that, after a man has reached the conclusion that all knowledge is equal to zero, he should be anxious to persuade himself that suicide is an innocent thing, a mere "diverting of a little blood from its ordinary channel." Upon the principles of such a philosophy, the condition of an oyster is far preferable to that of a man; the oyster has no power of thought, and cannot know the

These "Discourses" furnish melancholy evidence of the progress of infidel principles in the church. The time was when the denial of the *divine authority* of the Scriptures was a distinguishing badge of the enemies of Christianity; but that time has past. The devil has changed his tactics.

---

misery of thinking, which is doomed to hopeless uncertainty in all its conclusions, the misery of aspirations after truth which *must* be disappointed. Dr. Bushnell differs, it is true, from Mr. Hume. The one is brought to a negative of all belief, to absolute Pyrrhonism, by contradictions in nature; the other is brought to a negation of all disbelief, by *his theory* of contradictions in theology. But we may rest assured that Mr. Hume's conclusion is more logical than Dr. Bushnell's. The rule of logic, that "contradictories can never be both true or both false," is a rule which will hold till the structure of the human understanding has been entirely subverted. Two and two make four, and two and two make five, are propositions which can never be both true. There is no "depth of consciousness" (unless there be a depth lower than the *lowest*, as the "poetic insight" of Milton hints that there is) in which they can meet in *unity*. This we believe to be the instinctive and irresistible judgment of any sound understanding; and, therefore, it is our solemn conviction that the tendency of the *Discourses on God in Christ* is as mischievous as that of the *Treatise on Human Nature.* It may be well enough for the doctors of the Church of Rome to teach that contradictions may be both true, for their doctrines require such a notion for their defence; but it is a shame for one who professes to be a champion of the Protestant cause and of the rights of the human mind (his system indeed needs it, but he ought not to hold a system which needs it) to perpetrate such an outrage upon common sense. The distinction which he makes between kinds of truth, as absolute or relative, necessary or contingent, is a just distinction, but it does not help his case. A contradiction is a contradiction (we hope he will not object to this statement), and though it may be more readily detected in one class of ideas than in another, its nature is not changed. "No lie is of the truth." (1 John ii. 21.)

We deeply regret to see this theory of contradictions propounded in another form by Dr. Park, of Andover, in his *Theology of the Intellect and Theology of the Feelings.* We should not be surprised if some future historian of opinions should treat of these different systems in a chapter entitled, "On the Art of Lying Made Easy." Such a historian would deserve more respect for his judgment than for his charity. We do not say that these gentlemen are not honest; we judge no man; but we do say, and are ready to maintain it, that their principles make havoc of all fair-dealing amongst men.

He is still aiming at the same great end, still bent upon persuading men to prefer the farthing candle of their own reason to the sunlight of divine revelation; but he employs a different method of address. The "logical understanding," or what uninitiated and unsophisticated mortals call the "reason," was his great weapon before the star of cant arose above the horizon of philosophical speculation. Men sat in judgment upon the evidence and upon the subject-matter of the documents which professed to be the word of God. They proceeded upon the supposition that the record meant what the received canons of interpretation compelled them to conclude *was meant.* They knew nothing of the science of hermeneutical chemistry, which has been the source of so many splendid discoveries in our own day. The meaning of the record being ascertained, they brought it face to face with the logical judgments of the understanding, and decided either that it was no new substantive addition to their stock of knowledge, or that it was contrary to what they knew to be true, or that it was incomprehensible, and that, in any or all aspects of the case, it could not be the word of God. There was something bold, frank, manly, in that species of infidelity. The challenge was given to the friends of Christianity to meet its enemies on the field of argument; they met, and the issue of the controversy is very impressively proclaimed by the change in the mode of conducting the war. Satan has now entrenched himself behind fortifications which are impregnable against all the engines of the logical understanding. The enemies of the gospel have refused to be tried by the rules of logic, agreeably to the custom of offenders generally, renouncing the jurisdiction of the court whose verdict, they are certain, will be against them. They have taken refuge in a power of the mind, called the "pure reason," "intuitional consciousness," "poetic insight," etc. (for, like other things of questionable moral character, it goes under more names than one), which takes cognizance of spiritual realities, immediately and directly, as the eye does of color, or the ear of sound, or the taste of beauty in works of art. To make a logical objection to any of their doctrines would imply the absurdity of the enthusiastic mathematician, who, when coming out of the theatre, was asked by his companion how he liked the performance, and replied, "I do not see what it *proved*." They disdain to argue with us; for, argue as you will, with a man born blind, as to the true notion of scarlet, he will obstinately persist that it is like the sound of a trumpet. They can only pity us, and we can only bewail our misery, that nature should thus have curtailed us of our fair proportions, and left us without a faculty so necessary to our comfort here and our blessedness hereafter.

This species of infidelity does not deny the inspiration of the Scriptures; it denies the inspiration of no man; on the contrary, it affirms the inspiration of all men. This wonder-working faculty may lie dormant; it is actually dormant in the whole human race except in a few highly-favored individuals, such as Paul, Peter, John, Schleiermacher, Bushnell, Morell and others. It may exist in a great variety of degrees. Some, with the eye in a fine frenzy rolling, only see the *shapes* of things unknown; others, aroused to a higher energy of the intuitive faculty, see things unknown with no shape at all, or a shadow of a shape, or a very doubtful shape, like that of Milton's Death. When the faculty is excited, it becomes a powerful telescope, analyzing appearances, which, in those in whom it lies dormant, are mere nebulous lights, into clusters of brilliant suns. But we all have it, if we did but know it. Such being the case, there is no impropriety in infidels of this stamp becoming preachers of the gospel. And thus Satan gives the finishing touch to his policy; the serpent tracks his slimy way into the very pulpits of our churches; and Christ and his apostles, if they cannot be satisfied with places in the Pantheon alongside of the preachers themselves, are either violently ejected, or bowed, with the blandest courtesy, to the door. Infidels of this sort are more dangerous than those of the class of Herbert of Cherbury, because they are in the church, and because they do not, like him, openly reject the divine authority of the Scriptures, or pretend to a peculiar supernatural revelation made by God to themselves. They use the language of spiritual religion, and appeal to the experience of men, to their intuitional consciousness or poetical insight, not to the Scriptures, for the truth of what they say. Religion comes to be regarded merely as a work of art, intended to accomplish its effects by impressions upon the imagination, not by convincing the understanding, or arousing the conscience. Whatever pleases is truth, whatever excites displeasure or disgust is falsehood, or rather there ceases to be any inquiry as to what is truth. If the question is ever asked, "What is truth?" it is asked in the spirit of Pontius Pilate, and, like him, the inquirer does not wait for an answer.[1]

---

[1] It would occupy too much space to make quotations large enough to justify our representation of Dr. Bushnell's views on this point. He himself warns us, at the outset, that a man is not to be judged by single passages from his works, but that the impression is to be received from them as a whole; and this is specially true, he says, of a "many-sided writer" (that is, in the language of men, a writer who frequently contradicts himself), who is never "able to stand in harmony before himself (such is the nature of language), save by an act of internal construction favorable to himself, and preservative of his *mental unity*." . . . Therefore every writer, not manifestly actuated by a malignant or evil spirit, is entitled to this indulgence. The mind must be offered up to him, for the time, with a certain degree of sympathy. [That is, in plain English, we must, as the Oxford Apostles recommend, "maintain before we have proved, and believe before we examine."] It must draw itself into the same position; take his constructions, *feel* out, so to speak, his meanings [truly, it is a darkness of Egypt, that may be *felt*], and keep him, as far as may be, in a form of *general* consistency [a labor of Hercules]. Then, having endeavored thus, and for a sufficient length of time, to reproduce him or his thought, that is, to make a realization of him, some proper judgment may be formed in regard to the soundness of his doctrine.—(P. 89.)

Now let us look at the consequences of this doctrine. If the sensibilities of men are made the criterion of truth, the gospel will cease to be the gospel, good news of *salvation.* Where there is no *loss*, there can be no *salvation;* where there is no sense of loss, there can be no sense of the need of salvation. But what does the "poetical insight" pronounce concerning the doctrine of loss or damnation? It cannot see deep enough to see it. Hell is no suggestion of the "pure reason." It is not recognized by the "intuitional consciousness." It shocks the tastes and sensibilities of inspired preachers and philosophers. It is, therefore, the dream of a morbid fancy, a nursery tale of horror, suited to quiet refractory children, but utterly beneath the notice of a full-grown man, who has ascended to an eminence from which he gazes directly and immediately upon the soul, the universe and God. If they refer to it at all, it is for poetical effect, and then the reference is more to an unreal, imaginary hell, like that of the Paradise Lost, in which the devils are heroes in misfortune, nobly struggling for their rights against the tyranny of power, than the hell of the Scriptures, whose fires have been kindled by the

---

"They (human teachers) may be obscure, not from weakness only, which, certainly, is most frequent, but quite as truly by reason of their exceeding breadth, and the *piercing vigor of their insight.*"—(P. 91.)

Our readers, we think, will now excuse us from quoting; for they would hardly have the patience to read the whole book in a note. We fear, that even after reading the whole volume, they would not be able, unless they should be so fortunate as to possess this "piercing vigor of insight," to see down into that "depth of consciousness" where truth and falsehood lay aside their hostility, and lovingly embrace each other in "mental unity." For the statements of the text, therefore, we refer generally to that part of the second discourse which has the running caption at the head of the page, "Religion as in Art," from page 250 to 255, with the preceding pages from page 246.

As to the infidel tendencies of his principles, it is a very significant fact (if it be true, as stated in the public prints,) that his work is about to be published by an infidel book establishment in London.

breath of God's justice, to consume the transgressors of law, overwhelmed with merited shame and everlasting contempt. Hell, as implying the *curse* of God, comes, in this way, to be placed in the expurgatory index of pulpit ministrations. This is not a fancy sketch. A writer in the *Westminster Review*, the organ of the Radical party in Great Britain (April, 1850), in an article on the Church of England, ascribes the insufficiency of that establishment to the fact, as one cause, that its creed is behind the age, and its doctrines have become obsolete. One of these obsolete doctrines is that of a penal doom, threatened, against impenitent offenders, in another world. In proof that this doctrine does not form a part of the current, popular faith, and, therefore, ought not to be taught, he alleges the acceptation in which the term "salvation" is commonly held. "A meaning," he says, "far different from the historical definition of divines, is currently given to the word *salvation*—a word, however, which, after every softening, is not sincerely congenial with the highest religion of the time. Its direct opposition to *damnation* is very much lost; and, instead of denoting mere rescue from a penal doom, it is accepted as an expression for personal *union with God*, spiritual *perfectness of character;* or, without reference to any penal alternative, the simple *attainment of a blessed and immortal state.*" [The italics are the author's own.] The cold-blooded indifference with which this assertion is made—an assertion which stultifies the Bible, and makes it, indeed, a bundle of old wives' fables unworthy the respect of a masculine understanding—is calculated to fill every sober mind with the most melancholy reflections. "Salvation, a word which, after every softening, is not sincerely congenial with the highest religion of the time"! The highest religion of the time basing its pretensions to be so considered upon the repudiation of that doctrine which constitutes the discriminating characteristic of the Christian religion! Paul was "not ashamed of the gospel of Christ," because it was "the power of God unto *salvation*." When the angels descended to earth to announce the tidings of the birth of Jesus, it was not the advent merely of an illustrious prophet or a mighty king that filled them with rapture, but the advent of *Jesus*, Jehovah, the *Saviour*. "Unto you there is born this day a *Saviour*, who is Christ the Lord." The proclamation which the Saviour put into the mouth of all his apostles was, "He that believeth shall be *saved;* he that believeth not shall be *damned*." And yet, in the "highest religion" of the year eighteen hundred and fifty, there is nothing sincerely congenial with the idea of "*salvation*," and "the direct opposition of that term to *damnation* is very much lost"!

Some simple people might conclude that this man is an infidel. But their simplicity misleads them. It is true that he not only laughs at the notion of a penal doom, but speaks contemptuously of the Mosaic cosmogony, and of the unity of the human race, and of other plain statements of the record. But he is not an infidel; he does not deny the inspiration of the Scriptures. He has only been a follower of Bushnell, and performing, under his direction, experiments in the "chemistry of thought," neutralizing and "liquidating contrarieties." The whole article bears evidence of the author's recent perusal of the *Discourses on God in Christ*, and of his having been (to use his master's phrases) "drawn into the same position," "taken his constructions," "felt out his meanings," "reproduced him and his thought," and "made a realization of him." In the very paragraph from which the above citation is taken, the poetical theory of religion is formally announced.[1]

[1] The reviewer quotes some long passages from Dr. Bushnell's book, on the subject of *atonement*, with his cordial approbation. He is no fool, and is able to see that such a sentence of approbation is not at all inconsistent with the assertion that "salvation, after every softening, is not sincerely congenial with the highest religion of the time." With the usual recklessness or ignorance of the English, when matters and things in America are

Such is one very natural consequence of the poetical or artistic theory. Men dislike to think of hell, even as a fancy. The most skilful and finished painting of the horrors of the damned will not please. Admiration for the artist is lost in the terror inspired by the subject of his pencil. Some few men of sombre imaginations might be found, who could be charmed with *The Inferno* upon canvas; but the great majority of amateurs would much prefer a gallery furnished exclusively from the descriptions of the poet of *The Seasons.* Hence, artistic preachers must say nothing about it, and, when once thoroughly *ignored*, it will cease to be beloved or feared, and all inquiry about *salvation* will cease.[1]

Another consequence of this view of religion is the loss of a sense of responsibility for opinions. If judgments are to be framed upon *evidence*, a man is responsible for the state of mind, whether candid or otherwise, with which he examines the evidence; but in matters of mere taste and sensibility it is different. We usually regard the absence of refined taste or delicate sensibility as a misfortune rather than a crime. But if objective religion be a work of art, and we are to judge of it as we do of a painting, then we are not responsible for our judgments. There is no moral element at all in the process. Let us hear Dr. Bushnell as to the effect upon his own sense of responsibility: "As regards the views presented," says he, "I seem to have had only about the same agency in forming them that I have in preparing the blood I circulate and the anatomic frame I occupy. They are not

---

concerned, he styles Dr. Bushnell an "orthodox divine," and a "Presbyterian clergyman." As to his orthodoxy we say nothing; that depends upon the standard of comparison; but we most earnestly protest against his being called a "*Presbyterian.*"

[1] Men do not argue or feel so absurdly when their own temporal interests are concerned. The gibbet, the penitentiary, and the officers of police, no doubt, shock the sensibilities of thieves and assassins; but they are not abolished on that account, nor do they prove to be unreal bugbears to the transgressors of the law.

my choice or invention, so much as a necessary growth, whose process I can hardly trace myself; and now, in giving them to the public, I seem only to have about the same kind of option left me that I have in the matter of appearing in corporal manifestation myself; about the same anxiety, I will add, concerning the unfavorable judgments to be encountered; for though a man's opinions are of vastly greater moment than his looks, yet, if he is equally simple in them as in his growth, and equally subject to his law, he is responsible only in the same degree, and ought not, in fact, to suffer any greater concern about their reception than about the judgments passed upon his person." (Pp. 97, 98.)

We make no comments on this passage, but only quote the solemn words of the Son of God: "He that *believeth* not shall be damned." "If ye *believe* not that I am he, ye shall die in your sins." God grant that the opinions of these "Discourses" may not be laid to the author's charge!

But our author thinks that he finds his theory in the second chapter of the Second Epistle to the Corinthians; and, as he does not often refer so specifically and particularly to the law and the testimony, it may be well to notice the passage. That chapter contains, certainly, a very strong assertion of the necessity of the Spirit's illumination in order that the truth may be effectually understood. But we cannot see how it subserves Dr. Bushnell's purpose, except upon the supposition that the subject under consideration is the necessity of *inspiration*, and that this inspiration is given, though in different degrees, to all who are to understand spiritual things. We cannot admit that *he* is inspired, or that his notion of inspiration is a just one; and, therefore, we must be allowed to say that this noble passage of the logical, scholastic apostle of the Gentiles has nothing, as it appears to us, to do with his theory. It is not a gift of the Spirit bestowed upon a man to see what he pleases independently of the record, or to see what suits his tastes *in* the record, but a gift by which his understanding may apprehend the truth, and the heart may feel the goodness and sweetness of the things revealed in the word. Faith contains two elements, a conviction of the understanding and a sympathy of the heart; and the Spirit alone can produce either effectually. It appears to us that the doctrine of the "Discourses" makes the "spirit of a man" the judge of the things of God, which Paul says cannot be. We can refer our author to two places of the New Testament which seem to give more support to his *æstheticism* than the one upon which he mainly relies. They are Philippians i. 9, and Hebrews v. 14. The word rendered "judgment" by our translators in the first is *æsthesis* (αισθησις); the word rendered "senses" in the second is *æstheteria* (αισθητηρια.). And the apostle seems to teach that there is a faculty for the apprehension of spiritual truth analagous to the senses for the perception of external objects. But this is nothing more than the faculty of spiritual discernment of the second chapter of Second Corinthians, an illuminated and sanctified mind interpreting the logical revelation which God has given, with a tacit reference to the rapidity of its operation; a rapidity which is the natural result of "exercise," and which makes the faculty to resemble an instinct or taste. In cases where the record does not speak expressly or by necessary implication, the spiritual nature of a believer will often indicate to him the will of God. "Be not conformed to this world; but be ye transformed by the renewing of your mind, that *ye may prove what is that good and acceptable and perfect will of God.*" (Rom. xii. 2.) But this is the poles apart from the power contended for by our modern philosophers. It pretends to no vision of transcendental concrete realities; it is simply the power of judging, from our past familiarity with a person's character and opinions, and our sympathy with him, what his opinion would be in a given case, in reference to which we had never heard him express an opinion. In another form, it is the old maxim, "A sound heart is the best casuist."

We have greatly exceeded the limits which we had assigned to ourselves for the notice of these "Discourses," and conclude with expressing our earnest hope that the spirit of this Luciferian philosophy may extend no farther in the ministry of the church. Satan fell into condemnation, through pride (probably) of understanding. The stress of the temptation by which Adam fell and brought death into the world and all our woe, was in the imagined virtue of the fruit "to make one wise." It was listening to the suggestions of intellectual ambition, instead of following, with the simplicity of a child, the word of the Lord, which ruined him and ruined us in him. These great swelling words of vanity are rebuked even by the pagan sages, and betray the shallowness of the thinking from which they spring. Sure we are, they are the words neither of truth nor soberness. They are not the gospel of Jesus Christ; they are more like the ravings of Jean Jacques Rousseau. Christ crucified, Christ *made a curse* for us, Christ magnifying the law and making it honorable, Christ rising again for our justification and making perpetual intercession for us, Christ the Alpha and the Omega, the beginning and the end, the first and the last, the all and in all; this is "the wisdom of God and the power of God to salvation." It is the exhibition of sovereign grace in him, a grace bestowed freely, without money and without price; a grace which fixed upon the sinner before he was born and had done either good or evil; a grace which disdains commixture not only with human merit, but with human works; which lays the foundation and brings out the topstone; which imparts, develops and completes the principle of spiritual life—it is the exhibition of sovereign grace like this which brings the penitent prodigals of mankind back to their Father's house, with the confession, "We have sinned."

[NOTE.—As we have spoken in terms of some severity of Dr. Park's discourse, in a note to the preceding article, we deem it just to add, that since the article was written we have read a pamphlet of the author, containing forty-eight pages of remarks upon the strictures of the Biblical Repertory upon the Sermon. We are rejoiced to find that he holds more truth than we supposed, and a great deal more truth than the Doctor of Hartford. We, of course, receive the author's exposition of the leading design and main doctrines of the sermon, and the *dexterity* of his defence cannot be too highly appiauded. "*Si Pergama dextra,*" *etc.* But we must say, that our opinion of the tendencies of the performance remains unchanged. It is not fair to charge a man with inferences which he repudiates; but it is always fair to show, if we can, that such and such consequences do flow from his doctrines, and therefore that the doctrine is not true. It is the *reductio ad absurdum* of the mathematicians. One of the criteria which Dr. Park himself lays down in his last pamphlet, to discriminate between the true and the false, is "the *moral tendency* of a doctrine." To this test we are perfectly willing to submit the *Discourses on God in Christ*, and *The Theology of the Intellect and the Theology of the Feelings*.

"TAKE HEED TO THYSELF."[1]

PAUL exhorts Timothy to "take heed to himself and to his teaching"; and we are reminded of the distinction between that kind of training which has the man himself for its end—the development of his powers and the improvement of his character, and that which has for its end the making him a dexterous instrument for the doing of a particular sort of work; in other words, between a liberal and a professional education. These two are inseparably connected. What a man does depends upon what he is, and, therefore, it is of the first importance to take heed to himself. It is important, above all, in those who are seeking to be trained for the preaching of the gospel. Let me ask your attention, then, to the kind of discipline which constitutes taking heed to one's self, and to some of the means by which that discipline is to be acquired.

I. And first let me remind you of the fundamental necessity of godliness. "Theology is the science of religion," *i. e.*, it is the system of doctrine in its logical connection and dependence, which, when spiritually discerned, produces true piety. I say spiritually discerned, for there is a science of theology which is the result of the ordinary exercise of our faculties of knowledge, and the habit of which, like every other habit of science, is that of mere speculative knowledge. But when the truth of God is spiritually discerned by the gracious illumination of the Holy Spirit, and by a soul which has been renewed and inspired with love to God by the Holy Spirit, the habit which corresponds to it is the habit of true

[1] The substance of an address delivered to the students of the Seminary at the opening of the session of 1889–'90. It was published in the first issue of *The Union Seminary Magazine*, October–November, 1889.—ED.

religion. (Rom. vi. 17; 1 Peter i. 22, 23; James i. 18.) There can be no conviction of divine truth, or even any proper understanding of it, without regeneration. It is a common remark, and, when properly understood, a perfectly true one, that no man can preach effectively who does not preach "out of his own experience." What is Christian experience but the impression, according to Paul's figure, which the mould of the truth makes upon the heart. Not only ought the minister to have the root of the matter in him, but he ought to be growing in grace, and to have his grace in constant exercise. In Acts xiv. 1, even such preachers as Paul and Barnabas are said to have "so preached" that multitudes believed.

Never forget that the only reason why God has chosen men and not angels to preach his word concerning sin and salvation is that men alone can have experience of sin and salvation. Bunyan ascribed his success in awakening sinners to the fact that he had felt the fire of hell in his own conscience. McCheyne's success in winning souls to Christ was due, in great measure, to his habitual and deep communion with Christ, and to the consequent conviction of his preciousness as the Saviour of sinners.

In other professions the difference may be wide between the man and the workman; though in all the trades and professions it may be truly said that the godly man, other things being equal, will always be the best workman. Still there is a difference between the "end of the work" (*finis operis*) and the "end of the worker" (*finis operantis*). But in the preaching of the gospel these two ends coincide. For example, Paul was a tent-maker as well as a preacher. The end of his trade as a tent-maker was the making of tents; and that end could be accomplished by a pagan or an unbelieving Jew, as well as by Paul and Aquila. But the end contemplated by Paul, as a *man*, was the glory of God by a life of industry and honesty. In the preaching of the gospel the end of the work and of the worker was the same—the glory of God in the salvation of the church.

It is plain, however, that these two ends could not have coincided in his case, unless he had been a godly man and a minister of the word. The validity of a priest's ministration does not depend on his moral character, nor on his spiritual condition at the time of service—Hophni or Zadok, it is all one. But not so with a minister of the word. His power is moral and spiritual. Hence such exhortations as Acts xx. 28, 1 Tim. iv. 16, apply with peculiar force to ministers, and the last to candidates as well as to ministers.

Growth in grace is indispensable to growth in the knowledge of Jesus Christ, and what is Christian theology but the knowledge of Jesus Christ? The active exercise of the principles of piety is necessary to a steady faith in God's word. Never was it more necessary to remember this than now. Constant contact with Christ himself will make us superior to all the difficulties suggested by the understanding. Consider John vi. 60–69, where we have types of two classes: (*a*), Men of understanding only, and (*b*), Men of heart and conscience, who are intent upon eternal life. Compare Nathaniel in John i. 45–49: he was an Israelite, indeed, and yet stumbled at logical difficulties. These all vanished when he came into contact with Christ himself. Christ's reference to his season of sweet fellowship with him under the fig tree was enough to put to flight all his doubts, and the Saviour assured him of greater seasons than that, when Nathaniel should recognize him as the truth and reality of the mystic ladder of Jacob's vision. If such is the fundamental importance of piety in the study of theology, then the discipline by which piety is promoted must occupy a conspicuous place in the course of preparation for the ministry. *Pectus facit theologum.*

II. Let us now consider *the necessity and mode of discipline in piety*. The *necessity* of discipline need not be argued, if the necessity of piety be conceded. The Christian life is a warfare requiring incessant activity and vigilance. "Exercise thyself unto godliness" (1 Tim. iv. 7) is an exhortation suited to every wrestler in the Christian contest. The minister must lay his account for special "temptations and conflicts," unless either grace is overwhelmingly abundant or Satan judges him to be a workman that he need not fear.

As to the *mode*. The first is prayer: Luke xviii. 1; Matt. xvii. 21; Acts vi. 4; Eph. i. 16, ff.; vi. 18; 1 Thess. v. 17, *et mult. al.* If the word of God cannot be understood without the illumination of the Spirit, then prayer is necessary. (Psa. cxix. 18; Eph. i. 17, 18; Luke xi. 13.) If the word cannot be understood without a renewed heart, then prayer is necessary, for God only can renew the heart. If special grace is necessary for the arduous duties and tremendous responsibilities of the ministry, then special prayer is required on the part of those who are seeking the ministry.

"There are three things that make a minister," Luther is reported to have said, "prayer, meditation, and temptation." "*Bene orasse est bene studuisse*" is another saying that has been ascribed to him. The connection between prayer and study is worthy of particular attention from us. Students, especially the young, are very liable to the delusion that progress in knowledge is in direct proportion to the time spent in study. Hence, they judge the time given to exercise and recreation as time lost, and even pious students make their private prayers what their public prayers ought to be—short. This I say is a delusion. Some time, of course, is required for study, but successful progress requires a preparation of the mind for it. Hence, the time spent in exercise and recreation is not lost, but time gained. This is eminently true of prayer. It is the highest and noblest exercise of the soul. If communion with a superior human intellect is quickening and elevating to the soul, what must we say of communion with that intellect of which the most splendid human intellects are nothing more than feeble scintillations? Could Bunyan have written his *Pilgrim's Progress*, or Milton his *Paradise Lost*, or even Newton his *Principia*, if they had not been men of prayer? Nearly all the great discoverers, as distinguished from inventors, have been praying men; their faculties have been quickened and the intuitive power of their genius has been purified and made keener by coming in contact, so to speak, with the eternal fountain of intelligence and truth. This indirect influence of communion with God in promoting successful study can hardly be overrated. But, beside this, it cannot be doubted by any believer in God's word that God honors those who honor him as the Father of lights, and by a direct agency of his Spirit does quicken the mind, purge the vision and make it apprehend truth which would otherwise elude its grasp; as, on the other hand, he sends blindness as a judicial curse upon those who despise him and are determined to walk in the light of their own eyes.

The second element of the discipline of piety I shall mention is the constant reading of God's word in the English version. Be not startled at this statement. Are we not here, you are ready to say, for the express purpose of studying the Scriptures? Why, then, mention this particularly? I answer, that the very fact that you are here for the study of the Scriptures makes it all the more needful to exhort you to familiarity with the English version. The grammatical and critical study of the Hebrew and Greek texts in which you are to be employed will not answer the purposes of devotion. Your want of thorough acquaintance with these languages will be a constant obstruction to the flow of feeling. Your habit of searching into the exact meaning and shade of meaning of every word—a habit to be cultivated with much diligence—will have the effect, if not counteracted by other habits, of making your acquaintance with Scripture merely scholastic in its character and limited in its range, limited to the parts of the Bible which are critically studied in the seminary course. Hence, the importance of reading the Bible in a language with which you are so familiar that you will not have to think of the words at all. The kind of reading of which I am speaking is, in a certain sense, no doubt, superficial. Many words and even sentences will be passed over without being understood, and you will have to resist the temptation to stop and analyze. But bear in mind that you are reading now for the purpose of catching the tone and imbibing the spirit of the sacred writers, not for the purpose of ascertaining the meaning of what they say.

A child growing up in what is called "good company" hears and sees a hundred things it does not know the meaning of, but it is moulded, nevertheless, and acquires a certain tone and manner which will make people say, "This child has seen good company." Let your familiarity with the English Bible be such as to make men say that you have been with Jesus, and have been keeping company with prophets and apostles.

Another argument for the diligent reading of the English version is, that *it is the people's Bible.* Some preachers, who are scholars and learned men, are complained of by the people because they do not quote the Bible correctly. A misquotation of the common English Version impresses the hearer who is familiar with it in a manner similar to that in which a misquotation of a Greek or Latin classic impresses a scholar. It produces a jar or shock which is disagreeable, if not painful. Such misquotation is often the result of reading more in the original than in the English Version. This was said of the great preacher, Robert Hall. Constant reading in the version which the people use will prevent this. I would earnestly recommend, also, a daily exercise of committing to memory a portion of the English Version. This will promote correct quotation, and at the same time help you to form a pure and simple English style.

The ability to recite off-hand, from memory, paragraph after paragraph of Milton or Shakespeare has been considered an enviable attainment. Why should we value less a like facility in reference to the Bible? The English Bible, considered merely as an English classic, is fully equal, to say the least, to Shakespeare or Milton. It is incomparably superior for the purposes of a minister, because, among the masses of the people, it has ten readers where any other great classic has one. "The diction of the English Bible," as has been beautifully said, "with its simplicity, its dignity, its power, its happy turns of expression, its general accuracy, the music of its cadences, and the felicity of its rhythm, is the consecrated diction of devotion and religious instruction for all denominations of English-speaking Christians, God's greatest gift to the many millions of Britain and America. It lives on the ear like music that can never be forgotten; like the sound of church-bells, which the convert hardly knows how to forego; and the felicities often seem to be almost things rather than words. It is part of the national mind, and the anchor of national seriousness. The memory of the dead passes into it. The potent traditions of childhood are stereotyped in its voices. The power of all the griefs and trials of man's life is hid beneath its words. It is the representation of his best moments; and all that there has been about him of soft and pure and penitent and good speaks to him from out of his Protestant Bible. It is his sacred thing which doubt has never dimmed, and controversy never soiled."[1]

The third element in the discipline I am recommending is *faithfulness* in the performance of every duty imposed by the rules of the institution of which you have become mem-

[1] These exquisite words are to be found in "The Characteristics of the Lives of the Saints," an essay prefixed to Faber's *Life of Saint Francis of Assisi*. See Trench's *English Past and Present*, section i., page 39, of the eleventh edition, London. Trench says that in some of the earlier editions he had attributed them to Cardinal Newman.

bers. Some people think, and, it should seem, have good reason to think, that candidates for the ministry should be models of conscientiousness. Paul exhorts Timothy (1 Tim. iv. 12) to be an example (*τύπος*) to believers in word, behavior, love, faith and purity. It is not unreasonable, therefore, to expect that those who are seeking the ministry, and are in training for it, should cultivate the heart and conscience more assiduously than others. That this is universally the case, observation does not warrant us in asserting.

Note, therefore, in the first place, the weighty words of Jesus himself, whom you profess to obey: "He that is faithful in that which is least is faithful also in much." (Luke xvi. 10–12.)

The teaching of this passage is, (1), That faithfulness implies, in its very nature, an undivided heart. The spirit of obedience is a spirit which makes no distinction among the commandments. Its language is not, "This is great and important, and must be done; this is small and insignificant, and may be slighted or omitted." No! Its language is, "Then shall I not be ashamed when I have respect unto *all* thy commandments." (Psalm cxix. 6; and compare Matt. iii. 19; James ii. 8–11.) Indeed, a man's conduct in little things is a sure test of his spirit and character, and, therefore, of what he is likely to do in great things. If he is unfaithful in small matters we do not expect him to be faithful in great ones; for it is in the so-called small matters that the authority of the Master is most nakedly, and, therefore, most emphatically, expressed; and so obedience is exhibited more emphatically in such matters. It is said that in some Romish monasteries the first lesson that is given to a novice is the drinking of a bowl of bitter liquid, or even something more disgusting, such as licking the floor with the tongue. Such requirements show a knowledge of human nature. If the soul is to be broken into monastic obedience, nothing can be better suited to such an end than submission to arbitrary and distasteful requirements, which express naked authority. If obedience is rendered simply as obedience, then all distinctions of great and small disappear. So in matters of trust. It is required in a steward that he be found faithful; and faithfulness is violated as much in the embezzlement of a dollar as in the embezzlement of a thousand. He who will tell a small lie will tell a great one. The spirit of faithfulness is absolutely incompatible with unfaithfulness in the least as well as in the greatest. "*Falsus in uno, falsus in omnibus.*" The same conclusion is made good by the fact that the habit of committing great sins is formed by committing small ones. "*Nemo fit repente turpissimus.*" The divergence from the straight line of duty may begin with an angle so small as to be imperceptible; but, if continued in the same direction, the line will ultimately be at an infinite distance from that from which it diverged. Beware, then, of allowing yourselves to dally with the temptation of neglecting any duty because it is small.

(2), The Saviour teaches that improvement in character and position is the result of faithfulness in all things. The connection between fidelity in everything and improvement in character is too obvious to need illustration. It is simply one exemplification of the law of habit. You are familiar with the story of the artist who was observed to take great pains with some very minute and trivial parts of his work, and who, when asked why he spent so much time on trifles, answered that the trifles were necessary to perfection, and that perfection was no trifle. Jenny Lind sang once for a crowd of poor people, and was observed to sing with all her power. She was asked why she took so much pains. Her answer was, "I never slight my art." Golden words! Imitate God, who takes pains with everything—with the blade of grass as well as with the cedar of Lebanon; with the eye of an insect as well as with the eye of an eagle. An improvement in position is also the result of faithfulness in everything. David in the wilderness with the sheep was preparing for the throne. Promotion everywhere is the result of faithfulness in the lower form, and is all the more certain for not being aimed at. A young minister who occupies a small and obscure field of labor, and works with all his might, as if it were to be his field for life, and is ambitious of no other, is the man who is most likely to be promoted to a wider and more conspicuous field. The principle is announced by the Saviour on more than one occasion, and in more than one form. (See Luke xix. 17, 26; Matt. xxv. 21, 23, 29.) Faithfulness in the lower place is necessary to the attainment of the higher.

There are two aspects in which the exercises prescribed for the students in this institution may be regarded. (*a*), As merely scholastic—as intended to furnish the mind with professional knowledge and to form certain intellectual habits, exegetical, theological, homiletical, etc., and incidentally to serve as a gymnastic for the mind. (*b*), As *moral*—as intended to discipline the moral character by the formation of habits of obedience and faithfulness. As to the first, bear in mind that all your studies are prescribed by men of more age, of greater experience, of riper judgment, than yourselves; and that some branches of study, like some parts of the body—to use the figure of Paul—are none the less necessary for being feeble, uncomely, unattractive. Your aversion to a particular study may be a sign of a defect of mind which makes that study specially necessary for you in the way of a remedy, in the way of forming a habit which it is especially needful for you to form, and which cannot by any other study be formed so well. "*Abeunt studia in mores*," says Bacon (*Essay on Studies*), "studies turn into habits; nay, there is no stond [disinclination or restiveness] or impediment in the wit but may be wrought out by fit studies, like as diseases of the body may have appropriate exercises; bowling is good for the stone and veins; shooting for the lungs and breast; gentle walking for the stomach; riding for the head, and the like. So, if a man's wit be wandering, let him study the mathematics; for, in demonstrations, if his wit be called away never so little, he must begin again; if his wit be not apt to distinguish or find differences, let him study the schoolmen; for they are *cymini sectores* [dividers of cummin seed—'able to divide a hair twixt south and southwest side']; if he be not apt to beat over matters and to call upon one thing to prove and illustrate another, let him study the lawyers' cases. So every defect of the mind may have a special receipt." These considerations may justify us in doubting as to the wisdom of giving up the curriculum in some of our colleges, and in deploring the "fatty degeneration" (to use a happy expression of Shedd) of it in others.

But it is in the second aspect of the studies of this place, as a moral discipline, that I have treated them specially in these remarks. I beseech you to look at them in this light, and to consider the damage which may be done to your character, and, therefore, to your usefulness, by disregarding obligations which you assume by the very act of your coming here, and which you have made more serious by signing a solemn pledge to fulfil.

There are always special dangers attending changes in the manner of life and in the occupations of men; but these changes are more serious in prosecuting the work of God. You may expect, in entering upon a course of special preparation for the work of the ministry, to be *tempted* as you were never tempted before. Our great Exemplar was driven into the wilderness to be tempted of the devil immediately after his baptism and solemn inauguration into office. This is both a warning and an encouragement to us, "therefore take heed to thyself and to the doctrine."

THE TWO PROFESSIONS.[1]

"SEEING then that we have a great high priest, that is passed into the heavens, Jesus the Son of God, let us hold fast our profession." (Hebrews iv. 14.) Such is the exhortation of the apostle to the Hebrew Christians.

"Profession" includes two things: 1, The solemn and public declaration of adherence to that which is professed; 2, The thing itself which is solemnly professed. In this case, that which is professed is the Christian religion, as distinguished from Judaism; and that which is signalized as the prime characteristic of the Christian religion is the nature of its priesthood. Man, the sinner, is afraid to meet God, and feels the need of a mediator. The Israelites at the foot of the burning mount simply gave voice to the sentiment of mankind when they said to Moses, "Speak thou with us, and we will hear; but let not God speak with us lest we die." Hence, a priesthood and sacrifices are found wherever a religion is found amongst men. Neither Judaism nor Christianity is an exception to the rule. The practical question with the professing Christians to whom the Epistle of the Hebrews was addressed was whether they would hold fast to the priesthood of Jesus, the Son of God, or let it go, and return to the priesthood of Aaron. Let us compare the two professions, and see in what particulars the Christian is superior to the Jewish, though both of them were ordained of God.

1. The Jewish priesthood was one of mortal men. As they who held it "were not suffered to continue by reason of

[1] Outlines of a sermon preached in the chapel of Union Theological Seminary, and published by request of the students.

death," there must be many priests coming to the altar in succession. Besides, these priests were all sinners, and many of them very flagrant sinners; and "by reason hereof must, as for the people, so also for themselves, offer for sins."[1]

2. A priest must have "somewhat to offer." Wherefore the Jewish priests were "ordained to offer gifts and sacrifices."[2] These sacrifices consisted of domestic animals, bullocks, goats, sheep, etc. Their life was appointed to be a covering for the forfeited life of man.[3]

3. The efficacy of such sacrifices offered by such priests was what might have been expected. It would reach no farther than "the purification of the flesh,"[4] the removal of a bar to communion with the external and visible church. "The blood of bulls and goats could not take away sins," could not "purge the conscience."[5] The very fact of their constant repetition convicted them of imperfection, of inability to give peace with God. If they had been efficacious in removing guilt, they would have ceased to be offered, because that the worshippers once purged should have had no more conscience of sins."[6] Further, if the sacrifice was inadequate to give peace, it was for the same reason impotent to procure holiness. The flesh was purified, not the spirit. The offerer remained under the dominion as well as under the guilt of sin. He was unsanctified as well as unjustified; defiled as well as condemned. Truly the whole system, if it had been intended to be final and not provisional and temporary only, would have been an unreasonable service,[7] weak, unprofitable, beggarly,[8] a grim mockery of the sinner groaning under the torment of conscience, and sighing to be delivered from the body of death.

Let us now look at the priesthood that superseded it, the Christian priesthood.

---

[1] Heb. vii. 23; v. 3. [2] Heb. viii. 3. [3] Lev. xvii. 11. [4] Heb. ix. 13.
[5] Heb. ix. 14; x. 4. [6] Heb. x. 1, 2, 3. [7] Rom. xii. 1.
[8] Heb. vii. 18; Gal. iv. 9.

1. The priest is *one*, not many, because he is the eternal Son of God, "without beginning of days or end of life," "continuing ever," and therefore having "an unchangeable priesthood"; that is, a priesthood which "does not pass to another," which admits and requires no succession,[1] a priesthood "made not after the law of a carnal commandment, but after the power of an endless life." He is also very man as well as very God; "taken from among men," and "able to have compassion on the ignorant and on them that are out of the way," because he also himself was once compassed with infirmity[2]; was "tempted in all points like as we are, yet without sin; holy, harmless, undefiled, and separate from sinners"[3]; needing not, like the Jewish high priest, to offer up sacrifice first for his own sins and then for the people's.[4] He was also consecrated to his office by the oath of God, a solemnity not used in the consecration of the Jewish priests. What a pledge have we in all these circumstances that the interests of God's kingdom and the salvation of the church shall be safe in his hands.

2. The sacrifice. This is said to be "himself."[5] His human life was offered for us. The blood of bulls and goats could not take away sins; the life of a mere animal could not be a satisfaction for the life of a man created in the image of God. Neither God nor man could be satisfied with such an offering. It is man that has sinned, and it is man that must die. So thought the saints even of the Old Testament.[6] A divine man, a God man, must offer up his life—one who has power (right) to lay down his life and power to take it again.[7] The life of such a person is a perfect "covering" or atonement for the life of a human sinner,[8] and the life of no other person can be. The high priest of our profession is a glorious paradox. He is at once priest, sacri-

[1] Heb. vii. 3, 16, 24. [2] Heb. v. 1, 2. [3] Heb. iv. 15; vii. 26.
[4] Heb. vii. 27. [5] Heb. vii. 27; ix. 14; Eph. v. 2.
[6] Psa. xl. 5–8; Heb. x. 4–10. [7] John x. 18. [8] Lev. xvii. 11.

fice and altar. The infinite dignity of his person lends infinite value to his sacrifice. Hence,

3. The efficacy of his priestly work avails to the taking away of sin, the purging of the conscience, and the removal of the pollution of our nature. He is a priest unlike those of the Levitical law, who were "standing daily ministering and offering oftentimes the same sacrifices, which could never take away sins." He offered *one* sacrifice for sins *for ever*, and "sat down on the right hand of God, from henceforth expecting till his enemies be made his footstool; for by one offering he hath perfected for ever them that are sanctified."[1]

In this view of the infinite superiority of the Christian priesthood, it may seem strange that any exhortation to hold fast the profession of it should be thought needful. Yet a large portion of those very Christians to whom this exhortation was addressed apostatized from their profession. Stranger still, the largest portion of Christendom has fallen into the same deplorable error. If we estimate the number of professing Christians in the world at 300,000,000, and the numbers of the Roman and Greek communions at 200,000,000, we have as the result two apostates from God's priesthood for one who adheres to it. This is far worse than the apostasy against which the apostle warned the Hebrews; for that was an apostasy to a priesthood which had been once divinely ordained, and had acquired prodigious force from the observance of centuries; this, in Christendom, was an apostasy to a priesthood that never had the semblance of a divine sanction; nay, was set up in defiance of the warnings of prophets and apostles. For what is the priesthood of Rome? It is—

1. One of sinful and mortal men.
2. One ministering "unbloody" sacrifices.
3. Therefore sacrifices which cannot purge the conscience,

[1] Hebrews x. 11-14.

or purify the heart. This is confessed by themselves in the constant *repetition* of the sacrifices.[1]

God's priesthood, which *can* take away sins, has been forsaken for a priesthood which, by its own confession, can *not* take away sins! "Hear, O heavens, and give ear, O earth! I have nourished and brought up children, and they have rebelled against me. The ox knoweth his owner, and the ass his master's crib; but Israel doth not know, my people doth not consider." No wonder that the great apostle of the Gentiles denounces this error with burning words, in which "there are earthquake and hurricane, battle and blows." As he contemplates the enormous wickedness of such an apostasy, "his whole being becomes full of indignation, his breast heaves, his brow darkens, his feelings explode, and the flash and thunderbolt leap forth in the form of something like an exterminating curse, 'I would they were even cut off which trouble you'—excluded from the church of Christ or struck dead by the hand of God."[2] And yet this is the error which is patronized by the politicians and the secular press in this Protestant country; and even some Presbyterian theologians hold that the papacy may be recognized as a church of Christ! The journalists and politicians, some of them at least, know what the social, political, commercial effects of a reign of popery have been and are; yet they make a pet of it! Their maxim seems to be, "Let us have power *now*, and after us the deluge."

But it was not only the wickedness of the return to Judaism which roused the indignation of the apostle, but its absurdity also. He rebuked Peter for his dissimulation (Gal. ii.) as a virtual "building again the things they had destroyed," and so outraging common sense. He had "acted like men who had left a mud cottage that stood upon the sand, and had taken shelter in an edifice of solid stone built high upon a

---

[1] See Hebrews x. 1-4; ix. 28.

[2] Binney: Sermon on *The Law Our Schoolmaster*.

rock; and who after that, and in order to be safe from a dreaded inundation, actually went back to the thing they had abandoned, or encouraged others to trust themselves to it! The apostle saw an absurdity in this deserving the contempt of his understanding, mixed with a cruelty which at once roused and wrung his soul."

This leads us to note the *cruelty*, the devilish cruelty, of this apostasy of so large a portion of the nominally Christian church. If a Hebrew brought his offering to the altar, the canons of the Levitical law were violated; if the priest who sprinkled the blood upon the altar was no divinely-appointed priest, or if such priest, he violated, like the sons of Eli, the canons of the law in making the offering; or if the victim was not such as the law prescribed, there might be no expiation. But the worst that could happen to the sincere and honest worshipper would be the failure of the ceremonial expiation--the failure of the "purification of the flesh," the remaining under certain external ecclesiastical disabilities. His eternal salvation was not put in peril. God had never made *that* to depend upon the ministrations of a sinful and mortal priesthood. But according to the papacy, the salvation of men does depend upon the ministrations of such a priesthood; and to cap the climax of iniquity and cruelty, upon the ministrations of priests who according to their own principles can never know that they *are* priests, and therefore can never give any reasonable assurance to the people that they are so. Further, it teaches that the efficacy of the ministration depends upon the "intention" of the priest; and as his intention is not known to any one but himself, it cannot be known to the worshipper whether his sins are forgiven. Can any wickedness and cruelty exceed this? Surely no candid mind can fail to detect here the device of him who was a liar and murderer from the beginning.

To the inquiry, how such an apostasy from God's priesthood came to pass, it is not a sufficient answer to point to the avarice and ambition of the man-made priests. "By this craft we have our wealth." How were people "professing and calling themselves Christians," brought to submit to a priesthood usurping the office of Jesus the Son of God? The only sufficient answer is to be found in the enmity of the heart against God as a *holy* God. "Without holiness no man shall see the Lord." God's priest is one who sanctifies all for whom he acts; he is exalted at the right hand of the Father to give repentance as well as remission of sins. These two things cannot be separated in his glorious ministrations. That they cannot be is a matter of thankfulness and joy to all who desire to be saved from sin, and not merely from its penal doom. But it is very different with those who dread the tribunal of God, and yet are in love with sin. They admire a priesthood which shall not by the life of its members remind them of the inexorable demands of holiness, which shall usurp the kingly as well as the priestly office of God's king and priest, and claim the prerogative of dispensing with the precept of the law as well as that of remitting its penalty. "The fatal spell of popery is its absolving power;" but the potency of the spell lies in its pretended power to absolve from the obligation of obedience to God as well as from the penalty which he threatens against disobedience.

HEBREWS VI. 4-6.

"For it is impossible for those who were once enlightened, and have tasted of the heavenly gift, and were made partakers of the Holy Ghost, and have tasted the good word of God, and the powers of the world to come, if they shall fall away to renew them again unto repentance; seeing they crucify to themselves the Son of God afresh, and put him to an open shame." (Hebrews vi. 4-6.)

THIS is on many accounts one of the most interesting passages in the Epistle to the Hebrews. It was the main bulwark of Novatian and his followers in the third century, and the Latin church, in their opposition to the austere discipline of the Reformer, were disposed to deny the canonical authority of the epistle itself. In modern times it has been the arena of animated contests between the champions of free grace and Arminians, both parties acknowledging the epistle to be a revelation from God, but differing widely as to the true interpretation. Many a humble follower of the Lamb, ignorant of the disputations of the schools and anxious only for the prosperity of his own soul, has been made by these words to tremble for the stability of that covenant upon which he had reposed his immortal concerns as upon an immovable foundation. So that between weakness of faith and subtlety of the adversary many have been made sad whom the Lord hath not made sad. These considerations will furnish an apology, if any be needed, for a few expository remarks upon this passage.

It may be well, in the first place, to notice the connection in which the words are introduced. "*For* it is impossible." The apostle had just been compelled to arrest the progress of the discussion, by the reflection that the persons whom he was addressing had not reached sufficient maturity in knowledge to comprehend the statements. He rebukes them for their negligence, and exhorts them to learn the first principles of the doctrine of Christ, and to go on unto perfection; adding, "and this will we do if God permit." "For it is impossible." It is as if he had said, "Our negligence in the study of the mysteries of the gospel is an alarming symptom of an evil heart of unbelief in departing from the living God. Not to go on, is the next thing to going back. It may be that God will not permit us to go on. He may suffer us to fall from bad to worse, until that declension which began in sloth shall end in total and hopeless apostasy. For such a falling away from God is hopeless."

This view of the connection of the passage is pregnant with instruction. It will not be easy for those who condemn systematic doctrinal instruction in the pulpit, and contend for a sort of *disciplina arcana* in the department of biblical exposition, to reconcile their views with the argument and example of the apostle. They would, no doubt, have reserved such a subject as the character of Melchisedek for the meditations of the closet or the prelections of the schools. We cannot enlarge upon the subject here. We can only say, that in our opinion the capacity of the masses is much more commonly underrated than overrated, and that the ordinary ministrations of the pulpit much more commonly go under than over the heads of the people. An elevated standard both of knowledge and experience must be kept before their minds, or their stature, intellectual or moral, cannot be much increased. In every case they will fall below the standard, and therefore it is of the utmost importance that the standard should be high. We do not see the evils of superficial preaching (or practical, as it is most preposterously called) while the church is basking lazily in the sunshine of peace; but if the storm of persecution should ever sweep over the land, the multitude of apostates will reveal these evils in all their magnitude. But to return:

There are three interpretations of this passage which we intend to consider.

I. The first is that which regards the persons described as true believers, but supposes they are contemplated in their collective and organized capacity as a church, and not individually. According to this view, the apostasy of a true church is here described. In reference to this interpretation, we simply observe that a church which holds the truth may, unquestionably, apostatize in the course of time, and become so hopelessly corrupt as to make the attempt to reform it as a church presumptuous and absurd. This is the case with the Church of Rome, as we shall have occasion to illustrate before we close this article; but we cannot think that this is the meaning of the text, for reasons which will appear afterwards.

II. The second interpretation is that which regards the description as belonging to Christians, true believers, and that, too, as individuals. According to this view, the passage implies the possibility of hopeless apostasy in the case of those who have been born again by the power of God.

In reference to this interpretation, we observe that, as a general rule, it is not safe to convert the hypothetical statements of Scripture into categorical propositions. It does not follow necessarily, from the statement of this passage taken by itself, that a real falling away is possible, although we believe, from the consideration of the context, and from other places of God's word, that such an apostasy is possible. The warnings which are addressed to Christians by no means imply that the calamities to which the warnings refer can ever overtake them. It might as well be said that the prayer of our Saviour in the garden implied that it was possible for him not to die, not to perform that great work to which he was consecrated before the world was, and which he came into the world to perform. No; there was a certain fitness in the appalling agonies which were before him, to produce in his human nature the feelings which found expression in that prayer. And so it is with warnings of Scripture as addressed to those who are in Christ Jesus. They possess a fitness, in the calamities they threaten, to produce certain feelings in the breast of a believer, which operate as so many checks and barriers against his yielding to temptation and falling into sin. God keeps his children in the way of holiness and salvation, but he uses methods adapted to their complex constitution. He employs all the natural emotions of the heart in accomplishing his purpose. Surely those who defend this view of the passage under consideration would not assert that it is possible for the holy angels, or the spirits of just men made perfect, to fall from their happy position before the throne; and yet we can conceive that the contemplation of the immaculate holiness and inflexible justice of God, as illustrated in the fires of hell, may have an important bearing upon their perseverance in holiness and in the hatred of sin. God's purpose to save is irrevocable. He will infallibly keep his people unto salvation; but his people are creatures of hope and fear, and he uses these emotions to achieve the result. Even, therefore, if it should be granted that the persons here described are true believers, we could not settle the question whether it is possible for them to fall away, without appealing to the analogy of faith. All that is asserted is, that upon a certain state or condition certain consequences take place. It is not asserted that this state or condition can ever exist.

We believe, as has been already remarked, that such an apostasy as has been described is possible, because the context and the analogy of faith support this opinion. But, for the same reasons, we are certain that it is not of the true children of God that this apostasy is predicated. The apostle tells us so expressly in the verses below: "But, beloved, we are persuaded better things of you, and things that accompany salvation, though we thus speak. For God is not unrighteous to forget your work and labor of love which ye have showed toward his name in that ye have ministered to the saints and do minister." The apostle here informs us that the illumination and other spiritual endowments enumerated in the fourth and fifth verses are not "things that accompany salvation," that is, are not so inseparably connected with salvation but that they may belong to persons who never have been and never will be in favor with God. In other words, they are spiritual gifts, not spiritual graces. The love of God, on the contrary, which is manifested by ministering to the wants of his saints, is a spiritual grace, the fruit of union with Christ; and under the perfect and unchangeable government of God cannot fail of its reward. The grounds of this inseparable connection between grace and glory are pointed out in verses seventeen to nineteen. They are the promise and the oath of God, "two immutable things, in which it is impossible for him to lie." So that all have "strong consolation, who have fled for refuge to lay hold upon the hope set before them; which hope they have as an anchor of the soul, both sure and steadfast, and which entereth into that within the vail, whither the forerunner is for them entered, even Jesus, made a high priest for ever after the order of Melchisedec."

With this accords the whole analogy of faith. The believer is united with the Son of God, the Eternal Son of the Father, by a tie as indissoluble as that which unites the Father to the Son. He has died, been buried, and is risen again with Jesus. Christ has borne the penalty of the broken law, he has drunk the cup of his Father's anger to the very dregs, and is now exalted to the right hand of God. "Being raised from the dead"—to use the emphatic language of the sixth chapter of Romans—"he dieth no more; death hath no more dominion over him. For in that he died, he died unto sin once; but in that he liveth, he liveth unto God." All those things may be asserted of the meanest sinner, who is one with Christ by the indwelling of the Spirit, who proceeds from and dwells in Christ. This is obvious from the words which follow immediately the passage just cited: "Likewise reckon ye also yourselves to be dead indeed unto sin, but alive unto God through Jesus Christ our Lord." There is, therefore, no condemnation to them who are in Christ Jesus. When Christ can be degraded from his position at the right hand of the Majesty on high, when he can be made to abdicate his supremacy over principalities and powers, and might and dominion, and to become again a wanderer among sinful men, the object of their reproach, and finally the victim of their malignity; when the Father can forget his acceptance of the work of his own Son, an acceptance so solemnly proclaimed in raising him from the dead and giving him glory; then, and not before, can one who has been united with Christ become subject to the penalty of the law, and expiate that penalty in the everlasting pains of hell. "The gifts and calling of God are without repentance. He is not a man that he should lie, or the Son of man that he should repent. He who hath begun a good work in us will perform (or finish) it until the day of Jesus Christ."

The distinction between the *gifts* and the *graces* of the Spirit should always be observed. The former proceed from the operation of the Spirit *ab extra;* the latter, from the operation of the same Spirit dwelling in the believer, and thereby completing his union with Christ. The former produce no change upon the character. Balaam and his ass were both endowed with extraordinary gifts. The pagan prophet saw, in the vision of the Almighty, the future prosperity of the people whom he was employed to curse; he saw them spread forth as the valleys, as the gardens by the river's side, as cedar trees beside the waters; and over all he saw the Morning Star of Jacob rising, and shedding its beams upon the darkness. The glory of the vision was such as to excite, even in his mercenary soul, a transient aspiration after good, and he exclaimed, "Let me die the death of the righteous, and let my last end be like his!" And yet Balaam was still what he was before, an idolater of mammon, a lover of the wages of unrighteousness. He spoke with the voice of God to Israel, "Blessed is he that blesseth thee, and cursed is he that curseth thee"; but he was still a man in the gall of bitterness and the bond of iniquity. His dumb ass rebuked his madness with the voice of a man, but was a brute still. The *graces* of the Spirit, on the contrary, proceed from the new nature with which the believer is endowed. He has been born again by the power of God, "not of corruptible seed, but of incorruptible, by the word of God, which liveth and abideth forever." All earthly distinctions shall fade and perish, but the new nature, which the Lord Almighty has imparted to his sons and daughters, is as imperishable as his own being.

Gifts may be lost, graces never can. It is gifts, not graces, which are predicated of those who may fall away, in the passage under consideration. This brings us to the third interpretation.

III. This is given by Owen, and, as we believe it, in the main, to be the true one, we propose to dwell upon it more particularly. It supposes the persons described to be those who possessed extraordinary gifts of the Holy Spirit, endowments which have no natural, and, of course, no necessary connection with the enjoyment of God's love. That these endowments were the offspring of the operations of the Spirit is obvious from the last clause of the fourth verse, "were made partakers of the Holy Ghost." This clause stands midway in the enumeration, and seems to be intended to indicate the author, while the two clauses which precede and the two that follow indicate the nature, of the gifts. "To partake of the Holy Ghost," then, in the sense in which it is here used, is nothing more than to be the subject of his operations. Now, we are told in John xiv. 17, that "the world cannot receive the Spirit." The meaning is, as Owen suggests, that the world cannot receive him as to "personal inhabitation," and, accordingly, our Saviour adds, "but ye know him; for he *dwelleth with you*, and shall be *in* you." That the world does receive him as to his operations is evident from innumerable places of Scripture. Inanimate nature itself receives him. In the beginning he brooded over the void and formless infinite, and made it pregnant with life and beauty; it was by his hands that the heavens were garnished; it is by his all-pervading energy that the universe, with its nice connections, gradations, and dependencies, is sustained. Whither shall we go from this Spirit? "If we ascend up into heaven, he is there; if we make our bed in hell, behold, he is there; if we take the wings of the morning, and dwell in the uttermost parts of the sea, even there shall his hand lead us, and his right hand shall hold us." It is through this adorable agent that the power of the Godhead is exerted in the government of the world. Now, if such be the relations of the Spirit to the universe in the administration of providence that even ungodly men are not exempt from his operations, there is no reason why they should not be the subjects of his operations in things belonging to the administration of the spiritual kingdom of God. This is what is implied in the clause under consideration. It may be added that the prominence which is here given to the third person of the Trinity serves to impress the mind more distinctly with a sense of the awful dignity of that person, and, consequently, with the enormity of apostasy, as committed in contempt of his authority and grace.

The clauses which precede and follow state some of the characteristics of the operations of the Holy Ghost, of whom the apostates may have been partakers. The first is illumination, "who were once enlightened." There is a twofold illumination ascribed to the Spirit in the Scriptures. One is objective, and consists in the revelation which is made in the

Scriptures themselves. This revelation is ascribed to the Holy Ghost in 2 Peter i. 21, and other places. The other is subjective, and consists in opening the mind to receive the light. This also is ascribed to the Spirit, as in John xvi. 7–15; Eph. i. 17, 18. It is obvious that the apostle does not speak of the first, for this was common to all who had the Scriptures, or who sat under the ministrations of inspired teachers. It is to the inward subjective revelation that he refers. In reference to this inward illumination by the Spirit, the Scriptures speak of two kinds. One is penetrating in its nature, and accompanied with a transformation of the heart. The rays of the divine glory enter, as it were, into the frame and texture of the soul, so that it ever after bears the image of him who is light, and in whom is no darkness at all.[1] The other is a superficial transient glancing of the light, which may and often does influence the conduct, but makes no change in the character of the man. It is superior to that merely natural illumination which is the result of a studious application of the mind to the truths of revelation, inasmuch as it is the result of the spiritual agency of the Holy Ghost; but it is immeasurably below that illumination which the same glorious person imparts to the heirs of eternal life, since it leaves the heart as it found it, "a cage of unclean birds." This kind of illumination I suppose to be described in the account of the seed that fell upon stony places, in the parable of our Lord,[2] and illustrated in the case of Herod, who "heard John gladly, and did many things."[3] *

---

[1] See Gal. i. 16; 2 Cor. iii. 18; 2 Cor. iv. 4, 6.

[2] Matt. xiii. 20, 21. [3] Mark vi. 20.

* Though this article is incomplete, no apology is offered in presenting it here.

THE PEACE OF GOD.[1]

"Be careful for nothing; but in every thing by prayer and supplication with thanksgiving let your requests be made known unto God. And the peace of God, which passeth all understanding, shall keep your hearts and minds through Christ Jesus." (Phil. iv. 6, 7.)

CARE is the necessary result of a sense of responsibility combined with a sense of weakness. The brutes that perish know nothing of the burden of care, because they know nothing of responsibility. The end of their being is accomplished in obeying the impulses of a merely animal nature; and looking neither before nor after, their satisfaction is disturbed by no remorse for the past, nor anxiety for the future. The angels that excel in strength know nothing of care, though possessing the keenest sense of responsibility; because they know nothing of weakness. They are creatures, indeed, and, as such, are perfectly conscious of limitations upon their powers; but they know nothing of weakness in the sad significance of that word to mortal men. Their powers are exactly and critically adjusted to the measure of their obligations, and whatever they are bound to do is done with ease, and therefore with delight. But man is a sinner, weak, as well as responsible, and consequently cannot but be burdened with care.

By the very constitution of our nature, it is impossible for us to exist, much more to attain the highest ends of existence, in a condition of isolation or solitude. The author of our nature has ordained society as the sphere in which we are to live, and move, and have our being. But society gives rise to manifold relations, and these relations to manifold

[1] This sermon was preached March 8, 1863.

duties; and these duties bring with them a sense of responsibility so great as to be often harrassing and well-nigh intolerable. Man is born to care as the sparks fly upward. It is further worthy of remark that an increase of care is the necessary condition of the development of the individual man, and of the progress of society. The social relations of a savage state are few and simple. The man of the forest or the desert is roused to exertion by the pains of hunger, or the cries of his wife and children for food, or by the necessities of defence against the violence of his fellow-savage or the ferocity of the beasts of the field. His pressing wants in regard to sustenance or protection being satisfied, he relapses into a condition of torpor amounting almost to insensibility. The man of civilized life sustains many and complex relations which make the burden of care incessant; and in proportion as he rises in the scale of usefulness and honor, as his relations and duties are multiplied, his responsibilities become graver, and his cares heavier. No such cares as afflict the heart of the President of the Confederate States, in the present perilous times, are known to the chief of a savage tribe.

Care, then, being the inexorable law of our condition here, and an increase of care the law of development and progress, it seems strange that we should be exhorted to "be careful for nothing," and that, too, by a man exalted to such a pitch of usefulness and honor as to be burdened with "the care of all the churches." Must we understand it as an exhortation to abandon ourselves to a light-hearted epicurean disregard of the stern responsibilities of life? Are we advised to adopt the philosophy of the stoic and fortify ourselves against the assaults of care by a heroic resolution to recognize no distinction between pain and pleasure, and to accept all evil as only partial good? By no means. What, then, must be understood by this, "Be careful for nothing"? I answer, that the word rendered "careful" in the original signifies, according to its etymology, to "divide," and generally expresses that sort of care which divides or distracts the mind. It is opposed to the "peace which passeth all understanding." The epicurean notion of serenity, or tranquility of mind, in which the philosophers of that atheistic school asserted the chief good of man to consist, was an entire freedom from all care, a serenity incompatible with any serious views of human life, with any just views of its responsibilities, or any earnest endeavors to fulfil them. It was the balance of the two sides of an empty pair of scales. The "peace which passeth all understanding" is founded upon a conviction that, great as the burden of care may be, there is a counterbalancing support in the presence and sustaining power of a personal God. It is the equilibrium of the two sides of a pair of scales produced by heavy but equal weights in both. The soul is not relaxed, but tense. It is earnest and glowing in the discharge of its manifold duties, but dwelling safely, as in a garrison (see verse seven in Greek), from the assaults of torturing care.

I. But how is this peace to be obtained? By *prayer*, is the answer of the apostle in the text: "but in everything by prayer," etc.

The efficacy of prayer in relieving us from distracting care, and in securing the "peace which passeth all understanding," may be shown in several ways.

(1), As care is the result of a combined sense of responsibility and of weakness, prayer relieves us, because, while it brings us into the immediate presence of that God whose will creates the responsibility, it also assures us of his ability to help our weakness. It brings us into contact with a God whose providence cares for us in our minutest concerns. This is the argument of Peter (1 Peter v. 6, 7): "Humble yourselves, therefore, under the mighty hand of God, that he may exalt you in due time; casting all your care upon him; for he careth for you"; and of the Psalmist (lv. 22): "Cast thy burden upon the Lord, and he shall sustain thee; he shall never suffer the righteous to be moved"; of the Saviour himself (Matt. vi. 25–34), where the word rendered "Take no thought," is the same as that rendered in the text, "Be careful for nothing." He "helps our infirmities," or (as the figure seems to be in Rom. viii. 26) takes hold of one side of the burden, while we carry the other. And here I beg you to note the immense contrast between Paul and the philosophers who undertook in his day to relieve the burdens of mankind. The two schools of philosophy which were most popular in the Roman Empire, where he was publishing the glad tidings, were those already alluded to, the Epicureans and the Stoics (Acts xvii. 18); more popular than the more ancient and noble schools of Plato and Aristotle, because more ethical and practical. It was a time of trouble. The glory of the Greeks had departed; their liberties had perished first under the iron heel of the Macedonian, then of the Roman. The nobler class of the Romans themselves mourned over the extinction of the republic and the erection of a splendid but cruel despotism upon its ruins. Men's hearts were filled with disappointment and oppressed with gloomy forebodings. They looked to the philosophers for comfort. The Epicureans told them that all things, including the earthly lot of men, were the sport of chance, and that serenity of mind could only be found in seizing the pleasures of the passing day. "Let us eat and drink, for to-morrow we die!" This was the favorite philosophy of the Greek, mercurial, and fond of pleasure and excitement. The sterner and nobler Roman was more inclined to listen to the oracles of the Stoic, as he taught that all things, including not only the destiny of men, but the destiny of gods, were the slaves of a blind and remorseless fate, and that serenity of mind was possible only for those who stubbornly ignored the existence of pain and evil, who regarded all things as equally normal developments of the universe. Neither Epicurean nor Stoic spoke of prayer as an antidote of human care. Alas! they knew no God who could see, or hear, or help. The cries which agonized nature extorted from the sufferer were poured forth to an idle divinity, who took no part in administrating, as he he had taken no part in creating, the universe; or to a mysterious impersonal power, whose movements were at once necessary and resistless; or, at best, to "an unknown God." In contrast with these gropings in the dark, these desperate utterances of an earth-born philosophy which could find no remedy for the woes of man except in unmanning him, in annihilating and mutilating his nature; in contrast so sublime and exalted as to force the conviction upon us that he spoke by the inspiration of the Almighty—Paul announces the remedy in the text. Let us praise God, my fellow-travellers, through this vale of tears, that we have this clear shining in this dark place, till the day dawn and the day-star arise in our hearts! Let us praise him in these perilous times, when our liberties are threatened with a deluge from the North, and the dragon stands ready to devour the new-born man-child of the South; let us praise him that we can appeal to the righteousness of his throne and the might of his arm! Let us praise him, my fellow-Christians, not only that we have this revelation of God and his providence, but that he has enabled us, by his Spirit, to recognize it and to rejoice in it, while so many, even now, with the Bible in their hands, are drivelling still about chance, or fate, or force, or law, as the controlling agency in human affairs! Let us praise him that we know him not as the logical, abstract, passionless God of the schools, but as the living, feeling, yearning Father of the Bible, whose "soul is grieved for the misery of Israel," who sees the returning prodigal afar off, and runs and falls upon his neck and kisses him! who, in all our affliction, is himself afflicted; who says that whosoever toucheth us toucheth the apple of his eye!

We are abundantly justified in ascribing to prayer such an efficacy in relieving the burden of care, because,

(2), In the second place, it not only brings us into contact with a God who exercises a special and benignant providence over our concerns, but because it brings us to a God who sustains a special covenant relation to all who are in his Son Jesus Christ. The phrase "through Jesus Christ," with which Paul closes the exhortation, determines the complexion of all its parts. It is through Christ Jesus we are to make known our requests unto God, because he is the trustee of the covenant, and all its exceeding great and precious promises are in him yea, and in him Amen. He is the heir of all things, and in him all things are ours, whether Paul, or Apollos, or Cephas, or the world, or life, or death, or things present, or things to come; all are ours, and we are Christ's, and Christ is God's. "I will be thy God" is the formula of the covenant. God has given *himself* to his people as their all-comprehending good as well as their all-disposing Lord. He is their sun and their shield; he will give grace and glory; no good thing will he withhold from them who walk uprightly. The warrant and measure of our prayers, therefore, is this boundless covenant with all its promises, a covenant formed in the depths of eternity, sealed with the blood of the Lamb, and confirmed by an oath. (Heb. vi. 13, etc.) Having such promises (and these are only a few out of an almost countless number in the word of God), having such promises to plead in prayer under the pressure of our cares, how can we fail to find relief, and to experience that "peace which passeth all understanding." For all spiritual blessings, faith, love, repentance, gratitude, patience, increase of grace and perseverance therein to the end, we may pray without limit or condition. The fountain is infinite, and the only limitation upon our blessing is our capacity to receive. "According to your faith be it unto you," is the comprehensive charter. "All things are possible to him that believeth." We are not straitened in God; we are straitened in ourselves. But in reference to temporal blessings, health, food, civil liberty, etc., we have no absolute expression of the purpose of God, our Father, and must, therefore, pray in submission to his unknown will. We have the absolute assurance, however, that he will withhold "no good thing" from them that walk uprightly. When he denies us anything, then, he denies it because it would not be good. We know not what is good for ourselves all the days of our vain life which we spend as a shadow; and like passionate children we often cry for that which it would be ruin to obtain. When we go to our heavenly Father with our cares, we may go with the utmost confidence that he will either do what we ask or something far better; that if it should not please him to remove them, he will convert them into a salutary discipline for our distempered natures; that he will either take away the burden, or make it such a burden, to use the expression of one of the old fathers, as sails are to a ship or wings to a bird, serving to waft us the more swiftly to our home in the bosom of Christ. We know with a transcendent certainty that he who has given the greater will not withhold the less; that having spared not even his only Son, he will freely give all other things which his wisdom sees needful for us. "For we know that *all things* work together for good to them that love God, to them who are called according to his purpose."

And now, beloved, in reference to the dark shadow that rests upon our whole country, deeper, like the shadow of an eclipse, in some parts than in others, but gloomy and portentous in all. Here is the faith and patience of the saints. It is the work of him who bought us with his blood. The same voice that uttered amidst the dying agonies of the cross that memorable prayer, "Father, forgive them, for they know not what they do," has now mustered the hosts to battle. All power is given him in heaven and earth, and in the exercise of this power he is working out upon fields of blood, in desolated homes, in chambers of bereavement and sorrow, by scarcity of food and all manner of straits and necessities, the wondrous purposes of his grace. And in like manner as the devil was taken in his own devices in procuring the crucifixion of the Son of God, and was conquered in the very hour of his imaginary triumph, so, I doubt not, it will be manifest in the end, that this war, barbarous and cruel, which by his instigation our enemies are waging against us, is only another example of that righteous judgment of God by which the wicked and their master are snared in the work of their own hands. It is a time of winter with the people of God, of windstorm and tempest; the trees of his garden are stripped and bare, to all appearance dead; but glorious summer will succeed, and the golden fruits which will then adorn those new naked boughs will demonstrate the wisdom and the goodness of the great husbandman. The multiplication of their cares has multiplied their errands to the throne of their Father in heaven, and they have been strengthened with strength in their souls.

This great fact that God is our God in covenant is not only our consolation and support under the pressure of present cares, but the bulwark against torturing apprehensions of the future. He is not only the "I am," but the "I will be." He is known by his name Jehovah. His covenant name embracing in its composition the past, the present, and the future, "the Lord God Almighty, who is, and who was, and who is to come." Let your conversation be without covetousness, and be content with such things as ye have; for he hath said, I will never leave thee nor forsake thee. So that we may boldly say, "The Lord is my helper and I will not fear what man can do unto me." (Heb. xiii. 5, 6.) The promise contained in these words is full enough to keep house upon in the darkest times. Our version gives a very inadequate impression of strength. Two or more negatives in Greek strengthen the negation, instead of destroying it as in English. Now, in this promise, as expressed in the original, there are no less than five negatives. We might have a feeble imitation of the form by repeating the negations, thus: "*I will not, I will not* leave thee; I'll *never, no never, no never* forsake thee."

> The soul that on Jesus has leaned for repose
> I *will not*, I *will not* desert to its foes;
> That soul though all hell should endeavor to shake,
> I'll *never, no, never, no, never* forsake.

Surely such a God may well say unto us, "Take no anxious thought for the morrow!" The morrow of trouble, such as your gloomy forebodings depict it, may never come; but if it should come, God will be with it and with you in it. If prayer brings us into communion with such a God, it may well produce that "peace which passeth all understanding."

(3), As God chooses our cares for us as our covenant-God, and as prayer compels us to recognize that fact, so also prayer is the antidote to care, because it brings us to an issue with ourselves and compels us to recognize the fact that not only were those relations and conditions which are the source of our cares chosen, for the most part, by ourselves, but that they are still chosen, notwithstanding the cares they bring with them. Illustrate by children and servants. Dr. Palmer, in presenting this point, refers to the vision in the *Spectator*, in which men were seen depositing their burdens in separate heaps, and, upon being allowed to choose freely any of them, were seen each to choose again that which he had laid down before.

(4), The efficacy of prayer as the antidote of care may be further illustrated by its effect upon the general *tone* of the Spirit[1]. Every scholar knows the effect upon his own mind of communion with some master-spirit of our race, whether that communion be enjoyed with the living person through the medium of speech, or with the departed genius speaking through the written or printed characters, in which his precious life-blood has been embalmed and treasured up in

[1] See Palmer's Sermon on this text.

order to a life beyond life. He is gradually lifted up out of his own lower sphere into that of the Spirit of a nobler mould. The range of thought and feeling is widened and elevated. He is placed upon an eminence, from which he looks down upon the objects which formerly engaged his attention, diminished and dimmed by the distance, and descries new and more commanding objects, which the lowness of his position before would not permit him to see. The atmosphere is bracing, and an athletic tone is imparted to the whole man. The whole soul beats with a quicker and stronger pulse, and the man is amazed that trifles light as air could have hung like dull weights upon him.

If such, my friends, be the effect of communion with a superior human soul, a Bacon or a Milton or a Howe, what may we not expect from communion with the Father of Lights, with whom there is no variableness nor shadow of turning? The loftiest genius of earth is but a spark from that eternal mind; the noblest and most magnanimous sentiments that ever glowed in the hearts of apostles, prophets, and martyrs are but faint reflections of the love and majesty which reside in the bosom of God. Behold how the man who once breathed threatening and slaughter against the innocent followers of the Lamb now burns with generous indignation against the wrong done to the weakest and meanest of the saints. See how the soul once absorbed with the low ambition of upholding the glory of a narrow pharisaical bigotry now expands and swells with the great thoughts of redemption and pours itself out a libation upon the offering of the whole Gentile world unto God! How cheerfully he endures the ignominy of scourging, when by the simple utterance of the magic words, "I am a Roman citizen," he might have escaped it, and all for the honor of Christ and the safety of the little band of believers in Philippi! How gloriously does his triumph over the dungeon and the stocks express itself in rapturous songs of praise to him whose grace was thus magnified out of the very "belly of hell"! And why this change? The soul of Paul had been living in unceasing, prayerful communion with the Father of glory.

(5), Lastly, prayer is the remedy for care because, as is contained in the text, *thanksgiving* is a part of prayer. We cannot pray for more without being thankful for what we have already received. "In everything give thanks," in want and affliction, in prosperity as well as in adversity. A thankful spirit is a peaceful spirit from the very nature of the case. Balance your mercies against your cares, and you cannot fail to see that your mercies greatly preponderate. You concede this yourselves by still choosing as beforesaid the relations and conditions which are the occasion of your cares. Those relations and conditions must be attended with many mercies if you still choose them, in spite of the cares they bring.

THE CALL TO THE MINISTRY OF THE WORD.[1]

I. ALL branches of the Christian church which acknowledge the necessity of an order of ministers at all are agreed that no man has a right to be a member of this order unless he be called of God. This they consider established—

(*a*), By the fact that under both Testaments God has called ministers, partly ordinary and partly extraordinary, to perform the office of preaching his word and of teaching the people: Moses, Aaron, the Levitical priesthood, the prophets, apostles, evangelists, pastors and teachers. (Matt. xxviii. 19, 20; Eph. iv. 11).

(*b*), By the counsel of God of calling men to salvation by the preaching of the word. (1 Cor. i. 21; Rom. x. 14, 15).

(*c*), By the nature of the ministry. Ministers are *ambassadors* (2 Cor. v. 20), are stewards (1 Cor. iv. 1); both of which offices imply *authority*.

(*d*), By the causes of the calling, to-wit: the honor of God, the salvation of the church, the peace of consciences. *In respect to God*, that his supreme authority may be recognized; *in respect to men*, that the attention of the hearers may be arrested and held, and that they may receive the word with meekness and love (explain the difference between the effect of any rite considered in itself, and the effect of it as an ordinance instituted by authority); *in respect to the ministers themselves*, that they may be sure of their right to preach, of God's blessing upon their ministry, and of his protection against the hatred of the world and the dangers which threaten them. (Jer. i. 7, 8; Acts xx. 24).

[1] This article contains Dr. Peck's mature views on the subject of the call to the ministry.—ED.

We must be careful, however, in asserting the necessity of this calling not to confound the calling of Christian ministers with the calling of priests. The necessity of a divine call for ministers ought not to be supported by such a passage as Heb. v. 4 (which refers to the office of *priest*), nor by Jer. xxiii. 21 (prophet); nor should the danger of obtruding themselves upon the minister's office be enforced by such a passage as 2 Sam. vi. 7. The office of a priest is one thing, the office of a minister is another thing; the qualifications of the priest and the reality of his call could be certainly determined; in these particulars the case is wholly different with a minister of the word. The preaching of the word and the administration of the sacraments are offices which might be performed, and in some circumstances ought to be performed, under "the law of charity," by a private member of the church; the functions of a priest can be performed only by one who is called thereunto of God, and that immediately, without the intervention of the people. The law of charity has nothing to do with authority to offer an expiatory sacrifice. This function belongs only to him who has been appointed to it by the God to whom the sacrifice is offered.

II. It is agreed on the part of nearly all Christians that all believers are not called to be preachers. Women are forbidden to exercise the office (1 Tim. ii. 11, 12; 1 Cor. xi. 3–15; compared with xiv. 34, 35); novices are excluded (1 Tim. iii. 6), while they are novices.

III. How is a call to the ministry authenticated? How can a man reach a reasonable assurance that he is called?

(*a*), Not by a mere conviction that he may be more useful in the ministry than in any other calling. This notion puts the ministry on a level with every other lawful "calling." This very word implies the common impression of men in Christian countries that God appoints a work for every man, and when we say of a man that he has "mistaken his calling," we mean that he has misapprehended the nature and extent of the powers by which Providence indicated the work for which he was intended. But the powers by which a man is fitted for the secular callings of life are powers of nature or gifts of the "God of nature," involving nothing of the supernatural. A man cannot argue from the mere possession of such powers (if he does really possess them) that he could find larger or more effective scope for the exercise of them in the ministry than elsewhere. The ministry deals, indeed, with holy things, with things which immediately concern the glory of God and the salvation of men; but does it follow that because a man deals with such solemn realities he must of necessity do more good and be more useful? The history of the church gives a mournful answer to this question. The truth is, a man is useful in the ministry only when and because he has been called to it, not called because he thinks he can be more useful.

(*b*), One indispensable evidence of a call to the ministry is the possession of gifts suited to the work, and these gifts are *charisms* (*χαρισματα*) of the Holy Ghost. Let me explain. There are three classes of these charisms mentioned in the New Testament: (1), Those that make men Christians ("*gratia gratum faciens*"), such as justification, salvation, repentance, faith and love (Rom. i. 11, 12; v. 15, 16; vi. 23; xi. 29), called "graces" of the Spirit. (2), Miraculous gifts (1 Cor. xii. 4, 9, 28, 30, 31). (3), Gifts which qualify men for office in the church (called by Rome "*gratia gratis data*). (See Rom. xii. 6; 1 Tim. iv. 14; 2 Tim. i. 6; 1 Peter iv. 10; 1 Cor. xii. 28, 29.) Of these classes, the first are common to all genuine Christians, but ought to be conspicuous in a minister; the second were peculiar to the Christians of the apostolic age; the third belong to church officers. What is their nature? Answer in the words of John Owen ("Discourse on Spiritual Gifts"), they are *natural powers supernaturally improved.* Illustrate by the powers of the understanding, the conscience, the will, the sensibilities, speech. When we say supernaturally improved, we mean strengthened, purified, exalted, quickened by the Holy Ghost. (See 1 Cor. xii. 1–11.) This work of the Holy Ghost is included in the apostle's expression in 2 Cor. iii. 5, 6, and 1 Tim. i. 14.

(*c*), When these gifts exist there will be a "moving" to exercise them. This is common to all gifts; for our happiness consists in exercising our powers. (See Judges xiii. 25; 1 Tim. iii. 1.) (The "desire" will accompany the gifts.) A want of will and of effort to bring souls to Christ is a sign that a man has not been called to preach the gospel. A man may have this desire without being called to preach. All Christians have it in some measure; but the absence of it is conclusive evidence against a man's being called. A man may have this desire, however, and may labor as he has opportunity to glorify God in promoting the interests of his kingdom, and yet may shrink from assuming the tremendous responsibilities of the preacher's work. (See the cases of Moses, Jeremiah, Jonah and Ezekiel, Calvin and Knox.) Yet he may be called, notwithstanding. And this leads me to observe, in the first place—

(*d*), That there must be a strong conviction that it is one's duty to preach. This is indispensable to preaching with the tone of authority, to steadfastness, and to peace of mind in the exercise of the ministry. Says Dr. R. J. Breckenridge: "In every act we can perform on earth we are entitled to expect, before we can be required to perform it, and we are bound to have, before we venture to perform it, the testimony of a good conscience; and the clearness and force of our conscientious convictions should be analagous to the magnitude, the perplexity, the difficulty of the contemplated duty. For a man, then, to presume to be an ambassador for Almighty God, and that touching questions no less awful than the glory of his throne and the endless states of his rebellious subjects, without a settled conviction in his own soul that this fearful trust is laid on him by the King eternal, is insane audacity.[1] It is not a matter of great consequence when or how this conviction of duty arises. It may arise in a man's mind he knows not how, or it may arise from the manifest judgment of Christian friends, or from the voice of the Christian congregation (Knox), or from the solemn importunity of some minister of the gospel (Calvin and Farel), it matters not *how*; but the conviction must arise and assert itself (1 Cor. ix. 16). And it matters not *when*, whether before the scholastic preparation for the work begins, or after that preparation has been completed; whether before the judgment of the church has been uttered or afterwards, the conviction must be had before the work can be attempted. This conviction may exist in various degrees in different men, and in the same man it may be stronger at one time than another. "The assurance of a call to the ministry is like the assurance of our pardon and acceptance, subject to many fluctuations, preserved by faithfulness, dependent on humility and singleness of heart, a source of joy when clear, of agony when darkened or disturbed."[2] "Like as the kingdom of heaven itself is but as a grain of mustard planted in the broken heart, which must be watered by many a tear and watched amid long and anxious vigils as its roots strike down and its branches spread strongly and widely abroad, so this inward testimony of a divine vocation may be a whisper to the soul almost inaudible in the profoundest stillness of the spirit of man, lost, restored again, strengthened, repeated, struggling amidst the passions that toss it to and fro, and fighting against the sins that would quench it; following us, if need be, as God followed Jonah, till out of the belly of hell the right of the Almighty Dispenser is confessed."[3]

---

[1] "Discourse on the Christian Pastor," quoted in *Thornwell's Works*, Vol. IV., p. 34.

[2] *Thornwell*, Vol. IV., p. 33.

[3] Breckenridge in *Thornwell*, Vol. IV., p. 35.

The passages I have just quoted, specially the last, could not have been written but by men of very strong natures, and by men whose Christian experience was of a very deep and perhaps of a very tempestuous kind; and we should not be warranted in concluding that such an experience is necessary to every man who is called to the ministry, any more than we should be warranted in concluding that the experience of "Christian" in the *Pilgrim's Progress* is necessary to every pilgrim from the City of Destruction to the Heavenly City. As in the matter of one's salvation, all that is necessary is such a conviction of sinfulness and helplessness that we can never find peace except in entire and exclusive reliance on Jesus for pardon, purity, and strength; so in the matter of a call to the ministry, all that is necessary is such a conviction of duty as will prevent a man who resists that conviction from ever being at peace with his own conscience until he ceases to resist it. A man who is a physician may be satisfied that he has "mistaken his calling," and may regret that he had not adopted the profession of law, as he once thought of doing; but his regret is a very different feeling from that of a man who finds himself a lawyer or a physician, when he feels that he *ought* to have been a minister of the gospel. In this last case, the feeling is, I have *sinned;* in the other it is, I have *made a mistake.*

(*e*), "The testimony of conscience, however, is not final and conclusive." (Here read *Thornwell*, Vol. IV., from p. 35, beginning with the words just quoted, and as far as the end of the paragraph on p. 39, concluding with the words, "a special field of labor.")

That the testimony of others than the ordaining power is at least proper, if not necessary, to the due authentication of a call, seems to be conceded even by the Episcopal Church. Read the "form and manner of ordering priests"; the presentation of the candidate; the address of the bishop to the presenter; the answer of the presenter, and the address of the bishop to the people (which implies that they have at least a negative voice).[1]

So the question of the bishop and the answer of the candidate recognize the necessity of a conviction of duty on the part of the candidate. We see in these forms the relics of the ancient right of God's people to give their voice in the call of pastors, a right acknowledged by the patron saint of the Episcopal hierarchy, the lofty churchman, Cyprian, of the third century, and one of the last rights surrendered by the people, even in the city of Rome, the headquarters of papal tyranny and oppression.

It appears from what has been said: 1. That God alone can call a man into the ministry. 2. That God alone can confer the gifts needful for the work of the ministry. 3. That there must be *positive* evidence that a man is called. The doctrine is *not* "that every young man of talents and attainments should devote himself to the ministry without some special reasons to the contrary," but it is, "that no man, whether young or old, rich or poor, learned or unlearned, should presume to dispense the mysteries of Christ without the strongest of all possible reasons for doing so—the imperative will of God. No one is to show cause why he ought *not* to be a minister; he is to show cause why he *should* be a minister. His call to this profession is not the absence of a call to any other pursuit; it is direct and powerful to this very department of labor. He is not here because he *can* be nowhere else, but he is nowhere else because he *must* be here." 4. That this positive evidence of a call is twofold: that of the man's own conscience and that furnished by the church. The evidence of the church is given in a twofold form—through the body of existing rulers (in our church the presbytery), and through the people, or congregation. The judgment of the congregation may not always be rendered in the form of a regular call; as in the case of our foreign mis-

[1] *Book of Common Prayer*, Protestant Episcopal Church, U. S. A.

sionaries, a call to a pastoral charge is not given, for the very reason that they are known to be destined to a foreign field. But no man should be ordained to the work of the ministry who is supposed to be destitute of the approbation of God's people. The church has always condemned ordinations *sine titulo*.

IV. It is further to be observed that the New Testament does not make the wide difference between the call to the ministry of the word and the call to mere rule, or of the custody and distribution of the revenues of the church, which is commonly made. Ruling elders and deacons must be called of God as well as preachers; and their call must be authenticated in the same way, viz., by the testimony of conscience and by the voice of the church, through its courts and its congregations. Ordinarily, indeed, the conscience of one who has been called to the ministry of the word is awakened and impressed before the voice of the church is uttered; and it is no uncommon thing for an unconverted man to feel that if he should be converted he will be obliged to become a preacher of the gospel; and, further, the instances are not unknown of men who have refused to attend to the great concern of personal salvation because they felt that when converted they should be obliged to enter the ministry. An experience of this sort I have never heard of in respect to the office of ruling elder or deacon. You have never heard, I suppose, of a man coming before a session and announcing that he felt called of God to exercise the office of elder or deacon, before the church had signified its conviction that God had called him to it. This is all true, nevertheless; the difference is one only of chronology. In the case of one called to be a preacher, the conviction of the call often, perhaps generally, comes first, and the authentication by the voice of the church comes afterward. In the case of one called to be a ruling elder or deacon, the voice of the church comes first, and the conviction of the call afterwards. But, in other respects, the call is he same in all; that is, the elements of the call are the same, gifts of the Holy Ghost, conviction of duty, and the call of the church.

We have seen that the conviction of duty admits of various degrees among those who are called to the ministry of the word, and even in the same man at different times. So, no doubt, it may be truly said that the conviction of a call among elders and deacons as a class is inferior in strength to the conviction of a call among ministers of the word. This is what we might expect from the nature of the offices and from the nature of the gifts necessary to the proper discharge of the duties pertaining to the offices. The preacher's office is superior to that of ruling elder, in that while the preacher is an elder he is more (1 Tim. v. 17); and hence, in addition to the qualifications which fit him for rule, he must have those that fit him to preach. But we have seen under a former head that along with gifts goes the impulse to exercise them; and the higher and more plenteous the gifts the stronger will be the impulse to exercise them and the conviction that the possessor ought to exercise them. Hence, we ought to expect in the preacher stronger convictions than in the elder, and in the elder stronger convictions than in the deacon, in reference to a divine call to their respective offices.

If this is a true statement of the case, it follows:

(*a*), That the church ought to "look out men of good report" from among its male members, whom it may appoint to the preaching of the word as well as to ruling and to the custody and distribution of its revenues. (Acts vi. 3.) The judgment of the church must come in somewhere, why not at the beginning, as well as at the end?

(*b*), The ruling elder or the deacon occupies a much higher and more solemn position than is commonly thought, either by himself or by the people. (Explain and point out the indications of progress in the church, in its estimation of its officers, particularly compare the new book with the old in regard to *ordination* of elders and deacons.)

(*c*), The minister's office no more "sacred" than that of elder and deacon. Under the gospel, holiness does not attach to *office* but to *men*. It is not the holy apostolate, but the "holy *apostles*."

IMPERFECTION OF THE WORK OF SANCTIFICATION IN THIS LIFE—ARGUED.

I. FROM the inability of the holiest men to obey the law of God perfectly in this life. (1 Kings viii. 46; Prov. xx. 9; James iii. 2; 1 John i. 8.)

II. From the imperfection of sanctifying grace. Here the saints have only the "first fruits." (Rom. viii. 23, 24, 25; Heb. xii. 23.)

III. From the remnants of the "flesh" and of "the old man." (Matt. xxvi. 41; Gal. v. 17.)

IV. From the duties which continue to be incumbent on us in this life: (1), Prayer for *forgiveness* and *deliverance* (Matt. vi. 13); (2), Mortification of the flesh; (3), Making progress in holiness (1 Cor. iv. 24; Phil. iii. 12–14); (4), Fighting not only against the world, but against our own depraved desires. (Heb. xii. 4; Eph. vi. 12 ff.)

V. Specially from Rom. vii. 14–26. Proof that this passage is a description of Paul's experience as a regenerate man: From, (1), the use not only of the first person, but from the use of the present tense. In verses 4–6 he and other believers are described as having become "dead to the law," "married to Christ," "delivered from the law," "serving in newness of spirit," etc., in contrast with their former condition "in the flesh." Two objections might be suggested by the strong expressions of the apostle: (*a*), That the law was *sin;* (*b*), That the law was *death.* He answers "*a*" by stating the operation of the law upon him in his *status securitatis* (vs. 8, 9), and his *status sub lege* (vs. 9–13), using the *past* tense. (Compare "ποτε" in vs. 9.) He answers "*b*" (vs. 10, 13) by asserting that it was the sin that wrought the death—

that sin which the law revealed. He then illustrates the purity and spirituality of the law in the most impressive manner, by comparing it with his condition even in his *present* state (using, then, the present tense throughout to the end of the chapter), the *status regenerationis.*

The attempt has been made to evade the force of this argument by supposing either (*a*), an enallage of persons, or (*b*), an enallage of *tenses.* As to the first, Paul may be representing by the εγω a man who is a Gentile, a natural man, serving sin, or, at most, groaning under the yoke of the law. It is a sort of *metaschematism*, or transferring to himself in a figure (see 1 Cor. iv. 6) of what is meant of another. (Compare Rom. iii. 7; 1 Cor. vi. 12; xiii. 2; Gal. ii. 18.) Answer: (*a*), No indication of a change of persons as there is in 1 Cor. iv. 6 and the rest. (*b*), If there is such a change it might with equal propriety be supposed to have taken place at verse 9 and at verse 13. (*c*), In some of the places quoted as parallels, as 1 Cor. iv. 6, the apostle *includes himself*, so that even if there is an enallage of persons here, Paul may still include himself; and this would not help the cause of the objectors. (Compare 1 Cor. xiii. 1, 2; Gal. i. 8.) As to the second, the enallage of tenses, δουλευω for εδουλευον. Answer: (*a*), The supposition of such a change is a pure *petitio principii.* (*b*), There is a steady and uniform use of the *present* to the end, not to anticipate by saying that he says some things which cannot be said of an unregenerate state. (*c*), The objector will hardly venture to assert that there is an enallage of tenses in the first clause of verse 25, but the time of δουλευω in the second clause is the same as ευχ. in the first.

(2), From the ascription of this "εγω" of an "inner man" and a "law of the mind."

(*a*), The "inner man" is evidently the same as the "new man" in Eph. iv. 24 (compare Eph. iii. 16; 2 Cor. iv. 16; 1 Pet. iii. 4; Rom. ii. 29; Psa. xlv. 13; li. 6), and, indeed, what else can the phrase possibly mean? Grotius and others say it may mean the intelligent soul, sound reason, the light of nature, etc. If this is so, then "flesh," which is opposed to it, must mean the body, and "carnal" in verse 14 must mean *corporeal*, and to be "in the flesh" (vs. 5) must mean to be "in the body," the mind of the flesh (chap. viii. 6, 7), the mind of the body; and to walk "according to the flesh" (chap. viii. 4), to walk according to the body, etc. Apply it also to verse 18 of this chapter (vii.). It will follow from this interpretation, also, that the mind of the natural man delights in the law of God.

(*b*), "The law of the mind"—opposed to the "law of the members" (vs. 23) as the "law of sin" is opposed to the "law of God," and as the "spirit" is opposed to the "flesh." "The law of the mind" cannot be from the strength of nature (chap. viii. 7), for it is a law which wars against the law of the "members" and of "sin" (vs. 23). The "law of sin," says Spanheim, is indwelling sin; the "law of the members" is actual concupiscence exerting itself in the members; the "law of God" is the decalogue; the "law of the mind" is the internal conformity of the mind or the regenerate part with the "law of God."

(3), From the ascription to the εγω of things which are impossible to the unregenerate man, such as a recognition of the spirituality of the law, delight in it, love of the moral good which it presents, hatred of the evil which it condemns, &c.

(4), From the doxology in verse 25, which could burst from the heart of none but a regenerate soul; as it can be said of none but a regenerate man that he has the double principle in him by which he "serves" both the "law of God" and the "law of sin," and yet delights in the law and hates sin.

And before we go further, the general remark may be made on this whole passage: That there is evidently a mixture of good and evil in the εγω here described, very different from that described by the pagan poets and moralists (*video meliora*, &c.), and the advantage we have over our opponents, who refer the description to an unregenerate man, is plain. Whatever of evil our opponents allege against our view of it, we may admit without loss or damage to our view; but whatever of good we adduce from it, our opponents are unable to admit, without denying in great part the native corruption of man, and to such denials their interpretation strongly tends.

(5), The supposition that Paul describes the condition of the regenerate εγω suits the argument better, by making it more conclusive, as to the following particulars: (*a*), The impossibility of justification by our own righteousness. (Even the regenerate man's righteousness is imperfect.) (*b*), The spirituality of the law (so spiritual that even the regenerate man cannot attain unto it). (*c*), The defence of the law against the charge of being *per se* the cause of sin is rendered more complete (the "flesh" is the cause, for even the spiritual man, whose delight is in the law, sins by reason of the flesh that remains in him). No wonder that the law cannot annul the force of sin in an unregenerate man, when it cannot do it even in the regenerate, of whom Paul is an example, who knows by his own experience the impotency of the law.

Objections to this view.—I. From the appellation "carnal." (v. 14.) *Answer*, (*a*), Conceded that it is foreign to the nature of the regenerate man that he should be *altogether* carnal "in the flesh" (viii. 8), walking according to the flesh (viii. 4); but (*b*), Flesh is taken sometimes *substantively* (John i. 14), sometimes *qualitatively;* and here either for external and temporary (Heb. vii. 16; ix. 10; comp. Rom. xv. 27; 1 Cor. ix. 11), or in a vicious sense; and here, again, in the sense of vicious simply and wholly (viii. 7), "in the flesh"; or comparatively (compared with others or with the spirituality of the law), which is the sense intended in vs. 14, where "carnal"="body of death" in vs. 24; as "sold under sin"="captivity to the law of sin" in vs. 23. Hence, the same believers are called both "spiritual" and "carnal" (in 1 Cor. ii. 12; iii. 1, 3; where the idea evidently is that though these believers were spiritual, the apostle could not address them as spiritual, but rather as *carnal*, on account of the factious temper which was exhibited by them). Contrary predicates may be used of the same persons when they have contrary natures or principles dwelling in them. We say of a man that he is mortal and immortal, etc. Again, the apostle uses the *past* tense when he says that he was "in the flesh" (vs. 5); the *present* when he calls himself "carnal."

II. From the expression "sold under sin."

Answer: (*a*), No more difficulty about this than about the "carnal." If the "flesh" still remains in him, the sinful nature, the "sin that dwelleth in him," why should he not be "sold under it" and brought into "captivity" to it? (*b*), Being sold is not always of the same sort. Some sell themselves freely (John viii. 34; Rom. vi. 20; vii. 8; Eph. iv. 19; compare 1 Kings xxi. 25; 2 Kings xvii. 17); others are sold against their will as here (the verb is *passive*). They struggle against the bondage and hate it, and long to be delivered. (*c*), Grotius says the verb is reflexive and may, therefore, mean, have sold myself under sin. Answer: he himself says that it is = *αιχμαλ.* in the twenty-third verse, and if so, it is an involuntary captivity.

III. Other objections are founded upon such expressions as "doing evil," "not doing the good," "the indwelling of sin," not balanced by any such expression as "the good that dwelleth in me," etc. Answer: (*a*), General; see above as to the advantage we have over our opponents. (*b*), Particular; all these evil things are balanced by such expressions as "delighting in the law after the inner man," etc. See above.

CHURCH HISTORY.[1]

WHAT is history? History, in its widest acceptation, is a statement of facts; or, as the etymon of the word would seem to imply, a knowledge of facts, whether that knowledge be put into the form of words or not. This notion of history seems to lie at the root of the German word *geschichte*, which is derived from a verb which signifies "to happen," "to take place." It is in this sense that the term is used in natural science; and, in this sense, history lies at the foundation of all human knowledge which is worthy of the name. "For knowledges are as pyramids," says Lord Bacon, "whereof history is the basis." The prominence given to history, in this sense, constitutes the immense superiority of modern over ancient science. It is this which has given scientific renown, since Bacon's time, to men who, to use Sir William Hamilton's expression, were but "intellectual barbarians," compared with Socrates, Plato, or Aristotle. Those old masters were deficient in history; they accepted the results of an imperfect induction as expressed in the common language of their day, to too great an extent, and contented themselves too much with the mere analysis and unfolding of the elements contained in the existing general terms. This process was performed with an ability, with a subtlety of dialectic, and an energy of thought, which have made them the intellectual sovereigns of the race, "ruling from their urns" the mightiest spirits of all ages, and conferring, by the intellectual gymnastic their writings have furnished, even the training and vigor by which their doctrines have been assailed and overthrown. Yet while we

[1] Inaugural discourse, delivered May 14, 1861.

stand amazed at the excellence of the work, we must lament the meagreness of the stuff, the material out of which it was made. They built much wider than the foundation, and consequently built precariously. Their most labored fabrics have tumbled into ruins under the assaults of a less imposing and less ambitious method, the method of a sound historical investigation.

Facts, then, lie at the basis of all knowledge. The actual phenomena, the perceptions, the sensations, the volitions of the mind, are the foundation and starting-point of philosophy, properly so-called. The phenomena of the heavens are the foundation and starting-point of the science of astronomy. The history of man in organized communities is the only basis of a sound social or political philosophy. And so the actual occurrences which make up the history of the church of God (still using the term history in its wide sense) are the only basis of a sound ecclesiology.

But what is a fact? It is not always easy to say, in a given case, what the fact is. A celebrated physician (Dr. Cullen) was in the habit of saying "that there were more false facts than false theories." This saying is applicable to such cases as that of the Royal Society touching the question of the fish in a vessel of water. We may also say that a fact is often false because a theory is false. We cannot ascertain what a fact is without a theory; for a theory, as the term itself implies, is a *seeing*, is that by which we see intellectually. The nature of the fact is determined by the manner in which and the end for which we look at it. An act, or a substance, or a change in the appearance of a substance, may be referred to several classes and called by several names, by contemplating it in several relations, all of which relations are true and real; it may be a fact in physics, or in metaphysics, in political philosophy, or in theology. The farmer has one classification and the botanist another for the very same plants. Again, where the purpose

8

of the inquiries is the same, they may differ as to the nature of the fact. To take an example from Paley: We see two men at a distance; one gives a purse of gold to the other. This is the physical phenomenon. The one gives the money to the other for, say, one of three purposes: to pay a just debt, or as an act of charity to relieve distress, or to bribe the receiver to commit murder. The fact, then, *morally* considered, may be one of justice, or one of benevolence, or one of atrocious crime. Take another case: Jesus of Nazareth died upon the cross. Did he die merely as a martyr, sealing the sincerity of his convictions with his blood? or as an imposter and blasphemer under the Jewish law? or as a common felon, like the two thieves who were crucified with him? or as the substitute for his elect people, bearing their sins in his own body upon the tree? Was this Jesus God, or a mere man, or a super-angelic creature in human form? According to our answers to these questions will be our conception of the nature of the fact. In like manner, the facts of church history will be one thing to a papist, another to a Protestant; one thing to a pantheist, another to a Christian. The whole value of a fact for instruction and direction depends upon the relations of it, upon the theory of it. This shows the absurdity of exalting facts against theories in theology.

These illustrations lead me to observe that history involves much more than the mere recounting the things done. It must tell how and why; it must trace events to their causes. This is brought out in the Greek term for history, *ιστορεω*, implying inquiry, research. It is philosophy teaching by example. It is vain for any man to pretend that he has no theory, if he pretends to any knowledge of history at all. If he sees, it must be with eyes of some sort. He may see "men as trees walking," or he may have the jaundice, or he may be afflicted with "color blindness," or, like the man couched for cataract, he may see all objects in the same plane, and have no notion of perspective, but he cannot see without eyes. And the theory is the organ by which the mind sees the events of history. There is all the difference between the actual vision of a Christian and an atheist, when both are contemplating the history of the church, that there is between the actual vision of the hunter and his dog, when both are looking from the summit of some lofty hill upon a landscape spread before them. The same images, doubtless, are painted upon the retina of the eye of the dog which are painted upon the retina of the hunter's eye, but how different the *vision*. There must, then, be a theory; it may be provisional at first, a hypothesis merely, subject to verification or modification, or entire rejection by the course of investigation. But, as in the investigation of nature, you cannot observe or experiment without an end in view, you cannot question her without having some point in your question, so in the history of man you must study with at least a provisional theory. All that candor requires is that you be willing to give it up if it prove to be wrong.

The widest classification of the theories of history which it is worth while to make may be indicated by the terms theistic and atheistic; the theories which recognize God as one of the constant factors of history, and the theories which do not so recognize him. Under the latter we, of course, include pantheism, which has been the prevailing philosophy of the world from the beginning until now, and has had a larger share in moulding the church histories of the last half-century than any other. Pantheism is atheism; because it is the same in effect to say that there is no God and that everything is God. An infinite personal intelligence, creating all things and controlling all things, is alike denied under both suppositions. Under both suppositions alike,

> "Thinking is but an idle waste of thought,
> Nought is everything and everything is nought."

There is a plausibility, however, in the pantheistic aspect of atheism that there is not in any other aspect of it, because it seems to recognize the operation of a principle of order in the universe, of force under the regulation of law; while the other forms of atheism make all the changes in the frame of nature and in the history of the world the mere sport of chance. But this apparent advantage is altogether delusive. So far as the moral government of God is concerned, it is as completely repudiated by pantheism as by any other form of atheism. The only law it recognizes is the internal force of the one substance which constitutes the *το παν*, a force operating blindly and necessarily, and producing a development as fixed and unchangeable as fate. Hence, according to this theory, there is and can be no liberty, no responsibility, no personal immortality, in man. He is but a bubble that rises and glitters upon the surface of the great ocean of being, and is absorbed again. All distinctions between truth and falsehood, right and wrong, are abolished. Whatever is, is right. The pantheist calls darkness light, and light darkness; puts evil for good, and good for evil; sweet for bitter, and bitter for sweet. God, the soul, the universe, men, angels and devils, are all commingled in one amorphous mass, one void and formless infinite, over which no light, but darkness visible, sways its gloomy sceptre. The historian of the church, interpreting its phases according to this theory, sees in all its changes, external and internal, in doctrine, in worship, in government, in life, only successive stages in the process of development, all equally necessary, and, of course, equally normal. The church of the middle ages was as orthodox as the church of the apostles. Gregory I. and Gregory VII., Leo the Great and Leo X., Luther, Calvin, Knox, and Ignatius Loyola, were all equally true and righteous, because equally necessary phenomena of the one all-pervading substance in its process of development.

So powerful and so insidious has been the influence of this

philosophy in Germany, where church history has been more scientifically studied than in any other country, that even historians whom charity compels us to accept as Christians write often as if the course of events were a necessary unfolding and development according to an internal law, without the direction or control of any presiding intelligence whatever. Professor Schaff, for example, who is not only a fine scholar and a man of great learning, but, I have no doubt, receives, *ex animo*, the doctrines of the Heidleburg Catechism, is disposed to apologise for the errors and abuses in the church as belonging to a particular stage of development, where, as it appears to us, fidelity to the truth and loyalty to his Master would have required him to judge and to pronounce according to the law and the testimony. Mr. Nevin, who was for some time his colleague at Mercersburg, has gone much further, and has applied the pantheistic theory of development in such a way as to reach the result of a sort of mixture of popery and eutychianism.

Now, against pantheism and against atheism in all its forms, as applied to the interpretation of history, and especially of church history, all believers in a personal God, the Creator and Ruler of the world, are bound to protest. In opposition to them all, we assert that *will* is the great element of history; the will of God, the Ruler, and the will of man, the creature of God's power and the subject of his government; that these are the two factors which, by their combined operation, produce the result we call history. But history is but the evolution of the plan of God, settled from all eternity according to the counsel of his own will and his sovereign purpose, which must be accomplished alike in the accomplishment and defeat of all the purposes of man. As before God there is no contingency, there can be no such thing as an unexpected, unforeseen, unprovided-for turn in human affairs. It was by the determinate counsel and foreknowledge of God that the weeping friends and scoffing enemies of Jesus stood together before tha. cross upon which the great redemption was achieved. Moses and Pharaoh, Arius and Athanasius, Augustine and Pelagius, Luther and Leo X., Andrew Melville and Charles Stuart, were all instruments, free and willing, yet absolute instruments, of him who doeth according to his will among the armies of heaven and the inhabitants of earth, whose counsel shall stand and who will do all his pleasure; who hath made all things for himself, even the wicked for the day of evil.

There is a sense in which the notion of development and even organic development, of which you read so much in modern histories of the church, is a just notion. The processes of organic life are frequently used by our Saviour to illustrate the processes of his own spiritual kingdom. The growth of seed and of trees, the process of generation and of birth, and analogies of this class, are perhaps more frequently used than any other for this purpose. One of the most striking of his parables is that of the grain of mustard seed, the least of all seeds, and yet growing into a tree, in the branches whereof the fowls of the air may lodge.

Now, in all forms of organic life there are three essential conditions of development or growth. One is life, the vital principle; another is the form of the organization; the third is the sphere or set of circumstances suited to the nature of that life. In wheat, for example, we have the principle of vegetable life; the form of the seed (I use the term "form" in its philosophical sense), that which marks it wheat, and not rye or oats; the external conditions of soil, sunshine, rain, etc. All these conditions are necessary. Pound the seed of wheat in a mortar, you destroy the life and the organization together, or put the whole seed in the foldings of a mummy and let it remain there for centuries and it will not germinate. Take it from its resting-place, where it has been so long slumbering, and sow it in a soil suited to it, and you will see that its suspended vitality will again become active and prolific. So it is also in the animal kingdom; so, also, in the intellectual, and so, also, in the spiritual. The development of the church of God which constitutes its history, will, according to these principles, depend upon the life, the form, and the external conditions of the church. Of these in order.

1. The life of the church, the vital principle, is the Holy Ghost, or Christ living in her by his Spirit. Her life is not natural, but supernatural.

2. The form of the church is the word of God. This is the incorruptible seed which determines its nature, and all its manifestations; the mould into which it is cast.[1]

3. The external conditions are, summarily, all the means by which the word is kept in contact with the mind and heart of the church, whether these means be of special institution, like forms of worship, or of ordinary providence, like political or social arrangements.

Supposing, now, the existence of a certain *quantum* of vital force in the church, the kind and degree of development will depend upon her knowledge of the word of God. We should expect to find, therefore, different degrees of development in different ages of the church.

1. For, in the first place, the word itself has been undergoing a development. Beginning in the germ of the first promise in the garden of Eden, it unfolded itself from age to age, till it reached its full expansion, and the maturity of its bloom and fragrance, in the teaching of Christ and his apostles. It is growth, not mere increment by accumulation, from age to age. The whole gospel is in the first promise, as the whole oak is in the acorn, or the whole man in the infant of an hour old. The essential completeness of revelation from the beginning, and its consequent identity all along the ages, is the ground upon which we may assert at once the antiquity and the unity of the church. The gradual development of revelation is the fact by which we account

[1] See Romans vi. 17; 1 John iii. 9.

for the changing aspects in the external form of the church, thus ancient and thus one.

2. And, secondly, there is a development in the *knowledge* of revelation. This point I will illustrate in the eloquent words of Dean Trench's fifth Hulsean Lecture for 1845: "Our task must be to show how this treasure of divine truth, once given, has only gradually revealed itself; how the history of the church, the difficulties, the trials, the struggles, the temptations in which it has been involved, have interpreted to it its own records, brought out their latent significance, and caused it to discover all which in them it had; how there was much written for it there, as in sympathetic ink, invisible for a season, yet ready to flash out in lines and characters of light whenever the appointed day and hour had arrived. So that in this way the Scripture has been to the church as the garments to the children of Israel, which during all the years of their pilgrimage in the desert waxed not old; yea, according to rabbinical tradition, kept pace and measure with their bodies, growing with their growth, fitting the man as they had fitted the child, and this until the forty years of their sojourn in the wilderness had expired. Or, to use another comparison, which may help to illustrate our meaning, Holy Scripture thus progressively unfolding what it contains might be likened fitly to some magnificent landscape, on which the sun is gradually rising, and even as it rises is bringing out one headland into light and prominence, and then another; anon kindling the glory-smitten summit of some far mountain, and presently lighting up the recesses of some near valley which had hitherto abided in gloom, and so travelling on till nothing remains in shadow, no nook nor corner hid from the light and heat of it, but the whole prospect stands out in the clearness and splendor of the brightest noon."[1]

It is obvious from this view of the case that the true de-

[1] Page 75 of Dean Trench's Fifth Hulsean Lecture for 1845.

velopment of Scripture, since the canon was closed, is only a development in the *knowledge* of Scripture, the written word, and differs from the Roman and Anglican theory as widely as the Westminster *Confession of Faith* differs from the "Decrees and Canons of the Trent Council," or the *Book of Common Prayer*. There has been a progress in the knowledge of the church somewhat analagous to that which takes place in the individual Christian. Heresies, persecutions, social and political convulsions, as well as the calm studies of philologists and the researches of travellers, have contributed to it. Wilkinson and Champollion, Young and Roscelin, Layard, Laborde and Rawlinson, have all been elements in it. As to the distinctive doctrines of the gospel, they have always been learned most rapidly and effectively in the furnace. Its flames have brought out, to use the figure of Trench, "the characters in sympathetic ink," and revealed the presence of the Son of God in the midst. In this way apostate Babylon has been of more service to the saints in the development of doctrine than by all her infallible decisions of popes and councils. Thousands have written upon her dungeon walls sentences from the word of God, which the place itself eloquently expounded and which the eye of infidel curiosity has been compelled to read. Thousands will be thankful for the dragonades of Louis XIV. and the hell-hounds of Claverhouse as the means by which, in the providence of God and under the illumination of his Spirit, they have grown in practical appreciation of the preciousness of the promises, and of the comfort to be derived from knowing that there is an avenging judge. We know more and with more accuracy of the doctrine of the Trinity for the controversies of Arius and Socinius; more of the doctrine of grace for the heresies of Pelagius and the semi-pelagianism of Arminius; more of the true nature of ecclesiastical power for the usurping ambition of a Hildebrand; more of the true marks of the church for the misrepresentations of Bellarmine;

more of the morality of the Bible for the detestable casuistry of the Jesuits; more of the value of a personal God for the visions of Theodore Parker and Francis Newman. There has been a great develpment of Bible knowledge by the favor of its enemies, and we doubt not the development will go on till the church militant shall throw off the armor at the coming of the Lord and rejoice in the millennial glory. "And as it was at the Reformation"—I quote again from Trench—"with the Pauline Epistles, as it is now with the gospels, so I cannot doubt that a day will come when all the significance of the Apocalypse for the church of God will be apparent, which hitherto it can scarcely be said to have been; that a time will arrive when it will be plainly shown how costly a gift, yea, rather, how necessary an armor, was this for the church of the Redeemer. Then, when the last things are about to be and the trump of the last angel to sound; when the great drama is hastening with ever briefer pauses to its catastrophe, then, in one unlooked-for way or another, the veil will be lifted up from this wondrous book, and it will be to the church collectively what even partially understood it has been already to tens of thousands of her children—strength in the fires, giving her songs in the night, songs of joy and deliverance in that darkest night of her trial which shall precede the break of her everlasting day, and enabling her, even when the triumph of anti-Christ is at the highest, to look securely on to his near doom and her own perfect victory."

Corresponding, now, with this development of revelation itself, we find the church under different forms at different periods of the world: the patriarchal before Abraham, the Abrahamic, the Mosaic, the Christian. The polity and worship corresponding with the doctrine of the period, and the life of the church, as represented by distinguished saints, such as might be expected from the combined operation of the teaching, worship, and discipline of the period. The church before and after the coming of Christ is compared by the Apostle Paul to a human being before and after the period of maturity[1]; and God's dealings with it corresponded with its conditions—a child, a man, tutors and governors, freedom.[2]

Corresponding with the development in the *knowledge* of revelation will be the actual development of spiritual life. Illustrate by the history of the Jews, times of Joshua, times of Judges, of David, of Rehoboam, of the captivity; Christian church, age of the apostles, of Constantine, of the Reformation, of Westminster Confession, of this age. The general standard of knowledge is the standard and measure, *ceteris paribus,* of the general development. Preposterous to assert that any individual of the church of the nineteenth century (or any congregation) is in advance of the Christians of Augustine's time, or of any other past time, simply because the time is past. The whole nominal church for many centuries after Augustine was immeasurably inferior in all the elements of its condition to the church of his day.

3. In the third place, the external conditions of the church have contributed to modify the development. Instituted means, worship, etc.; ordinary providence, its relations to state; church in France after the Reformation, in England, in Scotland, in the United States. Prosperity, adversity, etc., etc.

From this view of the theory of development it follows that in a certain sense, and to a certain extent, the church of any given period is the child of all its past, and the father of all its future history, as the child of ten years old is the offspring of that ten years and the father of all the future. Yet we must never lose sight of the fact that the sovereign Spirit of God comes into the soul of a man, or of a church, and by the creation of a new life modifies the whole development. The boy of ten years may threaten to be a monster of

[1] See Gal. iv.

[2] See "Mission of the Comforter," in *Presbyterial Critic*, Vol. I.

wickedness, and afterwards be converted and be eminent for his devotion to truth and righteousness. So on a large scale of a congregation or a whole church, a development of a fatal sort may be arrested and reversed, and a new development begun.

In one sense, the development is always in direct proportion to the chronology. If history be only the unfolding of the plan of God, then every movement brings us nearer to the consummation. But the actual progress cannot be estimated without taking another element into consideration. This leads me to observe:

We must never forget that this world is a scene of perpetual conflict and struggle. There are, and have been from the beginning, two developments antagonistic to each other. The very first promise in the garden of Eden contained a prophecy of it: "I will *put* enmity between thee and the woman, between thy seed and her seed," etc. Man had entered into an alliance with the serpent, an offensive treaty against God; and this treaty would have remained unbroken forever but for a supernatural, gracious interposition of God, by which a new spiritual life was created in man, and he was restored to communion and friendship with his Maker. This spiritual life was a beginning of a development in the church which is destined to go on forever; and this is the development which it is the main object of church history to trace. But the old enmity to God was the germ of an antagonistic development, which is also destined to go on forever. In the individual Christian, while in the body, and in the whole church during the state of testimony and of trial on earth, the flesh and the spirit are struggling for the mastery; and in the church and the world the two developments are going on side by side, and will continue to go on till the final coming of the woman's seed, when death and hades shall be cast into the lake of fire. From Cain and Abel, down to the last prophet, before the coming of Christ in the flesh, who perished between the porch and the altar; and onward from the death of John the Baptist by the sword of Herod, and the crucifixion of the Son of God, to the present hour, has the conflict been going on; and the harp of prophecy is struck to alternate strains of joy or woe, as it announces the future continuance of the same conflict, until the shout of victory from the sacramental host of God's elect shall rend the heavens: "We give thee thanks, O Lord God Almighty, which art and wast, and art to come; because thou hast taken to thee thy great power and hast reigned;"—"Alleluia; salvation and glory and honor and power unto the Lord our God."

The *existence* of these two principles in the "kingdom of heaven" during its incipient stages on earth is announced by our Saviour in the parable of the drag-net, which drew both good and bad fish; the *development* of these two principles is announced in the parable of the wheat and the tares; "they shall *grow* together till the harvest," the wheat manifesting itself more and more to be wheat; the tares manifesting themselves more and more to be tares.

The same conditions of development exist in evil as in good—life, form, external circumstances. The form of evil is the opposite of the form of good; and as the latter is the word of God, so the form of evil is the denial, either expressly or by implication, of the word. So it was in the beginning. The word of God was, "In the day thou eatest thereof thou shalt surely die"; the word of the devil was, "Thou shalt not surely die," but "ye shall be as gods," &c. So all along the ages, the antagonistic element has obtained the ascendency, and the development of the church has been arrested or perverted just in proportion as she has allowed the word of God to be set aside by the "traditions of men."

These two developments, their struggles, the victory of the one, the defeat of the other, constitute the history of the church of God; and the history of the world is important mainly as it bears on the history of the church. Hence, in biblical history, the church always occupies the foreground of the picture; and nations and empires, their rise and fall, their successes and disasters, their temporary triumphs and final destruction, are all grouped according to the importance of their history in relation to the church of God.[1] If these views be just, it follows:

1. That the standard of criticism in the study of history, that by which we are to judge and estimate events, is the word of God, and the word of God only. It is not rationalism, or mysticism, or traditionalism, or the natural reason of the individual, or the religious life of the individual, or the religious life of the church in any particular period of its development. We cannot tell in any case how far the principle of evil has perverted or retarded the normal development of the church, without this unchanging standard. A reformation is a reform-ation, a bringing back again to the standard form, which is the word of God.

2. As the word of God itself is variously interpreted, and, consequently, the various sects, Lutheran and Reformed, Presbyterian, Prelatical, and Congregational, Calvinistic, and Semi-Pelagian, will each contemplate history through its own medium, or, as the phrase is, from its own standpoint, we, as Presbyterians, are obliged to look at history from our own standpoint, and estimate its results according to our own interpretation of the word. This is inevitable by the same necessity which in the first instance gave rise to variety of sect. All that is required of us is, that we be honest, candid, humble, docile, always. For we are as accountable to God for the exercise of our understandings as we are for the exercise of our wills.

A great deal of the common talk about the absence of prejudice and sectarian partiality comes from those who do

---

[1]See *Shedd's History of Doctrine*, Introduction, §§ 3, 4, 5, Vol. I., pp. 11–22.

not feel interest enough in the glory of God, or in the salvation of man, to take sides, and they are bigoted for indifference. But I envy not the man who can read the record of such a battle of ages without enlisting himself on one side or the other; without feelings of anger, or pity, or sadness, or exultation, as the scenes, one after another, pass before him. Indeed, no man can be indifferent, for all must be for Christ or against him. And even Gibbon, with the pretended impartiality of a judge, is always playing the advocate where Christianity and its enemies are impleaded together at the bar. The serene smile of philosophical indifference does not conceal the frown of malignity upon his brow, or the contemptuous curl upon his lip, when he speaks of Christianity. The sarcasm of Porson had as much truth as point when he said of him, "His humanity never slumbers except when Christians are persecuted and women ravished."

3. As has been already, incidentally, suggested, a supernatural interposition is necessary to produce a thorough reform. Neither an individual nor a church can be brought back to that *form* which we have seen is one of the essential conditions of the normal development, without a new life, or the supernatural revival of the life. The Reformation of the sixteenth century was not the reformation of the papacy, which was nominally the church of God upon earth. That body was the most intense and flagrant representative of the antagonistic development of evil, its life being the life of the devil, and its form the lies of the devil in opposition to the truth of God. The word of God had been repudiated, imprisoned, buried, and its very memory insulted. The reformation of that body, therefore, as an organization, had become utterly hopeless. It was apostate, the hold of every foul spirit, the cage of every unclean and hateful bird. But within her dominion, the line of the true development, feeble, hidden, despised, and, whenever it appeared, persecuted, was

still preserved. A monk here and there in his cloister pored over that mysterious book that was chained, like a felon, to the desk; and the hidden life that had been imparted by the Spirit of God was nourished and invigorated and finally, when Providence gave the occasion and opportunity, this life meets the life of many others in the glorious fellowship of the truth, and a whole continent awakes from the nightmare of centuries. A feeble flame is kindled in Germany, and another feeble flame in Switzerland; and then flame meets flame, and soon all Europe is in a blaze. Meantime, the old development goes on, till it reaches the climax of falsehood and blasphemy in the Council of Trent.[1]

4. The manner in which God prepares the way for great revolutions is also in harmony with the view of an organic development. It is one feature of this process of nature that the different elements of the organism are all begun at once, and grow from their appropriate centres, each to meet his fellow at the appointed time and place. We have an illustration of this law in the *post-natal* juncture of the sections of an infant's cranium. So also, in the preparation for the first advent of the Son of God, there was a development of Judaism, and a development of heathenism, and in heathenism of Greek and Roman history, and when all reached a certain point the "fulness of time" was come, and he who was the substance of all Jewish shadows, and the unknown satisfaction of the desire of all nations, was born. So, for the Reformation, the like process of preparation was gone through with. I may add that there is also in nature a preparation for the *external sphere*, as well as of the *life* and *form* of the organism. So, also, in history. The rigid principle of faith in an external revelation was furnished by the Jews; the possibility and facility of a logical theology

[1] Note.—Christianity is the only system, once lost, that has ever been revived or restored. There is no instance of a lost dynasty or philosophy or religion being restored in the history of man.

by the culture of the Greeks; the principle of government and organization (external) by the Romans, in the first example above given. The diffusion of God's word and the exposition of it, by means of the art of printing, the revival of letters, etc., in the last example.

5. It follows, also, from this view of history that its great stages will be *typical*, that is, the great end of development, the consummation to be reached, will, at every such stage, become more and more distinct; "the *idea* which is to be reached in its reality when the last and highest degree of development has been reached will become more and more manifest."[1] This is strikingly manifest in sacred history. The flood a type of the judgment,[2] so, also, the destruction of Sodom,[3] etc. The structure of prophecy corresponds with this. The profound observation of Bacon, that prophecy has a "springing and germinant accomplishment throughout all ages, but reaches its highest fulfilment in some one age." Hence the "manifold sense" of prophecy. Take Enoch's, for example, as recorded in Jude's Epistle. It was fulfilled first in the flood, and many times since; it will reach its height and fulness in the second coming of our Lord. If one event is typical of another, then a prophecy of the first event will be a prophecy of the second event also, provided, always, that providence is the unfolding of the plan of God, and prophecy a revelation of it.

Show wherein this "manifold sense" differs from the "double" or equivocal sense of the pagan oracles. Illustrate this general point by vegetable and animal life, particularly by the growth of the human being, whose early stages of growth are wonderfully prophetic. See Deut. xviii. 15–19, with Acts iii. 22, 23, for Christ as a prophet; Gen. xiv. 18–20, with Psa. cx. and Heb. vii., for the sacerdotal and regal offices combined; the whole Aaronic priesthood for the

[1] Kurtz's *Sacred History*, p. 33.

[2] 2 Peter iii.; Matt. xxiv. *et al.*

[3] 2 Peter ii.

priestly office alone; David and Solomon for the kingly office alone; Joshua and Zerubbabel (Zechariah) together for Christ as priest and king, "a priest upon his throne." All typical persons emerging in history at certain stages to indicate him, in whom all the lines of history meet. "Oh! the depth of the riches, both of the knowledge and wisdom of God."

6. Show how, from these views, any new development of life in the church requires the direct interposition of God. Hugh Miller's argument from geology against the transmutation of species, the germ from which the development begins must, in every case, be the product of the creative power of God. This furnishes us with a complete refutation of the pantheistic and quasi-pantheistic theory of the development of the church, which would make the Reformation under Luther a stage in the development of the same sort (I mean equally normal), or, in other words, a stage in the same line of development with the changes which took place in the church under Hildebrand—that is, the church under Hildebrand developed into the church under Luther, than which nothing can be more absurd. It might as reasonably be asserted that a serpent was developed into an eagle, or the egg of a hawk into a dove. The truth is, the Reformation was a revival, by the direct agency of the Holy Ghost, of the true line of development which had been apparently almost lost. Illustrate, also, in the case of the regeneration of an individual man; the beginning of a new life in him *must* be referred to the *creative* energy of God. "Whatsoever is born of the flesh is flesh." Spirit must be born of spirit. One kind of life cannot be developed (no matter how long a period of time be given) into another kind of life. Flesh will still be flesh at a remove of the thousandth generation. If at any stage the flesh is to become spirit, the Spirit of God must interpose. Hence all forms of pelagianism, denying as they do the total depravity, the total absence of holiness in

the sinner, and consequently the necessity for the immediate creative energy of the Holy Ghost in regeneration, are consistent. There is a germ of holiness in the heart, and it only needs to be developed. The man is to be educated, developed, *not* born again, created anew, raised from the dead. Bushnell's *Christian Nurture* is a pelagian view of nurture, not a Christian view. *O'cœcas hominum mentes!*

7. There can be no church, and, of course, no church history, where the word of God is not. The life and the form must go together. Therefore, those who hold that the heathen can be saved without the gospel hold that God, in their case, violates all the analogies of his works, both of creation and of providence. Suppose that God converts the heathen as he converts infants, how is the spiritual life of such children of his to be developed? There is neither form nor external conditions suited to the life which has been imparted. There are eyes, but no light; ears, but no sound; lungs, but no air. It will not do to say that people are sometimes born blind, dumb and deaf; for this is to be expected in consequence of the curse. But in the case of the heathen, the case by the theory, is one of salvation, of restoration from the effects of the curse. If, therefore, any heathen are saved, they must be taken immediately to heaven, where the development goes on by vision, as with infants dying in infancy, not by faith. If they continued to live in this world they must walk by faith, and faith implies a divine testimony. "Faith cometh by hearing, and hearing by the word of God." "Awake, thou that sleepest, and arise from the dead, *that Christ may give thee light.*" The only other supposition in the case conceivable is that each converted heathen has a special revelation made to him, by which he walks. This is altogether a gratuitous assumption; and even if it were so, there could be no "fellowship," unless he were commissioned to impart this revelation unto others. Then we should have apostles, prophets, etc., and another Bible for heathendom different from

the apostles of Christendom; all of which is inconsistent with the tenor of the great commission, "Go ye into all the world," etc., which implies that Jerusalem was to be the centre from which all knowledge of salvation was to be diffused unto the ends of the earth. In heathendom, therefore, there can be no church and no church history.

DIVISIONS OF CHURCH HISTORY.

By divisions of church history I do not mean the periods into which it may be chronologically divided, but the heads or rubrics under which it is to be mainly considered. These are suggested by, and follow from, the nature of history and of the church, as already explained.

1. The fundamental element is *the life.* But the nature of life is such as to be inscrutable to us in itself. "The wind bloweth where it listeth," &c. We can only know it by its manifestations and developments; and these are determined by the form and the external conditions.

2. The form is the word of God, as actually understood. And hence the leading rubric in church history will be the *history of doctrine.*

3. This, again, will depend, to a great extent, upon the external circumstances of the church. And here it must be observed that the form and the external conditions are, in a certain sense, coincident with each other in reference to the growth and development of the church. It is not so in vegetable or animal organizations. The seed determines the form both of the plant and the animal, but the external conditions are totally different; the soil, the air, the light, &c. But in the case of the individual believer, the word of God is at once the seed which determines the new nature, and the milk, the wine, the water, the strong meat, by which he is nourished and invigorated. The word of God in the soul is the form in the strict sense; and at first is imperfect and defective, but is destined to become more full and more

symmetrical by the ministry of the word externally, and the constant communication of life by the indwelling Spirit of God. Hence the external conditions, so-called, are only the circumstances by which the access of the word to the mind and heart of the church is facilitated or hindered as the case may be.

First and foremost among these circumstances is the *worship* of the church: preaching, singing, praying, sacramental rites, and contributions. The effect of preaching in this relation is too obvious to need any remark; and so with the reading of the word, which preaching more or less implies. Formal praise and prayer impress the truth more deeply upon the soul, by the very constitution of our nature. The word, for example, says God is holy, just, wise, and good. In praise and prayer we acknowledge that he is so; and that very acknowledgment, while it implies that we have some conviction and sense thereof (otherwise it were hypocrisy), has the effect of increasing that conviction and sense of the reality and glory of these attributes. The word says we are sinners; we worship, confess our sins, and that confession, sincerely made, deepens our convictions of sin. The word says, and the ordinance of the supper says, that Christ died for us, and that he is freely offered to us as our substitute. In praise and prayer, and in eating the bread and drinking the wine, we acknowledge the truth and grace of God in the gift of the Son, and express our grateful and joyful acceptance of the Saviour as thus offered, and thereby are strengthened in faith and gratitude and love. The word says that we are dependent upon God for everything, and that all our substance has been committed to us as stewards in trust, and that he will condescend to hold fellowship with us in the use of our substance for the extension of his kingdom and the glory of his name. We acknowledge the truth and grace of all this by *giving* of our substance, and thereby have more intimate fellowship with God, and increase of our faith, gratitude, and love. So, also, with visiting the fatherless and widows in their affliction, which James tells us is "*worship*[1] pure and undefiled before God and the Father"; baptism and the religious training of children.

Second, The *polity* of the church. I use the term polity for the reason assigned by Hooker in his celebrated treatise, that it is more general than "government" or "discipline," and includes everything pertaining to the external organization of the church; the exercise of all official power, the *potestas ordinis* as well as the *potestas jurisdictionis*. All ecclesiastical power is "ministerial and declarative," it is only the power of servants to declare and do, and help one another to do, their master's will. All the departments of this polity are designed to bring the word in contact with the mind and heart of the church to testify for God and against the devil, for the truth and against lies in all forms.

Third, The relations of the church to the world, and especially to civil government, and this chiefly under five heads. The church as *persecuted*, *tolerated*, *patronized* or *established*, *dominant* or *controlling*, and *free* or *independent*. Perhaps we ought to add a sixth, to express the condition of the church under the patriarchs, when it was confounded with the state in the common nursery of both, the family; and a seventh, to express its condition under many of the kings of Judah and Israel, a condition very peculiar, and in part sanctioned and in part not sanctioned by the authority of God. For instance, the doings of David, in arranging the courses of the priests and Levites and the order of worship in the temple. (See 1 Chronicles.)

This branch of church history is what constitutes, for the most part, what is called the "external history" of the church. It is very obvious, too, how this external history might, in many ways, affect the great matter of the contact of the word of God with the mind and heart of the church.

---

[1] See the Greek of James i. 27.

Fourth, The *literature* of the church; the writings of her officers, and members; and her symbolical instruments and formularies. The press, in this connection. I put the symbols in this category, not as the acts of the church through her courts and councils (in which relations they would belong to the second head); but as a part of the *litera scripta*, as influencing the general views of truth and the tone of faith. And according to this principle of classification we may also add the sacred Scriptures themselves. Add: Contemporary literature of the nations.

Fifth, As the result of all these circumstances and as reacting again upon them, we may add the extension and progress of the church.—*Missions.* "Freely ye have received; freely give;" "give and it shall be given you," the law of her life. Here, again, the likeness to the processes of vegetable life becomes very striking.

Such, then, are the leading topics of church history as suggested by a view of it as an organism, subject to the law of development or growth.

THE MORAL LAW.[1]

I. AMONG the numberless questions which may be asked in reference to the moral law is the question, "Why was its formal promulgation delayed so many centuries?" In answer to this question, it may be observed—

1. That the delay is in harmony with the analogy of other parts of revelation. We have already seen, in following the history of the plan of redemption, that this history furnishes the occasions, from time to time, of new disclosures of the scheme of mercy, and determines the form in which those disclosures are made. We do not presume to say why the plan of mercy was so gradually revealed, for God has not explicitly informed us. But there are dim intimations given in the Scriptures that, when the whole plan shall have been completed, the reasons will be found in the organic unity of the church. The writer of the Epistle to the Hebrews says that the ancient heroes of the faith "received not the promise, God having provided some better thing for us, that *they without us should not be made perfect*." (Heb. xi. 39, 40.) Every stage of the church's growth, like every stage in the development of a human being until he reaches maturity, has its imperfections, and perfection will be the privilege of none, until it can be the privilege of all in the resurrection at the last day. The fathers could not be made perfect without us, and we cannot be made perfect without the fathers. The Bible is full of proofs that the saints under the gospel are not absolutely in a better condition than the saints under the law; that is to say, the mere fact of being under the gospel is not necessarily an advantage. Abraham was

[1] This paper is taken from Dr. Peck's notes for his junior class in Ecclesiastical History.—ED.

the father of the faithful, and this is a privilege which belongs to no other believer. And what means this roll-call of the mighty dead in the eleventh chapter of Hebrews, if their faith is not proposed for our imitation upon whom the ends of the world are come? And, further, is it not a notorious fact that the saints of the gospel dispensation, in the highest heights and the deepest depths of their experience, can find no more appropriate expression of these heights and depths than the records of the experience of the old worthies in the Book of Psalms? Lastly, are not the final disclosures of the Apocalypse cast in an Old Testament mould throughout? As there is an advantage to the human being in the stages of infancy, childhood, youth, manhood, there is no reason to doubt that there is also an advantage in similar stages in the development of the church. The church is an organism, and it is the characteristic of an organism that each part is for the whole, and the whole for each part. There is the same reason, therefore, for a gradual revelation of law that there is for the gradual revelation of grace, though, in reference to neither can we affirm, without intolerable arrogance, that we know the whole case.

2. Another reason may be found, perhaps, in the constitution of society in the line of the chosen seed down to the age of Moses. This constitution was patriarchal. No proper political community, in the form of a nation, with a complex social organization, then existed. As the organization of society grows in complexity, and the relations of its members to each other are multiplied, a more extensive classification of rights and duties, as well as clearer and sharper definitions of both, become absolutely indispensable to peace and order. In addition to this, it also becomes necessary to give to the directive power more strength and authority by penal sanctions. In the bosom of a single family, and even in the circle of a single clan, the bond of blood is a mighty one; and the feeling of kindred is a powerful prompter to deeds of

kindness,[1] and a powerful restraint upon deeds of oppression and wrong. "We be brethren" was an argument not easily resisted. But as relations are multiplied and complicated, the sensible power of this peculiar relationship is diminished, and it needs to be supported, or to be wholly replaced, by the threatenings of pains and penalties. Hence the clear, stern voice of law.[2]

3. Again, the regulative power of the elder man, whether in the sphere of a single household or in the larger sphere of a clan or a "family connection," derived great force from the extreme longevity of the period. Adam lived until the days of Lamech, the father of Noah. It is impossible for us to appreciate the weight of authority which must have belonged to a man of such years and of such an experience. With what force must he have expounded the doctrines of the personalty and supremacy of God! With what force must he have spoken of the holiness, justice, goodness of the law which had been written, in the beginning, upon his own heart, and of the horrible malignity of sin which his own act had brought into his own nature and the nature of his race! Could he ever have forgotten through all the centuries of protracted life the horrors of that moment when he looked upon the mangled corpse of Abel, mangled by the hand of his own brother, murdered *because* his works were righteous and his brother's evil! Was not the conviction of the sinfulness of sin, then, branded upon his paternal heart? With what earnestness must he have inculcated the duty of *love* and testified against the breach of it!

---

[1] This word is derived from "kin" or "kind."

[2] The laws of the "Twelve Tables" were not written until 300 years after the foundation of the city of Rome (Smith's *Dictionary of Greek and Roman Antiquities*), and then they were not so much new laws as the embodiment in writing of laws previously existing (*jura* passing into *leges*). So, also, it was 300 years after the overthrow of the Western Roman Empire by the German tribes before the attempt was made to construct a general system of laws, and to embody them in a written code.—*The Capitularies of Charlemagne.*

4. Once more, God himself had testified against sin, which is a transgression of the law, by the "preachers of righteousness" not only, but by tremendous judgments. The deluge and the destruction of the *cities* of the plain were such testimonies. The one against lust and violence, the other specially against unnatural and monstrous lust. It is a striking fact that the only formal enactment against crime recorded in the patriarchal age is that which was given immediately after the flood, requiring murder to be punished with death. The reason of the command is also instructive. Both the precept and the reason were a protest against the *violence* of the "sons of men," against their hellish maxim that "might makes right," a maxim which degrades man to the level of the stronger beasts of the field, and utterly repudiates the fact of the divine image in him, of a moral nature capable of perceiving the glory and supremacy of righteousness. This command is a voice, uttered over the ruins of the race, against the dominion of brute force and in behalf of the dominion of God, which is a dominion of right.

The race, then, was not wholly without law before the uttering of "the ten words" upon the burning mount. The memory of the law written upon the heart of man at his creation was kept alive by the instructions of parents, by the warnings of "preachers of righteousness," by the translation of Enoch, by desolating judgments from the hand of the invisible lawgiver. The law of which the heathen Cicero speaks in such wonderful terms,[1] in a passage often quoted,[2] "right reason, conformable to nature, diffused among all, unchangeing, eternal, which, by commanding, urges to duty, by prohibiting deters from fraud, which has God himself for its author and administrator"—this law was, more or less clearly, perceived and recognized. The authority of conscience was not totally denied. But notwithstanding all, sin

[1] *De Republica*, III., 22.

[2] See, for instance, Fairbairn's *Revelation of Law in S. S.*, Lect. III.

increased, and it became necessary when God had redeemed his church out of Egypt to begin his instruction of them by a clear announcement, in the most solemn terms, of that great standard of holiness to which they were required to be conformed, and without conformity to which redemption would be incomplete, or, rather, could not be at all.

II. The next question which invites our attention is, "What is the form and substance of this law?" And here first,

1. Note the relations and offices of the lawgiver as stated in the preface, as constituting the grounds upon which obedience should be rendered.

(*A*), "I am Jehovah." This name expresses, fundamentally, self-existence, and therefore conveys the idea that he to whom it belongs is the author of all finite being. The people to whom the law is given are hereby reminded that they are the creatures of God, living, moving, having their being in him, and that this absolute physical dependence involves an absolute moral dependence also. This name serves to show that this law was not given to the Hebrews, as Hebrews, but as men, and, consequently, that it belongs not to those elements of the Mosaic institute which are provisional and temporary, but to those which are permanent and eternal. The sum of this law is *love;* and love to God is absolutely essential to the perfection and happiness of men. The law has been dispensed under many different forms, but in its essence it is as immutable as the nature of God and the relation of creature to creator.

(*B*), But beside this natural relation of the lawgiver to the Hebrews and to all men, there is a federal relation which he sustains to the church. This is expressed in the words, "Thy God." This formula would remind the people that he who was now speaking to them had made a covenant with Abraham, and had renewed it from time to time with Isaac and

---

[1]Fairbairn's *Revelation of Law in S. S.*, Lect. IV.

with Jacob. This covenant, while it was a matter of free promise on the part of God, as Paul argues in the third chapter of Galatians, yet involved, in the execution of its provisions, the conformity of the fœderate to the character of God as expressed in his law. The blessing promised to Abraham, according to Peter,[1] consisted "in turning away the seed from their iniquities," and was actually exemplified on the day of Pentecost in the conversion of three thousands of them. They were bound to keep the law, not only because they were men, but because they were in covenant with the lawgiver and heirs of the promises.

These statements serve to show the groundlessness of the notion that this law was given to the Hebrews merely as a republication of the covenant of works; and that the whole transaction was merely a rehearsal on the part of God and man fallen of what had before been done between God and man unfallen. When the Hebrews said, "all the words of this law we will do," something more was meant than a bare acknowledgment of an obligation still to keep the law, notwithstanding the loss of ability to keep it. It was a formal promise of the covenant people of God to make this law the standard of holiness, and to endeavor to conform to it. It must be ever borne in mind that the people here standing before God constituted a church, the identical church which was formed by the covenant with Abraham, and that the law was given in pursuance of the mercy promised to Abraham.

In addition, then, to the obligation springing from the fact that they were God's creatures, is the obligation arising from their relation to God as the giver of the promise of salvation.

(*C*), But, lastly, God presents himself distinctly in the relation of a redeemer, "who have brought thee out," etc. Not only is he the giver of promises, but the fulfiller of them. He has actually redeemed them out of Egypt, has delivered them

---

[1] Acts iii. 25, 26.

out of the power (εξουσια) of darkness into the kingdom of the Son. The law was given to a people who had not only received the promise of redemption, but who had been in fact redeemed. The error of the theory alluded to a little while ago becomes, in the light of this part of the preface to the law, still more glaring. So far from the law being only the memorial of a covenant hopelessly broken, and consequently designed and suited only to produce consternation and despair, it appears here as a revelation given to the people by their *redeeming* God, in order to teach them what redemption is, or rather in what real redemption consists, to-wit, redemption from the power of sin, which is a "transgression of the law. How perfectly does all this correspond with the representations of the New Testament! Jesus was so called because he should save his people from their sins. He gave himself as the paschal Lamb for his people, that he might redeem them from all iniquity, and purify them unto himself a peculiar people, zealous of good works. There is no happiness for the *sinner*. If we are ever to enjoy the *blessedness* of God we must have the *holiness* of God. He who sets himself against the law sets himself against salvation, and hence we find the Saviour beginning his ministry as Moses began his, by a promulgation of the law, or, at least, by a solemn announcement that he came not to destroy but to fulfil it, followed by an exposition of the spirituality of it in opposition to the infatuated glosses of the scribes and Pharisees. He begins with the beatitudes, indeed, but declares that the blessedness of the kingdom of heaven shall never be the portion of those who have no better righteousness than that of these blind leaders of the blind, these teachers of law who annul a portion of it and "teach men so." Can we desire stronger evidence of the fact that the church of the law and the church of the gospel is the same church, sustaining the same relation to a redeemer and to the law whose precepts he obeyed and whose curse he endured? Note, then, that the law given on Sinai was the utterance of *love*, as well as of justice; of love which had just manifested itself in an act of *redemption*. The pious Jew of that day might have said, with less force, indeed, than the Jews of the days of John the Apostle, yet he might have truly said, "I have a *new* commandment, because the darkness is past and the light shineth."[1]

2. As to the form of the law itself, the first thing that strikes us is that this form is prohibitory. This was determined, no doubt, by the fact that the people were sinners, and had manifested for generations, like the rest of the human race, a tendency to overt and flagrant acts of rebellion against God. "The law entered because of transgression," says Paul; not only to reveal it, but to restrain it. But that the form of prohibition implies the form of requirement, that the negative implies the positive, necessarily results from the very constitution of man's nature. Every moral act involves a choice, and the choosing of one thing involves the refusing of its opposite, the abstaining from one course of action involves the pursuing of the opposite course. Again, the moral life of man is a continuous one, and he must every moment be fulfilling or coming short of, keeping or transgressing, a divine law. He cannot be passive or neutral, for this would be the absence of moral activity, and inactivity in the moral sphere would be death. No man, therefore, can obey a prohibitory divine law by simply abstaining from the act prohibited; he must do the opposite thing. The substance of the law is *love*; and love cannot be satisfied with simply not doing ill; it must do the opposite good. Hence, our fundamental rule for the interpretation of the law, as recognized by theologians, is, that when evil is forbidden, the opposite good is to be understood as enjoined; and when

[1] See *Larger Catechism*, Questions 93-97. The view now given receives confirmation from Fairbairn's *Revelation of Law in S. S.*, pp. 84-86.

a good is required, the opposite evil is understood to be prohibited.[1] This principle of interpretation is clearly sanctioned by those civil laws of Moses which were intended to carry out, in social life, the principles and spirit of the decalogue. A man, for instance, must not only refrain from killing his fellow-man, but he must use means to prevent his losing his life.[2]

3. Note that all the sins of one kind are forbidden under some one sin, and all the duties of one kind are enjoined under one duty.[3]

4. All the rules here laid down are fully justified by the positive form in which the law is stated by Moses, as well as by Christ: "Thou shalt love the Lord thy God with all thy heart," &c., and "Thou shalt love thy neighbor as thyself." We are to abstain from *all* evil, and to do all the good our relations require at our hands. I say, all that our relations to God and our fellow-men require; for these relations determine the modes in which our love is to be manifested. The law is like the fabled tent in the "*Arabian Nights*," which could be so folded up as to be held in the hollow of the hand, and yet capable of being so expanded as to cover vast armies. It is one law to the angels in heaven, to the devils in hell, and to men on earth. Is is one law to men under the gospel, and to men without the gospel. Yet there are sins against the law as given to men which the fallen angels cannot commit, and duties which the elect angels are not required to perform. There are sins and duties which appertain to men who have the gospel which do not appertain to men who have it not. There are sins and duties which appertain to men in certain social relations which do not appertain to men who are not in those relations. As the

---

[1] See the Exposition of the Moral Law in the *Larger and Shorter Catechisms of Westminster*. (See, also, Fairbairn *ut supra*, Lect. IV., p. 87.)

[2] See Deut. xxii. 8., *et mult al.*

[3] See *Larger Catechism*, Q. 99, for this and other features of the law.

relations are ramified, the duties are multiplied as well as the occasions for sinning.

5. These relations are of three classes, giving rise to three classes of duties: (1), Our relations to God. (2), Our relations to our fellew-men. (3), Our relations, if we may be allowed the expression, to ourselves. Hence, moralists speak of "duties to God, to our fellow-men, to ourselves." All these duties are comprehended in love to God, to our fellow-men, and to ourselves.

(*A*), Duties to God: (*a*), His *being*; (*b*), His *worship;* (*c*), His *name;* (*d*), His *day.* As to the fifth commandment, there is doubt whether it belongs to the first or the second table. Parents may be regarded as *representatives* of God to their children, and then it will fall into the first; or the relation of parent and child may be regarded as the radical or fundamental social relation, next after the marriage relation which is implied in it, and, hence, as the representative of all the other social relations which flow out of it, and then it may be referred, as is generally done, to the second table. The Scriptures themselves make no division, unless Matthew xix. 18 and 19 be an exception. Jesus said, "Thou shalt do no murder, thou shalt not commit adultery, thou shalt not steal, thou shalt not bear false witness, honor thy father and thy mother, and thou shalt love thy neighbor as thyself." They speak of two tables, but do not indicate where the one ends or the other begins; perhaps, as has been suggested, to teach that the line is not to be very sharply drawn, and that the contents of the one gradually approximate and at last pass over to the other. We find even in the fourth commandment the duty of a kind consideration of persons in the humbler ranks of life inculcated upon those in the higher.[1]

(*B*), Duties to our neighbors, or fellow-men: (*a*), As to their *life;* (*b*), Their *chastity* and *honor;* (*c*), Their property; (*d*), Their *character* and *position* in life; and finally, (*e*), To

[1] See Fairbairn *ut supra*, p. 92.

show that the very seat and foundation of desire with reference to all these things are to be kept pure, the table closes with a command against lust, or inordinate desire.

(*C*), Duties to ourselves. There is no dispute touching the existence of duties to God and to our fellow-men, but that we ought to love ourselves, or that it is even lawful to love ourselves, has been disputed. The theory has been held by some that all virtue or holiness consists in "disinterested benevolence," and that all sin consists in self-love. Upon this theory we remark:

(*a*), That the sum of the second table takes for granted the natural necessity of self-love, its necessary existence as an element of the constitution which God has given us. "Thou shalt love thy neighbor *as* thyself." And so in the "golden rule," which is only another form of the same command, we are required to do to others what we would have them do to us. A principle which is essentially wrong could not be made the regulator of our duty in any sphere whatever.

(*b*), That self-love is thus a necessary part of our constitution is plain from the universal consciousness of mankind and from universal observation. Men *must* seek their own happiness. No man can desire to be miserable. To assert the contrary is to assert a contradiction in terms. God does not require us to cease to be men in order that we may be holy. He does not require us to be willing to be damned in order that we may be saved, or, in other words, to be willing to hate him in order that we may love him.

(*c*), The theory confounds self-love with selfishness, which are very different things. Self-love is a blind natural instinct, indifferent as to its moral quality, just as hunger, thirst, the love of approbation, the love of property, curiosity, etc., are blind natural instincts, and, like them, it is right or wrong according to the circumstances of its exercise. If self-love is indulged without subordination to the supreme will of God, if the simple desire of happiness controls us without subjection to the higher purpose of glorifying God, then it degenerates into selfishness. We are no longer "following nature," but are rebelling against nature in the true sense of the word; for nature is a *constitution*, and not a single appetite or bundle of appetites. The nature of a watch is not indicated by the form and movement of any one wheel, or by the form and movement of the mainspring, but by the arrangement of all the parts with reference to the great purpose of the machine, which is the indication of the time upon the dial. The balance-wheel, the regulator, is not only an essential point, but the control of the movement of the mainspring by the balance-wheel is necessary to make it a watch. If the watch were a sentient moral being, we might say of it that its virtue and its happiness consisted in this regulated movement, or, in the case of the absence or loss of power in the balance-wheel, that the rapid, unregulated movement of the wheels constituted its misery and ruin. Self-love is the great motive power in man, setting all the wheels of his being in motion. When regulated by the will of God it reaches its proper end, the attainment of the enjoyment of God in the glorifying of him; when not so regulated it is the source of "misery and woe." The selfish man is always miserable. To make happiness our chief aim is infallibly to miss it. "Man's chief end,"[1] etc. Here lay the great error, the πρωτονψευδος, of the ancient pagan moralists in their speculations concerning the *summum bonum* and man's relation to it. They saw that man's nature pointed to such a good, but they overlooked the fact that man's nature was a *constitution*, and that to "follow nature," which was their prevailing method, did not consist in following blind impulses and appetites, but in following the constitution of the nature, giving to all the elements and powers their proper places, and especially in giving to conscience its proper place and function as the regulator of the whole. If

[1] *Shorter Catechism*, Question 1.

they had done this, they could scarcely have failed to see that the *summum bonum* could be attained only by the pursuit of the *summum jus;* that supreme devotion to the *right* was the sure way, and the only way, to reach the *good.* Aristotle seems to have been the only one of the ancient sages who got a glimpse of the truth. His theory of happiness makes it the result of the normal exercise of the powers of man, "the reflex of energy," to use Hamilton's expression, not pleasure, which is the result of the gratification of particular appetites and comes altogether from without, but the health of the soul, consisting in the normal position and exercise of all the organs. It is peace, peace in the microcosm.[1]

---

[1] See Butler's *Sermon on Human Nature;* Hamilton's *Discussions;* Thornwell's *Sermons on Truth.* It must be borne in mind that when we speak of duties to ourselves, the very word duty implies subjection of ourselves to a lawgiver, and consequently that the indulgence of our self-love is to be regulated by the supreme love we owe to him. We are to love ourselves *as he commands or permits us to love ourselves.* So, also, we are to love our neighbors *as he commands or permits us to love them.* This principle is important, as evincing, (1), That benevolence is not all of virtue. God is all of love, but love is not all of God. Justice is a different thing from benevolence, although in entire harmony with it. The argument of the Universalist, drawn from the infinite love of God, against eternal punishment, is, therefore, nothing worth. It only proves that God does not *will* the death of the sinner. (2), That it is a gross abuse and misunderstanding of the "golden rule" to construe it as requiring us to do unto our neighbors what they *desire*, or what we should desire to be done to us, if we were in their places. The true meaning is, that we are to do to others what we might *lawfully* wish to be done to us, if we were in their places. What desires and wishes are lawful, and what not, must be determined by the law of God. This simple statement blows away whole volumes of absurd reasoning about slavery and other things. To act on any other interpretation of the rule would be impossible. It would disorganize society; and nobody acts on any other interpretation where *his own interests are concerned.* The Jacobin owner of a factory or foundry who employs "free labor," pours out his invectives upon the slave-owner, and discourses eloquently upon the golden rule; meanwhile he does not make his employees the owners of his property, albeit they greatly desire it, no doubt. What a jewel is consistency!

(*d*), "Disinterested benevolence" is an egregious misnomer. Benevolence is a feeling of good-will to others, a wishing well to them. It cannot, then, be other than "disinterested." The expression is altogether superfluous, in the ordinary sense of it. But if by the use of this term the idea is intended to be conveyed of a feeling or impulse whose exercise involves no gratification or pleasure to him who exercises it, it is again misapplied. Man is a social being, is intended to live and move in society, as well as to seek his own happiness or his own interest (if you prefer that expression), and hence God has endowed him with appetites and instincts which fit him for a social state, as well as with appetites and instincts which prompt him to seek his own good. If he has the appetite of hunger, without which he could not preserve his own life, he has also the impulse of benevolence, without which he could not live in society. And I beg you to observe that pleasure is the result of the gratification of all the appetites and impulses, whether the final cause of them be the interest of the individual or the good of society. If "disinterested," therefore, means unattended with pleasure to the person who gratifies the impulse, it is certain that there is no such thing as "disinterested benevolence," or, at least, that benevolence is no more disinterested, considered as an instinct or an impulse, than hunger, or thirst, or love of approbation or of property. A man is as disinterested in eating his dinner when he is hungry as he is in giving a dollar to a beggar, when he acts in both cases from the mere impulse of nature. In short, self-love and the love of others are equally original endowments of our nature, and both or neither are disinterested.

It must be conceded, however, and here is, perhaps, the true origin of the idea intended to be conveyed, that the effect of the fall of man has been to destroy the equilibrium of his powers, and to give undue preponderance to self-love, or to those appetites which belong to it, over the impulse to benevolence. This is shown very strikingly in the *habits* which are formed upon the basis of these principles, respectively. All our instincts and appetites, though in themselves blind, and, therefore, destitute of moral quality, may become, and are designed to become, the conditions of forming certain habits corresponding in character with them. And there can be no doubt that the tendency in man, a sinner, is to repeat the acts prompted by self-love oftener than the acts belonging to benevolence, and so strengthen or repair the respective habits. Then, again, a man may perform the acts corresponding with the habit of benevolence, when neither the *feeling* nor the habit is in him. In such a case there is, of course, no "disinterested benevolence," but then, be it remembered, that in such a case we may also affirm there is no benevolence of any sort. But where the habit of benevolence has been formed, and is cultivated to such a degree as to stamp its *character* upon a man, we may very properly call him a "disinterested" person, in contradistinction from one who has not formed and cultivated the habit. The theory, however, we are examining does not use the word in this sense, and if it did we should still quarrel with it, although upon very different grounds. Benevolence is very far from exhausting the idea of virtue, or selfishness the idea of sin.

The history of this word in New England, where it was reviewed and propagated in the last century, is very instructive. It began with the speculations of Jonathan Edwards concerning the nature of virtue, as being "love to being in general," and ended in the grossest utilitarianism and epicureanism. Such is the Nemesis that attends all outrages upon the nature God has given us. Avoid excessive simplification in your theories. It is not allowed to man in the present stage of his existence, and, perhaps, it never will be his destiny, to arrive at the absolute unity of truth, although the reaching after it is the indispensable condition of all scientific research, and the very law which God has imposed upon the restless intellect of man.

It has been clearly shown, I think, that there are duties which we owe to ourselves, and the sense has been defined in which we are to love ourselves. This class of duties is more than once referred to and enjoined in the New Testament, under the name of "sobriety," or "sober-mindedness." We are required to live "sober," as well as "godly" and "righteous" lives. To seek our own improvement, the subjugation of the lower appetites, the supremacy of the conscience, and, in a word, that normal adjustment and equilibrium of all our powers among themselves which is the result of the proper relation of our persons to God and to our fellow-men and to the "nature of things," in opposition to all one-sidedness and loss of balance, to all extravagance and excess, is sobriety.

What a wonderful harmony is here among our relations and duties! No collision nor conflict! For these different classes of duties are like so many concentric circles, of which man is the centre, and his agency, like a radius, sweeps around them all, and all at once, though with varying degrees of intensity and force. And as, according to the theory of La Place, the same law of gravitation which keeps the members of each solar system in their orbits around respective centres keeps also the solar systems themselves in their orbits around one great common centre, so the same principle of love orders and controls all the movements of the moral and spiritual system, while, with all its connections, gradations, and dependencies, it revolves around the throne of God.

In the light of this exposition of the form and substance of the moral law, who can doubt concerning the place it was designed to occupy in the Mosaic institutions? It must be radical and fundamental, since it reaches to the very root and foundations of man's being and of his moral relations. The judicial and ceremonial departments of that institute cannot but be subordinate to it, as the enactments of a legislature in a free commonwealth are subordinate to the constitution or fundamental law. The moral law was the constitution of the theocracy. God, the absolute monarch, had the right to proclaim how he should be served. The Jews were men, and the relations they sustained to God and to one another were primary and permanent relations, which could not be set aside by any special relations which God might ordain for them as Jews, as a nation designed for a temporary and provisional purpose. These special relations and arrangements, therefore, could have no other design than to secure the conformity of the Hebrews to the moral law, or, in other words, their holiness. This is true of the Hebrews considered in themselves, without reference to the typical character of that dispensation. But the Hebrew nation was a type of the kingdom of God, and that kingdom is founded upon the great law of love; as the kingdom will have no subjects who are not loyal in *heart*, both to his person and his government, we find that God does not proclaim this law as an absolute sovereign, but as the *chosen* ruler of his people, and their consent to the law is formally given, as if to the terms of a constitutional compact between them and the ruler whom they had chosen.

It may be added, that the fundamental importance of this law is further indicated: (1), By its being uttered by the voice of God himself, and then, twice written by his own finger on tables of stone. (2), By the number "ten," which is the number of completeness. (3), By the place assigned to it in the ark of the covenant, the symbolical basis of God's throne in Israel. The mercy-seat was the "covering" (or atonement) of this law, indicating that God's justice as the moral governor, expressed in this law, must be satisfied before mercy can be shown to the guilty.[1]

[1] On the Double Form of the Decalogue compare Ex. xx. 1–17; Deut. v. 6–21, and the questions to which it has given rise. See supplementary Dissertations in Fairbairn's *Revelation of Law in Scripture*, Dissertation I.

III. Some uses of the law which have been hinted at in the foregoing remarks deserve a more articulate statement. Such a statement will serve to show more clearly the sameness of the relation to the law sustained by the Hebrew and the Christian church, and so to vindicate the views we have expressed.

We begin with the statement of the uses of the law in the *Larger Catechism*, Questions 94–97. These uses are not peculiar to the Mosaic institute, although some of them are affirmed, with special emphasis of that institute, in the writings of Paul.

1. The law presented the standard of holiness to which the people were to be *personally* conformed. This is said in opposition to all those low and paltry views which make the decalogue a sort of civil code, merely defining the temporal relations, rights and duties of the Hebrews,[1] and other views which represent the law as having nothing to do with *persons*, but only with the nation, considered as a whole. It is not necessary to go into an elaborate refutation of these views, after what has been said of the form and substance of the law. It could require nothing less than holiness of *heart;* and, of course, this holiness must be personal. "Be ye holy, for I am holy," said the Lord; and what this means Peter tells us in the first chapter of his first epistle.

2. As it was given to sinners, it must also have served the purpose of convincing them of sin. "The law was added because of transgression, until the seed should come." How effectually this office was performed we may see in many of the Psalms, particularly in those called the Penitential Psalms, such as the fifty-first. Here we see the Psalmist deploring not the overt act only, but the radical corruption of the heart from which it proceeded, just as Paul, a whole millennium later and under the clear light of the gospel, describes the process by which he was convinced of the plague

[1] Michælis.

of sin, under the operation of the same spiritual commandment, "Thou shalt not covet." (Romans vii.) Compare the fifty-first Psalm with the seventh chapter of Romans, and say if the legal and evangelical dispensations differ as much as is sometimes alleged. Here are the same pungent convictions of sin and helplessness, and the same reliance upon the mercy of God, and upon the means of expiation he has provided, as the only ground of hope.

3. Intimately connected with this office of the law is another, the exasperation of sin. This is a never failing effect upon the unregenerate in all ages. "The carnal mind is enmity against God; is not subject to his law, neither indeed can be."[1] Sin erects itself like a serpent, in the presence of the law, and shows its fangs and spits its venom. So marked is this feature of fallen human nature, that the "*nite in vetitum*," the striving against that which is forbidden, and because it is forbidden, has been noticed by the pagan writers themselves. As the revelation of God is made clearer, the enmity of sin rises higher and higher, for it is God that sin hates; and the most flagrant outbreaks of sin have been those produced by revelation embodied in the person and character of the Son of God.

4. The law was designed to shut men up to the faith which was to be revealed. Nothing saved the ancient believer from despair but the word of promise and the symbolical ordinances in which that word was embodied. So under the gospel the sinner, convinced by the law, has no refuge but Christ, in whom the same word of promise has been fulfilled. To men crying in anguish, "What must we do?" Peter says, "The promise (*i. e.*, the promise of the Abrahamic covenant) is unto you and your children."[2]

It may be objected to all this that Paul presents, in many places of his writings, views of the law which seem to imply a relation of the law to the Hebrews totally different from

[1] Romans viii. 7. [2] See Gal. iii. throughout.

the relation which it sustains to Christians under the gospel.[1] Upon passages of this sort I remark—

(1), That it must be conceded that the Hebrew dispensation was more legal in its aspect than the Christian. This arose from the fact that it was the condition of infancy or childhood. The child, though he be an heir, must be under tutors and governors until the time appointed of the father.[2] Given a child possessing by the constitution which he has received from God an understanding capable of apprehending its relations to its parents, a conscience capable of recognizing the duties which grow out of those relations and the obligations to fulfil them; a child, moreover, possessing that filial affection which is natural, and, so far, a tendency to comply with the commands of its parents, and yet under the influence of evil passions powerful enough to overbear and defeat that tendency to obey; given, I say, such a child, then it is evident that the most prominent feature of its education will be a rigorous legal discipline, by which it shall be compelled, as it were, to cultivate a regard to the authority of its parents, to form habits of doing the things which are commanded, and of refraining from doing the things which are forbidden, and all this as a necessary preparation for the enjoyment of the inheritance which the love of the father has provided. The child is subject to a law imposed for its own good, a law which is the expression of love, and which can only be truly obeyed in the spirit of love; yet a law which is often obliged to assume a sternly imperative or prohibitory form. Its powers are the powers of love; yet they are real powers, real expressions of displeasure against sin, which at once dishonors the parent and ruins the child.

It is further manifest, that under such a system of discipline, if the passions be powerful enough to acquire and to maintain ascendency over the principle of obedience, the effect of the law must be to exasperate them. By the very

[1] See 2 Cor. iii. and Gal. iv. for examples. [2] Gal. iv.

constitution of human nature these passions become stronger by the resistance they encounter, and the proud waves fret with ever-augmenting violence against the barriers which are designed to stay them. The ultimate effect to the child must be the total ruin of his character. Hence, it has almost become a proverb that children who have been religiously educated, if they break through the restraints of such an education, are apt to become the very worst, to sin with desperate greediness.

Now, this is the kind of discipline to which the Jewish church was subjected. The glorious results of this discipline, in many cases, are recorded in the Old Testament in a long line of worthies and heroes of the faith, in a great "cloud of witnesses" whose testimony and example have been the inspiration and support of many a Christian baptism of blood, or martyrdom of fire. Yet it is too true that, in a large number, the evil was mightier than the good, and the law was made unto them a minister of condemnation and death. It was *made* thus unto them by their own perversion of it. It was not the design of the lawgiver, or the tendency of the law itself, as the apostle shows in the seventh chapter of Romans.

(2), That this is the meaning of the apostle, in such passages as those above referred to, is further manifest from the fact that he is speaking, not of the moral law only, but of the whole law of Moses. Now, the ceremonial law had fully as much of gospel as of law in it, of the promise of grace as of the word of command; and yet this part of the law had the same effect upon the carnally-minded Jews as the moral law. No one can read the searching invectives of the prophets (*e. g.*, Isaiah i.) against the abuses of the ceremonial law without seeing that the perverseness of the people made it a ministration of death. And to make assurance doubly sure, the like effect is affirmed even of the gospel itself, by this very apostle himself, in the context immediately preceding the passage referred to in 2 Cor. iii. (See 2 Cor. ii. 16.)

THE JUDICIAL LAW OF MOSES.[1]

THIS law is so denominated, perhaps, because it consists of judgments or decisions rendered by God himself as the sovereign of the Hebrew theocracy, in particular cases clearly specified, in which there might be some doubt touching the application of the moral law. They are called *mishpatim*, the "statutes" or "judgments," in Exodus xxi. 1, bearing the character of judgments in relation to the "ten words" going immediately before. It is otherwise called the civil or political law, because it chiefly concerns the social and civil relations of the Hebrews as the members of the same civil community or body politic. It may be considered as embracing all the enactments or statutes of Moses which are not referred to the moral law or the ceremonial. It is a large subject, but the points to which our attention is now to be directed are, summarily, the following:

1. That such a law was given at all is to be accounted for by the peculiar relation of the Hebrew nation to God, a relation *altogether* peculiar. "And Moses went up unto God, and the Lord called unto him out of the mountain, saying, Thus shalt thou say to the house of Jacob, and tell the children of Israel, Ye have seen what I did unto the Egyptians, and how I bare you on eagles' wings, and brought you unto myself. Now, therefore, if ye will obey my voice indeed, and keep my covenant, then ye shall be a peculiar treasure unto me above all people; for all the earth is mine: and ye shall be unto me a kingdom of priests, and a holy nation. These are the words which thou shalt speak unto the children of Israel." (Ex. xix. 3, 4, 5, 6.) While civil govern-

[1] Taken from Dr. Peck's notes to his junior classes in Ecclesiastical History.—ED.

ment is the ordinance of God (Rom. xiii.), in the sense that the social nature of man necessarily gives rise to it, yet as to the form which this government may assume in all other nations, and the special laws by which the ends of government may be secured, God has prescribed nothing except that the civil magistrate shall have the power of life and death, and that it shall be his duty to inflict the penalty of death for the crime of murder. *Regulative* principles of government are implied in the moral law, and in the general tenor of Scripture teaching, but the *constitutive* principles of government there are none, except in the case of the Jews. The case of the Jews was made an exception, because they were to be separated from all other nations for the specific purpose of being a type of the kingdom of God and a preparation for it. Hence, a purely natural civil development could not be allowed, as it would interfere with the execution of this purpose. If the Hebrews had been permitted to determine their own polity and laws, they would soon have lost their distinctive character and become mingled with the Gentiles. In point of fact, we find that they did lose it in a very great degree, in spite of all the legal regulations which were prescribed to prevent it. The great powers of the old world struggled for the possession of the land of Palestine, just as the great powers of the modern world have struggled for it, and are now watching one another with intense eagerness and jealousy in regard to it. It was to prevent the Hebrew power from becoming a member of the "political system" of the Orient that the judicial law was given, but given, to a great extent, in vain.

2. Note, that this judicial law does not regulate *everything* belonging to the civil administration of the people, or, in other words, does not absolutely arrest their natural civil development. Jethro, the father-in-law of Moses, gives him advice which he receives and acts upon, although Jethro was a heathen, and Moses was a divinely-commissioned and

divinely-inspired lawgiver. This shows that there were some things connected with the social well-being of the Hebrews which were not determined by the revealed will of God, but left to be determined by the sagacity and experience of men under the guidance only of the natural reason. Again, when the people passed from the patriarchal and confederate forms of government into the monarchical, the transition was a natural one and allowed of God, although with a note of disapprobation. It was disapproved, no doubt, because the preceding constitution was abstractly better adapted to the purposes of a theocracy, and because the demand for a king on the part of a people enjoying theocracy indicated an absence of the true theocratic spirit, a want of appreciation of their calling and privileges, and a tendency to assimilate themselves to the nations from whom they had been separated. In like manner, the Christian church went astray from the platform of government which God gave it through the apostles, and went astray from a spirit of conformity to the world, and yet God has not utterly forsaken it, nor taken away his word and Spirit. The judicial law seems to have been given, not to serve as a complete code of civil enactments, but to protect the constitution, the moral law; to carry out or apply its principles, and to prevent such *natural* legislation as might be incompatible with the great purpose of the theocracy, and ultimately work its ruin. These general ends may be illustrated by the brief examination of a few particulars.

(*a*), In the first place, it might be asked whether the love enjoined in the decalogue, and constituting its substance, must be felt and exercised towards enemies, strangers, &c. The judicial reply is, that a neighbor, even if he be an enemy, ought to be helped. If his ass or ox strays, he ought to aid in the recovery of the lost property.[1] Revenge is forbidden, and love to all enforced.[2] In matters of judgment, in the

[1] Ex. xxiii. 4, 5. [2] Lev. xix. 18.

administration of the law, a careful discrimination as to degrees of guilt is inculcated,[1] and all partiality in favor of the poor, as well as in favor of the rich, is sternly prohibited.[2]

(*b*), Another class of enactments concerns the punishments to be inflicted for the deliberate infraction by act of the commandments of the decalogue. The penalty of death was inflicted for the violation of those precepts which were fundamental in the theocracy, among which are to be numbered the first five. To be guilty of such sins[3] was to be guilty of high treason against God, the sovereign. Some violations of the commandments of the second table were also punished with death, as murder, adultery, men-stealing, bestiality, and extreme cases of violence and oppression. All judgment was administered in the name of the Lord.[4] In Exodus xxii. 8, 9, where our version has "judges," the Hebrew has (verse 7, 8, in Hebrew) Elohim, and the plain implication of the passage is, that causes for judgment in Israel are brought to God, even if a human tribunal takes cognizance of them. The tendency of such punishment is to produce a profound sense of God's righteousness and of the evil of sin, and when it is considered that every sin against God is a capital offence, the fact that all open sin was not *capitally* punished under a theocracy was an exhibition of the mercy and forbearance of the king. It is hardly necessary to say that such severity of punishment would be altogether unbecoming in any government which is not a theocracy; and there has never been but one theocracy *de jure*, though the folly of men has attempted others.

(*c*), Closely connected with this point is that class of statements which are based upon the *lex talionis*, or law of compensation, "An eye for an eye," etc. Such laws are not to be literally interpreted, for the simple reason that their literal

---

[1] Ex. xxi. 12–14; Ex. xii. 2. [2] Ex. xxiii. 2–9; Deut. i. 17; Deut. xix. 7–19.
[3] Ex. xxii. 20; Deut. xiii. 9, 10; Ex. xxxii; Deut. iv. 25, 28, &c.
[4] Deut. i. 17.

execution would violate the principle of compensation which they are designed to express and sustain. Such an execution would exemplify the maxim, "*summum jus, summa injuria.*" A man with one eye who should be guilty of putting out the eye of a neighbor who had two, and should be punished according to the letter of the law, would be injured much more severely than the man whom he had himself injured; for he would be totally blind. The loss of a hand to a mechanic would be much more severe than the same loss to a scholar. The Jews never interpreted these statutes literally. They regarded them simply as the embodiments of a principle of justice which was always to be observed in the administration of the law; as an echo in the civil sphere of a great principle exemplified in the moral government of God himself, the principle of retribution in kind.

And this leads me to observe that the characteristic which pervades the judicial law of Moses is that of *justice*, the giving to every man according to his deeds, that is, the desert of his deeds, without reference, or with a very subordinate reference, to the prevention of crime or the reformation of the criminal. This law knows nothing of that sickly sentimentalism which sympathizes with the criminal instead of sympathizing with virtue; which has tears to weep over the murderer, but none for the murdered man or the murdered law. It knows nothing of an epicurean *utility* which can "calculate" the value of an innocent life that has been sacrificed, or helpless virtue which has been trodden down under the heel of oppression; but it responds to the original unperverted moral instincts of our nature, the instinct of resentment, of indignation of wrong as wrong, the feeling that the sinner *deserves* to be punished for his sins, whatever the consequences of his sins may be to others. Seneca says, "No prudent man punishes sin because it is sin, but in order that sin may not be committed; for the past cannot be recalled, but the future may be anticipated and evil prevented."

This is, perhaps, pardonable in a heathen; but the same folly is often uttered by nominal Christians who ought to know better. The truth is, that no government on earth has the smallest right to inflict suffering upon a human being from any consideration of expediency alone, or chiefly. "The minister of God," as the magistrate is called (in Romans xiii. 2), is a minister of justice and not of expediency. God's universe is no epicurean republic where magistrates may employ themselves in weighing pains and pleasures, and balancing one evil against another; but it is an universe in which right is to reign supreme because it is *right*, and wrong is to be put down and crushed because it is *wrong*. Incidentally, subordinately, in details, expediency may come in as a guide, but a *criminal* code which is based on expediency alone, or chiefly, is very like a contradiction in terms. Criminal is no longer criminal, but inexpedient or unhappy. The moral law ever raised its voice in Israel in behalf of the right and the lovely, and whatever social evils were tolerated in the commonwealth of the Hebrews were tolerated under protest from that supreme law. This leads me to observe, next:

(*d*), That we must carefully distinguish between what the judicial law establishes and approves, and what it only bears with and regulates. This distinction is suggested in Matt. xix. 7, and in our Saviour's conversation with the Pharisees about divorce. The Pharisees ask, "Why did Moses command?" etc. Our Lord answers, "Moses suffered," etc. There is the distinction between commanding or prescribing, and suffering or permitting. The "hard-heartedness of the ancient Hebrews, which is assigned by our Saviour as the reason of some of the Mosaic statutes concerning marriage, is, according to some interpreters, a general intractable, rebellious spirit among the people; according to others, cruelty, specifically against wives. It matters not how we take it. It was, in either case, a sin against the moral law;

it was an infraction of the great law of love. How, then, you ask, could it be a reason for tolerating a wrong? The answer to this question is a very important and fruitful one. It is this, that the civil government of a people must be accommodated, more or less, to the character, genius, civilization of a people. Abstract theories, plans, platforms of government, may do very well to amuse the leisure of philosophers, or serve as a standard after which a people may strive; but Platonic republics and Utopias can never be put into operation successfully while men remain as they are. A government must be the *fruit*, the organic product of a people's history in order to be maintained. It is *sinners* that all human governments undertake to govern, and some evils have to be tolerated. It is an instructive fact that even God himself did not, as a civil governor, ordain the immediate extripation of all evils. He testified against them in the moral law, but did not authorize the magistrates who represented him in the judicial law to remove them by force. The reason given is the hard-heartedness of the people. The attempt to remove them by force would have produced greater evils than the partial toleration of them. Polygamy, for example, obtained among the Hebrews when Moses was sent to them as a lawgiver. Moses had but one wife, his brother Aaron had but one; they set a good example. Moses gave them statutes whose tendency, and, perhaps, design, was to discourage polygamy, but he allowed a facility of divorce, which was virtually polygamy. This our Lord says was inconsistent with the "beginning," when God created one man and one woman; and that primeval record, together with the record that the first instance of polygamy occurred in Cain's apostate line, was a perpetual testimony against the evil; still it was allowed. That the tendency of the whole institute was against polygamy is evident from the fact that it ceased after the Babylonish captivity.

To avoid misapprehension, let it be further observed, (1),

That according to the distinction commonly made between *mala per se* and *mala prohibita*, polygamy and all the marriage connections enumerated in the eighteenth chapter of Leviticus belong to the latter class and not the former. They are *mala prohibita*, not *mala per se*. It is inconceivable that God should tolerate an evil which is, in itself, morally wrong. (2), There is an analogy between God's disapproving of polygamy and yet tolerating it, and his disapproving of a monarchy and yet yielding the point. A monarchy was out of harmony with a theocracy, in which, as the word implies, God was king. Polygamy was out of harmony with the relation in which God stood to his people as their husband. The marriage union, as originally ordained of one man and one woman, was designed not only for the comfort and happiness of mankind, but to be a type of the union of Christ and his church. This last, indeed, was the archetype, of which marriage was the antitype or copy. Polygamy was, therefore, an obscuration of a great spiritual truth, as well as a departure from the original model of nature. But as the Jews, through the hardness of their hearts, were prone to polygamy, so for the same reason they were prone to spiritual polygamy and adultery. This last, however, was a *malum per se*, and punished with great severity. (3), Again, there are evils which the church, in God's name, is bound to testify against, which cannot be punished by the church. Every pastor knows that there are many sins which cannot be made the occasions of discipline. All he can do is to testify against them, and arraign the offenders at the invisible tribunals of conscience and of God. The fact that polygamy was tolerated, so far as the infliction of penalties was concerned, may, perhaps, be accounted for in this way.

The importance of the view here presented can scarcely be exaggerated. Infidels represent these and similar statements as given to the Hebrew church, as such, and make an argument, from our Saviour's condemnation of them, against the inspiration of one or both Testaments, and Christians are often perplexed by the difficulty. But, if we bear in mind that the Hebrew church existed in the bosom of a people not more civilized, perhaps, than the Chinese, we see at once that God, as their civil ruler, could not have done otherwise than he did without converting all the people and anticipating the millennium by several centuries.

In order to illustrate this point more fully, I refer you to another statement of the judicial law, that concerning the "avenger of blood." Here read Fairbairn, *Revelation of Law in the Sacred Scriptures*, pp. 105–112.

Slavery has been referred to this head of statutes by many writers (by Fairbairn, for instance), but I think improperly. Slavery, as between Hebrews, was put under restrictions, for, according to the theory of the theocracy, all the Hebrews were the Lord's freemen. Perpetual bondage was allowed in the case of a Hebrew only by his voluntary consent. In respect to the bondage of the heathen people, the Mosaic laws seem scarcely to have interfered with it, except so far as the pervading spirit of philanthropy in those laws would have a tendency to soften the rigor of the system and prevent oppression. For the same reason that Moses exhibited no zeal for any system of civil government in the abstract, he showed none for a commonwealth in which there should be no slaves. This kind of zeal was left for modern Jacobins and fanatics.

Upon this subject, I would recommend to you the able discourse delivered by Dr. Stuart Robinson to a congregation of British anti-slavery people in Toronto, Canada, in February, 1865, entitled "Anti-Slavery Theories vs. Inspiration," in which the following points, besides others, are clearly established, viz.:

1. That slavery existed in the church anterior to the civil code of Moses, and was recognized in the covenants which form the fundamental charter of the church visible. More-

over, the very redemption out of Egypt was the redemption of a nation of slave-holders from political bondage. So preposterous is the comparison, made in certain quarters, between this deliverance and the emancipation of the slaves in the Southern States by the brute force of the Northerner.

2. That the bond service of Hebrews under the civil law of Moses was not slavery in the proper sense at all. The prohibition against reducing a Hebrew to slavery was not on the ground of natural right, but of special religious faith.

3. That a system of perpetual slavery was recognized and regulated by the civil code of Moses, substantially the same with the system in these Southern States, nor was such slave-holding deemed inconsistent with the strict holiness symbolized in the ritual law.

4. That this system continued to exist in the Mosaic church till the close of the Old Testament inspiration, and formed a part of the social order of the Jews in the time of Christ.

5. That though the question of slavery in these must have been forced upon the Lord's attention in the exposition of Moses, he did not repeal Moses' permission of slavery as he repealed the permission of divorce and polygamy, nor claim to teach a purer ethics than Moses. He blessed both master and slave, and in his preaching referred without rebuke to the relation of master and slave.

Dr. Robinson has also shown that the views he defends were views held by all the ablest and best critics and commentators down to the time of the commencement of the anti-slavery agitation; and even since this agitation began, the whole orthodox biblical learning of the church, with the exception of a few who have been prevented by partisan feeling, has expounded Moses in the same way.

It also results from his argument that slavery is *not* a dead issue morally and religiously.

THE APOCALYPSE.[1]

GOD'S KING IN CONTRAST WITH THE WORLD'S KING.

THE Apocalypse, which is designed to set forth the general features of the history of the church from the time of John's exile, at the close of the first century, until the second advent of the Saviour in victory and glory, opens with a description of the church's king, under whose administration the battles are to be fought, and the victory achieved. Let us notice some of the particulars in this description:

I. He is said to be like unto the "Son of man." This phrase is constantly used by the king in speaking of himself during his ministry of humiliation on earth. It is generally taken for granted that he uses it, merely in humility, to express his real participation of the nature of man; to give the world assurance of a man; at once of the identity of his nature with that of Adam and the race which has proceeded from his loins, and of the restoration of that nature, in his divine person, to its primeval dignity and perfection. This it doubtless does express, but there is more than this in it, if we are not greatly mistaken. It is in the Old Testament, and especially in the prophecies of Daniel, that the full significance of this denomination is to be sought. The internal connection between Daniel and the New Testament, in a great measure overlooked by the older theologians and commentators, has, in recent times, been made the object of careful study; and the intimate relations between that prophet and the seer of Patmos have been clearly shown and

[1] Dr. Peck was much given to the study of the Apocalypse in the earlier years of his ministry and teaching. This and the following paper have been taken from his lectures on the book.

illustrated by Auberlen, in a treatise specially devoted to that topic. And it is to this pious and learned writer that we gratefully acknowledge our indebtedness for many of the views we are about to suggest.

First, Then, let it be borne in mind that this description of John is the description of a king chiefly, and not of a priest only, as it is often represented to be, without any labored attempt to prove it. Some of its features, no doubt, remind us of the Levitical priests; but there are others, such as the sword coming out of his mouth, which harmonize much better with the office and functions of a king. Besides, the general scope and purpose of the whole book, as a delineation of the conflicts and victories of the church, naturally suggests that her head, under whose auspices her warfare is accomplished, is presented to us here, chiefly in his *royal* majesty and glory, reigning in his church and over his enemies and hers.

Second, This king bears the form of a *man*. This carries us back, at once, to the original promise of dominion, which was given to the first Adam when he came perfect from the hand of God; a dominion founded upon the image of God, in which he was created. That image necessarily implied self-control on the part of man himself, the supremacy of the moral faculty, the subordination of all the lower faculties, and the absolute subjection of the whole man to the will of his Creator. If Adam had not fallen, his dominion would have been limited only by the necessary limitation of his powers as a creature; and that dominion would have been, really and truly, the dominion of God in man, or God through man. In his civil relations, especially, he would have been the minister and representative of the supreme governor of the world. But Adam fell; lost the image of God; lost dominion over himself, and lost the dominion which had been given him over the world, in the fulness in which it had been originally conferred. Still, the memory of that splendid inheritance was not lost, and the dream of its restoration has, from that day to this, continued to haunt the sleep, and captivate the waking imagination, of his children. It stimulated, perhaps, the ambition of Nimrod, "the mighty hunter"; it prompted the schemes and sustained the patience of the Babel-builders; it appeared to their proud successor, Nebuchadnezzar, in the colossal *human* image of gold, silver, brass and iron mixed with clay; and it has almost seemed to be realized in the "universal empires" of the Persian, the Macedonian and the Roman. This gorgeous dream is realized only in Jesus of Nazareth, to whom every knee shall bow, and every tongue confess. This is the "Son of man" whom Daniel, in vision, saw coming in the clouds of heaven to the ancient of days, and receiving dominion and glory and a kingdom, which shall never be destroyed:[1] this is the "Son of man" whom the Daniel of the New Testament saw in Patmos.

Third, It is evident from this whole description that this "Son of man" is more than man; that he is also God. He is the proper object of John's worship. He holds the keys of hades and of death. The man who is invested with universal and absolute dominion over mankind must be the object of divine honors. The shadow of this truth also can be plainly observed in the history of the world. Man became, indeed, a worshipper of himself so soon as he became a sinner. The very inducement to sin was expressed in the words, "Ye shall be as *gods*, knowing good and evil." The "tree of knowledge" was the symbol of the great truth that God's will was that which made good and evil to man. Whatever God commanded was good, because he commanded it; whatever he prohibited was evil, because he prohibited it. Now, sin is the denial of this; the sinner makes himself his end, and his own will the law by which good and evil are to be determined. He seeks to rule not only without God, but

[1] Daniel vii. 13, 14.

against God, because in the place of God. But man, with all his pride and insolence, is consciously weak, and feels that the claim to universal dominion on the part of the individual is simply contemptible. Hence, the necessity of association of a combination of forces; hence, the gathering in the plain of Shinar, and the building of the tower, as at once the symbol and the bond of the union of interests and resources. Hence, again, the "universal empires," in which a Nebuchadnezzar, a Darius, an Alexander, an Augustus, becomes the representative of the aggregated forces of humanity, and is deified by his subjects *as* the representative of these forces. The subjects become the worshippers of man, to whom the dominion belongs.

But all these delusions are one after another overthrown, and it is demonstrated by the fall of those vast empires that the "heavens do rule," and that these gods on earth are but men in the hands of the God of heaven, "who doeth according to his will among the armies of heaven and the inhabitants of the earth; and none can stay his hand or say unto him, what doest thou?" The idea of the government of a man who exercises the dominion of God, and is the proper object of worship, is realized in the "Son of man," and this is the full significance of this phrase. It is to such a ruler alone that "loyalty," in the truest and highest sense of that much-abused word, is due, because in him dwelleth all the fulness of the Godhead bodily. He alone has the right to demand the homage and devotion of the *heart;* and all merely human rulers who demand it are usurpers and servants of the dragon, who has given them his power and seat and authority. It is the dragon who speaks through them, and says to all men, as he said to Christ when he showed him the kingdoms of this world and the glory of them, "All these things will I give you if you will fall down and worship me." But of this more hereafter, when I come to speak of the world-power in opposition to the Christ of God.

II. The description of this "Son of man" as king implies that his kingdom is altogether spiritual in its origin, ends, and means. He is described as being "in the midst of the seven golden candlesticks," as having "eyes like a flame of fire," as having "a sharp two-edged sword" proceeding "out of his mouth." He is the "Amen," the "Faithful and True Witness." When he stood before the bar of Pontius Pilate, and was asked by that magistrate whether he was a king, his answer was, "Thou sayest that I am a king. To this end was I born, and for this cause came I into the world, that I should *bear witness unto the truth.* Every one that is of the truth heareth my voice."[1] The meaning of which is, (*a*), That the great purpose of his administration was to establish an empire, whose subjects should be, in conviction and feeling, exactly what the truth required them to be; that they should think, believe, feel, and act in exact accordance with the relations which they sustained to God and to one another, which relations the truth is intended to express. That the subjects of this empire should experience that "heaven on earth," which consists in having their minds "move in charity, rest in Providence, and turn upon the poles of truth," not constrained by force to obey the law, but prompted and impelled by love, and enjoying that only true freedom, the freedom which is found in the absolute harmony of the soul with the eternal standard of the true, the beautiful, and the good, in the nature of God. (*b*), That the means by which this empire is to be established is the testimony of the word of God. The King himself is the incarnate Word, and came into the world to bear witness to the truth. The word that proceedeth out of his mouth is the "sharp sword" by which the beast and the false prophet are to be slain, the "arrows" by which "the people are to fall under him."[2] Since his ascension into heaven, this testimony is borne by his church, symbolized by the seven golden candlesticks,

[1] John xviii. 37. [2] Psalm xlv.

the light-bearers in the midst of this dark world. He is the *lumen illuminans;* the church, the *lumen illuminatum;* he, "*το φως*"; it, "*το λυχνιον*"; he, the central sun; it, the moon which reflects its light. When his people are called to stand before kings, they are prepared for it by eating the "little book," which is sweetness in the mouth and bitterness in the belly. When they conquer, it is by the word of their testimony, in which they love not their lives unto the death. What strange associations of ideas do we find in the Scriptures in connection with this kingdom! "Gird thy sword upon thy thigh, O most mighty, with thy glory and thy majesty; and in thy majesty ride prosperously because of truth, and meekness, and righteousness; and thy right hand shall teach thee terrible things."[1] The sword of might, majesty, and glory, accomplishing its work by and for the sake of truth, meekness, and righteousness. It is the "Lamb" that conquers; and this Lamb conquers by being *slain*, and conquers again and again by the slaying of his witnesses. "Oh! the invincible might of weakness." "Oh! the depth of the riches of the wisdom and knowledge of God. How unsearchable are his judgments, and his ways past finding out. For who hath known the mind of the Lord? or who hath been his counsellor? or who hath first given to him and it shall be recompensed again? For of him and through him and to him are all things, to whom be glory for ever. Amen."

Let us turn now to the consideration of the kings and kingdoms of this world in contrast with God's king and kingdom. The contrast is presented first in Genesis iii. 15, in the seed of the woman and the seed of the serpent—the one *human*, the other *beastly*. But we must look to Daniel in the Old Testament and to John in the New Testament for the fullest exhibitions of the characteristics of the world-powers.

---

[1] Psalm xlv.

I. In the second chapter of Daniel the world-power in opposition to God is revealed in a dream of Nebuchadnezzar, and as all prophecy has a psychological, as well as a historical starting-point, we need not be surprised to find in a revelation made to a powerful monarch, exulting in his greatness, and knowing no greatness but the greatness of man, the world-power presented under a colossal *human* image. The image is made of various materials, for the most part durable and splendid; but it is *one* image, to indicate the unity in nature and principle of the power in all its changing forms. The materials gradually become baser as we descend from its head to its feet, to indicate, perhaps, the natural degeneracy in that which exalts itself against God, both in spirit and in strength. The feet which support it, made partly of iron and partly of clay, the weakest portion of the image, indicate how precarious is the standing and stability of the whole. The image which Nebuchadnezzar afterwards made was probably suggested by this image which he saw in vision, and he required his subjects to worship it as the representative of the supreme and invincible power of *man*. God's kingdom in the same vision appeared under the lowly and even contemptible form of a stone; a stone, however, which dashes the image in pieces, and becomes a mountain filling the whole earth. These are the kingdoms from the standpoint of the world.

II. In the seventh chapter we have another vision of the same powers given to Daniel himself, and also in harmony with his own psychological position. The world-power is not now an imposing *human form*, but a *beastly*, or rather several beastly forms. "It was given to the prophet," says Auberlen, "to penetrate further into the inner essence of things; to see that the kingdoms of the world, notwithstanding their defiant power, are of a nature animal and lower than human, that their minds are estranged from and even opposed to God, and that only in the kingdom of God is the true dignity of man revealed; and accordingly, the kingdom of God appears to him from the outset, and in the very selection of images, superior to the kingdom of this world. For though the beasts excel man in physical brute force, and though measured by this standard he seems but a frail mortal, yet he has essential spiritual power. The colossal figure that Nebuchadnezzar beheld represents mankind in its own strength and greatness; but, however splendid, it presents only the outward appearance of a man. But Daniel, regarding mankind in its spiritual condition, saw humanity through its alienation from God degraded to the level of reasonless animals, enslaved by the dark powers of nature. It is only in the kingdom of God that man gains his humanity and destiny; it is only from on high that the living perfect Son of man can come. Passages like the eighth Psalm, taken in connection with the history of creation (Gen. i. 25–28), which forms their basis, show how vividly the Israelites were presented with the consciousness of the superior dignity of our nature, and especially over the animal world given to man by his covenant relation to God. And as a counterpart to this, men are viewed as becoming like the irrational beasts whenever they do not come to God and take heed to his ways.[1] Humanity is impossible without divinity; it sinks down to bestiality. For this reason we find the obstinate heathen nations represented as beasts, even before Daniel's time (Psa. lxviii. 31), the Egyptian monarch is called the great dragon (Ezek. xxix. 3; xxxii. 2), the lion among the heathen; compare, also, Isaiah xxvii. 1; xli. 9. An animal may be stronger and inspire more terror than any man, it may show much sagacity, but it looks always to the ground, hears no voice of conscience, and knows no relation to God. What truly elevates man is his humility and his power of knowing the will of God which raises him above earthly objects. But the moment he says, like Nebuchadnezzar, "Is

[1] Psalms lxxiii. 22; xxxii. 9; xlix. 21.

not this great Babylon which I have built!" he loses, morally, his relation to God; he exalts himself, and all that is really lofty in him is destroyed, he becomes a beast. Whenever he ceases from his subjection to God, he yields his affections to objects lower than himself, and thus degrades himself.[1] The insolent monarch of Babylon was taught this lesson by the remarkable dispensation recorded in the fourth chapter of Daniel, when he was "driven from *men*, and did eat grass as oxen, and his body was wet with the dews of heaven, till his hairs were grown as eagle's feathers, and his nails like the claws of birds." The lesson was not in vain, as we find in the thirty-seventh verse, "Now, I, Nebuchadnezzar, praise and extol and honor the King of heaven, all whose works are truth, and his ways judgment; and those that walk in pride he is able to abase." This outward abasement of Nebuchadnezzar was the symbol of spiritual self-degradation of which he had been guilty in making himself a god.

III. Still another symbol of the same power we find in the thirteenth chapter of the Apocalypse. In Daniel's vision there are four beasts; but it will be observed that he passes rapidly over the first three, and the chief emphasis is laid on the fourth: "for it is in the fearful shape of the last beast that the world-power will fully manifest that its whole nature is opposed to God, and we are prepared for this climax by the order in which the metals are mentioned in the second chapter, where they are successively of a baser nature." Now, in the Apocalypse there is but one beast, corresponding mainly with the fourth of Daniel's vision, and partaking of the nature of Daniel's first three, the lion, the leopard, and the bear. This seven-headed and ten-horned beast probably represents the power or force of the world embodied in a political organization, as the beast described in verse eleven of the same chapter represents the cunning or wisdom of the world. The one rises like Daniel's beast out of

---

[1] See Auberlen, pp. 35, *et seq.*

the "sea," the population of the globe considered in an unsettled, tumultuous, revolutionary state; the other rising out of the "earth," out of the people in an ordered and settled political condition; but both the offspring of the dragon, the old serpent, who gives his force (*δυναμιν* v. 2) to the one, and his subtlety to the other.[1]

It will be seen from the foregoing statements that the symbols of Daniel and John are not to be confined to any particular governments, though they have been more strikingly exemplified and illustrated by some governments than by others. The universal empire of Rome has realized more fully the symbols of the fourth beast of Daniel, and the beast out of the sea of John, than any other; but any government which is of a beastly nature may realize the symbol. Any government which trusts in its strength and resources, in its wealth, in its armies, in the perfection of its material civilization; which boasts of being the best government on earth, and on the ground of this imaginary perfection claims not only the outward obedience of the subject or citizen, but the homage and devotion of the heart; which demands that this homage of the heart shall be expressed under the sanctions of an oath, and be testified by certain forms of worship rendered to the flag or any other image or representative of its majesty and glory; every such government bears upon its front the "name of blasphemy," is an usurper of the prerogatives of the Almighty, and in claiming to be God becomes, like the dragon of which it is the image, a serpent crawling on its belly and feeding upon the dust. Such a claim was practically set up, a few years ago, for the government of the United States by many of its representatives, civil and military, and, what is infinitely worse, by the

[1] Here read *Auberlen*, pp. 263–272, and *Fairbairn on Prophecy*—his explanation of the seven-headed, ten-horned beast—pp. 309–314. Then, in reference to the lamb-like, two-horned beast, read *Fairbairn on Prophecy*, pp. 332–338; *Auberlen, Daniel and John*, pp. 305 *et seq.*

church, by that very body whose calling is to witness for the supremacy of the "Son of man" as "King of kings and Lord of lords"; and which, as the wife of the Lamb, cannot talk of loyalty to any other lord but the Lamb without misprison, at least, of treason and adultery. "O shame! where is thy blush?"

It is strange that interpreters should have restricted the scenes and symbols of the prophets to the "Roman earth," that portion of the earth which was covered by the dominion of Rome. As prophecy was intended for the whole church in all places and in all times, what hinders its symbol from being exemplified on the continent of America with its teeming millions? or in China, with a population equal nearly to one-third of the entire population of the globe? Is it Rome only that has decreed that "all, both small and great, rich and poor, free and bound, should receive a mark in their right hand, or in their forehead; and that no man might *buy* and *sell* save he that had the mark or the name of the beast or the number of his name"?

Once more, this subject explains, in great part, at least, the martyrdom of God's people. It is in this way, chiefly, that an effectual testimony is borne for God as supreme against the insolent usurpations of the world. I say *chiefly*, for the whole life of a Christian ought to be a testimony against the world which *lieth* in the wicked one; and without sacrifices of some sort it is difficult to see how a man can testify effectually to others, or feel with any pungency himself, the rightful supremacy of Christ. "If any man love the world, the love of the Father is not in him. For all that is in the world, the lust of the flesh and the lust of the eyes and the pride of life, is not of the Father, but is of the world." Now, if none of these lusts be crucified, where is the evidence, either to the man himself, or to others that he recognizes the will of God to be supreme? But it is in martyrdom that this testimony is most emphatic, because it is surrendering life itself. The issue in any case of martyrdom is simply this: is God or the world, the Son of man or the beast, supreme and entitled to the homage and loyalty of the spirit of man? The freedom of the man is in his spirit, and consists in love and reverence for the true and the right, and above all for God, the eternal standard of truth and righteousness. You may confine, or mutilate, or kill the body; but you have not touched the nobleness or freedom of the man so long as the spirit remains faithful to its convictions. It is invincible by all the power of man, so long as it chooses to resist. It is only conquered and enslaved when it makes a voluntary surrender; and no other than a *voluntary* surrender is possible. Hence the tests applied by the beast are generally very simple; not at all hard to do, provided only there is a *will* to do them: an oath, the offering of a little incense, the saluting of an ensign,—anything which implies the *voluntary* act of the person. Anything short of such voluntary act fails to open the gates of the citadel; it remains impregnable and its inhabitant is free, and continues free, conquering even when he dies.

It was to instruct us in this lesson that we have the touching incidents in the life of Daniel and his friends recorded in the third and sixth chapters of his prophecies. Placed in the providence of God in the very heart and centre of the world-power, and surrounded by the proofs and signs of its might and majesty and glory, they might have been pardoned for thinking that the true divinity was here and not among the weeping captives of Judea; that in the palace of Nebuchadnezzar, and not among his slaves, was the all-disposing Lord and the all-comprehending good. But not so thought the captives, freer far in their chains and in the furnace of fire than the monarch upon his throne. With a majesty transcending the majesty of the king, they say, "O Nebuchadnezzar, we are not careful to answer thee in this matter. If it be so, God whom we serve is able to deliver us from the burning fiery furnace, and he will deliver us out of thy hand, O king. But if not, be it known unto thee, O king, that we will not serve thy gods, nor worship the golden image which thou hast set up." Thus they teach us by their example that we dare not yield *positive* homage to the power of the world by worshipping the image of the world; as we are taught by the example of Daniel himself in the sixth chapter that we dare not yield *negative* homage to it by neglecting to worship God.

Such as Nebuchadnezzar was, such as Darius was, the representatives of the world-power have been ever since. The dragon is the father of it; and he has been a liar and a murderer from the beginning. It did appear at one time that the nature of the beast had changed, or, at least, that his power had been greatly impaired, for the seer saw one of the heads of the beast "as it were wounded unto death," which symbolizes, no doubt, a change in regard to the worldly power's ostensible relation to the church (for in that respect alone is it represented under the aspect of a beast); the dropping for a season its wonted appearance of hostility to the kingdom of God; the ceasing for a time to act as a beast, which it could only do by assuming either a truly religious or a professedly religious character. And something corresponding to this took place when the sixth head of the beast tended towards the seventh and last, and the empire tottering to its fall, fresh races strove to form themselves into new states and dynasties. It seemed, then, as if the beast had received a deadly wound. The beast then "was not and yet was" (Rev. xvii. 8, 11), for the deadly wound was presently healed, and the old spirit returned as a kind of "Christianized paganism." (Fairbairn, pp. 29, 30.)

THE APOCALYPSE.

No. II.

PROPHETIC PICTURES OF THE CHURCH VISIBLE AND INVISIBLE.

I. The Church as Presented in the Epistles to the Seven Churches.

WE meet with several delineations of the church visible in the Apocalypse, setting forth its various states and conditions, as more or less pure or corrupt, more or less peaceful or disturbed. The first is contained in the second and third chapters in the Lord's epistles to the seven churches of Asia. That these epistles have a symbolical character, that the seven churches, while they had a real existence and were specifically concerned in the encouragements, warnings, and instructions addressed to them, were considered as types and representatives of the whole church visible, is, we think, very evident.

1. We argue from the number *seven.*[1] It appears, then, that the number seven is the number of completeness and of the covenant.[2]

2. We argue from the complete and exhaustive representations of the epistles. There is no condition of the church as a whole, or any part of it, which is not mirrored in these two chapters. Explain and point out the errors of the periodists, and the historico-prophetical interpretations of those epistles,[3] which are not to be confounded with the view here represented.

[1] Here read Trench on the *Seven Churches*, pp. 83-91.

[2] Read Trench (*ut supra*), pp. 293-296.

[3] See Trench (*ut supra*), pp. 296 *et seq.*

3. No other reason, than a symbolical design, can be given for the selecting of the churches here named. Some of them were prominent; some, the majority, obscure. They were selected, then, we may suppose, on account of their presenting types of the prevailing states and conditions of the church visible from John's time to the end. We find here the scattered traits, both good and evil, which are embodied in the subsequent part of this book, in the concrete symbols of the woman clothed with the sun, and the woman riding upon the scarlet-colored beast, of which I shall speak, if the Lord will, more particularly hereafter.

It is unnecessary to my present purpose, and would be foreign to this department of the course, to go into any detailed exposition of these epistles. I will content myself with indicating some of the signs of a pure church, and, in contrast with these, some of the signs of a declining or corrupt church.

1. The church of Ephesus is a type of the whole church visible, or any part of it, when a zeal for purity of faith is not coupled with love. It tried them who claimed to be apostles and were not, and proved the falseness of their pretences, and did this with labor and patience, showing that it was a genuine zeal for Christ, and not a mere church spirit, or *esprit de corps*. It is also mentioned by the Saviour that they "*hated* the deeds of the Nicolaitans, which he also *hated*"; a satisfactory evidence of their full sympathy with him. The visible church bears its testimony effectually only when it *loves* the truth and *hates* error, and this love of truth and hatred of error can exist only in the hearts of those who have had a saving experience of the power and glory of the truth. And yet even this honest zeal for the truth is compatible with a decay of love. The decay of the "first love" is not the loss of the vehemence and fervor of the love which is felt by the believer at his espousal to Christ; for this is necessary by the very constitution of our nature. Novelty and fresh-

ness gives a vivacity and freshness to our feelings, which must yield to time and familiarity. We must distinguish between the passive sensibility or emotion, and the habit to the formation of which the passive emotion is destined to lead. Illustrate by the connection between the affection of pity and the habit of benevolence. A man and his wife who have lived together for fifty or sixty years, in the exercise of mutual love, do not seem to love each other nearly so much as a couple who have been married only two weeks, yet the real difference in the strength of the love in the two cases would be made manifest if one of each couple should die. In the case of the younger, the grief of the survivor would soon be healed; in the case of the other, the grief, if not fatal to the survivor, as it often is, could never be entirely healed. The reference of our Saviour, in this case, is to the strength of the first love as manifest in "*works*," and hence he says: "Repent and do the first works." The habit of love (which is "the fulfilling of the law") had not grown in strength as the fervor declined. This is a dangerous symptom, both in the individual believer and in a church, and the church of Ephesus is more severely threatened (threatened even with extinction) than that of Thyatira, in which the opposite state of things existed; in which the Saviour commends the active ministry of love, and rebukes the want of zeal against error.

2. The epistle to Smyrna presents us with the type of an *ecclesia pressa*, a church suffering for its testimony to Christ; a church "poor in this world and rich in faith," and struggling with a church pretending to be the church of God; resisting those who "say they are Jews and are not, but are the synagogue of Satan;" a type of many churches under the dominion of Papal and Protestant apostasies.

3. In the church of Pergamum[1] we have a type of a church which is, in the main, steadfast in its allegiance to Christ,

[1]For this orthography see Trench *ut supra*, p. 153.

and suffering persecution, not from a false church, but from the heathen; but with so little zeal for the truth as to tolerate the atrocious free-thinking and licentiousness of the Balaamites and Nicolaitans; a church in which there is evidently a "Broad Party," patient of everything but faithful *discipline.* How large a portion of the church visible, even among Protestants, has answered to this type you will see in the course of church history.

4. In the church of Sardis we have the type of a church which has the outward appearance of life, but is really dead. There is something startling in the mention of a church which had a name to live, was regarded, it may be, as a model church, "not wanting in the outward manifestations of spiritual life, while yet all these shows of life did but conceal the realities of death. So he, before whose eyes of fire no falsehood can endure, too surely saw."[1] Yet all was not entirely dead, as the exhortation implies, "Be watchful and strengthen the things (or persons) that remain (as many as are not yet dead, though at the point of death), that are ready to die." How large a portion of the church visible has answered, or still answers, to this description, Christ, the head, alone knows.

5. The church of Philadelphia is one which, with little strength, in the world's esteem, does a great deal for Christ. Its anxiety for Christ's glory, and for the prosperity of his kingdom, is rewarded by an open door for the utterance of its testimony, by the reluctant confession of its powerful adversary that Christ's power is on its side, and that it is the object of his special love and providence; and by the precious promise that it shall be kept "from the hour of temptation which shall come upon all the world to try them that dwell upon the earth."

6. The church of Laodicea, like that of Sardis, has no commendation from the Lord; but, unlike Sardis, has not

[1] Trench, p. 208.

even a name to live; the type of a church rich in this world, but a pauper in faith; without sufficient zeal to provoke persecution or to maintain a conflict; enjoying the good things of this life and satisfied with these as its portion; indifferent to all the claims of her head, lukewarm and "giving a vomit" to her jealous king; yet a church in which the ordinances are observed, and in which the gracious Saviour continues to plead for admittance into the hearts of sinners and to invite them to fellowship with himself.

In a general view of the whole we may note:

1. That the condition of the church visible is a *mixed* one. Two of these churches only, Smyrna and Philadelphia, pass without rebuke. Two of them only, Sardis and Laodicea, pass without commendation. This corresponds with the teaching of the parables of the wheat and the tares, and of the drag-net. It corresponds, also, with the condition of the churches to whom the apostolical epistles are addressed, as described in the body of those epistles.

2. That the condition of the churches which are commended is one of *conflict* more or less severe. Sardis and Laodicea have none. There is not enough life to resist evil, either from within or from without. The conflict is most prominent in the churches of Smyrna and Philadelphia, which are commended without rebuke. It is taken for granted in the promise appended to every epistle that conflict is the law of the condition of the church visible. "To him that overcometh," and to him only, is the promise given. It must be so. The eagle cannot mount aloft but by the resistance of the air to the stroke of his pinions. Neither can the Christian reach perfect conformity to Christ but by resisting and overcoming the world, the flesh, and the devil. As he was, so must we be in this world; and he, though he were a son, must learn obedience by the things which he suffered. Let no man, then, be moved by the afflictions of the church.

II. THE CHURCH AS SYMBOLIZED BY THE "WOMAN CLOTHED WITH THE SUN," ETC.—REV. xii.

We have already seen that the kingdom of God is set forth in Daniel and John under a human form, and the world-power under a beastly, corresponding with the primeval representation in Genesis iii. 15.[1] The kingdom of God falls naturally into two parts, the king and his subjects, who are also his children, or the bridegroom and the bride, the head and the members, or body. So, also, the symbolization is twofold in the twelfth chapter of the Apocalypse: (1), The king or bridegroom as a man-child, or, literally, a "male son" (*υἱὸν ἀῤῥενα*, verse 5), an apparently pleonastic expression, to denote emphatically the perfection of his manly nature (additional explanation of the force of the phrase, "Son of man," already considered); and the bride or church as a *woman*. The first is the antithesis of the dragon, the other of the beast. This corresponds with the *usus loquendi* of both the Old and New Testaments.[2] Note, also, that the terms of the symbolization in Revelation xii. imply that the visible church is the same under the Old and New Testaments. For it is the same woman who gives birth to the "male son," and who flies into the wilderness, *i. e.*, who flies from the nation of the Jews, which had been for centuries her settled habitation, into the wilderness of the Gentile world.[3] The woman is exhibited, first, in the perfection of her calling, corresponding with the description of the church in the inscriptions of the apostolical epistles, as the exhibition of it in the Saviour's epistles to the seven churches of

[1] See *Fairbairn on Prophecy*, pp. 308–'19.

[2] Ex. xxiv. 15, 16; Num. xiv. 33; Isa. l. 1; liv. 1; Jer. ii. 2, 20; Ezek. xvi. and xxiii.; Hosea i. and iii.; Psa. xlv.; The Song; John iii. 29; Matt. ix. 15; xxii. 1; xxv.; 2 Cor. xi. 2; Eph. v. 25–32, *et mult al.* See *Auberlen*, pp. 240–'43; *Fairbairn on Prophecy*, pp. 319, 320.

[3] See Isa. xl. 3; xli. 17–19; xlii. 10–12; xliii. 19, 20, 21, and compare Matt. viii. 11, 12; xxii. 43; Acts xiii. 46, 47; xxviii. 25–28; compare, also, Rev. xii. 14 with Exod. xix. 1–4.

Asia corresponds with the descriptions of the actual state of the churches in the body of the apostolical epistles, specially those to the Corinthians and Galatians; and as the harlot of the Apocalypse corresponds with the exhibition of the almost apostate church of Israel in the Old Testament under the same image.

1. She appears as a "woman in *heaven*," as her Lord and espoused husband comes "down from heaven and is in heaven" (John iii. 13), in the same blissful and elevated region with her divine head, for there her citizenship lies as well as his. (2), Her condition is in accordance with her place; she is "clothed with the sun," with a divine and celestial glory, with the light of the Sun of Righteousness (Isa. lx. 1); she "has the moon under her feet," by which is meant, according to some, the heathen religions, which, so far as they have any truth, only reflect the light of the religion which Christ, the Sun, sheds forth upon the darkness of the world.

This light, too feeble and uncertain in itself to be a safe guide to men in the great concern of salvation, is entirely superseded by the light of the sun which shines around the woman, and she, therefore, has the moon under her feet; has a position in the light of God far above that of those who have nothing but "the light of nature" to be their guide. She aims at a *summum bonum* far higher than the purest heathenism ever knew, and has a purer method by which to attain unto it. According to others, the moon being a satellite of the earth, and belonging to her, is the symbol of the brightest things which are "of the earth earthy," the riches, the culture, the *honors* of the flesh; and the church has all such things beneath her feet, because she knows their emptiness and unsatisfying nature, and has had a nobler portion revealed to her. Again, she has her head emblazoned "with a crown of twelve stars," denoting, no doubt, in the first instance, the twelve apostles, and in the next, those whom they represented as called to shine and rule with Christ. The stars are those through whom the testimony of the church is primarily and chiefly uttered; they are about the head of the woman, and for this reason the devil's efforts are directed chiefly against them.[1] The woman with the twelve stars is the same as the city with twelve gates and foundations; the one is the exalted and transfigured church, the other the church militant.[2] These passages, again, compared together, furnish another proof that the church of the Old and New Testaments is the same; the twelve *tribes* and the twelve *apostles* go together. How sad and awful the contrast between the woman and the harlot!

III. THE TRUE CHURCH VISIBLE, SYMBOLIZED IN REV. XI. 1, IN CONTRAST WITH THE FALSE AND CORRUPT CHURCH.

The points[3] to which I would direct your particular attention here are, (1), The number of witnesses; (2), The substance of their testimony; (3), The period of their testimony; (4), The effect of their testimony; (5), The reward of their testimony.

1. The *number* of the witnesses. They are in the symbol only *two*. This number is supposed by some to denote two lines of witnesses, the East and the West; but, much more probably, by others the number is taken from the Mosaic law, which required the testimony of at least two. The symbol indicates that the witnesses would be few, but sufficient to fulfil the legal conditions of a valid testimony. "Where two or three are gathered together," etc. (Matt. xviii.) The disproportion of the witnesses, as compared with the mass of nominal Christians, would be as great as between the number of those who had access to the temple and the number in the outer court, or as between Jews and Gentiles. This is

---

[1] Rev. xii. 4; compare Rev. i. 20; Dan. xii. 3–viii. 10; Matt. xix. 28, and *Auberlen*, p. 246; see, also, Rev. xxi. 2, 9, 10, 12, 14.

[2] Compare Eph. ii. 20.

[3] Here read Fairbairn's *Prophecy*, pp. 370–376; Elliot's *Horæ Apocalypticæ*, Vol. II., pp. 198–206.

an important fact, as we shall see hereafter, in deciding during a long period of church history which was the true church.

2. The *substance* of their testimony. This is indicated in several ways: (*a*), Their testimony is a testimony concerning Jesus; Christ calls them "*my* witnesses." The language of Rev. xi. 1, implies that the "temple," the "altar," and the "worship," were the burden of the testimony. The temple was the symbol of two great facts, that God had revealed himself to man, and that man could approach God; or, in other words, that God was conversable with man; that God was with men (Immanuel, God with us). It is here predicted, then, that these witnesses would testify that Jesus is the only "temple"; that he is "the true sanctuary which the Lord pitched and not man"; that it is only in him that God communicates his will to men for their salvation, and only through him that man has access to God. This testimony was against the usurpation of the nominal church in challenging to himself the prerogative of revealing God, and requiring his members to receive the decrees as the infallible interpretation of God's will, on the one hand, and on the other, in making mere piles of stone and brick *temples* of God, and so localizing the worship of God and destroying its spirituality. The next particular specified is the "altar," either of sacrifice or of intercession, or both. The witnesses testified to the reality and perfection of Christ's sacrifice against all the errors which virtually denied it, such as the sacrifice of the mass, and to the reality and perfection of the intercession of Christ, as against the doctrine of the mediation of saints and angels. Next, in reference to worship, the true nature of Christian worship as free and spiritual, as against the carnal, slavish worship of the nominal church, etc., etc., and specially against the right of man, either in church or state, to prescribe forms of worship, this being the prerogative solely of Christ as king. All Christians are worshippers by their very calling, a

royal priesthood, having free access to the temple, even into the holiest of all, and "worshipping therein." (*b*), In Rev. xii. 17, this testimony of Christ is associated with "keeping the commandments of God." One part, and, in a sense, the chief part, of the testimony is the supremacy of God in Christ as the king. The great question between the faithful witnesses and the enemies of God is whether man or God is to be obeyed, and this, whether the particular question is one of doctrine or life, faith or practice. But this we have sufficiently considered before, when considering the conflicting claims of the Son of man and the beast.

3. The *period* during which this testimony is given. This period is described as that during which the Gentiles (the uncircumcised, the heathenists, paganized Christians) tread down the "holy city" (the true church of Christ); a period of "forty-two months," as it is called in verse second, or of "one thousand, two hundred and sixty days," as it is in verse third of this eleventh chapter, or the time of the true church's abode in the wilderness (chap. xii. 6), or the whole dispensation of conflict and trial, which extends from Christ's ascension to the millennium. This number and the other numbers of this book seem to be symbolical, and it is fruitless labor to attempt to fix the dates according to a historical chronology. Probably these periods were given, not to afford any absolute information as to time, but only a relative, that the period of the church's suffering and depression bears the same relation to the period of her glory and triumph on earth that forty-two months, or one thousand two hundred and sixty days, bear to one thousand years. This is enough to sustain the faith and patience of the saints; more might serve only to gratify an unprofitable curiosity. Prophecy is not history, but only a description of some of the leading characteristics of history. It was not given to make us prophets in reference to particular events, but to encourage our faith in a presiding and controlling providence. If this in-

terpretation be sound, the pervading characteristic of the present dispensation is that of testimony at the expense of suffering; this is the time of sackcloth and mourning in the absence of the bridegroom; the church will put off the sackcloth and be girded with gladness (Psalm xxx. 11) only when the bridegroom returns. It is not the church, but the harlot, that says, "I sit as a queen, and have no sorrow."

4. The *effect* of the testimony, verse 5, *et seq.* (*a*), Upon the enemies of God. Here read Elliott (*ut supra*), pp. 203-205. (*b*), Upon themselves, verses 7–10. As Christ was, so must they be in this world.

5. The *reward* of their testimony, verses 11–13. (*a*), A resurrection. (*b*), An elevation to the sphere of God in Christ. (*c*), The fall of the powers of the world and a revenue of glory to God.

IV. THE APOSTATE CHURCH UNDER THE SYMBOL OF A HARLOT. REV xvii.

Read Auberlen, pp. 274–296; or, Fairbairn's *Prophecy*, pp. 376–387.

V. THE CHURCH THE BRIDE OF THE LAMB IN HER STATE OF IDEAL PERFECTION.

1. Revelation iv. We have seen that the epistles to the seven churches (in the second and third chapters) present a view of the church visible as it should exist during the dispensation of the Spirit. The subsequent part of the book, from the fifth chapter onwards, presents us with the leading characteristics of this church's history till the work of purification shall be accomplished, and she shall be presented as a chaste virgin to the bridegroom. The fourth chapter presents the church in its perfected state. The second and third chapters give us the beginning; the fifth and onwards, the middle; and the fourth and twentieth and twenty-first, the end.

(*a*), The first thing in this vision is the "throne," the seat of supreme, sovereign, universal empire of God; the source of all the changes and movements on earth as well as in heaven, "the lightnings, thunderings, and voices," which agitate and alarm our world. But we must note, that while it is the throne of supreme and absolute dominion, it is the throne of the covenant God of the church. The rainbow, the sign of the covenant, is "round about" it, splendid and sparkling like an emerald. It is the throne of the "Son of man," who has been made "head over all things for the sake of his body, the church." This is the throne he now occupies, although appearances seem to be against such a supposition; and it will be, one day, acknowledged that he occupied this seat of absolute authority and power, and that the clouds and darkness, the lightnings, thunderings and voices which startled the world were the result of his unsearchable decrees. In confirmation of this view, compare the representations of the next chapter, where the "Lamb as it had been slain" appears "in the midst of the throne" as the "Lion of the tribe of Judah," opening the book and loosing the seven seals thereof, *i. e.*, as the spirit of the symbolization demands, not only revealing, but issuing and executing, the decrees of the seals, and of the trumpets and vials which they include. Christ is a "royal priest," a "priest upon his throne," as a priest, the Lamb; as a king, the Lion of the tribe of Judah; a king because a priest, satisfying the law, yea, magnifying it as a priest, and thereby acquiring the right to administer the law in heaven, earth, and hell, as a king. He is worthy to take the book and open the seals thereof, because he was slain, and redeemed the church by his blood.[1]

(*b*), The next thing in the vision is the body of the redeemed represented by four and twenty elders. Note here that all the imagery of the Apocalypse is drawn from the Old

---

[1] Compare Phil. ii. 5; Col. i. 15–20

Testament, and in not a solitary instance, from paganism, that is, any peculiarity of paganism; for many images, drawn from the more obvious phenomena of nature and of human society are common to both. The tribes of Israel are taken as a symbol of the church, and the rulers of Israel as the representatives of the church. The number twenty-four may have been chosen to express the priestly character of the redeemed, the priests under the Old Testament having been divided into twenty-four courses. The kingly character is expressed in the last part of the verse, "they had on their heads crowns of gold." Compare the song of the same body in the next chapter, in which they say, "Thou hast made us unto our God kings and priests." All the elect of God are "predestined to be conformed to the image of his Son,"[1] not only in rectitude and perfection of moral character, but, if I may so express it, in office and function also. As he is a priest, king, and prophet, so are they. As priests, it is their office to worship God, to offer spiritual sacrifices acceptable to God by Jesus Christ. Even here on earth they are to do everything in the spirit of worship; whether they eat or drink, or whatsoever they do, they are to do to the glory of God, in the exercise of conscious dependence upon him, and in the spirit of thankfulness for his marvellous mercies. Much more is their eternal employment in heaven to be that of worship. They are also kings. They sit round about the throne on "*thrones*" (not simply "seats," as in our version), and they have crowns of gold on their heads. They have been with Christ in the conflict, they have conquered with him, and they reign with him. The shepherd of Salisbury Plain spoke in the spirit of a king when he said, "The weather to-morrow will be such as pleases me, for it will be such as pleases God; and whatever pleases God pleases me." The will of the redeemed will be lost in the will of Christ; whatever he wills shall be done, and, therefore, whatever they will shall

---

[1] Romans viii.

be done. His obedience to the law is the foundation of his kingly authority; and his obedience is their obedience and the foundation of their reign with him. He has put down sin, death, the world, the devil and hell, by suffering and patient submission, and so have they in him; and they sit as conquerors on the throne with him.[1] As kings reigning with Christ, they are put in possession of all the sources of the highest and most exquisite enjoyment for ever and ever. Note the amazing mercy, wisdom, and power of God in overruling the fall of man and the ruin of sin, in making it the means of exalting the redeemed to higher glory than Adam and his race could ever have enjoyed, if they had never fallen. Angels are never said to *reign;* the saints occupy *an inner circle* about the throne, nearer to it than the angels, who are not kings and priests, because not redeemed by the blood of the Lamb. "Marvellous are thy works, Lord God Almighty!"

(*c*), The next thing in the vision is the symbol of the efficient agency by which the church has been brought from the very pit of pollution and shame to this pitch of glory; the seer saw "seven lamps of fire burning before the throne," which were explained to be "the seven Spirits of God." Seven, as we have seen, is the number of perfection and of the covenant, denoting here the manifold variety and inexhaustible fulness of the Spirit's gifts provided for the redeemed in the covenant with Christ. This symbol is here used with special reference to the illumination of the church (lamps of fire), and with peculiar beauty and propriety is the number seven used in connection with the consummate condition of the church. The old creation was completed in six days, and on the seventh God rested, with infinite satisfaction in his finished work, shining with the impress of his wisdom, holiness, power, and goodness. But now is the new creation finished, shining more gloriously in the image of God than the old either did or could, and all under the al-

[1] Compare Chapter iii. 21. Read, also, Chapter xv. 2–4.

mighty power and the infinite wisdom of "the seven Spirits which are before the throne." Now begins, indeed, what Lord Bacon so beautifully calls the "Sabbath work" of God, "the illumination of his Spirit," an illumination which is not merely a giving of light, but an infusion and incorporation of the light into the very texture of the soul itself, so that the soul itself becomes luminous, shining like the face of Moses when he came down from the mount, only with no veiled and transient glory, but with a glory unveiled and lasting; nay, evermore growing from one degree of glory to another. "The pure in heart shall see God," and shall evermore become purer and purer, as this "vision beatific" opens, more and more, upon the pure heart.

(*d*), This idea of purity as a necessary element of the illumination and blessedness of the saints seems to be specially symbolized by what John saw next, "a sea of glass like unto crystal," probably a laver of brass highly polished and shining like glass. The imagery continues to be taken from the tabernacle or temple. The laver signified the necessity of personal and inherent purification, in order to qualify a worshipper for an acceptable approach to God, who sat upon the throne in the holiest of all; as the altar of burnt offering signified the previous necessity of expiation and satisfaction to the same end. The symbol here, therefore, expresses the essential nature of the work by which the Spirit of God brings the church to its perfection; it is a work of *purification*. The betrothed church is to be cleansed before she can be united forever to the Bridegroom.[1] This is the grand design of ministry, oracles, ordinances, and providences; without it there can be no happiness. The saints must be like God in holiness, if they are to be like him in blessedness.[2]

(*e*), The perfection of the life of the redeemed seems to be specially symbolized in the living ones, the next feature in

[1] Compare Ezek. xvi. 1; 2 Cor. xi. 2, 3.

[2] See 1 John iii. 2, 3, *et mult al.*

the vision signalized by the seer. The word ζωα is unhappily rendered in our version "beasts," the English word which is properly used elsewhere in this book as the equivalent of the Greek θηριον. Our translators, no doubt, used the word in this place as equal to *animal*, but unhappily, as the living creatures here described have parts and appearances which animals properly have not, and besides, are represented as rational in the highest sense and in the highest degree. The features of this symbol are substantially those of the cherubim, which we have seen, in a previous part of our course, to be symbols, probably, of the perfection of creaturely life.[1] Compare the seraphim of Isaiah vi., which are no doubt the same as the cherubim, and Ezekiel i. The impression which all these representations make upon us is that the composite symbol had the prevailing aspect of a human being; and the symbol here must either set forth the state or exercises of a certain portion of the redeemed, or the perfect life which is common to them all. If the first, then the class of the redeemed symbolized is the most exalted class, and their life is the type of the most exalted creaturely life. This would amount, practically, to the same view as the other interpretation. The highest intelligence (man, eyes), the greatest courage and majesty (lion), the greatest patience of labor (ox), and the greatest activity and loftiness of devotion (flying eagle). The Rabbins say that these four parts of the symbol constituted, respectively, the devices on the standards of the four divisions of the Israelites during their march through the wilderness. If this be so, the symbol would be an appropriate representation of the whole body of the redeemed which are elsewhere in the book symbolized by the tribes of Israel. The chief features of the symbol here are the "wings" and the "eyes." If the uses of the wings here are to be determined by the explanations of Isaiah vi. 2, they express reverence, concealment from

[1] See Fairbairn's *Typology* on the cherubim.

mortal view, and activity in the service of God;[1] or, as the Chaldean paraphrase has it,[2] "with two they covered their faces, *lest they should see;* with two they covered their body, *lest they should be seen;* and with two they *served.*" What more appropriate to the higher creaturely life in the presence of God than the highest and readiest activity combined with the lowliest *reverence* and modesty? The piercing intelligence of these living ones is indicated by the multitude of eyes. It is the privilege of the perfect church *videre videndum*, to see the Son, to know even as it is known, no longer by means of a glass in an enigma, but face to face. Standing at the centre of the universe, with a vision purged of the last films of *error*, with the light of eternity poured like a flood upon the whole scheme of God's gift and providence, no wonder they rest not day nor night, crying, "Holy! holy! holy! Lord God Almighty!"

(*f*), This leads naturally to the consideration of the worship of the perfected church, which is described in the concluding verses of the chapter. The adoration of the "living ones" enlists the hearty sympathy of the whole body (according to one view); or the perfect life of the redeemed prompting the adoration (according to another), it expresses itself in an entire consecration of the whole body to the service of God. In either view the worship of heaven (and in an imperfect degree all true worship on earth) expresses itself in adoration, thanksgiving, and consecration. Adoration has reference to God as he is in himself; it is a glorifying of God for what he is, the opposite of all those defective, or dishonoring, or hard thoughts of him which are common in the world, and not seldom disfigure the lives of believers themselves. God is seen to be perfectly lovely, as he is unlimited in his sovereignty and dominion. He is felt to be *worthy* to receive glory and honor and power. *Thanksgiving* has reference to what he is and has been to his people. We

[1] Alexander's *Commentary on Isaiah, in loco.* [2] Alexander, *ut supra.*

never shall know fully what it is to give thanks until we join that happy company; because till then we shall never know the boundless riches of his goodness and grace. *Consecration* is the entire surrender of the whole of man to God, founded upon the fact that he has "created all things," and that the only end for which "they were created" and continue "to subsist" is his own pleasure. The saints will feel then, as they never felt it here, that it is *right* that it should be so; that it is their reasonable service.[1] They will be amazed that they could ever have supposed for one moment that their own ease or comfort, reputation or safety, were worthy to be considered at all in comparison with the service of God. If it were possible for the agony of shame to be endured in heaven, they would be ashamed to think that they had ever called anything they ever did on earth, even giving their bodies to be burned, or to be torn by wild beasts, a sacrifice. Standing before the Lamb and in full view of the doom from which his blood has delivered them, and of the glory and blessedness to which that blood has exalted them, the noble army of martyrs themselves will wonder that their resolution to die for Christ ever cost them a moment's hesitation. How monstrous, then, will appear all theories in theology or morals which relegated God and his sovereignty and glory to a subordinate position, or elevated man, his will, or his interests (so-called), to a practical supremacy! There will not be the shadow of a doubt, *then*, that God made (and had a right to make) all things for himself, even the wicked for the day of evil. Hallelujah will burst from every heart, as the smoke of the torment of the wicked ascendeth up forever and ever. The lost did not consecrate themselves to God; this will be felt to be enough for the vindication of the judge for giving them *themselves* for their inheritance in eternal separation from him. They refused to recognize him as their all-disposing Lord and

[1] Romans xii. 1.

their all-comprehending good; and now they must "eat of the fruit of their own way, and be filled with their own devices."[1] This absolute and complete consecration of the saints to God is one aspect of their kingly dignity and office. They "cast their crowns before the throne"! This is not the abdication, but the highest and most glorious exercise, of their royal functions. This is supreme felicity.

2. Rev. v. 8–14. Here, again, we have the worship of the redeemed church in glory. The features of this description which demand special notice are, (*a*), The worship of the *Lamb* (verses 8, 12, 13). To deny that the Lamb is truly and only God in the face of this passage is the result only of judicial infatuation. Every Christian is a worshipper of Christ by the very instincts of his new nature. To believe that Christ has redeemed us from hell and conferred upon us an eternal inheritance of glory and blessedness, of liberty and purity, and not worship him, is simply impossible. (*b*), The communion in worship with the angels. In the description of the communion of saints which we find in Hebrews xii. 22–24, "an innumerable company of angels" is one of the leading features. They form a part of the whole family of God in heaven and earth, sundered in spirit and fellowship from God's human children by sin, but reunited with that portion of them who have been restored by the blood of Christ and the spirit of adoption. The Scriptures do not warrant us in saying, as Lord Bacon thinks, that they are gathered under Christ as their head, in the sense of being confirmed in their state of acceptance with God by his righteousness. The representation here is against that view, as they do not join in the special song of the redeemed. But we *are* warranted in saying, that new views of God's wisdom, power, and goodness, in short, new views of his glory, have been given them in the plan of redemption; that the rapture of their praise and thanksgiving has been thereby augmented,

[1] Read Revelation xix. 1–4.

and that Christ as universal king is their head for the sake of his body, the church.

3. Rev. vii. 9–17. This, at first view, would seem to be a description of a portion of the church distinguished from the sealed in verses 3–8; but I think that they are the same. The definite numbers of the sealed might produce the impression that the whole number of the elect and saved was small. This impression the vision of the white-robed and palm-bearing multitude before the throne would seem to correct. It was a multitude which no man could number. Another feature of the description is the contrast between the conflict and the triumph, the tribulation and the consummate felicity, of these palm-bearers. The poet Burns is reported to have said that he could never read this exquisite description without tears.

4. Rev. xiv. 1–5. Here the one hundred and forty-four thousand sealed ones appear again upon the scene. The prominent features here are the faultless purity of the redeemed, and the ecstatic joy which has rewarded their faithful following of Christ while they were on earth. The reason of the introduction of this scene in this place seems to be the contrast between the sealed, who are virgins, with the apostates and traitors, who constitute the harlot. Their faithfulness is contrasted with her treachery, their joy with the dreadful doom of her and her followers. (Compare the parable of the rich man and Lazarus.)

6. Rev. xxi. 10–27. The same church in its consummate perfection is here called the "Lamb's wife," and the "New Jerusalem." The following points are to be noticed here: (*a*), It is a "city." So represented as opposed to the wilderness in which the church resides during the twelve hundred and fifty days, and to the city of Babylon, the mystical, which pretended to be the church of God, but is now gone into perdition. A city conveys the idea of a compact organization, of the abundance of wealth and of all that can minis-

ter to the safety and comfort of the citizens, and of the greatest splendor and glory. The life of a city is the highest form of life among men. There all the conditions of human development are found in perfection, and, specially, security and activity. (*b*), In this city, it is next to be observed, there are twelve foundations to the walls, twelve gates, and twelve angels at the gates; and twelve thousand furlongs, or fifteen hundred miles in height, length and breadth constitute the measure of it. It is a cube made up of squares, with thousands, as the units of measurement. This shows that the city is not the symbol of the abode of the church, but of the church itself, composed of the sealed ones and of them only.[1] The size of the city is immense. All the cities in the world are mere villages in comparison; it contains "the multitude which no man can number." (*c*), It contains no *temple*. No medium of revelation on the part of God to man; no medium of access on the part of man to God is needed where the contact and communion of God with man is immediate. (*d*), There is no need of the sun or moon, of any of the light-bearers of this world, when the city is bathed in the light of the Lamb. (*e*), There is no shutting of the gates by day, for there is no enemy; and as for the night, there *is* none. No fatigue, and, therefore, no needed repose. The inhabitants "rest not" in their activities, but are perpetually glorifying God in an ecstasy of praise. The intellect is ever widening and expanding, ever pluming itself for loftier flights; and as new and enlarging views of the wisdom and glory of God burst upon the eye of the enraptured soul, a new song of praise bursts from the lips and thrills upon the strings of the harpers before the throne. (*f*), Again, the purity of the city, as the foundation of all this blessedness and glory, as in other representations of the church, is presented here. No pollution and no lie can enter into it. Holiness pervades all and reigns supreme. (*g*), The site of the city is the earth;

[1] Compare Eph. i. 13; iv. 30; 2 Tim. ii. 19, etc.

this very earth, which has drunk the blood of the Son of God and of the saints, which has been the scene of the revels of the powers of darkness, and has been converted by the sin of man into a Golgotha and a Tophet, shall be a *new* earth. The "sighs and groans of miserable men" shall be exchanged for songs of everlasting joy. "The tabernacle of God shall be with men, and he will dwell with them, and they shall be his people, and God himself shall be with them, and be their God. And God shall wipe away all tears from their eyes, and there shall be no more death, neither sorrow nor crying, neither shall there be any more pain, for the former things are passed away."

7. Rev. xxii. 2. The scene once more changes, or rather another scene, within the one just considered, emerges, and the last book of the Bible closes, as the first opens, with the paradise of God and the tree of life. But the paradise regained is more glorious than the paradise lost. It is a paradise in a city (vs. 2, 14); it is a paradise with "a pure river of the water of life," and the "tree of life" bears *twelve* manner of fruits and yields her fruit every month, and the leaves of the tree are for the healing of the nations.

"Now unto him who is able to do exceedingly above all that we ask or think, according to the power that worketh in us, unto him be glory in the church by Christ Jesus throughout all ages, world without end. Amen."

THE PLACE OF ANCIENT GREECE IN THE PROVIDENTIAL ORDER OF THE WORLD.[1]

THAT the vast scheme of providence, according to which the affairs of our world are administered, contemplates the rise and progress of nations, the changes and vicissitudes in the life of organized communities, is conceded even by those who deny, in contradiction to the dictates of sound reason as well as the plain declarations of holy writ, that this scheme embraces within its ample scope the smallest events in the life of the meanest and most obscure individual. The most savage tribe has a history which, however barren of incident or instruction to the world at large, and however destitute of any appreciable influence upon the condition and destiny of the human race, is under the direction of that power which

> "Lives through all life, extends through all extent,
> Spreads undivided, operates unspent,"

and is destined to unfold its results throughout an infinite duration.

In the sublime vision of Ezekiel, providence was represented under the figure of "wheels within a wheel." The humblest man is one of these wheels, not a mere spoke in a wheel; but has a life, a sphere, a movement, a purpose to fulfil, which, though connected with the system of which it forms a part, and co-operating in the production of the grand result, is still, in a very important sense, a life, sphere, movement and purpose of its own. Nations, again, are larger wheels, with their own peculiar life and sphere, each having a distinct mission to accomplish, and all conspiring,

[1] From lectures on Ecclesiastical History.

"cycle and epicycle, orb in orb" to demonstrate the wisdom, justice, goodness and power of him who, from a throne enshrouded in clouds and darkness, directs, controls and governs all.[1]

There are three nations of the ancient world to which these principles will be applied by the consent of every man who admits a providence at all. These are the Jews, the Romans and the Greeks. It was not an accident that the superscription upon the cross of Christ was written in the dialects of these nations. These were the elect nations, whose religion, culture, language, laws and institutions were destined to impress themselves upon the whole race of mankind, and which, for this reason, were entitled to stand as the representatives of all the tribes and families of that race. That mysterious sufferer who hung upon the cross was to be, and to be acknowledged, King of all, and not of the Jews only. His praises were to be chanted in every dialect from the rising of the sun to the going down of the same. The treasures of philosophy, eloquence, poetry, history, the "pre-

[1] Mr. Gladstone very justly as well as beautifully observes: "Something that may be called religionism, rather than religion, has led us for the most part, not, indeed, to deny in terms that God has been and is the God and Father and Governor of the whole human race, as well as of Jews and Christians, yet to think and act as if his providential eye and care had been confined in ancient times to the narrow valley of Jerusalem, and, since the Advent, to the Christian pale, or even to something which, enforcing some yet narrower limitation at our own arbitrary will, we think fit to call such. But, surely, he who cared for the six score thousands in ancient Nineveh that could not distinguish between their right hand and their left; he without whom not a sparrow falls; he that shapes, in its minutest detail, even the inanimate world, and clothes the lily of the field with its beauty and its grace, he never forgot those sheep of his in the wilderness; but as, on the one hand, he solicited them and bore witness to them of himself by never-ceasing bounty and by the law written on their hearts, so, on the other hand, in unseen modes he used them as he is always using us, for either the willing, or if not the willing, then the unconscious or unwilling, furtherance and accomplishment of his designs. The real paradox, then, would be, not to assert, but to deny, or even to overlook, the part which may have been

cious life-blood of the master-spirits" of the world, "embalmed and treasured up in these tongues in order to a life beyond life," were all to be consecrated to the service of him who consecrated himself for the redemption and glorification of man.

In considering the place occupied by these three nations in the providential order of the world, their relation to the cross of Christ, as has been already suggested, obtrudes itself first on our notice. The life and death of Christ occupy, according to the Scriptures, the central point in the history of the world. The earth was created to be a theatre upon which might be displayed to principalities and powers in heavenly places the manifested wisdom of God. But, looking at the life and ministry of Jesus from a merely human point of view, it cannot be denied that they constitute an era

---

assigned to any race, and especially to a race of such unrivalled gifts, in that great and all-embracing plan for the rearing and training of the human children of our Father in heaven which we call the providential government of the world. Such preparation, asserted and established upon the solid ground of fact, may be termed prophecy in action, and is, if possible, yet stronger for the confirmation of belief, and yet more sublime in aspect as an illustration of almighty greatness, than prophecy in word. But in this providential government there are diversities of operations. In the great house there are vessels of gold and silver, vessels of wood and earth. In the sphere of common experience we see some human beings live and die, and furnish by their life no special lessons visible to man, but only that general teaching in elementary and simple forms which is derivable from every particle of human experience. Others there have been who, from the time when their young lives first, as it were, peeped over the horizon, seemed at once to

'Flame in the forehead of the morning sky,'

whose lengthening years have been but one growing splendor, and at the last who

'leave a lofty name,
A light, a landmark, on the cliffs of fame.'

Now, it is not in the general, the ordinary, the elementary way, but it is in a high and special sense, that I claim for ancient Greece a marked, appropriated, distinctive place in the providential order of the world." (Gladstone's address in *Eclectic Magazine* for February, 1866, p. 138.)

more fruitful and permanent in its consequences than any other in the history of the world, an epoch, indeed, a period, at which the world halted, and then turned and entered upon a new career. We cannot look around us without seeing the evidences that the glory of Jesus, considered merely as a man, transcend beyond all computation the glory of all the heroes, either in the sphere of thought or action, whom the world has agreed to worship. Even German rationalism confesses that "Christ is the centre of history."

What place, then, did ancient Greece occupy in relation to Christianity? The answer to this question may be distributed into several heads, among which I will select only a few.

1. First, then, in general, providence seems to have designed to show by the history of the Greeks how far the faculties of man, in their greatest vigor and their widest excursions, can go. The most cultivated nations of christendom acknowledge the Greeks still, and, we venture nothing in predicting, will continue to acknowledge them as their teachers. These nations, indeed, know a great deal more than their masters. Many a school-boy, in these times, knows many things which escaped the comprehensive grasp of Aristotle or the sublime and excursive genius of Plato. But the "march of mind" and the "progress of knowledge" are very different things. Many of the most enlightened men of the post-Baconian period, who have filled the world with their renown, and who are justly entitled to the gratitude of their race, are only "intellectual barbarians" compared with those "dread and sceptred sovereigns, who still rule our spirits from their urns." If we wish to educate the faculties of man, to develop their strength by tasking and exercising it; if we wish to cultivate the sense of the beautiful, and to enable them to attain to that which Cicero represents to be the perfection of all the operations of the mind, the "becoming," the "fit," the "decorous," we must

give our days and nights to the Greek models.[1] This is the unanimous judgment of all men who are entitled to pronounce judgment in the matter; and all the utilitarian talk of this century and of this country to the contrary is mere trash. "The Greeks," it has been well said, "were a peculiar race, a chosen people, to whom the image of ideal beauty was first revealed, and who cherished it even as the highest and holiest and divinest of things, with a devotion in which it is hard to tell whether deep love or just and exquisite discernment predominated. The Attic muse (*αρχαια και αὐτοχθων*) was only another name for unbounded and unblemished excellence in every art that addresses itself to an elegant imagination, and every science that tasks the powers of a subtle intelligence, in sculpture and statuary, in music and painting and architecture, in all the varieties of poetry and eloquence, in geometry and metaphysics, in short, throughout the whole range of speculative philosophy."[2] The highest ambition of the moderns has been to make some approximation to the orators, poets, historians, and philosophers of Greece, at least as to form and style.

But, now, why did God so richly endow this wonderful people? He is a sovereign, and chose them as the repository of the beau-ideal, and through them to teach the race what this ideal was, as he chose the far inferior race of the Jews (inferior in this respect) to be the repository of the truth concerning himself, concerning the moral condition of mankind, and concerning salvation; and as he chose the Romans as the repository of the art of government and law, civil and political. This was one reason. But the Scriptures give us another, and that is to show mankind that the human mind, in its best estate, in the very highest development of its noble powers, cannot only not find out God, but cannot even re-

---

[1] *Caput est artis decere, ut dixit Roscius. De Orat., lib.* 1., c. 29, cited by Legare in his essay on "Roman Orators," *Southern Review*, November, 1828.

[2] Legare, as above cited.

ceive what God reveals concerning himself. The intellectual princes of this world could apprehend, and in strong terms express, the necessity for men of more light; but if they had lived when the Saviour was on earth, we have no reason to doubt that they would have joined in crucifying the Lord of glory. For their own teaching demonstrated that there is no necessary connection between greatness of intellect and enlarged knowledge, on the one hand, and love of virtue, on the other. It is not only Aristophanes who makes fun of sin, but the grave and reverend Socrates who defends it. And if the principles of Plato's Utopia could have been carried out, his republic would have been as foul as the stye of Epicurus. Did not the wisest of the Greeks adhere to the traditional theology of their nation? and what is that "elegant mythology," as Gibbon calls it, but an apotheosis of the vilest passions of human nature? a putrid corpse adorned with the fairest flowers of human wit? What were many of the most exquisite masterpieces of Grecian genius and skill in sculpture, painting, and architecture but splendid monuments of the corruption of man and of his apostasy from God? It was, therefore, a decree of the wisdom of God that the world, by wisdom, should not know him. If the Greek mind could not find him out, it was certain that the mind of no other people could. It was a demonstration on the grandest scale of the misery and impotence of man with respect to everything which concerns his life as an immortal being. And this demonstration was a negative preparation of the greatest importance for the coming of Christ and the publication of Christianity.

2. But, secondly, Ancient Greece was also a *positive* preparation for Christianity, and that in several ways.

(1), This very mythology, of which we have spoken, although in its general spirit and tone corrupt and corrupting to the last degree, was yet not altogether and absolutely false. The shadows of the truth were constantly flitting across it, reminding its votaries of something higher and purer than itself, recalling them to a memory of a lost paradise, and prophesying of a paradise to be regained; there were voices from out of the darkness which spoke of the possibility of restoration to the image of the divine, if their ears had not been too dull to hear. Bishop Horsley is a forcible, and Archbishop Trench an elegant, interpreter of these voices, the one in his sermons on the "Unconscious Prophecies of Heathendom" in reference to the coming of Christ, the other in his "Hulsean Lecture" on the same subject. What idea more fundamental in the Christian scheme than the incarnation of God, and yet what idea more familiar to the Greek mind. The people of Lycaonia, who supposed that Paul was Mercury, and Barnabas Jupiter, fell into an error extremely natural in the inhabitants of a country which had been the scene, according to the traditions preserved by Ovid and others, of many visits of the "father of gods and men."[1] Again, we find the ideas of expiatory sacrifice by blood, even of expiation by human blood, of a golden age, of a future state of rewards and punishments, of a vanquisher of death and the grave, *et cet.*, the shadows of the sacrifice of Christ, of paradise lost, of heaven and hell, of Christ as the conqueror of death, *et ut;* so that when the first preachers of Christianity announced the doctrine of "God manifest in the flesh," of his expiatory sacrifice, *et cet.*, they announced nothing wholly foreign to the established associations of the Greek mind. All these ideas in the Greek mythology were altars to unknown truths; and the great mission of the apostles was to expound this unknown mythology, and point their hearers to the substance of all these shadows. No man can read Paul's speech to the Athenians in the seventeenth chapter of the Acts without feeling how much of the truth the dim traditions of his audience had preserved; while he cannot fail to recognize, in the manner in which the announce-

[1] Conybeare and Howson, *St. Paul*, Vol. I., pp. 229, *et seq.*

ment of the distinctive doctrines of the gospel was received, the instinctive opposition of the heart of man to salvation and fellowship with God. The difference between the preparation for the advent of Christ among the Jews and among the Greeks, with respect to theology, is shown in one singular circumstance, noticed by Mr. Gladstone in his late discourse on retiring from the Rectorship of the Edinburgh University. It is this, that while among the Greeks the idolatrous worship of *man* was the most common of all, we find it seldom or never among the Jews; the reason of which may be that God designed to manifest himself in a human form, in very deed to become man, and to present to the world a man who might be worshipped without idolatry, a phenomenon altogether marvellous and unique, by which the weakness of man, unable to grasp the conception of a purely spiritual God, and prone to create for itself a visible and tangible object of worship, might be reconciled and harmonized with the highest and most perfect truth. If providence had permitted the Jews to go the same length in an anthropomorphic idolatry as in Sabaism and in the worship of animals, the coming majesty of the incarnation would have been degraded by base associations. A pure theistic system was maintained; a redemption to come was embraced by faith; and in a religion laden with ritual and charged with symbol or rite, no symbol was permitted to exhibit to the senses, and through the senses to the mind of the people, the form of him who was to be the worker of the great deliverance. Thus was kept vacant till the appointed time, in the general belief as well as in the scheme and theory of religion, the sublime and solitary place which the Redeemer of the world was to fill."[1] On the other hand, among the Greeks, whose providential mission was not to maintain a pure theism, idolatry was ordained to assume this anthropomorphic shape in order to keep alive, in the absence of a

[1] Gladstone, *ut sup. cit.*

written revelation, the memory of the protevangelium of primeval paradise, that the seed of the woman should bruise the serpent's head, that the principle of evil was to receive a deadly shock in its vital part, and this at the hands of one who should be born into the very race that he would come to deliver.

(2), In connection with this thoroughly anthropomorphic feature of the Greek mythology may be noticed another feature of the Greek mind growing out of this, and that is its exalted idea of excellence. "I know not," says the writer already quoted, "what true definition there is for any age or people of the highest excellence in any kind, unless it be perpetual effort upward in pursuit of an object higher than ourselves, higher than our works, higher even than our hopes, yet beckoning us on from hour to hour and always permitting us to apprehend in part. I venture the opinion, that the fundamental cause of the transcendent excellence of the Greek artist lay in his being, by his birth and the tradition of his people, as well as with every favorable accessary, both in idea and in form, and in such a sense as no other artist ever was, a worker upon deity conceived as residing in the human form. It is hardly necessary to observe how the rich and many-sided composition of the Greek mythology favored the artist in his work, by answering to the many-sided development of the mind and the life of man. Unconsciously, then, to himself, and in a sphere of almost parochial narrowness, the Greek, not only earned himself an immortal fame, but was equipping from age to age a great school of art, to furnish principles and models made ready to the hand of that pure and high civilization which was to be, and over the preparation of which all the while divine providence was brooding like the Spirit on the face of the waters, till the fulness of time should come." "It was this perpetual presentation of the highest to the Greek artist that cheered him and rewarded him, and yet, while it cheered him and rewarded him, still ever spurred him on in his pursuit. Whatever he had done, more remained to do: *Nil actum reputans dum quid superesset agendum.* The desire of ambition was fulfilled; he had always more worlds to conquer. The divine was made familiar to him by correspondence of shape; but, on the other side, its elements, which it was his business to draw forth and indicate to men, reached far away into the infinite."[1]

There are two important applications of this fact in connection with the place of Greece in the providential order of the world. One is, that the truth which was shadowed forth in this idea of art is found in all its reality and glory in the person of Jesus Christ. We know not, for the Scriptures do not inform us, and even the traditions of the ancient church are conflicting in regard to it, whether the physical, corporeal form of Jesus was a model of manly beauty or not. But one thing we know with certainty, that his character was perfect. Love to God, supreme and perfect, and perfect love to man, constituted the mould into which his whole being, as a man, was cast. He was the model man, in a sense higher than the Greek ever dreamed, because moving in a higher sphere than the Greek ever moved in. His was the character of God, chastened and tempered in the effulgence and glory of its rays by shining through the nature of man. A mighty conqueror, but conquering by "the invincible might of weakness," as Milton says; the greatest of all benefactors, but the greatest of all benefactors because the greatest of all sufferers for man; a king for whom the heroic ages even of Greece furnished no parallel, "riding prosperously, because of truth and meekness and righteousness, whose sceptre was not only a right sceptre, but wielded by one who *loved* righteousness and *hated* wickedness." To realize, then, the sublime and inspiring idea of the Greek artist in its highest degree, the man Jesus must be studied by him

[1] Gladstone, *ut supra.*

who is working for immortality. In the production of a form and character upon that model, the artist is truly "working upon deity," not only "*conceived as residing*," but *actually residing*, in the human form. Thus will he, in his own life, "draw forth and indicate to men" the elements of the divine, "which reach far away into the infinite."

The other application is suggested by Mr. Gladstone himself, in another part of his discourse. It was by this anthropomorphism pervading their religion, combined with a remarkable fulness, largeness, subtlety and precision in their conception of human nature (the natural result of their seeing the divine in the human), that the Greek became "the great intellectual factor of the Christian civilization." "If we survey," he says, "with care and candor, the present wealth of the world, its intellectual, moral, and spiritual wealth, we find that Christianity has not only contributed to the patrimony of man its highest and most precious jewels, but has likewise been what our Saviour pronounced it, the salt or preserving principle of all the residue, and has maintained its health, so far as it has been maintained at all, against corrupting agencies. But the salt is one thing, the thing salted is another; and as in the world of nature, so in the world of mind and of human action, there is much that is outside of Christianity that harmonizes with it, that revolves, so to speak, around it, but that did not and could not grow out of it. It seems to have been for the filling up of this outline, for the occupation of this broad sphere of exertion and enjoyment, that the Greeks were, in the councils of providence, ordained to labor; that so the gospel, produced in the fulness of time, after the world's long gestation, might have its accomplished work in rearing mankind up to his perfection, first in the spiritual life, but also, and through that spiritual life, in every form of excellence for which his varied powers and capacities have been created." "The loftiest work of providence was entrusted to the

Hebrew race, but there was other work to do, and it was done elsewhere. It was requisite to make ready the materials, not only of a divine renewal and of a moral harmony for the world, but also for a thorough and searching culture of every power and gift of man, in all his relations to the world and to his kind; so as to lift up his universal nature to the level upon which his relation as a creature to his Creator, and as a child to his Father, was about to be established." These considerations constitute a triumphant vindication of the wisdom of Christian nations and of the church for centuries, in making the study of the language and literature of the Greeks the chief instruments in the education of the young, and the assaults upon the wisdom of this custom have generally been made either by conceited ignorance, or drivelling superstition.

(3), The next and last thing which I mention as indicating the connection of Greece with the greatest of all the works of providence is its *philosophy*, using this term in a sense wide enough to include *logic* or *dialectic*. The merest tyro in the history of Christian theology knows that, to a very great extent, Greek philosophy has determined not only its terms, but its form and shape. Alexandria was the fountain of this theology; and the name of this celebrated city suggests the wonderful history of the Macedonian who, with his Greeks, made the conquest of the eastern world, diffused the language of the Greeks everywhere, and prepared the way for the Greek translation of the Old Testament Scriptures, and for the administration of those Greek princes of Egypt who made that ancient empire once more a centre and source of light to the nations of the earth. The names of Philo Judæus, of Origen, Clement, Dionysius, and Athanasius, to mention no others, all of Alexandria, tell the story of Greek culture, and of its influence upon the theology of the church. It was through the instruments and forms of thought furnished by Aristotle and Plato that the scientific expression of the high mystery of the Trinity was, after generations of fierce controversy, finally reached in the elaborate creed of the council of Constantinople. So, also, in the christological discussions of the succeeding age, which resulted in the formal condemnation by the church of the Nestorian and Eutychian errors, we find the same dialectic playing a conspicuous part. At a still later period, during the Middle Ages, who does not know that the Greek philosophy, either in the Platonic spirit of the Psuedo-Dionysius, or in the Peripatetic spirit, first of the Arabian scholars, and then of the European and Christian thinkers of the schools and monasteries, determined the cast of dogmatic theology? and although the Reformation produced a rebellion against tho authority of Aristotle, yet it was rather a rebellion against the preposterous height of authority to which that great genius had been exalted than against the authority itself. Truly, there are few facts more wonderful in the history of the world than the vast and absolute sway of that imperial mind over well-nigh all the thinking of Europe and Asia for so many centuries; an empire vaster and more absolute than that of his pupil, Alexander the Great. Soon after the first effervescence of the Reformation had subsided, we find him regaining his authority in the universities, and holding it down to the times of Des Cartes and of Lord Bacon. By Lord Bacon, indeed, the defectiveness of Aristotle's *Organon* was demonstrated, and the *Novum Organum* set the human race upon a new and glorious career of discovery in all knowledges, the fruits of which we see everywhere around us. But the deductive logic of the Stagirite still continues, and will continue to the end of time, to be the most impregnable, as well as the most amazing, structure ever reared by a single mind. And that mind seems now, once more, about to regain a large portion of the influence it had lost. In the schools of Germany his spirit and method have been, for more than half a century, as mighty, if not mightier, than those of Francis of Verulam.

By all the influences then, of the theology of the church for more than fifteen centuries is the influence of Greek thought to be measured. But, it may be asked, has this been an influence for good? Would it not have been happier for the church and the world, if the free, spontaneous, simple, child-like faith of the church in the days of Clement of Rome, Ignatius, Polycarp, *et cet.*, had continued through all time? The answer is, that even if it had been desirable, such a faith was impossible. The reason of man *must* be exercised in the interpretation of the rule of faith, not only in discovering the meaning of the text by the rules of philosophy, but in deducing, from what is expressly set down, that which by necessary implication is contained in it; and this deduction can be made in no other way than by the laws of thought. Then, again, it was the purpose of God that the church should reach its ultimate perfection through conflict, not only with the persecuting powers of the world, which should be allowed to use the sword and fire and fagot to test the sincerity and constancy of Christ's witnesses, but with the more formidable, because more insidious, enemies who should attempt by argument to subvert their faith; and nothing is risked in the assertion, that infidel and heretical assaults upon the faith of the church have been of incalculable advantage to her in many ways. One is in bringing out the doctrines of that faith more clearly to her own consciousness, by compelling her to analyze and define them. "The science of contraries is one," and a truth is fully known only in contrast with multiform and many-sided error. Such a clear and complete statement of Christian truth as the Westminster Confession of Faith would have been impossible in the first century. These assaults have compelled the church to take an inventory of her possessions, and have made her know how rich she is. Another advantage is that the truth has become truly her own by the attempt to wrest it from her. The battles which must be fought to retain it are not fought with the weapons and resources of logic only, but with the sweat and labor of the heart. This is true not only of divine truth, but of all truth connected with the well-being of man, that it demands, if it is to be retained, the love and energies of the heart, as well as material resources. Hence the perpetual fighting over again, from age to age, of the battles of liberty and truth, whether in the world or in the church. It is true of individuals also. They do not possess the truth in a high sense, until they have fought for it. It is only the man who has doubted profoundly who believes profoundly. Luther *rehearsed* in his solitary cell, and in his own heart, the conflicts of the Reformation long before those conflicts took place upon the public theatre of Europe. So will it be, until the conqueror, the mighty King of kings, shall appear to be glorified in his saints and to be admired in all them that believe.

THE REFORMATION IN THE SIXTEENTH CENTURY,[1]

CONTEMPLATED IN SOME OF ITS CAUSES AND RESULTS.

WHEN we speak of second causes, it must never be forgotten that the concurrence of at least two of them is necessary to the production of an effect. Hence we speak of the *causes*, not the *cause*, of the Reformation, because we are here concerned with secondary causation only. The first cause we, of course, acknowledge to be God. The Reformation was a great work of his Holy Spirit, a mighty revival of the work which he had been doing ever since the utterance of the first promise in the garden of Eden. It was a re-form-ation, a restoration of the church to the word of God, which constitutes its form, as the Holy Ghost constitutes its life. But the work of God amongst men is performed under the conditions of time and place. And there are very many circumstances attending and concurring, in regard to some or all of which we might confidently affirm that they were causes *sine quibus non*, conditions without which the great event would not have taken place, or, if it had taken place, would not have been the same event, or been followed by the same results.

Our Saviour in his parables frequently likens the processes of the kingdom of heaven to the processes of vegetable and animal life. And it is not without authority, therefore, and that the highest, that scientific historians and writers on the philosophy of history have contemplated history under the notion of an organic development, in which the life, the form and the external conditions constitute the main subjects of consideration. We refer to this mode of contemplating his-

[1] Appeared in the *Southern Presbyterian Review*, October, 1871.

tory here only for the purpose of calling attention to that striking circumstance in the formation of organisms of which physiologists tell us, the circumstance of all its parts or organs being developed, each from its appropriate centre, and all growing *pari passu* to meet each other in the integrity of the organism as a whole. God builds the vegetable or animal in a way totally different from that in which the most skilful artisan builds any of his works, because God alone has the prerogative of imparting life. Hence, we are all familiar with such forms of expression as "events coming to the birth," "being *ripe* for execution," "the fulness of time," etc.

In "the fulness of time" God sent forth his Son. Christ came when the world was ripe for his advent, and the stupendous birth could no longer be delayed. The history of the world had been growing for ages towards this event from three distinct centres. Three distinct lines had been converging upon this great moment in the life of the human race—lines unconsciously recognized by the Roman governor when he wrote the superscription over the cross in the three languages which represented them.

So, also, in the case of the Reformation. The world was long in gestation before that great birth took place. There were several lines of providence which converged to produce that great revolution. Sudden as its outbreak appeared to the court of Rome, and even to some good men, almost despairing of the church, it was not sudden, as we now clearly see.

Before we glance at some of the causes of the Reformation, let us hint at some of the limitations under which these causes must be considered. Each one of these causes is itself an effect, as the Reformation itself becomes in its turn a most fruitful cause. The view of the mind in all such inquiries is necessarily artificial and arbitrary. Looking to the future, its point of departure seems a fixed base from which all that follows proceeds. Looking to the past, its present position seems but the result of what has gone before. Its present position is the juncture of two eternities, the child of the one, and the father of the other. In the ascending scale each cause becomes an effect; in the descending scale each effect becomes a cause. This view is the only one which can make history a rational study, a study adapted to the reason. The inquiry after causes (which includes the inquiry after results) is that which distinguishes reason in man from reason in brutes; and human reason can never be satisfied until it reaches a cause which is not also an effect. This procedure of the reason is beautifully illustrated by Villars:[1]

> "A man entirely unacquainted with the course of a river, arriving upon its banks, and seeing it here flowing in an extensive plain, there confined in a narrow channel, in another place foaming at the leap of a cataract, such a man would regard the first turn of the stream where it might lie concealed by a gorge from his eye as the origin of the river; the cataract would produce a similar illusion. Having reached the source at last, he would consider the mountain from which it issued as the primary cause of the river. He would soon, however, reflect that the bowels of the mountain must soon be exhausted by so constant a stream. He will observe the accumulation of clouds, the rains, without which the drained mountain would furnish no source. Thus, then, the clouds become the primary cause; but it is the winds which, by sweeping the vast seas, produce the clouds, and it is the sun which draws them from the sea. But whence comes this power in the sun? Thus he is soon drawn into the inquiries of speculative physics, by his search after a cause, after an absolute principle from which he may deduce, in the last resort, the explication of so many phenomena."

The like limitation must be laid down in reference to the *results* of this great revolution. The human reason, as it is never satisfied in the research of causes until it reaches a cause which is not in its turn also an effect, so in the research of results, it is never satisfied until it reaches an effect which is not also a cause. It seeks an *end* as it seeks a *beginning*. But we must end very far short of the end, as we

[1] *Essai sur L'Esprit et l'Influence de La Reformation*, p. 1, s. 1.

began very far short of the beginning. "Art is long and time is fleeting."

Using the term cause in the wide sense as before defined, we notice as the first cause—

I. The universal corruption which had existed in the church and in society for ages. This corruption was so enormous as to work its own cure.[1] The issue was reformation or death. The church, which was designed to be a wholesome leaven in the centre of the depraved mass of humanity, and, by its powerful though silent working, to transform the mass into the likeness of itself, became an evil leaven, and transformed the mass into the likeness of its own corruption. The opinion which some genteel and fashionable people, both in England and in this country, are so industriously propagating, and so many simpletons are believing, that the religion of the Middle Age was a simple,

[1] Bossuet, in his *Histoire des Variations*, *L. I.*, quotes Cardinal Julian as saying to Pope Eugene IV. that the disorders of the German clergy were so great as to stir up the hatred of the people against the whole ecclesiastical order; and that if these disorders were not corrected there was reason to fear that the laity would attack the clergy after the fashion of the Hussites, as they were already boldly threatening to do; that if the German clergy were not properly reformed, *another heresy would soon arise, far more dangerous than that of Bohemia;* that men would begin to believe that they would be offering a sacrifice acceptable to God in abusing and plundering the ecclesiastics as a race odious to God and men, and sunk in the depths of wickedness; that this hatred of the people for the sacred order would extend itself to the court of Rome, which would be regarded as the cause of all these evils, *because it neglected to apply the needful remedy.* "God," adds the Cardinal, "prevents us from seeing our perils, as he is accustomed to do to those whom he intends to punish. The fire is kindled before our eyes, and we run into it." This was Julian's idea of the manner in which the evil would work its own cure. The world was calling for a reformation of the church "in *head* and members"; but the blind guides would not reform the *head.* Hence that "other heresy more dangerous than Husstism" *did* arise, which proceeded upon the supposition that the See of Rome was the fountain of corruption, and must be either reformed or destroyed.

fervent, devout religion, worthy of the imitation of all ages. is a sheer and mischievous delusion. The religion of that age is not to be estimated by a noble hymn here and there like the "Dies Iræ," or by an occasional excerpt from an Anselm, or a Bernard, or a Richard of St. Victor, breathing a true spirit of love and devotion to Christ. Nobody doubts that God had his chosen ones all through these ages of gross superstition, will-worship, and idolatry, who were sufficiently enlightened to weep in the solitude of their cells over the darkness and corruption of the times, and sufficiently bold to testify against it. But the tears and testimony of these good men are themselves proofs that the mighty current which they were endeavoring to stem was too strong for them; not to say that they were themselves so much infected with the prevailing errors as to render their testimony, in a great measure, nugatory and vain. Let us notice some of these testimonies in regard to the condition of the court of Rome, the very head and centre of the church.

These testimonies are so numerous that one scarcely knows where to begin or to end. We cite, however, two or three as they are given in the *Pope and Council*, a work emanating from a Romanist source, and written in the interest of the Liberal or "Old" Catholic party on the continent of Europe, the party represented by such names as those of Döllinger and Hyacinthe. We have not the means of verifying these testimonies, but we apprehend that no one who will compare the characters of the men whose names have just been mentioned with the characters of those who have set themselves for the defence of the late council at Rome will be at all troubled by any denial on the part of these last of the genuineness of the testimonies.

Among the bishops of the time of Innocent IV. (pope), 1243–1254, there was not one more highly honored than Grostête, Bishop of Lincoln, nor one for a long time more devoted to the pope; indeed, so devoted that he acknowledged, in acordance with the Gratian and the Gregorian system, that he held his episcopal jurisdiction by delegation from the papal. This man, disgusted with the corruptions which, like a poisonous miasma, penetrated from the Roman court into every portion of the church, and especially with the hypocrisy exhibited in declaring the taking of interest for money a mortal sin, while the papal usurers and brokers were exhausting the churches and corporations in all countries with usurious imposts, wrote a letter to the pope shortly before his death, reproaching him with his tyranny and sharply warning him to repent.[1]

Jacob of Vitry (afterwards made a cardinal), after making some stay at the court of Rome, wrote to a friend (1216) that "it had lost every vestige of real church spirit," and that "its members were so busy with secular and temporal things, with kings and kingdoms, law-suits and quarrels, that they scarcely allowed a syllable to be spoken about spiritual things." Later, when Pope Nicholas III. wanted to make John of Parma, General of the Minorites, a cardinal, he declined, saying, "The Roman church hardly concerns itself with anything but wars and juggleries; *for the salvation of souls it takes no care.*"

St. Hildegard, the famous prophetess on the Rhine, highly honored by popes and emperors, prophesied of the popes as early as 1170: "They seize upon us like ravening beasts, with their power of binding and loosing, and through them the whole church is withered. The pride of the popes, who no longer observe any religion, will be brought low." So St. Bridget, the northern prophetess, who lived in Rome some two centuries later, calls the pope worse than Lucifer, "a murderer of the souls entrusted to him, who condemns the innocent and sells the elect for filthy lucre." Durandus

[1] See, besides, the curious story of an old monastic chronicler touching a visit of Grostête to the pope after his (Grostête's) death, in *Pope and Council*, and in Milman's *History of Latin Christianity*, VI., 293.

(bishop) says "the Roman court interprets *omnia traham ad me ipsum* (John xii. 32, in the Vulg.) as authorizing its appropriating the rights of all others exclusively to itself, and that the Roman church is reviled in every country; that every one is ashamed of her, and charges her with corrupting the whole clergy, whose immorality has exposed them to universal hatred." Yet this Durandus maintained the "Donation of Constantine," and the rights which flowed from that stupendous fraud.

But we need make no more citations from Romanists to show that even in their judgment the "head-centre" of the church was wholly rotten in their day. The love of money was the master-lust of those who boasted of being the successors of Peter and Paul, the two apostles who have left the most solemn warnings on record against this very lust. But the infatuated people continued to believe that the popes were the successors of Peter and Paul, while their lives were the lives of Ananias and Sapphira, of Simon Magus, and Demas. Protestants have been unjustly charged with originating that interpretation of the Babylon of the Apocalypse which makes it the symbol of the Roman church. Every reader of church history knows that this interpretation was very common among the Franciscans of the Middle Age. Even St. Bonaventura (1274), whom the popes had loaded with honors, and who was bound by the closest ties to Rome as a cardinal and general of his order, did not hesitate, in his Commentary on the Apocalypse, to declare Rome to be the harlot who makes kings and nations drunk with the wine of her whoredoms. For in Rome, he said, the dignities of the church were bought and sold; there did the princes and rulers of the church assemble, dishonoring God by their incontinence, adherents of Satan, and plunderers of the flock of Christ. He adds that the prelates, corrupted by Rome, infect the clergy with their vices; and the clergy, by their evil example of avarice and profligacy, poison and lead to perdition the whole Christian people. It was not, therefore, from a blind Ghibelline party spirit that Dante, too, applied to the popes the Apocalyptic prophecy. He had read Bonaventura, and puts directly into his mouth in paradise the denunciation of the covetous policy of the court of Rome.[1] And to the same effect Petrarch is quoted, calling Rome "the impious Babylon, nest of treasons, in which all the poison of the world is cherished, in bondage to surfeit and drunkenness, an execrable harlot, full of luxury and riot, an asylum of all heresies, a prison in which every good thing is extinguished, and every evil and abominable thing is nourished, a rebel against Christ and his apostles, in order to make divinities of Venus and Bacchus."[2] In unison with these invectives of the poets of the Renaissance in the fourteenth century, hear also the wailings of the Italian monk:

Quisquis opes sacras nummo reperire profano
  Quærit, eat Romam, sacra sunt venalia Romæ,
Templa, sacerdotes, altaria, sacra, coronæ,
  Ignes, thura, preces, cœlum est venale Deusque.

Compare Revelation xviii. 11–13. No wonder, when everything was put up for sale in Rome, that men who had any fear of God or sense of decency should identify the church in that city with the city described in this chapter of the Revelation.

We have dwelt upon this feature of the horrible wickedness of the court of Rome, because the love of money, when it takes full possession of a man, or of a body of men, banishes everything which is holy, just, and good. It is a demon whose name is legion. "They that will be rich," says Paul, "fall into temptation and a snare, and into many foolish and hurtful lusts which drown men in destruction and perdition. For the love of money is the root of all evil, which, while some coveted after, they have erred from the

[1] See *Pope and Council*, pp. 227, 228. [2] See *Tur.*, Vol. IV., p. 14.

faith, and pierced themselves through with many sorrows." (1 Tim. vi. 9, 10.) Hence, there was no evil passion which did not run riot in Rome. Conspicuous among these was the lust of uncleanness, a lust associated in the Bible constantly with avarice, and in the Greek tongue expressed even by the same word. "Sacerdotes, episcopi *avari, veneri ventrique dediti ignominiâ notati tribuque moti sint*," says a Council of Cologne.[1] The Council of Aix-la-Chapelle, A. D. 836, says of the nunneries, that "in some places they seemed to be rather brothels than monasteries."[2] The nunneries generally became brothels, we imagine, when they became rich; and they generally became rich, though organized under the vow of poverty as well as under the vow of chastity.[3] The history of the papacy from 881–956 is called by modern historians the period of the "Papal Pornocracy," because the popes, during this period, were generally governed by their mistresses or harlots, and are called by some of their own people "apostatic" instead of "apostolic."[4]

The apostle mentions "erring from the faith" as another evil flowing from the love of money. The numberless illustrations of this connection between the greed for money and heresy, which the history of mediæval Rome affords, may all be passed over except one, and that one is, *instar omnium*, since it was the occasion for the outbreak of the Reforma-

[1] Cited by Brucker, *Hist. Phil.*, 3, 602.

[2] Harduin, *Concilia*, tom. 4, p. 1397, No. 7, 8, cited in Murdock's Trans. of Mosheim's *Ch. Hist.*, Cent. IX.

[3] For specimens of the Anacreontic songs of the holy monks, see Wright's Early Mysteries, and other Latin Poems, cited by Milman in his *Lat. Christianity*, B. 14, c. 4.

[4] Baronius (Anno 900) acknowledges that the Holy Apostolic See suffered things *indigna, turpia, deformia, execranda, abominanda;* but ascribes them to the fact that the emperors elected the popes! The truth is, however, that the emperors in this very century *reformed* the popedom. See Professor Bryce's *Holy Roman Empire*. The history of the popes may well gravel the defenders of papal infallibility. One of the champions of Rome is said to have answered the objection to this dogma drawn from the noto-

tion. We allude, of course, to the sale of indulgences. Licenses to sin had been formerly issued for ages, certainly since the time of the infamous Pope John XXII., who, among all the Johns who sat in the Roman See, was, perhaps, the worst, with the exception of John XXIII., condemned and deposed by the Council of Constance, for simony, extortion, poisoning, adultery, incest, etc. This sale of indulgences was a monstrous and all-comprehending iniquity. 1. It involved, on the part of the pope, a blasphemous usurpation of the prerogatives of God, both as Lawgiver and Saviour. 2. It abrogated the whole gospel of grace by making its privileges a matter of money. The affair with Tetzel in Germany, and with Samson in Switzerland, is sometimes represented as one of those small occasions upon which great revolutions begin (like Hampden's ship-money); but we cannot imagine a more appalling form in which the hatred of the devil for both God and man could present itself in opposition to the gospel than this pretended claim to remit all punishment of sin for money. It was nothing less than a dethroning of him whom God had exalted a Prince and a Saviour, and an enthroning of him who was a liar and a murderer from the beginning. It was making a mock of sin, and a pouring of contempt upon the blood and agony of the incarnate Son of God. The world could endure no more. Tetzel and Samson were the last drops of bitterness which made the cup run over. Men had for ages been gnawing their tongues for pain under the scorpion stings

---

rious *ignorance* of theology which distinguished the clergy of the city of Rome, by alleging the case of God's speaking through Balaam's ass. But here is a case of abandoned wickedness, not of brutish ignorance--a far worse case. We suppose the answer may be found in the fact of God's speaking through Balaam himself, in spite of his love of the wages of iniquity. What other view could Bossuet have had when he wrote the introduction to his *Histoire des Variations?* Surely, he must have forgotten that the first pope, St. Peter himself, said, that "*holy* men of old spake as they were moved by the Holy Ghost." (2 Peter i. 21.)

of papal and priestly tyranny; and they welcomed the testimony of Luther and Zwingle as the voice of messengers from the skies.[1]

II. Another cause is to be found in the testimony of those bodies of Christians in the Middle Age known as "Witnesses for the Truth." The testimony of the more enlightened men in the church of Rome, to which reference has already been made, had very little effect, because they not only continued in the communion of the church, but upheld the supremacy and practical infallibility of the popes. As the papacy was the chief source and bulwark of corruption, there could be no chance for a reformation, while the reformers continued te revere and maintain its prerogatives. The empire of Rome papal was mightier than the empire of Rome pagan. The dominion of the latter was the dominion of the sword; the dominion of the former was the dominion of opinion. From the time that Charlemagne condescended to receive the name and crown of the Emperor of the West, until the time of Hildebrand, all Europe believed that the world had been subjected by God himself to the rule of pope and emperor as his vicars—the one in the spiritual, the other in the tem-

[1] It is instructive to compare the effect of Luther's preaching in Wittenberg with the effect of Savonarola's in Florence about twenty years before. They both preached against indulgences. The one was honored and applauded, the other burnt. They were so near together in time, that we can account for the difference in effect only by the difference in place and people. Luther preached to Germans living at a great distance from Rome, Savonarola to Italians. "Never," says Villars, "were there so many atheists as in the country and neighborhood of the sovereign pontiffs." "The nearer people are to Rome," says Machiavel (quoted by Villars), "the less religion they have. The scandalous example, and the crimes of the court of Rome, have been the cause that Italy has lost entirely all the principles of piety and every sentiment of religion. We Italians, then, owe this obligation to the church and to priests that we have become reprobates and villains." (Discourse on the First Decade of Livy, B. 1, c. 12.) Truly, "reprobates and villains" are terms not too harsh to be applied to men who could take part with such a man as Pope Alexander VI. against such a man as Savonarola!

poral, sphere. From the time of Hildebrand to the reign of Boniface VIII., all Europe believed, with here and there a dissentient, that the two powers were not coördinate, but that the emperor was subordinate to the pope. Even the monarch that resisted the execution of his decrees within their territories, with few exceptions, acknowledged his supremacy. "They kissed the pope's feet"—to use Voltaire's words—"while they tied up his hands." One of the most impressive proofs of the power of this opinion is the extreme reluctance of Luther to break with the pope. The Holy See laughed at all the testimonies while it continued to be adored by the witnesses. It was only the witnesses who denounced the papacy as anti-Christ that were dragooned and burnt.

But there were such witnesses. The Cathari, the Paulicians,[1] the Waldenses, the Henricians, the Albigenses, and other bodies, contended with more or less purity and zeal that God was greater than the pope. The policy adopted towards these witnesses was that of the liar-murderer: first to slander, then to kill them. We know little about any of them, except the Waldenses, which is not derived from the indictments of their enemies. But as malice is blind, these indictments are not so skilfully drawn, as to hinder us from seeing that they had at least more truth than their enemies. The slanders are not only incredible, but monstrous.

The points in which their testimony was defective or erroneous were chiefly those which concerned ordinances of worship which God had ordained and the papacy had grossly perverted and abused. As, for example, the papacy had made the whole of religion to consist in external rites; had substituted the tithing of mint, anise and cummin for judgment, mercy, and faith; had converted the church, which Christ had designed to be his witness-bearer, and an institute for calling and training his elect, into a vast sacramental ma-

[1]On this body, see Faber's *Waldenses and Albigenses*, and Elliott's *Horæ Apocalypticæ*.

chine for turning out Christians; they went sometimes to the other extreme of rejecting the sacraments altogether. As baptism of infants was held to be their regeneration, some of them rejected infant baptism altogether. Countless thousands sealed their testimony with their lives, but their testimony was not lost. Whole bodies were exterminated, but others sprang up in their room. One of these bodies lived on in spite of fire and sword, and lives still: the inhabitants of those valleys in which the noble Claude of Turin, in the ninth century, had borne his faithful testimony against the idolatry of Rome. How does the providence of God encourage us to testify for the truth by this history of the Waldenses, and by the fact that these witnesses, whom the relentless persecution of ages has not been able to destroy, are now, while we write, preaching the glad tidings under the very walls of the Vatican, from which issued so many cruel thunderbolts against them! Truly, as the apostle says, "we can do nothing against the truth, but for the truth." These witnesses did not reform the church, only because "the fulness of times" had not come. But when Luther appeared, they were ready with a hearty welcome to him as a new witness (and in an unexpected quartor) for truths for which they and their fathers had suffered the loss of all things.

III. The next cause we shall notice is that great movement of the human mind which has been called the "Renaissance," or the "Revival of Letters." It is to be observed, in estimating the true force of this movement, that there is no necessary connection between the illumination of the mind, which is merely natural and secular, and the reformation of the heart and life. The Romanists in nominal christendom still greatly outnumber the Protestants, though the human mind, under the impetus it has received from the Protestant movement, has been intensely active, and has achieved marvellous victories in every department of science. Revealed religion is not subject to the law of progress in the same sense that other departments of knowledge are subject to it, and for this reason, that it is revealed. "It matters not at all," says Macaulay, "that the compass, printing, gun-powder, steam, gas, vaccination, and a thousand other discoveries and inventions, which were unknown to the fifth century, are familiar to the nineteenth. None of these discoveries and inventions have the smallest bearing on the question, whether a man is justified by faith alone, or whether the invocation of saints is an orthodox practice. We have no security for the future against the prevalence of any theological error that has ever prevailed in time past among Christian men. We are content that the world will never go back to the solar system of Ptolemy; nor is our confidence in the least shaken by the circumstances that even so great a man as Bacon rejected the theory of Galileo with scorn; for Bacon had not all the means of arriving at a sound conclusion which are within our reach, and which secure people who would not have been worthy to mend his pens from falling into his mistakes. But we are very differently affected when we reflect that Sir Thomas More was ready to die for the doctrine of transubstantiation. He was a man of eminent talents. He had all the information on the subject that we have, or that, while the world lasts, any human being will have. The absurdity of the literal interpretation was as great and as obvious in the sixteenth century as it is now. No progress that science has made, or will make, can add to what seems to us the overwhelming force of the argument against the real presence. We are, therefore, unable to understand why what Sir Thomas More believed respecting transubstantiation may not be believed to the end of time by men of equal abilities and honesty. But Sir Thomas More is one of the choice specimens of human wisdom and virtue; and the doctrine of transubstantiation is a kind of proof charge. A faith which stands that test will stand any test."[1]

[1] Essay on Ranke's *History of the Popes.*

At this very day, in sober Christian communities, and under the shadow of the halls of science, a band of strolling, thieving gypsies will carry off no small amount of revenue derived from telling people's fortunes. People who can have their fortune, told are not proof against any superstitions, however absurd or pernicious. "A very common knowledge of history, a very little observation of life," says the brilliant essayist before cited, "will suffice to prove that no learning, no sagacity, affords a security against the greatest errors on subjects relating to the invisible world. Johnson, incredulous on all other points, was a ready believer in miracles and apparitions. He would not believe in Ossian; but he believed in second sight. He would not believe in the earthquake of Lisbon; but he believed in the Cock Lane ghost."

Another consideration of great importance not noticed by Macaulay is, that the heart has fully as much to do with faith in God's truth as the head. The natural posture of man in regard to this kind of truth is one of hostility. The truth comes as a *conqueror*, and is therefore received as an *enemy*. Even Hobbes confessed that if it had been contrary to men's interest and lust of dominion that the three angles of a triangle should be equal to two right angles, they would either have denied that truth, or burnt the books of mathematics.

When, therefore, we mention the Renaissance as one of the causes of the Reformation, we do not mean to assert any necessary connection between the two, but only that, in the ordering of divine Providence, the former was not merely a forerunner, but a powerful promoter of the latter. The revival of learning was, in its own nature, purely worldly and secular. The days and nights of the great majority of the scholars were given to the study of the pagan writers of Greece and Rome. Erasmus was, no doubt, to the end of his life, more of a pagan than a Protestant, in spite of his labors on the records of the Christian faith. Ulrich von Hutten, in the merciless sarcasms of the *Epistolæ Obscurorum Virorum* had little zeal for the gospel, and Luther declined his aid. *Non tali auxilio.* Indeed, the very name by which they were known indicates this view of the spirit of the revivalists. They were "humanists"; men cultivating a merely human literature, and cultivating it in the interests of humanity as contradistinguished from the interests of the church, which had for ages controlled all thinking and enslaved it. The movement was a rebellion of the human mind against a tyranny which refused to acknowledge that God had presided over the mind of Greek and Roman pagan, as well as over the mind of Greek and Roman Christian. The Hebrew and Greek Scriptures were studied in the same spirit, for they, too, were practically proscribed, and in many places proscribed by statute.[1]

Still, the Hebrew and Greek Scriptures *were* studied. Whatever the *animus* of Erasmus, his Greek Testament was a powerful instrument in promoting the Reformation. As

[1] "Even the faculty of theology at Paris declared at this time that religion was undone if the study of Greek and Hebrew were permitted. A monk in Hochstraten's army of ignoramuses said, 'They have invented a new language which they call Greek; you must be on your guard against it; it is the mother of all heresy.' I observe in the hands of many persons a book written in that language, and which they call the *New Testament.* It is a book full of daggers and poison. As to the Hebrew, my dear brethren, it is certain that all those who learn it become instantaneously Jews."

"This is a sample," says the Prize Essayist of the French Academy, "of the papal spirit of that age."

For such a spirit as this the Renaissance had infinite contempt, as well as for the spirit of mediæval mysticism. Aristotle himself, though a Greek, was hurled from his throne, because his name was associated with the dismal quarrels of Scotists and Thomists. People were content to gratify their tastes and their senses, caring little for worship, and still less for doctrine. They did not revolt against the church, but they had no enthusiasm for her; and they had enthusiasm for whatever was fresh and graceful and intelligible. See Bryce's *Holy Roman Empire*, p. 312. The literary clique of Weimar, with Gœthe at the head, a circle of polished scholars with no religion above the "elegant mythology" of Greece, will give us a good idea of the religious character of the leaders of the Renaissance. Gœthe professed his readiness to worship a model of Myron's statue of a cow and her sucking calf!

in the days of good King Josiah, so now the discovery of the "book of the law" made a stir among the dry bones.

IV. The last cause we shall mention is the political condition of Europe at the beginning of the sixteenth century. It would require more space than can be accorded to this article to go into anything like a full discussion of the causes which produced the political condition in which the Reformation found the nations of Europe. We beg leave to refer the reader who may wish to investigate this subject to the very interesting work of Professor Bryce, of Oxford, on the *Holy Roman Empire*. All we can now attempt is a very rapid sketch.

The prime necessity of western Europe, after the fall of the western division of the old Roman empire, was *unity*. Society had been thrown back into chaos by the invasions of the northern tribes, and the only law which was recognized was the law of the strongest. Wave after wave of violence and blood swept over the land from the north, and a fiercer deluge threatened to overwhelm it from the south, in a Saracen invasion. In the eighth century arose the first of the great Carlovingian line of princes, Charles Martel. In the battle of Poictiers he gave an effectual check to the Moslem power. But it was reserved for the genius of his grandson, Charles the Great (Charlemagne), to conceive the idea of restoring the western empire, and so of restoring civil order. His comprehensive mind perceived that the scheme could not in any way be so speedily accomplished, if accomplished it could be at all, as by enlisting the aid of the church in the west, and especially the aid of its leading bishop at Rome, the centre of the old empire. The church was the only organization that could pretend to anything like extensive power combined with unity. It was the only body that could confront the violence of the times with the power of opinion. And Charlemagne had the sagacity to understand that the empire of Rome could be restored, even in shadow, only by the force of opinion. When that colossal structure tumbled into ruin, it had done what no great empire had ever done before: it had unified the races subjected to its sway. It had made what was, in the republic and in the earlier empire, a proud distinction, the common possession of all the natives of the Roman world. The working of the equalized and equalizing Roman law contributed to bring about the same result, the assimilation of the races, and the merging of Greek, Jew, Scythian in Roman. The Greek and the Jew made the only successful resistance to this mighty process of fusion. Now, this tendency was precisely that which the gospel itself fostered. It was a catholic dispensation of the true religion; and the church which it produced, unlike the Jewish church of one nation, was the church of all nations. It was not wonderful, therefore, that, on the one side, the Roman should be considered Catholic; and that, on the other side, the Catholic should be considered Roman. In short, Roman and Catholic meant the same thing, in different aspects. Considered as a Roman, a man was the subject of the emperor; considered as a Catholic, he was the subject of the Roman bishop.

But these two dominions were only different sides of the same dominion. Ever since the time of Constantine the idea of a theocracy had been growing in the church. Its first form was pagan, the form of the old Roman republic, derived originally from the Tuscan lawyer-priests, the old Italian *Ulema*. This was the only form in which Constantine himself knew it. But after the establishment of the Christian religion it took on a Jewish form, and the relation sustained by the emperor to the church was like that of David and his successors to the priesthood in the Jewish theocracy. The kingly and priestly offices which were united in the invisible head of the theocracy reigning in heaven were separated in his representatives on earth. The kingly was given to the emperor; the priestly to the bishop of Rome. The Greek differed from this view only in challenging the priestly office for the bishop of new Rome, Constantinople.

This was the *theory* in the west after Charlemagne's time, and, as Professor Bryce has shown, theory was more potent in the Middle Age perhaps than in any other period of the world's history. Hence, the emperor was considered as a sort of head of the church *in temporalibus*, as the Roman bishop was head of it *in spiritualibus*. The church convicted of heresy, and the emperor made the crusade with fire and sword. If this theory had been fully carried out, and the two heads of the church, or ecclesiastical kingdom, had continued to coöperate as they did in the days of the great Charles himself, the bondage of Europe would have been, as far as we can see, perpetual and hopeless. But, happily for Europe and the world, Hildebrand arose, a pope of unbounded ambition as well as of surpassing ability, who could not endure *two* heads of the church; and from his time down to the Reformation the theory which has been above expounded, while it continued to captivate the imaginations of solitary dreamers in their cells, was seldom respected in practice, respected by popes of the emperor's creation, and not always by these.

The empire fell with the fall of the Hohenstaufen. Founded or revived by Charlemagne as an universal monarchy in A. D. 800; again erected in A. D. 962, on the narrower but firmer basis of the German kingdom, by Otto the Great, its pretensions were maintained for several centuries by a line of monarchs of unrivalled vigor and abilities, against the rebels in Italy and the ecclesiastical power. But each successive emperor entered the strife with resources scantier than his predecessors; each had been more decisively vanquished by the pope, the cities and the princes. That it did not expire utterly with the fall of the Hohenstaufen, but lived on for six hundred years more, till it became a piece of antiquarianism hardly more venerable than ridiculous—till, as Voltaire said, all that could be said about it was that it was neither "holy," nor "Roman," nor "empire"—was owing partly to the belief, still unshaken, that it was a necessary part of the world's order, yet chiefly to the connection, which was by this time indissoluble, with the German kingdom. But even as German king the power of the emperor was broken. He had been compelled, by his struggles in Italy, to relax the vigor of his resistance against the turbulent ambition of the nobles in Germany, to grant them privileges which they abused. So that at the era of the Reformation we find one of his electors able to bring so great an emperor as Charles V. to terms on the field of battle. His hereditary jealousy of the popes, combined with the independence of his own princes, humanly speaking, prevented the Reformation from being extinguished in its very beginning. Nay, it does not seem paradoxical to assert that the hostility of Charles to the new movement, under all the complications of his position, was more favorble to that movement than a merely nominal patronage of it might have been.

The view we have presented will derive additional confirmation from a comparison of Germany with France at this period. Under Charlemagne these two countries were under the same government, or rather (as unwilling as the French are to acknowledge it) France was a part of the German empire, and the great Charles was a German. The Franks were Germans, and conquered the Gauls, who had been conquered before by the great Caius Julius. Towards the close of the ninth century the Carlovingian empire was extinguished, and France began to assume the position of an independent state, under the genius of the House of Burgundy. By the year 1272, when the first of the House of Hapsburg was placed upon the throne of the empire, France was stronger than Germany. "Rudolf," says Bryce, "was as conspicuously a weaker sovereign than Philip III. of France, as the Franconian Emperor Henry III. had been stronger than the Capetian Philip I. In every other state of Europe the tendency of events had been to centralize the administration and increase the power of the monarch, even in England, not to diminish it; in Germany alone had political union become weaker and the independence of the princes more confirmed."

The internal political weakness of Germany was the strength of the Reformation. The internal strength of France was the weakness of the Reformation in that country. In Germany it grew and became firmly established after many a storm of fire and blood; and now we behold a new German empire strong enough to humble France in the very dust, erecting itself in the midst of Europe as a Protestant power; while France, which put out the light of the gospel with blood, is *becoming Ultramontane and surrendering those "liberties"* which her kings and bishops defended for centuries against the ambition of popes and cardinals!

And here, for the present, we make an end.

PROGRESS IN THEOLOGY.

IT is alleged (*e. g.*, Newman Smythe, in the *Catholic Presbyterian* for March, 1883) that there must be *progress* in theology, because it is a science, and all sciences are subject to the law of progress.

"The facts are given to us in nature and the Bible, and we must interpret those facts for ourselves according to the light we have, more or less. The facts of astronomy, for example, have always been the same, but the science of astronomy has been progressing for ages," etc.

1. We concede that theology is a science in so far as it is *systemized* knowledge. No body of divinity is presented to us in the Bible. The creeds of the Reformation era or the Westminster Confession, as compared with the Apostles' Creed, indicate progress.

2. But it is not true that in theology the facts are left wholly to the interpretation of our own reason, as they are in science. The great fundamental facts are interpreted for us; the theory is given as well as the facts; and this interpretation is the key to the interpretation of all the facts which are not interpreted. Take the Epistles to the Romans and the Hebrews as examples for the meaning of Christ's work, his incarnation, life, death, resurrection, etc. Indirectly, we have the moral condition of the race of man, the work of the Spirit, etc. There has been progress in the knowledge of these interpretations, and consequences not expressly stated in Scripture may be deduced from them; but we have the fundamental theology *given*, and all developments must be in harmony with them. (See 2 John, vs. 9, and Jude, vs. 3, in the Revision.) In science no such germinal

theory is *given* or revealed. It is all an affair of the reason, and the most widely accepted theory is liable to give room for some other which will explain the facts more completely. Even the law of gravitation, operating inversely, as the square of the distance, may be superseded by some other law, for God has not revealed the law. But no such thing can take place in theology, because God *has* revealed the theory. The very idea of progress implies some fixed points, a *terminus a quo*. If the starting-point is movable, the distance between that and any advanced point may remain the same, and hence no progress, *e. g.*, the law of gravitation in astronomy, of definite proportions in chemistry, etc. If there is any point fixed in theology, it is the idea of God; and yet these men of progress will have it (see Bruce, in the *Catholic Presbyterian*, *ut supra*) that the idea of God in the orthodox theology is not "ethical," etc.; so the idea of the incarnation, according to Newman Smythe, involves the notion of the incarnation as a necessary emanating process in the nature of God, so going back to Osiander and the old mystics. *Such* progress would ruin any other science.

Illustrate further by the dogma of the Trinity. The fixed points from which the church started were the unity of God and the divinity of Christ.

3. Progress in science has been made in a twofold way: (1), By ascertaining the meaning of certain facts, and then (2), by using this interpretation to explain other facts. The first belongs to Kepler, Newton, Davy, Faraday, Harvey, etc.; the second to the ordinary workers in science. But in theology the great *discoverers* have been inspired men (1 Cor. ii. 9–16), and the theologians since, if they have been sound, have only aimed at understanding their discoveries and applying them. True progress in all the sciences which concern *men*, their nature and their relations, consists in applying principles already known. Now and then a discoverer arises even in moral philosophy (*e. g.*, Butler, law of

habit); but generally the progress has consisted in applying and developing principles already known. Hence, there is no opposition between progress and conservatism properly understood. Conservatism is the conserving of *principles;* progress is the extending of the application of these principles. (John xvi. 13.) The meaning of the phrase is not "into all truth," but "to the whole truth"; *i. e.*, (1), The apostles should be led to the whole truth necessary to their personal salvation and to their office as the revealers of God's will, in virtue of which they became, along with Jesus, "the chief corner-stone," the foundation of the church's faith in all ages. (2), The people of God in all ages should, in the study of the rule of faith, be led to the whole truth necessary for them in their varying circumstances, temptations, etc. There is a *development of theology*, though not that of the papists or of the pantheistic doctors of Germany. (See Trench's *Hulsean Lectures*, Lecture I., pp. 74ff.)

4. This view is confirmed by the fact that those who contend for progress in theology in the ordinary sense have generally ended in denying the faith of the church in capital points. (See Tallock and Newman Smythe, especially the latter, in the *Catholic Presbyterian* for February and March, 1883.) By the way, the progress of the latter writer is shown by Watts (in the April number of the *Catholic Presbyterian*, 1883) to be a *re*gress, in some particulars, to the old Lutheran theology. So Tyndal, among the men of "advanced thought," has gone back to Democritus (360 B. C.) for his theory of the universe. Truly, "The Lord taketh the wise in his own craftiness."

5. The theology of the Bible is "the science of religion," and, therefore, must remain substantially the same. As in all the progress of science and civilization the essential features of man remain the same; as man has not become, and never will become, wise enough to dispense with bread and water, so whatever progress theology may make, or pretend

to make, man will always need just such a Saviour as is presented in the Bible, one who offered himself a sacrifice to satisfy divine justice and to reconcile us to God, and ascended to heaven to send down the spirit of regeneration and sanctification and consolation.

On technical precision in theology, as connected with the spiritual life of the church, see Shedd's *History of Doctrine*, Vol. I., pp. 247–'48; Hodge's *Systematic Theology*, I., pp. 166ff.

SCHAFF'S CREEDS OF CHRISTENDOM.[1]

DR. SCHAFF'S design is a grand one. He proposes to set before us in these volumes, not the results of the thinking of the individual minds, not what the most illustrious doctors of the church have thought upon questions no less awful than the being of God and the eternal destiny of man, but the products of the mind of the church itself—of that vast community which professes to be the witness of God and of his Christ in the midst of a world full of darkness, pollution and shame.

These creeds are not the expressions of *opinion* upon problems which have engaged and confounded the inquiries of philosophers. They are confessions of *faith* in the solutions of those problems by him who is the source of all truth as he is the source of all being; solutions contained in a book divinely inspired, divinely authenticated, and divinely interpreted. The church, in these creeds, declares that faith for which her members are willing to die, and for which hundreds of thousands of her members have willingly died; that faith which has confronted the lies of the devil from age to age, and will continue to confront them until the King of truth shall appear to settle the controversy forever. These creeds are the banners of the church. They have passed through many a storm of fire and blood; and to him who is acquainted with the history of the church there is scarcely a line which does not tell of some struggle with the powers of darkness. No record is more worthy of our study.

---

[1] *Bibliotheca Symbolica Ecclesiæ Universalis. The Creeds of Christendom, with a History and Critical Notss.* By Philip Schaff, D. D., LL. D., Professor of Biblical Literature in the Union Theological Seminary, N. Y. In three volumes. New York: Harper & Bros. 1877. Appeared in *Southern Presbyterian Review*, April, 1878.

The design of our author, it is needless to say, is not altogether new. There are very many collections of creeds. But, so far as we know, his plan is more comprehensive than any which has been attempted before. His work, as the title implies, is a symbolical library of the church universal. It contains, besides the principal creeds of the great historical churches, those also of many of the small "sects" and offshoots of those churches, and even the confessions drawn up by individual doctors who are supposed to have had, or known from history to have had, a sort of representative significance. The comprehensiveness of the plan can be better indicated by some extracts from the table of contents. The creeds are contained in the two last volumes. The first of these contains the "Creeds of the Greek and Latin Churches." Under this head we find: I. "Scripture Confessions"—of Nathaniel, Peter, Thomas; the Baptismal Formula; the Mystery of Godliness; the Elementary Articles (Heb. vi. 1, 2), etc. II. Anti-Nicene and Nicene Rules of Faith and Baptismal Creeds—Ignatius of Antioch; Irenæus of Gaul (three formulas); Tertullian (three formulas); Novatian; Eusebius of Cæsarea; Cyril of Jerusalem (two formulas); Epiphanius of Cyprus (two formulas); Apostolical Constitutions, etc. III. Œcumenical Creeds—The Apostles'; Nicene; Chalcedonian; Athanasian, etc. IV. Roman Creeds—including the Papal Syllabus and the Vatican Decrees of 1870. V. Greek and Russian Creeds—Mogilas, Dositheus, Philaret. VI. Old Catholic Union Creeds of 1874 and 1875. The second volume contains the creeds of the Evangelical Protestant Churches. Under this head we find: I. Creeds of the Lutheran Church. II. Creeds of the Evangelical Reformed Churches (besides the well-known principal symbols, such as the two Helvetic, Heidelberg Catechism, the Gallic, Belgic, etc.); the sixty-seven articles of Zwingli, 1523; the ten Theses of Berne, 1528; the Lambeth Articles, 1595; the Irish Articles, 1615, etc. The author gives us also the Westminster Confession in Latin as well as in English, and the Shorter Catechism of the same great assembly of divines. III. Modern Protestant Creeds—Congregational Confessions (Savoy, 1658; Boston National Council, 1865; Oberlin National Council, 1865); Baptist Confessions (Philadelphia, 1786; New Hampshire, 1833; Free Will Baptist, 1866); Quaker, Moravian, Methodist, 1784; Reformed Episcopal, 1875; and last, but by no means least, we imagine, in Dr. Schaff's estimation, "The Nine Articles of the Evangelical Alliance," 1846. Our readers will perceive from this table that our author has performed a valuable service to the church, and especially to our ministers. No pastor ought to be without a collection of the creeds. Yet very few of them are near enough to public libraries to have access to the collections of Hase, Niemeyer, Strütwolf, Augusti, etc. Still less have they salaries large enough to admit of their buying books such as these. But here is a book which contains all that is necessary for the ordinary uses of a pastor; and if he be too poor to buy, and has not the good fortune to have a friend of a longer purse who will give it to him, let him "sell his garment and buy one." It is a sword that he cannot afford to be without.

In these two volumes, however, Dr. Schaff appears only as a faithful collector and editor. It is in the first that he appears as an author; and it is the first, therefore, which claims chiefly our notice as reviewers. It is entitled "A History of the Creeds of Christendom." No one who is acquainted with the author's labors in the field of church history can entertain a doubt as to his fitness to write such a history. His learning and his industry are known to all men and are worthy of all praise. His impartiality is exemplary. This is, no doubt, due in some, perhaps in large, measure, to the integrity, purity, and simplicity of his character. But he is not a little indebted, we think, to his German education for it. In his native country, learning is so general, so extensive, so thorough, and literary activity and competition so great, as to secure speedy protest and exposure for any misrepresentation of facts, whether wilful or undesigned. Scholars there acquire a very wholesome habit of cautiousness in making statements of facts, or in proposing theories which, instead of affording a plausible explanation of the facts, do them manifest violence. There are exceptions, of course, to all rules; and polemics may be found in Germany to-day as bitter as Calovious and as one-sided as Godfrey Arnold ever were. But the prevailing tone is what we have described. Even the infidel, by his impartial (or indifferent) researches, has advanced the cause of truth; and the scholars of the papal communion in Germany have exposed themselves, by their moderation and candor, to the perils of the prohibitory or expurgatory index.

Our author's charity is also large—too large. It does almost literally and absolutely "think no evil." He seems to forget at times that "charity is no fool;" that the "sins of some men are open beforehand, going before to judgment;" that there are human "dogs" to whom we are forbidden to give that which is holy, and human "swine" before whom we are not allowed to cast our pearls; and who, therefore, can be known or righteously judged to be dogs and swine. Even charity must discriminate, or incur the risk of rejoicing (or of making others to rejoice) in iniquity as well as in the truth. Universal praise is universal detraction, because it reduces all men to a level. As one example of the spurious charity we have ventured to ascribe to our author, take the statement on page 153 concerning Pius IX. and Cardinal Manning: "Both these eminent and remarkable persons show how a sincere faith in a dogma which borders on blasphemy may, by a strange delusion or hallucination, be combined with rare purity and amiability of character."[1]

[1] Dr. Schaff says in another place (Vol. I., p. 165), of the dogma of infallibility. "It involves a blasphemous assumption, and makes the nearest

Our readers, then, will please note that a man's purity of character is not necessarily destroyed, or even seriously impaired, by the sin of blasphemy. For Dr. Schaff finds at least two men guilty of this sin, who are not only of pure character, but have "*rare* purity of character." And this blasphemy, be it observed, was not a sudden explosion produced by powerful temptation, and then immediately bewailed in dust and ashes, but deliberately meditated and resolved upon by the pope, who assembled the dignitaries of the whole body throughout the world to see him do it, and to sustain him by their suffrages in doing it; and constantly repeated and defended by the cardinal, who is not only a blasphemer, but an apostate. What can Dr. Schaff mean? That a man's faith has nothing to do with his moral character? Then what mean the innumerable declarations of Scripture about the necessity of *faith* in order to salvation? "He that *believeth* shall be saved; he that *believeth not* shall be damned." What mean these three thousand pages about creeds from our author's own hand? Is it all mere history? Have these blood-stained confessions, after all, nothing to do with purity of character? Our author will not say so. He thinks worthier of the truth and his own labors than to think so. What can he mean? That the pope and the English cardinal are not given to sensual vices and brutal pleasures, as so many popes and cardinals have been? That Pius is not such a pope as Borgia, nor Manning such a cardinal as Cossa? Or is purity so rare among popes and cardinals that average decency is to be regarded as *rare* purity? Or is Satan to be considered a person of rare purity because he is free from these vices? Perhaps the meaning is upright-

approach to the fulfilment of St. Paul's prophecy of the man of sin, 'who, as God, sitteth in the temple of God, showing himself that he is God.'" (2 Thess. ii. 4.) Justly and manfully spoken. He also calls the papacy (p. 185)—the whole system, as we understand him—a "colossal lie." We cannot pretend to the overflowing charity of our author; we are glad to have his authority for characterizing the system as it deserves.

ness in dealing with men. Then we ask, is a man's dealing with his fellowmen of more consequence than his dealing with God? Because a man respects the rights of his fellows, is he to be deemed of rare purity of character, although at the same time he is guilty, as Dr. Schaff believes he is, of an audacious usurpation of the prerogatives of his Maker? But, is it even dealing fairly with men, is it respecting their rights, to demand submission to a mortal like themselves claiming to be infallible, not only without evidence, but against the overwhelming evidence of reason, history, and Scripture, as bishops in the Vatican Council themselves demonstrated?

Dr. Schaff's good words in behalf of these two worthies remind of us of the like in one of Jeremy Bentham's biographers. After having said that "he had no doubt of Jeremy being an atheist," he proceeds: "We may be sorry for such things; but *if they are otherwise good men*, our sorrow will lead us rather to pity than to rage or hatred for them. As well might we rebuke those who are troubled with fever, as them that require to be convinced by touch, or taste, or ciphering, of the existence of a deity. Why may not men be suffered to believe what they please, or what they *can*, rather, about God and a future state, and all the mysteries of theology, as about any other subject of dispute or inquiry?" Dr. Schaff would be very ready with an answer to this foolish and wicked question. He has no sympathy whatever with those who assert that a man's creed is a matter of no consequence. If he had, he would never have taken the trouble to prepare these bulky volumes on creeds. And yet he has laid down a general proposition which involves two enormous errors. The *first* is, that blasphemy is not incompatible with rare purity of character; and the *second*, that the sincere belief of the blasphemous dogma is some sort of excuse for holding it and proclaiming it. Upon the first we have said enough. A few words upon the second.

By a sincere belief is meant, of course, a belief which is

not pretended or feigned. Now, we all admit that sincerity is better than hypocrisy. If a man professes to believe a lie, knowing it to be a lie, he adds the sin of hypocrisy to the sin of holding a lie. But how comes it to pass that any man believes a lie about God, especially a man who has in his hand what he professes to believe is a revelation from God, given for the very purpose of teaching him the truth concerning God? How came the pope to believe the enormous lie of his own infallibility, if he was neither a dotard nor a madman? Had he never read the Bible? Had he never read the history of his predecessors in the Roman See? If he had never read anything, the speeches of the anti-infallibilists in his own council might have convinced him. That he was not convinced—that he believed himself infallible—can only be accounted for by that awful judgment which the apostle describes in 1 Thess. ii. 11, 12. Our own opinion is, however, that the pope and the Jesuits who rule him no more believe that the occupant of the Roman See is infallible than they believe that "virtue is its own reward," or that "honesty is the best policy."[1] The decrees of the Vatican Council are simply culmination of the aims which the Jesuits have pursued with unrelenting cruelty and craft from the very foundation of their order. They have always professed to be "*perinde cadavera*" in the hands of the pope, because they always intended that the pope's hands should be moved by themselves. They professed obedience to the pope's commands, because they would see to it that the pope should command nothing except what they suggested or

[1] De Maistre (*Du Pape*, C. 1) explains infallibility to be the same in the spiritual order that sovereignty means in the civil order. He demands for the papal body only "that it should be allowed the right which is conceded to all sovereignties, of acting as if they were infallible. All government is absolute; and the moment it can be resisted under the pretext of error or injustice, it exists no longer." (Schaff, Vol. I., p. 166.) If this were all that the claim of infallibility means, then, indeed, the Jesuits would be firm believers in it.

approved. They aimed at making themselves masters of the whole body and of the world; and the shortest method of accomplishing that aim was to have but one authority in the body, and to govern that authority. They have succeeded at last. There is but one sword, extending to the ends of the earth, with the hilt at Rome.

But whatever may be Dr. Schaff's charity for the persons or the blasphemers, he has none for the blasphemy. He gives no quarter to the Vatican decrees. We do not remember to have read a more conclusive argument than that which he gives us against the audacious and blasphemous claim of infallibility in the first volume of this work. Even here, however, we must be permitted to enter a *caveat*. In noticing the papal argument for infallibility, based upon such passages as Luke xxii. 31, Matt. xvi. 18, John xxi. 15,[1] our author concedes the truth of "Peter's primacy among the apostles," and admits that "this is the truth which underlies the colossal lie of the papacy." He proceeds, indeed, to show that "the position which Peter occupied no one can occupy after him." But truth will not permit us to concede any such primacy as that which the papists claim for him. He was no more than *primus inter pares*. Dr. Schaff himself demonstrates this. He says, what so many writers have said before him, that "the New Testament shows not one single example of an exercise of jurisdiction by Peter over the other apostles, but the very reverse; that that apostle, in his epistles, disowns and prophetically warns his fellow-pres-

[1] We ought not to have said "based upon." The truth is, as Whately has somewhere observed, the errors of Romanism are not based upon Scripture; not even upon false interpretations of Scripture, but have arisen altogether independently of it. But having arisen, support is sought for them in Scripture. Hence, when the false interpretations of papal doctors are exposed and overthrown, we make very little impression upon them. When all the Scripture props are knocked from under them, they stand as they did before; a very conclusive evidence that these proofs were not the support upon which they rested.

byters against the hierarchical spirit (1 Peter v. 1–4); that Paul and John were perfectly independent of him; that Paul openly rebuked him at Antioch," etc. The primacy of Peter, as the New Testament really presents it, is not at all what the papists want. Their policy is to quote the passages and ring the changes upon them without inquiring what they mean. It is only a variety of what Whately calls "the fallacy of quotations." For what purpose, then, the concession that these passages contain "a truth which underlies the colossal lie of the papacy"? We can ascribe it to nothing but an amiable mania of the author for concessions. He cannot prove even the sin of blasphemy upon a man without taking off his hat and making his obeisance to him. For ourselves, we confess that we have more sympathy with the language of Paul to Elymas, when we are called to deal with impostors and hypocrites, who, for filthy lucre, are perverting the right ways of the Lord, and turning men away from the faith.

Another signal exception to the strictly historical character of the first volume is the fine argument against the dogma of the immaculate conception of the Virgin. The history of the bitter contests concerning this dogma in the papal body furnishes a striking commentary upon its boasted unity, and goes far towards justifying the sarcasm of the Edinburgh reviewer. "Their unity is the unity of chaos. There was but one chaos; but in that one there was infinite confusion." Even our amiable author cannot find in this "colossal lie" a single element of truth. It is a pure invention of the same audacity and wickedness which has deified the Virgin; nay, set her above God and his Christ. Dr. Schaff's treatment of the dogma, both historical and polemic, is in his very best style, and is worthy of all praise.

The part of this volume which will be most interesting to our Presbyterian people is that in which the author treats of the Westminster Assembly and Standards. He has evidently taken great pains with it; and it would not be easy to find anywhere, in the same space, an account of the great men of that Assembly, and of the immortal symbols they produced, more impartial, or, we may add, more lively. We cannot, indeed, concur in all he says about the Confession and the Catechisms, for we are in full sympathy with them; and he is not, and does not profess to be. But we think that we all owe a debt of gratitude to him for doing justice to a body of men who, though they extorted the admiration and praise of John Milton, yet afterwards, by their fidelity to truth, incurred his displeasure, and have been misrepresented and maligned ever since by a class of writers who had as little sympathy with Milton as with them. "Whether we look at the extent or ability of its labors," says our author of the Assembly, "or its influence upon future generations, it stands first among Protestant councils. The Synod of Dort was, indeed, fully equal to it in learning and moral weight, and was more general in its composition, since it embraced delegates from nearly all Reformed churches; while the Westminster Assembly was purely English and Scotch, and its standards are to this day little known on the continent of Europe.[1] But the doctrinal legislation of Dort was confined

[1] "It is characteristic," says our author here in a foot-note, "that Dr. Niemeyer published his collection of Reformed Confessions, the most complete we have, at first without the Westminster Standards, being unable to find a copy, and issued them afterwards in a supplement. Dr. Winer barely mentions the Westminster Confession in his *Symbolik*, and never quotes from it. If German church historians (including Gieseler) were to be judged by their knowledge of English and American affairs, they would lose much of the esteem in which they are justly held. What is *westward* is a *terra incognita* to most of them. They are much more at home in the by-ways of the remote past than in the living church of the present, outside of Germany."

The Westminster Confession was probably better known (in the Latin translation) on the continent in the seventeenth century than it is now. We remember seeing it quoted by Beaulieu, in his *Theses Sedanenses*, in support of his view of the nature of saving faith, as against the view of Luther and Calvin.

to the five points at issue between Calvinism and Arminianism; the Assembly of Westminster embraced the whole field of theology, from the eternal decrees of God to the final judgment. The Canons of Dort have lost their hold upon the mother country; the Confession and Shorter Catechism of Westminster are as much used now in Anglo-Presbyterian churches as ever, and have more vitality and influence than any other Calvinistic confession." (P. 728.) He also quotes Hallam as saying that "the Assembly was perhaps equal in learning, good sense, and other merits to any Lower House of Convocation that ever made a figure in England"; and then adds the opinion of "one of the best-informed German historians," expressed in these words: "A more zealous, intelligent, and learned body of divines seldom ever (*sic*) met in christendom." Such testimonies more than counterbalance the insolent and malignant slanders of Clarendon and his copyists.

Dr. Schaff finds some fault in the theology of the Westminster Assembly besides its doctrine concerning the relation of church and state, which has never been accepted by the Presbyterian Church in America. We feel strongly inclined to follow him into that field. We think it would not be difficult to show that the Assembly is right and that he is wrong. But it would lead us away too far from the purpose of this article. We must be permitted to say, however, that he is evidently not as much at home in the department of dogmatic theology as in that of church history. In the latter it would be hard to find his equal; in the former it would be easy.

Before passing to the more general remarks that we propose to make upon this work, we shall notice some of its slighter but very pleasant features. The style is very remarkable for a German who was old enough, before he made his home in this country, to have acquired a brilliant reputation in his own. It is almost always grammatical, generally idiomatic, sometimes even elegant. Occasionally he uses a phrase which is wholly colloquial, and once or twice one which borders on slang. This is not strange. The only wonder is, that such blemishes are so rare. We think that the amiable author's expatriation has been a benefit to himself, to the country of his adoption, and to his own native country. His style has gained immensely in clearness. Perspicuity, it must be acknowledged, is not a prominent characteristic of the style of our German friends. It is impossible that it should be, so long as the principle upon which they construct their sentences seems to be that of putting in each all that it can possibly be made to contain. De Quincey's humorous description is hardly an exaggeration, at least in its application to the style of the theologians and philosophers. "The character of German prose," he says, "is an object of legitimate astonishment. Whatever is bad in our own ideal of prose style, we see there carried to the most outrageous excess. Herod is out-Heroded, Sternhold is out-Sternholded, with a zealotry of extravagance that really seems like wilful burlesque; . . . a sentence is viewed by Kant, and by most of his countrymen, as a rude mould or elastic form, admitting of expansion to any possible extent; it is laid down as a rude outline, and then, by superstruction and *epi*-superstruction, it is gradually reared to a giddy altitude which no eye can follow. . . . It is like an act of parliament, where the exceptions, the secondary exceptions to the exceptions, the limitations and the sublimitations, descend, *seriatim*, by a vast scale of dependencies," etc. Sentences of this sort, he suggests, are not only of great calibre, but of very large *bore*. The want of perspicuity is also due, no doubt, to the fondness for speculation (in the German sense of this word), the "*mens pasta chimœris.*" "The English," said Jean Paul, "have the empire of the sea, the French of the land, the Germans of the air"—and of the clouds. The "obscure" of their philosophy may be made "palpable"; but it cannot be made clear by any artifices of style. Even Cousin cannot do it without the aid of the philosophy of common sense, although a Frenchman, and, therefore, either clear or—nothing. Dr. Schaff's thorough study of English literature, and his intercourse with the English and American people, have helped him mightily. We cannot remember a single sentence in this large volume of which the meaning, if not intuitively obvious, cannot be discerned without difficulty. We have noticed some instances of not very happy translation in the volumes containing the creeds, but these are from another hand, not his own.[1] And now, as he has become so familiar with the English tongue, we cannot refrain from expressing the hope that he will address himself to the task of completing his history of the Christian church. If it is easier for him to write in German than in English, let him finish his great work in German; and then we shall venture to hope that he may still find as happy a translator as Mr. Yeomans.

Another pleasant feature of the historical introduction are the anecdotes (*ἀνέκδοτα*), biographical, academic, literary, which are so plentifully sprinkled over his pages, especially in the foot-notes. They are interesting in themselves, and serve to relieve the strain of attention which is demanded by the grave matters of history or disquisition. We mention but one specimen of these *anecdota*. It concerns the famous words, "*in necessariis unitas, in non necessariis libertas, in omnibus caritas*,"—the motto of peace-loving men for so many generations, and dear, of course, to our author. The words have generally been attributed to Augustine, but, it

[1] For example, in the translation of the French Confession, "justice" is several times rendered "justification," instead of *righteousness*. So, also, in Article XIX., the words "*il convient tenir notre vie du lui, comme de notre chief*," are rendered, "we must hold our life from him (Christ), as from our *Chief*," where *head* would have been the better rendering. So again, "*les uns*" is rendered "the ones," which may be literal, and may be tolerated in colloquial English, but seems out of place in a grave document like this.

seems, erroneously. Lücke has devoted a special treatise to them, their age, their author, etc., and traces them to Rupertus Meldenius, the obscure author of "*Parænesis votiva pro pace ecclesiæ ad theologos Augustanæ confessionis*" (before 1635), in which the sentence occurs, "*Si nos servaremus in necessariis unitatem, in non-necessariis libertatem, in utrisque caritatem, optimo certe loco essent res nostræ.*" (I., p. 588.)

We propose now to gather some of the lessons which this collection of creeds and their history are suited to impress upon us.

1. And, in the first place, we are impressed with the necessity for creeds, if there be a necessity for the existence of the church itself. "*Ecclesia sine symbolis nulla.*" The church is an assembly, and an assembly consisting of persons who believe and have communion or fellowship in their belief. How is it possible that this fellowship can exist without a statement or expression of what is believed? Such a statement, be it long or short, is a creed. Those bodies of professing Christians, therefore, who boast, like the Campbellites, of having no creed, are really disclaiming the character and status of a visible church. There is no bond of fellowship in the faith if their boast be well founded. The truth is, it is not well founded. Men may associate for many purposes, for the accomplishment of which no faith (in the religious sense) is required. Men of all complexions of religious faith may unite to build a railroad, or throw a bridge across a river, or even to establish a civil government. But they cannot constitute a church without faith and without agreement as to the things which are the objects of faith. The Campbellites are, therefore, agreed as to certain doctrines which they profess to believe, or, at least, as to certain doctrines which they profess to disbelieve. Their positive creed may be very, very short, and their negative very, very long; but a creed they must have, or they could not continue to subsist as a religious association. It must be confessed,

however, that so long as they refuse to inform us what their creed is, or continue steadily to deny that they have any, we are compelled to take them at their word, and to refuse to them the character and title of a visible church; while, in the exercise of that charity which believeth all things and hopeth all things, we believe and hope that there may be true children of God among them. It is a very significant fact, that in this voluminous work which we are reviewing, projected upon the most comprehensive scale, and written by a man of the most comprehensive charity, all he can find to say about the "Disciples" is contained in this short sentence: "These are very numerous in the West; they reject all creeds on principle."

Again, the great function of the church is to bear witness to the truth. She is the representative on earth of the "Amen, the Faithful and True Witness," her head invisible in heaven. He is the light, she is the lamp; he the *lumen illuminans*, she the *lumen illuminatum*. She cannot perform this office by holding up a collection of writings and proclaiming, "This is my faith"; nor can she fulfil it by the preaching and writings of her ministers. They may misrepresent her testimony through ignorance or malice, as they have done a thousand times. She must have a standard by which the ministers themselves are to be judged, and to which all men may appeal. In short, she must have a creed.

Further, there must needs be heresies in the church. Heretics, as distinguished from infidels, profess to believe the Scriptures. How can they be separated from the church except by a creed? Hence, "forms of sound *words*" have been in use in the church from the beginning. The matter of Scripture has been stated in *words*, about which there could be no mistake or misrepresentation as to their meaning. Men affect to doubt, as has been well said, whether the Bible teaches the church doctrine of the Trinity or the doctrines of the Calvinistic system. But who doubts whether the Nicæno-Constantinopolitan creed teaches the former, and the Westminster Confession the latter? Aye! the church has been able to find *words* which, like the spear of Ithuriel, have compelled the spirit of evil to reveal itself. A jot or tittle, an iota, the smallest letter in the Greek alphabet, inserted in the middle of a word, was an excruciating test of orthodoxy in the fourth century, and, in spite of the sneers of Gibbon, subserved the purposes of fundamental truth. The presence or the absence of the iota in a man's confession determined whether he confessed Christ to be the almighty God or a mere creature.

Creeds are necessary, then, for a testimony, for the very existence of the church as an organized visible body, and for its defence against the inroads of heresy.

2. We learn the necessity for growth and development in creeds. In the infancy of the church, as in the infancy of the children who are trained from age to age in her bosom, the creed is naturally short and simple. Her faith, like the faith of infancy, is spontaneous, unreflective, unscientific. The "Apostles' Creed" exactly represents it. It is not only free from what have been called "the speculative elements" of doctrine, but omits some of the fundamental doctrines of Christianity. It was simply impossible that the church should be always satisfied with such a creed, if it was ever to pass beyond a state of infancy. The Arian and Pelagian had no hesitation in subscribing to it. But if Arianism had never arisen to insult the majesty of the Redeemer, if no other form of heresy had assailed the foundation of the church, the theology of the church must have been developed by the very laws of the human intellect. Her spontaneous, unreflective faith had to be justified to her own mind. In reference to the relation (for example) of the Son to the Father in the Godhead, the church could not think long without feeling the difficulty of reconciling its mono-

theism with the worship of two persons, each of whom was represented in Scripture as the proper object of worship, and therefore God. The law of non-contradiction is a fundamental law of thought, and the mind is restless and impatient until it discovers the principle by which the apparent contradictions are reconciled. Many unsuccessful attempts may be made before the law of harmony is ascertained, but there is no rest for the mind until it is ascertained, or until it is demonstrated that, in the nature of the case, it can never be ascertained. The conclusions of the Nicene Council, therefore, were conclusions which the church would have reached in the course of time, if Arianism had never arisen to compel the definition of the doctrine of the Trinity. It is vain to say that it would have been better for the church if she had always been content with the faith of her childhood, or, in other words, if there had never been any scientific theology; that a great many errors might have been avoided; that the "*rabies theologorum*," which afflicted the soul of Melancthon so grievously, would have had no cause for its existence. It would be as wise to say that it would have been better for mankind if there had been no science of chemistry, because that science has made men more expert poisoners than they could have been without it. Thinking is necessary to the progress of the race, and we must submit to the evils and abuses which attend it for the sake of the incalculable good which is its legitimate result. If the church refuses to have a sound theology, the devil and his instruments will take pains to provide another sort of theology for her.

And this leads us to observe, that, in point of fact, the church had no choice. Her faith was assailed. The "gates of hell" left nothing undone to subvert its very foundation. It had to be defended or surrendered. The result was not only the preservation of the faith, but a clearer knowledge of it, and a development of it. A clearer knowledge, because it had to be examined on more sides than one; on as many sides, in fact, as it had been assailed; and as "the science of contraries is one," the knowledge of the one contrary involves a clearer knowledge of the other. A development of it, because this is the necessary result of the many-sidedness of the examination. To illustrate our meaning, take the answer of the Westminster Shorter Catechism to the question (21st), "Who is the Redeemer of God's elect?" Here, in almost every clause, the "form of words" is determined by some error or errors by which the truth has been opposed—Arianism, Patripassianism, Nestorianism, Eutychianism. So, also, in the question which follows (the 22d), the form of statement is determined by the errors of the Docetists, the Apollinarians, etc.

As the theology is developed under these conditions, it would be unreasonable to expect that the creeds should remain stationary. The creeds of the church could not be the same after the christological discussions of the fifth century that they were before, any more than the church could be satisfied with the Apostles' Creed after the Arian controversy had arisen. So, also, it was impossible that the doctrines which belong to soteriology should not have greater prominence in the symbols of the Reformation era than in any preceding era. If there is no life in the church, or if her life is characterized, like that of Thyatira, by a zealous ministry of love at the expense of fidelity to the truth, then, indeed, she may not feel the obligation to testify for any other doctrines than those which are absolutely necessary to distinguish Christianity from Judaism, Paganism, and Mahometanism. We are constrained to believe that many of the union schemes of our own day have no better origin; that they are essentially humanitarian in spirit, and place the welfare of man above the glory of God. Theology, which is the knowledge of God, is relegated to a position subordinate to philanthropy, which is the love of man. This is a fatal error. For the good of man can never be promoted by any measure which obscures the glory of his Maker and Redeemer. The only effectual method of securing the interests of holiness is to bear a faithful witness for the truth. Truth is the mould of holiness, and without holiness no man shall see the Lord. The world has never seen a truer philanthropist than that great Apostle of the Gentiles, who, when the truth was in question, "gave way by subjection, no, not for an hour." A philanthropy without God has deluged a land with blood and marked its progress with dead men's bones.

It would really seem as if the lessons of history had been given in vain to these peace-makers. The course of the church is strewn with the wrecks of such schemes. They have all failed, because they have all demanded that the church should suppress her convictions of truth and annul her history; that the boy of ten should go back to the period of puling infancy, or that the man of mature years should abdicate all the dignity and strength which experience and reflection have conferred upon him. But the thing is impossible; and if not impossible, it is not to be desired. The first, original, genuine childhood has great charms; but a second childhood is a pitiable thing to contemplate. The simplicity of youth cannot be copied by age. Manhood has its cares and its conflicts, but they are cares and conflicts which ennoble and elevate. Reflection conjures up a host of doubts and difficulties to torment us; but who, on that account, would be willing to abjure reflection? John Locke wrote a treatise to persuade the church that no larger creed was necessary than the single article, "I believe that Jesus Christ is the Son of God." Why was he not satisfied with the same brevity and simplicity in philosophy? His "Essay on the Human Understanding" has certainly been anything but an "*Irenicum.*"

We have said that the course of the church is strewn with the wrecks of union schemes. Let us glance at some of them. One of the first is encountered in the Arian controversies—that of the "Homoians." This was a proposition to abandon the use of only one word—*ousia*—which had been the cause of so much dissension, and a word, moreover, whose use involved an audacious claim of ability to comprehend the incomprehensible. Why not lay it aside and adopt a formula in which Homoousians and Homoiousians might unite, and so extinguish the war which was a scandal to the world? The scheme was, for a time, successful. The powerful influence of the emperor, the intrigues of the bishops of his court, the adhesion of the bishop of Rome, Liberius, the reluctant subscription of the councils of Seleucia and Rimini, finally made Homoiism the acknowledged creed of the empire, as Homoousianism had been before. But in twenty years from the victory of the emperor and his episcopal politicians, Homoousianism triumphed in the council of Constantinople. The christological controversies of the following century gave rise to similar attempts. The Monophysites and Dyophysites were to be reconciled by a "Henoticon," according to which the history for the last hundred years was to be forgotten, the church was to go back to the Nicæno-Constantinopolitan creed, and all controverted points were to be carefully avoided. This Henoticon was the beginning of the schism between the eastern and western churches. A similar fate attended the conciliatory measures of Justinian, in the sixth century, and of Heraclius and Constans, in the seventh. The "Typos" of the last-named emperor was designed to quiet the Monothelite disputes, by restoring the *status quo*, that is, by commanding divines to speak and write as if the controversies of the preceding thirty or forty years had not taken place.

After the Reformation, we have the like schemes for uniting the different branches of the nominal church and the same kind of basis proposed, if not for organic union, at least for "correspondence"—the oblivion of the past and the cessation of controversy. The scheme of Calixtus was to go back to the first five centuries—the "*consensus quinquesecularis.*" This was practically to annul the history of the studies and conflicts of a thousand years. The labors of that great martyr in the cause of peace to realize his idea is almost incredible. Yet with what result? He "spun himself and his life out into one pitiful controverted conclusion." He was obliged to fail, because he was contending against the elementary forces of nature, and his proposals for peace became the signal for one of the fiercest wars that ever raged in Germany. One might have supposed that a man of great learning, as Calixtus undoubtedly was, would see from the first that his idea could never be realized before the millennium, and that then there would be no use for it. The creeds of the first five centuries were in possession of the church and every branch of it, and they were received by all. But this very fact was fatal to the scheme of the peace-maker. The reason is a very plain one. *Notwithstanding* the common reception of the Œcumenical creeds, the church was divided into Roman, Greek, Lutheran, and Reformed. The very fact of division, in spite of the *consensus quinquesecularis*, if properly considered, was enough to chill the ardor even of a Calixtus. The differences were as real as the agreements, and they could not be waved away by the wand even of such a wizard as he. This is the stubborn fact which his scheme had to encounter and against which it was doomed to be wrecked, and deserved to be. If he could have persuaded the churches that the differences were unreal or unimportant, then union or correspondence might have been established in *faith*. But the churches ought not to have united or corresponded upon any other basis than that of faith. The only body calling itself a church which has succeeded in suppressing differences not upon the basis of faith is the papacy. But with what results? One result was the monstrous doctrine of the dualism of truth—that the same proposition might be true in theology and false in philosophy, and *vice versa;* or the other monstrous doctrine, which has been ascribed to Occam, that God can make and unmake truth as it pleases him, and can authorize the church to do the same. Another was the extinction of all love for truth and faith in it, and the erection, in the name of Christ, of a kingdom worldly in its aims, worldly in its means and policy, and caring nothing for God, heaven, or hell, except so far as these great ideas may aid its visible head and his advisers in accomplishing the schemes of their ambition and gratifying their lust for gold.

3. The last remark we make is that, while the study of this collection of creeds cannot fail to impress us with the differences which exist among Christians upon certain points of faith, it must impress us also with the real *consensus* of the evangelical churches upon others, and the most important. He who will take the pains to examine the creeds of these churches will find evidence enough that they have not only been governed by the same external standard, the word of God, but that they have been led also by the same Spirit. He will also find that there is more real unity in the different branches of the Reformed body than there is in the one body of Rome, and that, too, in regard to the fundamental point, the way of salvation. Innocent III., in the thirteenth century, the historians inform us, was opposed to the formation of what he called "any new religions," meaning new religious orders. The term was more happily chosen than he was aware of. Each one of these orders was a "new religion" in the sense of "denomination" as used by Protestants, except that they all agreed to submit to the pope. But they were none the less jealous of each other on that account. The wars of the Dominicans and the Franciscans about the nature of sin and grace, fundamental elements of doctrine, soon justified the caution of the cunning pope, to say nothing of their controversies concerning the immaculate conception of the

Virgin. Then we have the controversies about sin and grace renewed between the Dominicans and the Jesuits in the sixteenth century, which was quieted according to the recipe of *Punch*—"the best way to crush a thing is to get a committee to sit on it." The congregation "*de auxiliis*" sat on the controversy for many years and smothered it. But it revived again in the next century between the Jansenists and the Jesuits, and the wish of Voltaire was at one time apparently almost realized, "to see the last Jansenist in the bowels of the last Jesuit." The unity of Rome is the unity of staves in a barrel. The staves are kept together by the hoops. There is no life, no organic unity, in the body considered as a religious body. There is life enough in it considered as a political corporation which is aiming, like its pagan predecessor, to establish an universal dominion, an iron despotism which shall not suffer the slightest vestige of liberty to remain on earth. Not the slightest vestige of a church now remains at Rome, except the name.

The unity of the evangelical churches, on the other hand, is the unity of life. It is the unity of a living organism, not only admitting, but requiring, diversity. It is not a great iron wheel of which the different parts are only spokes, having no other motion than that of the wheel itself, but a complicated structure of wheels within a wheel, like that of the prophet's vision, each having a sphere and a movement of its own, but all instinct with the spirit of the living creature. The individuality of the parts is preserved, yet all conspire for the accomplishment of the end designed for the whole. Each member of the system traverses its own orbit, obeying the attraction of the central sun, an attraction mighty enough to counteract the centrifugal force which, if left to its own operation, would drive them asunder forever. The *consensus* of the apostate churches, on the other hand, is a *consensus* in the denial of the great doctrines of salvation, and perfectly compatible with mutual anathemas of each other, as well as with a common anathema of those which hold the truth.

Let us hope that no further attempt will be made to disturb the true *consensus* of the Reformed churches, by forcing a union which must be more or less insincere. Let us avoid the fatal error and the odious hypocrisy of Rome. Let us never forget that "fraternal relations" does not mean organic union or even "correspondence," but the loving recognition of one evangelical church by another as a true church of Christ. Above all, let us never forget the supreme importance of the truth itself, in which the glory of God and the salvation of men are so deeply concerned—of that *doctrine,* which, however postponed in the esteem of many to the interests of peace, is, after all, as Calvin said, the "*sacrum vinculum fraternitatis beatæ.*"

CHURCH AND STATE.[1]

THE fundamental relations implied in the distinction between "the things which are God's, and the things which are Cæsar's," have been recognized, more or less clearly, from the beginning of the history of our race. These relations are that of man to man in a state of society, on the one hand, and, on the other hand, that of man to God. They have been designated by different names, and have been the objects of divers kinds of legislation, according to the diversities of age and country; but, whether known by this name or that, whether, in practice, partially separated or totally confounded, the relations themselves have been, and could not but be, apprehended. The relation of man to man would force itself upon the notice by the necessities of every day's existence; the relation of man to God would be developed in the operations of conscience, arraigning the offender before an invisible tribunal, and pointing him to a coming retribution. Yet it cannot be denied that in reference to few objects of human thought have attempts at articulate exposition been more unsuccessful than in reference to this; or that the wisdom of the wisest man has still more signally failed, by any kind of political machinery, to realize perfectly the theories which make the most plausible approximations to the truth.

It is only in modern times, indeed, that the philosopher has undertaken to grapple with these relations with a view to the practical separation of the spheres of the temporal and the spiritual, the civil and the ecclesiastical, the church

[1]Appeared in the *Southern Presbyterian Review*, October, 1863. It deals with a subject handled in Dr. Peck's *Ecclesiology*, but throws additional light on it. Hence, it is included in this volume.—EDITOR.

and the state. In the ancient forms of civilization, in its leading types, the Oriental, the Greek, and the Roman, we look in vain for any discrimination between these powers. In the East, the cradle of the human race, and the seat of vast empires, where the patriarchal idea and the patriarchal sentiment pervade and mould the whole fabric of society, the monarch is not merely the highest religious functionary, but a divinity, the object of worship to his subjects. In Greece, the cradle of philosophy, and the scene of the proudest triumphs of speculative thought, we find a similar, though not so complete an identification of the civil and the religious. The miraculous subtlety of Aristotle was as unequal to this discrimination as it was to the discovery of the fact and the necessity of a physical creation *ex nihilo*. Among the Romans, whose extraordinary genius for government made them the masters of the world, we find a still larger infusion of orientalism than among the Greeks, and far less of a speculative tendency, and, consequently, a more complete confusion of the relations which belong to man as a sojourner on earth with the relations which belong to him as the subject of a supreme invisible power. In illustration of this point we take the liberty of quoting a paragraph or two from an essay on Roman legislation by that able lawyer and accomplished scholar, Hugh S. Legaré, of South Carolina. We offer no apology for the length of the quotation, as it is the legislation of Rome, more than all other causes combined, which has determined the posture of all christendom for ages upon this great question:

"The legislation and history of Rome are altogether unintelligible without a distinct apprehension of the causes, the extent, and the consequences of this extraordinary influence—[the influence of the class of the hereditary priests and jurists of the republic, the *ulema* behind the throne greater than the throne itself]. All nations are governed more by manners and opinions than by laws, and the Romans above all other nations. But their manners and opinions were formed and directed by this *caste* of lawyer-priests, an institution quite oriental, transmitted to them through Tuscany, at once by inheritance and by education. In every part of their annals, from the earliest struggles of the *plebs*, in the freshness and vigor of youthful health and enthusiasm, under their immortal tribunes, down to periods of degeneracy and servitude, the same spirit is everywhere visible. Religion, law, subordination, or all these names in one, *discipline*, civil and military, at home and abroad—'this was their sorcery.' Created to teach the law to all coming time, they regarded it with instinctive awe, approached its oracles as those of their gods, and yielded to it a devoted, yet magnanimous and enlightened obedience. Hence it was that revolution after revolution occurred; that the assemblies of the curiæ were superseded by those of the centuries, and these in turn overshadowed by those of the tribes; that the veto of a single tribune, clothed himself in no armor but that of religion (inviolable, *sacrosanctus*), could bring on universal anarchy by preventing all elections, and leaving every office vacant; that repeated secessions of the *plebs* to the mountain appropriately called *sacred*, or to the Janaculum, took place; that for centuries together the story of Roman politics, omitting the wars altogether, is, in the hands of Livy, and even of Dionysius, by far the most thrilling and sublime of historical romances; and yet that, in the midst of so many elements of disorder and violence, not one drop of blood was shed in civil war, and the glorious commonwealth,

> 'Rising in clouded majesty, at length,
> Apparent queen, unveiled her peerless light.'"

Again, speaking of the *libri rituales* (to the Romans what the Mosaic ritual was to the Hebrews), Mr. Legaré says, after Festus: "They teach the rites with which cities are to be founded, and altars and temples dedicated; the holiness of the walls of towns; the law relating to their gates; how tribes, wards, and centuries are to be distributed; armies organized and arrayed; and other, the like, things relating to peace and war." Then adds: "We see the same influence extending itself over the very soil of the Roman territory, and making, in the technical language of their augury, one vast temple of it. It was consecrated by the auspices; it could become the property only of one who had the auspices, that is, a patrician or *Roman*, properly so-called; once set apart and conveyed away, it was irrevocably alienated, so that sales of the domain were guaranteed by religion, and it was sacrilegious to establish a second colony on the place dedicated to a first. Auspices could be taken nowhere else but on some spot which *they* had rendered sacred. The city, by its original inauguration, was also a temple; its gates and walls were holy; its *pomœrium* was unchangeable, until higher auspices had suspended those under which it was first marked out. Every spot of ground might become, by the different uses to which it was applied, sacred (*sacer*), holy (*sanctus*), religious (*religiosus*). To the assembly of the *curiæ*, the presence of the augurs was, of course, indispensable; that of the *centuries* could not be held, unless the augurs and two pontiffs assisted at it, as it was dissolved instantly at their bidding, on the occurrence of any sinister omen. The first *agrimensor*, says Niebuhr, was an augur, accompanied by Tuscan priests or their scholars. From the foundation of the city, the sacredness of property was shadowed forth in the worship of the god Terminus, and that of contracts protected by an apotheosis of faith. In short, the worthy Roman lived, moved, and had his being, as the Greek writers observe, in religion."

We have, as yet, made no allusion to the history of the Old Testament, because, while, as to its subject, it belongs to the East, it is, as to its origin, the word of God, and therefore cannot be expected to contain any merely philosophical views upon this or upon any other question; and further, because the dispensation which it is its main purpose to reveal and to illustrate was altogether peculiar, and was designed to be temporary. But the very fact that it contains the history of an oriental people makes it specially instructive, if found to present or to imply views of the connection of the civil and ecclesiastical powers different from those generally prevailing in the East. And the additional consideration that we have, in those venerable records, the primæval history of our race, will furnish an ample apology, if any apology be necessary, for a brief notice of it.

We learn, then, that the whole race was once confined to the limits of a single family, and that all the intricate and manifold relations of human society which have been developed in the progress of civilization once lay here in the germ. The family was the nursery, both of the secular and of the spiritual power. But these powers were combined in the person of the *paterfamilias*, who was both king and priest, governing and ordering his household in regard to the things of this life, and instructing them and leading them in the knowledge and worship of God. In process of time, even after the visible church had been formally set up in the family of Abraham, we meet with that mysterious person, Melchizedek, who was at once king of Salem and priest of the most high God. In him the powers of these twin ordinances of God, the church and the state, appear still united, but discernible as distinct and separable. Then, under the institute of Moses, we find the sacerdotal functions given to a separate order of officers, and the whole ministry of the tabernacle to a particular tribe; while the elders, the representatives of the patriarchal system, seem to have continued the exercise of civil functions. We do not pretend that there was an entire separation of the secular and the spiritual. It is possible that the synagogue, with its mingled jurisdiction over civil and ecclesiastical affairs, may even then have existed, as that jurisdiction was based on the patriarchal principle upon which the whole Hebrew commonwealth was organized. But we assert that we have here in the books of Moses what we find nowhere else in the East, a class of high and honorable functions in the matter of divine worship, with which the highest officer in the state dared not intermeddle. It is certainly a striking circumstance that, in a theocracy like that of Israel, its public forms should recognize to so great an extent the distinction between civil and sacred functions. As a theocracy, it could not easily admit of their entire separation; and it must be borne in mind that, as the state was organized with a view to the interests of the church as supreme, if any argument be drawn from Judaism in support of the union of church and state, it is rather in favor of the ultramontane than of the Erastian theory. In this respect paganism presents a strong contrast to Judaism in giving supremacy to the civil. But in both, as also in Mahometanism, the two powers are so combined that their history cannot be separately written. There is no history of the synagogue, or the mosque, or the pagan temple, as there is of the church.

So thoroughly rooted had the union of the two powers become by immemorial custom and tradition in the thinking, feeling, and entire life of mankind, that there can be little doubt of the wisdom and love of that dispensation by which the Christian church was exposed, almost from the beginning of its existence and for the first three hundred years of its career, to the bitter persecution of the civil power. The line was thus clearly drawn between God and Cæsar, and it was demonstrated that the church could live, not only without alliance with the state, but in spite of all its power and hate. But no sooner did Cæsar profess himself the friend of Christ and his cause, than the old idea of union was revived, and Cæsar assumed once more the exercise of power in the church of God. Then came the reaction of the human mind, too violent to rest in the centre of truth, and swinging to the opposite extreme, still holding to the union, but making the civil subordinate to the ecclesiastical. The popery of Hildebrand, of Innocent III., and Boniface VIII., was the Nemesis of the Erastianism of Constantine, Theodosius, and Justinian. The doctrine, however, of these emperors was only the old Roman doctrine of the first centuries of the republic, with the change of Christianity for paganism. After the desperate struggle between the popes and the emperors, which kept the world in an uproar during the Middle Ages, came the earthquake of the Reformation. Even that great revolution did not dissolve the union of church and state. It continued to exist in some countries, as in Germany, Holland, England, and even in Scotland, to hinder the progress and mar the purity of the work of God, and in others, as in France, to extinguish it almost altogether.

It was in the church of Scotland that the independence of the spiritual power was first proclaimed in modern times. John Erskine of Dun declared to the Regent Mar, "There is a spiritual jurisdiction and power which God has given unto his kirk, and to them that bear office therein; and there is a temporal jurisdiction and power given of God to kings and civil magistrates. Both the powers are of God, and most agreeing to the fortifying one of the other, if they be rightly used." Andrew Melville dared to say to King James: "There are two kings and two kingdoms in Scotland; there is King James, the head of the commonwealth, and there is Christ Jesus, the King of the church, whose subject James the Sixth is, and of whose kingdom he is not a king, nor a lord, nor a head, but a member."[1] "For the space of more than a century," says Mr. Robinson, "this noble army of the martyrs attested the spiritual freedom of Christ's kingdom in the face of every effort of Cæsar to crush out the truth. But the seduction and arts of power at length accomplished what the violence of power could never do; and in the act of settlement of the Scottish kingdom under Queen Anne, the only testimony for this great truth was silenced, and, in consequence, the Scotch church of the eighteenth century degenerated even to the point of spiritual death. Nothing could more forcibly illustrate the power of current and generally-admitted error in blinding the eyes of intelligent men against the plainest results of their own principles than the fact that, when the slavery of the church to the power of the state could no longer be endured, and the memorable exodus of the Free Church of Scotland occurred, even then Chalmers and his compeers could not go all the length of the apostolic idea of church freedom, but clung, as, indeed, their disciples

[1] Stuart Robinson's lecture before Maryland Institute, p. 18.

still cling, to the idea (while they practice voluntaryism) that the state should support the church, as though it were possible for the church to depend upon the state for support and still be independent."

Such being the history of the case, it ought not to create surprise, if the public mind, even in the freest and most enlightened nations of modern times, should not appear to have a clear comprehension of the principles which control this subject, or that, in practice, there should be so great a neglect of those principles. Momentary glimpses of the truth may be discerned along the ages, even in the darkest ages, under the pressure of persecution, when the weak were compelled to take refuge from brute force under the ramparts of sound principles; but the light which shines clearly in the darkness is lost again in the blaze of recovered power, and the persecuted of yesterday are the persecutors of today. Decrees of councils, bulls of popes, rescripts of emperors, decisions of jurists, opinions of publicists, dogmas of the civil and dogmas of the canon law, all conspire to join together what God has put asunder—the things that are his and the things that are Cæsar's. And now, in the middle of the nineteenth century, and in America, we who have been accustomed to boast that it was our mission as a people to teach the world the truth upon this subject have witnessed among ourselves, if not the revival of the maxims of the canonists and civilians, at least the adoption of measures which can only be acquitted of atrocious wickedness and folly by the truth of those maxims. "So far," says Vattel, "as religion is seated in the heart, it is an affair of the conscience, in which every one should be directed by his own understanding; but so far as it is external and publicly established, it is an affair of the state." It is upon this maxim that the officers of the usurper at Washington have proceeded, when they have dragged from their pulpits and banished from their churches the ministers of Christ because their prayers sinned against political orthodoxy, either in the way of omission or of commission. And, on the other hand, the church, forgetting that her power is strictly a power only to declare and do her Master's will as revealed in his word, has usurped the functions of the state and fulminated its curses against all who hold the heresy of state sovereignty. Then, among ourselves of the Southern Confederacy, there are those who seem ambitious to revive the absurdities of the fifth monarchy fanatics, and to exclude from the councils of the state all except the saints; and others, who speak as if a particular form of religion were destined to be the religion of the Southern Confederacy, or, at least, of its army and navy. And doubtless there are among us, as in the old Union, tender-conscienced atheists also, who are shocked at the recognition of a God at all in the administration of the government.

All these facts go to show the importance of standing and looking for the old paths, that we may walk therein. The revolutionary temper of the public mind prompts us to look for something new; but we want nothing new. We are not Jacobin destroyers, despising the wisdom of the past; but like William the Silent and the Dutch, like Hampden and Sidney and Somers, like Washington and the glorious fathers of the first war for independence, it is our mission to "maintain" and to restore. We need no new principles; but we do need to review and to remember the old, to refresh ourselves and renew our youth at the fountain of truth. This is our apology for asking the attention of our countrymen once more to the principles which constitute a true theory, or an approximation to a true theory, of the connection of church and state. We say an *approximation* to a true theory, because there is room for doubt whether a scientific expression can be given to the nature and limitations of either church or state, so clearly and so sharply defined as to afford rules of universal application. One of the factors of the problem still waits for a thorough analysis and construction; and the political history of this country would seem to demonstrate that we do not comprehend the nature of the state. But we may approach the truth by considering the points in which the church and the state agree, and then the points in which they differ.

I. The church and the state agree in these three points:

1. That they are ordained of God. 2. That they are ordained for his glory. 3. That they are ordained for the good of mankind. These statements will not be disputed by any of our readers; and we shall not stop to argue them.

II. They differ in the following points:

1. That the state is an ordinance of God considered as the creator, and, therefore, the moral governor of mankind, while the church is an ordinance of God considered as the saviour and restorer of mankind. The state is ordained for man as man; the church for man as a sinner in a condition of inchoate restoration and salvation. The state is for the whole race of man; the church consists of that portion of the race which is really, or by credible profession, the mediatorial body of Christ.

We say that civil government is designed for man as man. We find it existing in the germ, when the race consisted of one man and one woman. The woman was in a state of subordination to the man. This subordination was not the penal consequence of transgression, as is evident from 1 Timothy ii. 11–14; where Paul argues that the transgression was the consequence of the violation, by the woman, of the order established by heaven; of her ambitiously forsaking her condition of subordination, and acting as if she were the superior or the equal of the man. If it should be asked where was the necessity or the propriety of an order implying subordination in beings who were created in the image of God, in knowledge, righteousness, and true holiness, the answer is, that the propriety was founded upon the diversities of capacity in intellect and other endowments of human nature, which it pleased God should exist in the man and the woman. If man had not fallen, it would have been his duty still to bring up his children in the knowledge of God, and to *direct* them in the way in which they should glorify their Maker, albeit these children, by the terms of the supposition, would all have been holy and without inclination to go astray; nay, more, in no danger at all of apostasy from God. In other words, if all creatures, because they are creatures, need direction from God, there is not only no absurdity in making some of them the instruments of directing others, but there are traces of the wonderful wisdom and goodness of the creator in such an arrangement. Society is not an unison, but an exquisite harmony; a grand instrument of various chords for the harping of hymns and hallelujahs to the God and Father of all. Even among the unfallen angels, we have reason to believe, there are thrones, dominions, and principalities, and powers—order in the form of a celestial hierarchy. Man having fallen, however, and the love which constituted the very spirit and temper of his mind having given place to enmity, something more than *direction* was now necessary. He needed *restraint*—his appetites must be bridled and coerced. The law of the two tables, which, in his state of innocence and uprightness, had been written upon his heart, summarily, in the *positive* form of *love*, must now be written externally, in detail, upon tables of stone, and in a *prohibitory* form—"thou shalt *not*." And in reference to the second table, which prescribes the duties growing out of the relations of man to man, it became necessary that overt acts of transgression, which were not only morally wrong, but injurious to society, should not only be discountenanced by prohibition, but restrained and prevented by punishment. Hence arose a government of force.

The case, then, stands thus: "In any condition of our race, the social nature of man must have given rise to the secular power. In a state of innocence it would have been simply a *directing* power, a constitution designed merely to carry out and fulfil, without confusion, the blind instincts or impulses of love, love of self and love of "neighbor." In a fallen state, it has become, of necessity, a *restraining* and *punishing*, as well as a directing power. But in both conditions and in both forms it is an ordinance of God, "the author of the constitution and course of nature." It is the nature of man to exist in society, and society is necessary to his existence. But society cannot exist without order and law of some sort. Therefore, government is necessary to man as society, and, for this reason, is as natural to man as society. It may not be an *original* endowment of man, but it is *natural;* and if natural, then the ordinance of God. The perception of distance by the eye is not an *original* endowment of man, but the organ is so constituted that, in the course of time, it necessarily acquires it; and it is, therefore, *natural* to man, and therefore the ordinance of God. Civil government, then, is a branch or department of the moral government of God, the creator and ruler over man. God governs man by mechanical laws, by chemical laws, by vital laws, and he governs him by civil laws. He who leaps from a precipice, or drinks a glass of poison, and dies, dies under a law of God which *executes itself*. He who murders his brother, and dies on the gallows, dies under a law of God, *executed by the hand of man*. In all these cases, death is a penalty inflicted by God for the violation of a rule of his government, physical or moral.

Once more: If this be a just view of the subject, civil government is a great *moral* institute, not a mere expedient of human sagacity and wisdom for the prevention of evil. It is this low, wretched, utilitarian view which has contributed its full share to the ruin of the late United States government, in which the criminal law was fast becoming as pure an affair of utilitarian regulation as the civil. But the government of God, as creator, is a government of justice; and the civil magistrate, who is his minister, servant, *διακονος*, has no right to inflict any punishment which justice does not sanction, and is bound to inflict the punishment which justice requires. This remark is made for the sake of one important inference, and that is, that every civil government on earth is bound explicitly to recognize its responsibility to God as the moral governor of mankind. It is perfectly monstrous that the power which bears the sword and assumes the awful prerogative of taking human life, either in peace or war, should not acknowledge itself to be the servant of the sovereign Lord of life and death; that the power which represents the majesty of justice should not recognize its responsibility to him who is the eternal fountain and standard of all righteousness. One of the sins, doubtless, for which the vengeance of God descended upon the Federal government, was the atheism of its fundamental law; and it is a matter of devout thanksgiving unto God that the people of the new Confederacy have had the grace given to them explicitly to acknowledge their dependence upon him, both in their Confederate Constitution and in their Confederate escutcheon. We have written "*Deo vindice*" upon the flag which our noble countrymen have borne aloft on a hundred bloody and victorious battle-fields. Let us never forget that God, our "Vindex," is the punisher of our sins, as well as the protector of our rights, and the avenger of our wrongs. Let us also remember that it is not enough to bear this solemn truth upon our banners; we must bear it upon our hearts, lest we meet the fate of those of old, who "flattered him with their mouths, and lied unto him with their tongues."

So much for civil government as the ordinance of God, the creator, preserver, and moral governor of mankind. The church differs from it in this, as has been said, that it is the ordinance of God, as the Saviour of men, in the person of Jesus Christ, his only-begotten Son. It contemplates man, not as upright, in his original condition of innocence, nor simply as a fallen being, but as "the prisoner of hope"; or, more strictly still, as the "heir of salvation," really or by credible profession. Its great function is to teach, to convince, to persuade, "to bear witness to the truth." Its triumphs are the triumphs of love; it drags no reluctant captives at the wheels of its chariot; the design of its ordinances, its oracles, its ministry, is, through the efficacious operation of the Holy Ghost, to bring its captives into hearty sympathy with its King, and so to give them a share in the glory and exultation of the triumphs of the King. It has nothing to do with the power of the *sword;* its symbol is the *keys.* Its discipline is not the discipline of avenging justice, asserting the unbending majesty of the law, but the discipline of a mother, whose bowels yearn over the wayward child, and who inflicts no pain except for the child's reformation and salvation. The authority of her King is spiritual. His voice is, "Son, give me thy *heart*"; and by the power of his Spirit he sweetly and powerfully constrains those whom he chooses for members of his kingdom "to call him Lord." They who are his, or profess to be his, have, or make a credible profession of having, the great law of love written upon their hearts, and, therefore, need more the *directing* than the *restraining* power of the law.

The difference in this point between the civil and the ecclesiastical power may throw some light on the question which has been agitated in our church of late as to the duty of recognizing the kingly office of Christ our Lord in the civil constitutions of the country. Christians are all agreed that Jesus, their Saviour, is King of kings and Lord of lords, not only in the sense that he is the greatest of kings, but in the sense that all earthly kings and lords are subject to his authority. But the question is, whether civil rulers derive their authority from him as mediator, or whether they derive their authority from God as moral governor of mankind. The latter seems to us to be the truth. Christ says that "his kingdom is not of this world." This is his solemn testimony before a civil magistrate whose authority he recognizes. (See John xix. 10, 11; Rom. xiii. 1, etc.) Now, was Pilate, as a representative of the Roman government, acting as an officer of the kingdom of Christ? If so, to what perplexity are we reduced in the interpretation of such a text as John xviii. 35–37! If any authority is "of this world," it certainly is the authority of the civil magistrate. If it should be said that, as Christ is "*head* over *all* things unto the church," his supreme headship should be acknowledged by all "powers that be"; we answer, first, that it ought to be done where it can be honestly and truly done; and we doubt not that the day is coming when all "the kingdoms of this world will become the kingdoms of our Lord and of his Christ," and "all kings shall fall down before him, and all nations shall serve him." But how is it now? "No man calleth Jesus Lord but by the Holy Ghost," says Paul in 1 Cor. xii. 1. Are there more than a very small minority of the people of the Confederate States who are, in the judgment of charity, persuaded by the Holy Ghost that our blessed Saviour is Lord and King? What then? Will the acknowledgment of Christ in the constitution make us a "Christian nation"? Have not the kings of France enjoyed the titles of "eldest sons of the church" and "most Christian kings"? What shall we say of Henry VIII. and Philip II.? O Christ! what crimes have been committed in thy name! No; there is no magic in the name of Christ emblazoned in our constitution and on our banners to transform us into a Christian people. Many a foul heart has beaten under the "cross" of the crusader; fouler far than beat under the crescent of the Saracen. To make the change proposed in our constitution would have one of two effects: either to make us a nation of hypocrites, or to exclude from our public service every sort of ability which was not found associated with a cordial reception of Christ as king, or, at least, with a sincere recognition of his authority. Are we prepared for either alternative? We believe that, as civil government was ordained for all men and not for the saints only; as there is a moral constitution in all men which responds to the authority of God as moral governor, and they can recognize him as such without the saving power of the Holy Ghost; and as God, the God of nature and providence, has endowed men with capacity for government who are not Christians; all that is necessary in the way of an explicit acknowledgment of responsibility is the acknowledgment of our responsibility to God as the governor of nations. But we shall have more to say on this subject under the next head.

2. The next point of difference between church and state is in the rules by which they are to be respectively regulated in the exercise of their functions. The rule of the church is the word of God, the Scriptures of the Old and New Testaments. This is the statute book of the visible kingdom of Christ. The rule for the state is the "light of nature," or the human reason. The power of the church is, strictly and only, "ministerial and declarative"; the power of the state is magisterial and imperative. The church has no power to *make* laws, but only to *declare* the law of God. All her acts of government are acts of obedience to her Head and King. The state has the power to make laws as well as to declare them; has a legislative as well as a judicial power. Hence, the form of government for the church, the regulative and the constitutive principles of her organization, are not matters to be determined by human reason, but to be derived from the Bible as the constitution and statute-book: while, in the state, these are matters to be settled by the history and condition of political communities. The life of the state is natural, and it is left to assume an organization for itself. The life of the church is supernatural, and God prescribes an organization for it.

If it should be asked, whether the Bible is no rule for the civil power—whether the secular magistrate may proceed, in all cases, as if God had not revealed his will in writing—the answer is, assuredly not. In the first place, the light of nature is made much more clear by the revealed will of God. For example, in respect to the justice and expediency of capital punishment for the crime of murder, the Bible not only gives its sanction to this penalty, but it makes it the duty of the magistrate, as the sword-bearer, to inflict it. So, also, as to the lawfulness of defensive war. The sword-bearer is bound to wage such a war. According to the light of nature, interpreted by the Bible, the Quaker theory of war is not merely a sickly sentimentalism, but a rebellion against the organic law of society and government. The law of marriage is another example. In the second place, the erroneous teaching of the light of nature is rectified by the Bible. In the case of a weekly rest, for example, the word of God demonstrates that such a rest belongs to man as man, was ordained before his fall, and is necessary to his well-being. Reason and experience have amply demonstrated the same truth, that "the Sabbath was made for man"; but it is doubtful whether the fact would have been recognized by the light of nature alone. In the third place, every man who has received this revelation is bound to accept it as a revelation from God, and to regulate his faith and practice by its authority, either in a positive or in a negative way. In some of his duties the Bible is a positive rule; in others, it is a negative rule. Touching the whole matter of the method of salvation, the whole question as to what is necessary to be believed or done in order to obtain eternal life, the Scriptures are a *positive* guide, teaching what is to be believed or done, and *all* that is to be believed or done to that end. Touching the life that now is, the avocations necessary to sustain the being or promote the well-being of society, agriculture, commerce, manufactures, civil and criminal laws, the man, if he be a civil magistrate, or whatever else, is to be governed by the *negative* authority of the Bible. He can do anything the Bible does not *forbid.* The principle contended for by Hooker and the court party, in the time of Elizabeth, against Cartwright and the Puritans, for the regulation of the church, though a false one for the church, was true in application to the state—that anything may be lawfully ordained which is not forbidden in the word. We say false in its application to the church, because contrary to the injunction that "nothing be added to the requirements of God"; the word being a *positive* charter, and therefore signifying prohibition by *silence.* It is true in its application to the state, because the Bible is not, for the state, a *positive* rule.

Let us now, for a moment, return to the question which has been discussed, and consider it in the light of those principles. Should the supremacy of Christ, as King of kings, and the supreme authority of the Bible, be formally and explicitly acknowledged in our civil constitutions? We answer, again:

1. By all means, if it can be truly and honestly done. If all the sovereign people could say "amen" as heartily, or even as sincerely, to such an addition to the section on "liberty of conscience" as they do to the section as it now stands in the constitution, there would be no objection to it, except that it was not necessary—that it was not an essential function of a civil constitution to make such a declaration. If the body that framed the constitution had been able sincerely to declare, in presenting it to the States for their ratification, that they, the members of that body, had felt their responsibility to Christ as king in framing that document, such a declaration would have been a noble testimony from individual citizens, and a happy augury for the people. But, evidently, the value of such a testimony would depend upon its *sincerity;* and to have introduced it into the constitution itself as the solemn utterance of "we, the people," when it was notorious that not one-half of the peo-

ple even professed to believe it, what were this but to incorporate hypocrisy in the fundamental law? Would to God that our statesmen who profess to be Christians might be more courageous, as individuals, in bearing their testimony for Christ!

2. As the doctrine of the supremacy of Christ is a doctrine of pure revelation, it forms no part of the essential functions of civil government to teach it or profess it. The supremacy of Christ is founded upon his work as a priest for the salvation of his elect. The state is a branch of the moral government of God as the righteous judge of all, and is bound to recognize God only in this capacity. The church, which is the body, or professes to be the body of the saved, is bound to recognize the Saviour, prophet, priest and king. This is her very vocation, to be a witness-bearer, and the Bible regulates her testimony and her profession. The state must not contradict her testimony, and that is all the state is bound to do. What is the definition of the church visible in the *Westminster Confession of Faith?* "The visible church consists of all those throughout the world that *profess the true religion*, together with their children; and is the kingdom of the Lord Jesus Christ," etc. Now, if our brethren could carry their point, the state and church would be, at least logically, confounded; for the same definition would answer, in a great degree, to both of them. They both *profess the true religion*, that is, the revealed religion of *salvation*, with mercy and not justice as its prominent feature. Nor is the proposed profession of the state a meagre one. Implicitly, it is the whole gospel; explicitly, it is as full as was the profession of the church for hundreds of years. And if the state begins to make a profession of the Christian religion, it is impossible to predict where it will stop. The only safety for liberty and for religion is in rigidly enforcing the maxim that the Bible is, in the sense already illustrated, a *positive* rule for the church, a *negative* rule for the state.

But we are asked, if the state is bound to respect the negative authority of the Scriptures, where is the impropriety in her *professing* that respect? We answer, that it is one thing to be *bound* to perform a duty, and quite another thing to be *prepared* to perform it. Every man who hears the gospel is bound to confess Christ before man; but we are in the habit of warning men against coming to the Lord's table unless they are believers. We repeat, that the church is the body whose vocation it is to profess faith in Christ and in his word; and any other doctrine will have the effect of confounding the church and the state. If any legislator, or judge, or governor, chooses to profess his responsibility to Christ for his own public acts, a responsibility he really feels, let him do it. We should render our hearty thanks to God for every judicious public act of this kind. But let it be remembered that it is his own personal responsibility he is confessing, and that he is not speaking for those who feel no such responsibility.

It may be added, that we have not intended, in anything that has been said, to deny that the state is a moral personality; that there is an "organic life," or a "public conscience" belonging to political communities. All this is freely admitted. But it has been shown, we think, that this moral personality is subject to the government of God as a government of justice, of natural justice; that this public conscience and organic life are to be regulated and controlled by the light of nature, interpreted and corrected by the word of God, when the state is in possession of that word.

The view advocated by some of our brethren, of the personality of the state, which makes it something totally different at once from the administration at any given time, and from the whole body of the people, so that the state may be Christian, while the administration and the people are Jews, Turks, or atheists, is a view which passes our comprehension. Such a theory might, with some color of plausibility, be maintained under a despotism like that of Louis XIV. of France, who boasted that he was the state. But what is the state, according to the Confederate constitution? What is the state, according to the terms of the proposed amendment to the article on liberty of conscience? These are the terms: "Nevertheless, we, the *people of these Confederate States*, distinctly acknowledge our responsibility to God, and the supremacy of his Son, Jesus Christ, as King of kings and Lord of lords; and hereby ordain that no law shall be passed by the Congress of these Confederate States inconsistent with the will of God, as revealed in the Holy Scriptures." What can be clearer than that the state, here, is the "*people* of the Confederate States"? Not the whole mass of the population—women, children, foreigners, slaves—but the political corporation, the *populus*, the *demos*, the body of voters—a minority of the whole population. Now, of this minority a large majority are rebels against Christ. Yet this is the body whose religion, it is insisted, must be the Christian religion, whatever the religion or no-religion of the people may be! It is the body, at least, which must *profess* the Christian religion! Or shall we say that the constitution itself, the parchment roll on which the fundamental law is written, is the state, whose religion is Christian, although "the people" who ordain it are not? We confess that all this sounds to us very much like the old realism of the schools, which asserted for abstract ideas a substantive existence, different from and independent of the concrete things in which they were manifested and exemplified. We say this with a veneration amounting to awe for the memory of that great genius and noble man of God, whose illustrious name gives support to this movement for an amendment of the Confederate constitution.

The two points of difference, which we have attempted to illustrate, between the civil and the ecclesiastical power, comprehend some others, which, although already incidentally referred to, are worthy of an articulate statement. For example:

3. The church and the state differ in their *sanctions*, as well as in their *authority* and their *rule*. The sanction of ecclesiastical government is *moral*, appealing to the faith and the conscience, a parental *discipline*, designed for the good of the offender. Its symbol is the "*keys*." The sanction of civil government is *force*, appealing to the bodily sensibilities of the subject or the citizen; a *penal* administration, designed to vindicate the majesty of justice and the supremacy of law, with a very incidental, if any, reference to the good of the transgressor. Its symbol is the "*sword*." It is so perfectly obvious that the employment of force is abhorrent, from the whole nature and genius of the church, that even the fiends of the "holy office" were compelled to profess the greatest horror of shedding the blood of heretics, and piously turned them over to the secular arm.

4. "The scope and aim of civil power is only things *temporal;* of the ecclesiastical power, only things *spiritual*. *Religious* is a term not predicable of acts of the state; *political* and *civil*, not predicable of acts of the church." (See Robinson, *ut supra*.) The proclamation of the president in regard to days of fasting and prayer is a religious act; but then it is not an act of government. It is merely an invitation or request addressed by a citizen in high place to his fellow-citizens. If it were done as an act of government, it would be an usurpation of the prerogatives of the church. On the other hand, if the church does a political act, it is guilty of an usurpation of the prerogatives of the state. Rebellion (which, by the way, is a totally different thing from revolution, the latter always implying the existence of a civil government under whose authority the revolutionists are acting, and thereby excluding the very idea of treason)—rebellion is always a *sin* as well as a *crime;* and a church member may be disciplined for rebellion, but the fact must first be found

by the civil authority and accepted by the church. Nothing can be more presumptuous and absurd than the decision by a church court sitting in the city of Philadelphia as to the allegiance of one of its members, who is a citizen of Virginia. If he is obeying the laws of the State of which he is a citizen, no power on earth can convict him of the crime either of treason or rebellion. One more illustration may be added. The act by which ministers of the gospel, as such, are excluded in some of the States of this Confederacy, perhaps in all, from civil office, is an usurpation by the civil power of the functions of the church. If it be a sin, an infraction of solemn vows, for ministers to hold civil office, as we believe it is, it is, nevertheless, a sin which it is the function of the church, not of the state, to rebuke. As to the grounds of expediency upon which this disfranchisement of ministers has been defended, we only say that the history of the world, if candidly studied, will show that the church is in much greater danger from the ambition or the stupidity of politicians than the state is from the ambition or avarice of ecclesiastics.

But enough. The theory of church and state illustrated in the foregoing pages is the Virginia doctrine as we understand it—the doctrine of the Presbytery of Hanover in their memorials to the legislature of that grand old commonwealth from 1775[1] to 1785, in which last year Mr. Jefferson's "Bill for Establishing Religious Freedom" became a law. It has been called the "American" theory; but the history of the Northern States has shown that the current theory there has been rather the "semi-theocracy" of New England, according to which, as Mr. Robinson observes, "the church becomes an agency for keeping the proper party in power, a congress-

[1] The work of the Presbytery of Hanover in advancing this doctrine began at least as early as 1774, as witnesses the paper drawn by the Presbytery at the house of Col. Wm. Cabell, of Amherst, in November, 1774. This paper was discovered by Mr. Wm. Wirt Henry, and published in the *Central Presbyterian*, May 16, 1888.—EDITOR.

managing society, a public-opinion-manufacturing society. Hence, its three thousand clergymen's memorial to congress, its religious press devoted to Fremontism, and its treasury of religious funds to carry the election in Pennsylvania."

Whether the views expressed in this article be sound or not, there can be but one opinion among intelligent men as to the necessity of reviewing these old controversies, and of feeling once more for our foundations. If what we have written should contribute in the smallest degree to a safe and satisfactory conclusion, we shall be amply rewarded for our trouble.

THE GENERAL ASSEMBLY OF 1856.[1]

General Observations.

THE number of commissioners present at the opening of the sessions of the Assembly of 1856—one of the largest since the disruption—was less than two hundred. The number of votes cast for moderator of the Assembly which has just adjourned was two hundred and thirty-two. This full attendance at the beginning was, doubtless, due to the extraordinary facilities for travel furnished by the capital and enterprise of the great commercial metropolis of the country, and to the natural curiosity felt by the more distant members to see the city of which all the rest of the United States is a sort of suburbs.

This is the first meeting of the Assembly in the city of New York, and we doubt not that the good Presbyterian people thereof will not only be willing, but even anxious, to welcome it again, if we may judge by the heartiness and largeness of their hospitality to the members at this meeting. We feel assured, also, that good has been done by this meeting to the churches connected with us in that city. City churches are too apt to live for themselves, to be vigilant and active in promoting their own prosperity, and to forget that a single congregation, however large or rich, is but a small fraction of the great Presbyterian Church in the United States of America. There is a tendency to isolation of effort, and consequent alienation and jealousy of feeling in every quarter of our church among the particular congregations; but this tendency is aggravated by many circumstances in a crowded commercial population. The absence of a vigorous social life, the very feeble play of those affections and sym-

[1] Appeared in the *Presbyterial Critic*, May, 1856.

pathies which can only be nourished by a vigorous social life, the conventional forms which have been substituted in its stead, to some extent insincere, because conventional—these are among the circumstances which go to increase the unhappy tendency referred to. There are gentlemen in New York, we have reason to fear, who do not know that the Presbyterian Church in the United States has its Foreign Missionary office in that city, although they contribute to its funds. Now, if anything can annihilate such narrowness of views, it is a meeting like this of the representatives of a church extending over a territory of three millions of square miles, and we earnestly trust that not only the members of this body, but the Christian friends who entertained them, have a wider conception and a sweeter sense of the fellowship of the saints since this meeting has been held.

As to the effect of the meeting on the city at large, it was probably the same as the effect of all other sorts of conventions, that is to say, nothing. An enthusiastic gathering of thousands at the city hall, with all the noisy pomp of music and cannon, would never be known to the inhabitants up-town but for the press. There were several assemblies ecclesiastical in session at the same time in New York during the month of May; but the great monster was scarcely more conscious of their presence than the ox in the fable was of the presence of the fly upon his horn. It is impossible to determine how many assemblies might pour into that city without in the slightest degree disturbing its equanimity. For purposes of general impression there can be no doubt that any other place in the country ought to be preferred to New York for the meeting of the General Assembly.

In looking over the Assembly one of the most striking features to an observer was the large, perhaps unusual, number of grey heads. No man could doubt that a body of men was here who worked hard and endured privation for Christ's sake; and it was a pleasant reflection that no man ever worked or suffered for that blessed Master in vain, and that the time was coming when a premature old age, brought on by incessant labors in his cause, should be rewarded with the joys of immortal youth and vigor. If our infidels, who are always canting about "earnest-minded men," would look in now and then upon an assembly like this during the devotional exercises, they might, perhaps, be led to suspect that men who worship a God above them may be as "earnest-minded" as those who worship themselves, the divinity within. While we say this, it gives us great pain to add that there is not in the lobbies, nor always even in the house, that silence during the worship of God which eminently becomes such a body of representatives of his people. The lobby nuisance will have to be abated, or there will be an end to all reverent worship or profitable debate.

One remark more of a general kind. No one could fail to be struck with the conservative temper of the body in regard to the subject which is now agitating the whole country. Henry Clay is reported to have said that he would never despair of the Union until the Old School Presbyterian Church was rent asunder. And in this "deliverance" he showed more sagacity than in some others which have become more famous. Long may she be a bond of union to these States and a blessing to the world!

THE OPENING SERMON.

The propriety of publishing opening sermons by the authority of the Assembly admits of serious question. It is often the case that retiring moderators make the sermon the vehicle of their own views, touching certain points which are subjects of debate between different parties in the church, or between the church and the world. The sermon of Dr. Boardman at the opening of the Assembly of 1855 was an instance of the former; the sermon of Dr. Rice at the opening of the last Assembly, an example of the latter. The Assembly, as such, ought not to be committed before the world to certain doctrines, or to certain methods of handling doctrines, by a vote upon a mere complimentary resolution. No man likes to refuse to join in a vote of this kind, and yet the effect of it is to commit him, as a member of the body, to the doctrines or methods of the performance proposed to be published under its imprimatur. If the theory of the church propounded in Dr. Boardman's sermon had been brought before the Assembly last year for discussion and formal vote, there would have been a large and respectable minority against it; and when it comes to be thoroughly examined, the whole church, we doubt not, will reject it. And yet the resolution to print, so far as we know, was adopted *nem. con.* In regard to Dr. Rice's sermon, we may say, that the impression made by its delivery was, upon the whole, a happy one and a wholesome one. But as a *discussion*, we think it was defective, even for a sermon. His text was, "Preach the word"; his leading topics, the "matter" and "manner" of preaching. He professed his intention to say little or nothing about the "matter," and to devote himself chiefly to the "manner"; but, in point of fact, as it appeared to us, he said a great deal about the "matter" and comparatively little about the "manner." This, however, is a mere affair of arrangement and logical distribution. A large part of the sermon was occupied with defining the true position of the public expounder of the word in regard to philosophy and science—a very delicate point in the present posture of opinion. The prominent postulate here was, that on all questions science and revelation should each be regarded as supreme in its own sphere, and its decisions final. Sometimes, consequently, science must correct its conclusions by the voice of revelation, and sometimes the interpretation of revelation must be modified and corrected by the discoveries of science. But the preacher did not propose any criterion by which we might determine to which of the two classes any given question is to be referred. The divine, Sumner for instance, will insist that it is in the last degree improbable that there should be no authentic record of so stupendous a series of facts as are implied in a cosmogony; and if there be such a record, our whole business is one of interpretation; we are to interrogate the record according to the established usages of language. This record having been made by the Creator himself—for in the nature of the case none other could be authentic—its deliverances must be final, and the geologist must bring his facts into harmony with it. The geologist, on the other hand, maintains that the record he has found written upon the stony tablets of the earth is equally authentic, and more perspicuous; and, therefore, Moses must change his voice. Now, will Dr. Rice tell us how we are to arbitrate between the divine and the geologist; upon what principle or by what criterion we are to decide to which *sphere* these questions belong? If he can do this he will impose a debt of gratitude upon Christian geologists and geological Christians all over the world.

Again, in another part of the sermon, he justly defined the office of reason in respect to revelation to be twofold: *first*, to examine the evidences of revelation, and *second*, to interpret it. But he did not tell us what this term "evidences" includes. Are the *contents* of the record any part of the evidence? If so, then what are the limitations under which the reason of man is to judge of these contents considered as evidence, or, which amounts to the same thing, considered as determining the interpretation? The infidel geologist says Moses, interpreted according to the laws of the Hebrew language, is wrong; therefore, he did not write by inspiration of God. The Christian geologist says Moses, as commonly interpreted, is wrong; therefore, we must seek another interpretation. The principle upon which they both stand is the same, the authority of reason. Now, what are the limitations upon this authority? Will Dr. Rice tell us?

The truth is, we are too sensitive altogether about the pretensions of science; and especially now about the pretensions of geology. There is no contradiction among the *facts* of nature; the contradiction lies in the theories which men have framed to account for them. We may rest assured that the Bible, which is even now necessary to reconcile the apparently contradictory conclusions of different sciences, geology and ethnology, for example, will ultimately be found to be in perfect harmony with the highest and maturest conclusions of them all.

If any apology be necessary for making these remarks, we refer to the fact already mentioned, that the Assembly has ordered the sermon to be printed, and thus made it, in some sort, a part of its proceedings. And we may add, that the reputation of Dr. Rice, as well as his official position before the Assembly, gives weight to everything he speaks or writes.

THE BOARDS.

These institutions occupied, as usual, a very considerable share of the attention and time of the Assembly. The address of the Rev. J. L. Wilson, one of the secretaries of the Board of Foreign Missions, was listened to with great interest. No man who loves the Lord Jesus Christ can help rejoicing in such intelligence as the report of this Board communicates to the churches. The Lord has demonstrated his faithfulness in performing his promises to his people; and it should have the effect of increasing their faith, patience, diligence and zeal. The resolutions reported by the various committees to whom the annual reports were referred were adopted, as is generally the case, without discussion, and, we may add, without examination. The only apparent exception to this remark—and it was only apparent—was a speech of two or three minutes in length by the Rev. Dr. Thornwell, of South Carolina, by way of protest against the control of the Board of Education over secular education, and against the assumed duty and constitutional power of the church to exercise any control over this department of the interests of society. He insisted that the whole affair of general public education belonged to the state, and not to the church; and that the Board of Education had been created for the sole purpose of assisting candidates for the Christian ministry while engaged in the prosecution of the necessary course of study. He stated that he did not intend to make an argument upon these points, though he was prepared to do so; and no argument was made. The resolution objected to is as follows:

"5. *Resolved*, That while the Assembly continues to approve of the course of the Board in establishing schools, academies and colleges on a definite religious basis, a sound discretion is necessary as to their number and location; and lest the observations of the Board in this relation should be exposed to invidious misconstruction, it should be distinctly understood that the church does not undervalue the importance of any institution of learning which, though not subjected to ecclesiastical supervision, recognizes the authority, and inculcates the principles, of God's written word, much less disparage the common school system as adapted to useful ends, so long as the Bible is not excluded."

It will be observed that this resolution is so construed as to be incapable of division; and the vote, therefore, was, of necessity, a vote either for or against the whole. We do not know whether "the land of Joab" was in it or not, but it marvellously resembles most of the statements of the Board of Education upon this delicate subject, mixing up the true and the false, the unquestionable and the doubtful, in one mass, and forcing the church to the disagreeable alternative, either of accepting some error, or of rejecting some truth. We cannot understand these perpetual saving clauses in regard to common school education, while the effort is systematically made to draw off from it the support of the Presbyterian Church. If all the evangelical denominations set up for themselves, and leave the common schools to the care of themselves, or to the care of the world and the devil, of course these common schools must become a curse. We cannot but hope that our church will pause and consider the drift of this whole scheme, and will refuse to abandon the glorious mission which the past history of our country demonstrates that God has committed to her. Let her not cut herself off from the sympathies of the great American people.

We cannot pass from this subject without expressing our gratification with the remarks made by Dr. Dabney, of Virginia, upon the low standard of qualifications for the ministry practically established by too many of our presbyteries, or, in other words, upon the easy admission of candidates to the privileges of the ministry. He showed that the effect of slight and merely nominal examinations was to degrade the whole office in the eyes of that very class of young men whom we should be most anxious to get into it. What anybody can get is not worth anybody's striving for. The wider we open the door, the fewer men of generous minds will come in. In our anxiety to increase the number of ministers, we should beware of degrading the office in such a manner as to discourage any but ordinary men from seeking it.

Dr. Peyton Harrison, of the same State, protested against the current notion, that only indigent young men are to be expected to offer themselves to the Lord, in the service of the ministry. And it deserves to be considered, whether we have not, in our plans and prayers, practically limited the Holy One of Israel, in choosing his ministers, to a certain class, to young men, and poor young men. The sooner we get rid of the idea of a class-ministry the better. We cannot help thinking, that a large infusion of that sort of tone which is acquired in the honorable practice of the other learned professions would greatly improve the tone of the ministry, by counteracting the tendencies of the exclusively professional, we had almost said monastic, education acquired in the seminaries.

There was one circumstance connected with the operations of all the Boards during the last year which will gratify all the "strict-constructionists" in the church, and that is, that they have dispensed, in whole, or in part, with paid collecting agents, not only without detriment to their revenues, but to the positive increase of them. The Assembly does some good things as well as bad, without knowing precisely at the time what it *is* doing. It has called attention, by its action of 1854 and 1855 on systematic benevolence, to principles which will work an entire revolution, ultimately, in the plans and schemes of the church for sustaining and propagating the gospel. These principles are very far from being fully comprehended as yet, but they are working. Let us have faith in God, and wait!

INADEQUATE SUPPORT OF MINISTERS.

The Rev. Dr. Junkin offered a resolution, which the house agreed to, for the appointment of a committee to draft a pastoral letter to the churches in reference to this subject. Dr. Dabney was made chairman of this committee, and reported a paper containing many hints and suggestions, which our congregations would do well to consider.

There can be no doubt that the ministry is inadequately supported; but there is as little doubt, in our own mind, that the whole blame ought not to be laid upon the people. The first question in regard to any particular preaching is, whether it is worth paying for at all. There is not a little of what is called fine preaching which is not worth the money expended upon the sexton, fuel, and light, simply for the reason that it is not the gospel. Unfortunately, preaching of this sort is generally well supported; for the world loveth its own.

There is very little of this preaching, we rejoice to believe, in our own church. But there is a kind of preaching which is evangelical as to its matter, but anything but that as to its manner and form. It makes no impression upon the people, and they cannot be expected to value the truths it is designed to convey. There is no earnestness, no freedom, no urgency of exhortation or entreaty, nothing to make the people feel that they are in contact with a living soul. It is utterly idle to expect that a genuine gospel ministry will be sustained, unless the people live and grow under it. A few men may be found, in almost every community, who are willing to contribute to the support of the church and its ordinances from a general consideration of the happy influence of these institutions upon society; but such comprehensive views are rare. In the great majority of cases all depends upon the man himself, first of all. Let him be baptized with the baptism of the Holy Ghost, and preach Christ, with all his heart, and soul, and mind, and strength; give himself wholly to his work, and throw himself upon the people for his living. Next, let the people grow in grace; let them be "rooted, grounded, settled in the truth, *abounding therein with thanksgiving*,"—as they will be very apt to be under such a ministry—and nothing can hinder them from coming up to the full support of the gospel among themselves but want of means, or want of instruction in regard to this particular duty. If they are poor, then the Lord accepteth according to what they have, and not according to what they have not. If they do not know that it is their duty to minister in temporal things to those who minister to them in spiritual things; that the Lord has ordained that they who preach the gospel should live of the gospel; that contribution to the cause of God is a regular, stated ordinance of worship, like prayer or singing; whose fault is it? Their own fault, no doubt; but the fault also of the preacher, who ought not to shun to declare any part of the divine counsel.

But it is a delicate matter, it is said. It might be so considered, if it were not a divine ordinance, and designed fully as much for the edification of the people who give as for the comfort and usefulness of the minister who receives. Even if a minister were able to live without a salary, it would still be the part of mercy to the people to require them to give according to their ability. If a man, therefore, understands the spiritual relations of this ordinance of giving, and believes in it as a means of grace, provided by the "Author and Finisher of faith," there need be no delicacy in the matter.

Let these conditions then concur: life in the preacher and life in the people, along with proper instruction as to their duty, and a competent measure of pecuniary ability, and there will be no difficulty on the score of support. The great trouble is the want of life. We are expecting the grace of liberality to flourish while all the other graces are languishing; we are looking for a vigorous arm when a mortal paralysis has smitten the heart. Let us give up our galvanism and pray for the Spirit of life. There can be no substitute for that. We need never distrust the grace of God in the hearts of his people; only let us appeal always to their *faith* in the word of Jesus and their love to his person. But if professing Christians believe not in him and love him not, what right have we to look for any better treatment? The disciple is not greater than his teacher, nor the servant than his master. It is *enough* that the disciple be as his teacher, and the servant as his master. It would be a wretched thing for us and for the church if we were allowed to ride in triumph upon our high places, while the honor of our royal Master was in the dust.

PROVISION FOR DISABLED MINISTERS AND THEIR FAMILIES.

Upon the reading of the annual report of the trustees, to whom the funds contributed for the relief of disabled ministers and their families are entrusted, a committee was appointed to prepare and present a plan to the Assembly by which the wants of this class of sufferers should be provided for more effectually. Dr. Rogers, of Philadelphia, as chairman of this committee, made a report in which, after setting forth the poverty and distress which actually exists, and arguing the right of worn-out ministers to a competent support, and the corresponding duty of the church to afford it, a plan was recommended for a permanent fund; this fund to be raised by a contribution of not less than five dollars from every minister, and one of not less than ten dollars from every church annually for five years; and to be distributed according to certain rules laid down in the same paper. The plan was simply the constitution of an insurance company.

The report was adopted by parts, but when the question was about to be taken upon its adoption as a whole, the motion was made and carried to re-commit the paper to the committee. The committee reported the second time substantially the same plan, and, after very considerable discussion, the subject was committed to another committee, consisting mainly of ruling elders, to report to the next General Assembly. The only portion of the original committee's report adopted by the house was the rhetorical preamble to the resolutions, and that not without some expurgation. We cannot refrain from expressing our surprise that a paper of this kind should be ordered to be spread out upon the Minutes. It ought to have been put in the appendix, if printed at all.

The whole discussion showed—and there was more said upon this subject, first and last, than upon any other—that a majority of the Assembly were afraid of *permanent* funds. Wherever the church has been, or is established, endowed by the state, no objection is made to such funds; but under any purely voluntary system men feel, even when they have not the perspicacity to perceive, that they are foreign to the genius of the system, and are liable to great and dangerous perversion and abuse. It was, indeed, argued that we must have permanent funds, that we could not have seminaries, etc., without them; but it was conceded that they were dangerous; and the history of seminaries is a signal proof of it. Dr. Thornwell argued that a permanent fund ought always to be avoided in providing for *contingent* wants; it ought only to be resorted to in the case of wants or demands permanent in their nature, and existing and operating according to a settled law, capable of being ascertained and defined. He contended that seminaries belonged to this last class, and the wants of disabled ministers to the category of contingencies, to be met as they arose. He argued against such a fund, also, from the well-known principle of political economy, that a public institution for the relief of poverty has the effect of increasing the evil. And a fund of the kind proposed by the committee would be apt to bring men into the ministry of our church whom we did not want. It would be a great calamity to weaken that spirit of self-denial and of trust in God which is now so honorable a characteristic of our ministry, and which contributes so largely to their respectability and usefulness. He conceded, it was conceded by all, that our brethren in affliction, their widows and little ones, ought to be and must be taken care of; but he held that the sympathies and charities of the people of God would not be found wanting when the cases of distress became known. It was the duty of the church to provide for the poor saints, and this duty would be performed without a permanent fund.

It appears to us that a great many random assertions are made by our brethren in discussing this subject. We do not believe it to be true, for example, that ministers, as a class, leave their families in a more helpless condition than any other class of the people of God; and the people of God are not, as a class, forsaken, nor are their seed, as a class, beggars of their bread. That they are not rich is true; but that is no calamity. God, who loves them, does not intend that they shall have their portion in this life. He has a better and an enduring substance in store for them. They who have their portion in this life, whose belly is filled with hid treasure, and who leave the rest of their substance to their babes, are "men of the world." Again, it is no disgrace to be poor or to live upon the charities of the church, if the Giver of all has denied to us the privilege of working. If we are able to work and do not, we have no right to eat. If we are able to work and do work, we shall eat. If we are not able to work, then are we Christ's poor, and must live as he lived, upon the charities of his people. We must not fret against that sovereign, and, we doubt not, merciful constitution of society which has made poverty a permanent element in it, especially since Jesus has made the poor the representatives of himself, and has said, "Inasmuch as ye have done it unto these, ye have done it unto me." So long as it stands upon record that the Son of man had not, on earth, a place to lay his head, how can any child of God doubt his love because he is poor? It is *enough* that the servant be as his master. A great deal was said in the debate in the Assembly about ministers and their families being thrown upon "the cold charities of the world." This is not the true statement of the case. They are thrown upon the charity of those who love the Lord Jesus Christ, and that charity is not "cold." It was a charity to which the Saviour was willing, amidst his dying agonies, to commit her who bare him.

We think, therefore, that our chief concern as rulers in the house of God should be to have the living and working ministry adequately supported; and the rest should be willing to be numbered among the poor of the flock, and to be provided for as they are. At any rate, the plan of an insurance company is not the thing. If a man has no conscientious scruples about insurance, he can be accommodated by others than the trustees of the Assembly. One remark more, and we dismiss this subject. If any systematic effort is to be made for the relief of the class in question, it ought to be made by synods or presbyteries, and not by the General Assembly. The Church of Scotland is no model for us in matters of this sort. It covers a territory not much larger than the State of Maryland, and may act as an unit in everything. Our church covers a vast expanse of country, and the sentiment of sympathy operates with comparative languor and feebleness between the distant parts. It would be well on this account if, following the analogy of our political system, we relied more upon the energies of the local bodies and less upon the Assembly. If, for example, the interests of education and of domestic missions were managed by the synods for themselves, with some small central committees of the Assembly to be the means of communication between the weak and the strong, the business would be much more effectually done, to say nothing of the great saving of expense. But in the matter before us, in which so much depends upon the natural operation of compassion, the nearer the parties needing assistance are brought to the parties who are to give it, the more certain is the result. We do not believe that any *Assembly's* fund, of any kind, will ever answer the purpose.

THE QUALIFICATIONS FOR VOTERS FOR CHURCH OFFICERS, AND THE RELATION OF BAPTIZED PERSONS NOT PROFESSING FAITH IN CHRIST TO THE CHURCH.

An overture was sent up from the Presbytery of Londonderry, asking the Assembly to express its judgment in reference to these points; and the Committee of Bills and Overtures recommended that the Assembly content itself with the following deliverances:

1. That only communicating members have a right to vote for ruling elders.

2. That inasmuch as the pastor sustains the relation of teacher as well as that of ruling elder, there is no impropriety in the non-communicating supporters of his ministry voting for him, provided that no communicating member be excluded.

3. That a baptized person not professing faith in Christ stands in a relation to the church analogous to that in which a minor in the state stands to the state.

As the official Minutes of the Assembly have not yet appeared, we have been compelled to rely upon our memory for these statements, as for many others contained in this article. There can be no doubt, however, as to their substantial accuracy.

The report of the committee was put upon the docket, and was not taken up until the last day of the sessions. It was evident, from the conversation which then took place, that there would be very considerable debate upon these propositions, and, as the house was not prepared at that late stage in the proceedings to go into it, the motion was made and carried to lay the whole subject upon the table, with the expectation that it would come up again at the meeting of the next General Assembly. This fact, together with the fact that one of these questions was before the Assembly of last year, justifies us in throwing out some hints which may contribute a little towards a final and satisfactory decision upon the subject.

1. In regard to the qualifications of voters for ruling elders, there is scarcely any room for a difference of opinion. Chapter XIII. of the Form of Government provides that "every congregation shall elect persons to the office of ruling elder, and to the office of deacon, or either of them, in the mode most approved and in use in that congregation." (Section 2.) If nothing more were said, it might be supposed that "the mode," here, included the question of qualifications. But the form of installation in the fourth section is

conclusive in favor of the interpretation of the Assembly's committee: "The minister shall address to the *members of the church* the following question, viz.: Do you, the *members of this church*, acknowledge and receive this brother as a ruling elder (or deacon), and do you promise to yield him all that honor, encouragement, and obedience *in the Lord*, to which his office, according to the word of God and the constitution of this church entitles him?" Now, independently of the express designation "members of the church," applied to the electors, the question itself is one which, by its very terms, is incapable of being properly answered in the affirmative by any other persons. We wish this point to be remembered, as it is an important circumstance in the consideration of the question touching the qualifications of voters for pastor, so far as that question is one of constitutional law. Let it be observed, also, that the terms "church" and "congregation" are used interchangeably in this chapter. The "congregation" shall elect; the "members of the church" shall answer. We do not intend to assert, however, that these terms are, either in general use or in the use of our book, precisely equipollent. We think that the framers of the constitution intended to use them interchangeably when they had reference to a *particular* society of believers; but that the term "church" was used only of the whole body, consisting of a plurality of particular churches or congregations. Compare Chapter VIII., Section 2, where it is said that the governing assemblies "exclude the contumacious and impenitent from the *congregation of believers*." If the persons excluded be elders, deacons, or private members, then the congregation from which they are excluded is, of course, a particular congregation. If they be ministers, then the congregation is the church, represented by the presbytery (not the session); and as this is an unusual sense of the word, our fathers thought it was well to add the epexegetical clause, "of believers." The exception proves the rule. No instance, we think, can be found in our book in which the term "congregation," without any explanatory phrase, is used of the whole church, considered as a unit, or of any portion of it larger than a particular society under the jurisdiction of a session. But of such a particular society the term is used interchangeably with the term "church." See the footnote to Form of Government, Chapter XII.

But even if the constitution were less explicit than we have found it to be upon this question of the voters for ruling elders, we should still have no difficulty in settling it in the light of the great principles of our system and of the word of God. There is a broad distinction made in the New Testament between the church and the world, the sphere of God and the sphere of Cæsar. Our Saviour makes the distinction so broad as to exclude not only the interference of the state as such, but also the interference of the *world* as such, in whatever form that interference may be attempted. "My kingdom is not of this world." Any power or "patronage" exercised by those who are not subjects of this kingdom, citizens of this commonwealth, members of his household of faith, is an usurpation, a tyranny, incompatible, *de jure*, if not *de facto*, with its freedom and independence. Let the history of all religious establishments, even that of Scotland, witness the truth of this proposition. It is nothing to the purpose to say that this is state patronage, but, in this country, where no such thing is possible as usurpation by the state, there can be no harm in non-professing people voting for elders. The ready answer is, that the latter sort of patronage is the more dangerous because it is exercised wholly *without responsibility;* while patrons, under the authority of the state, are, at least in name, responsible to that authority; and, further, because the state patrons *may be* God-fearing men, whereas these church patrons of ours are *ex vi terminorum*, without Christ and without God in the world. If, then, a body of voters outside of the church of

Christ, which is his kingdom, a body of voters not subject to the jurisdiction of ruling elders, can *impose* a man as a ruler upon the church, where is its freedom? If one body of men are bound to obey a ruler which another body of men have chosen to rule them, what becomes of the cardinal principle of liberty, that the ruled have the right to choose their own rulers; that the people are to be governed by representatives elected by themselves? Will it be said that this argument proceeds upon an extreme case, and that in the vast majority of instances the feeling of the outside supporters of a church is not antagonistic to the interests of the church members? The answer is, that these so-called extreme cases are not infrequent in the choice of a pastor; and extreme cases are the crucial tests of principles. Let us never forget that our revolutionary fathers "went to war against a *preamble*." Death is preferable to the loss of a few shillings of ship-money where the right to exact the payment involves the right to make slaves of freemen.

The principles laid down in the chapter on the civil magistrate (XXIII.) in our *Confession of Faith* are applicable to the whole subject of outside control over the affairs of the church. "As Jesus Christ hath appointed a regular government and discipline in his church, no law of any commonwealth should *interfere with*, let, or hinder, the due exercise thereof among the voluntary members of any denomination of Christians, according to their own profession and belief." Any influence, any custom, operating with the force of a law upon the church from without, most certainly comes under the condemnation of this sentence. Trustees exercising certain functions under a state law of incorporation, or pew-holders invested with certain rights of property under the same law, may imagine that they have a right to exercise certain privileges in a corporation existing under the law of the great king, Christ, *qua* trustees and pew-holders; but if they have, then verily the people of God have no king but

Cæsar, and freedom is "of all our vanities the motliest, the merest word that ever fooled the ear from out the schoolman's jargon."

We have dwelt the longer upon the first proposition of the committee because it afforded the occasion of calling attention to some of the great principles which control the whole subject of the committee's report; and because it will require us to say less on their second proposition, which is:

2. That as the pastor sustains the relation of teacher as well as that of ruling elder, there is no impropriety in the non-communicating supporters of his ministry voting for him, provided that no communicating member be excluded.

As the pastor is a ruling elder, it will not be denied that the principles already laid down in regard to the election of that officer apply, and apply with greater force, to him. Being generally superior, in point of education and of knowledge of ecclesiastical law, to the other elders associated with him in the government of the congregation, and having greater advantages for the acquisition of personal influence among the members of the church than his colleagues and equals in authority, and being, officially, *primus inter pares*, it is of vastly more consequence to those who are subject to the jurisdiction of the session over which he presides to have a free election, to resist all outside interference in choosing him as moderator, than in choosing the other members. And the more especially as in the event of his malversation in office he is to be tried, not by the session, like his colleagues, but by the presbytery, a court in which only one representative of the aggrieved congregation can sit. Practically, in many cases, either through the modesty or neglect of the ruling elders, or the fault in some way of the pastor himself, he is the session. If he should be a bad man, and yet with talents enough and of the right sort to secure the support of the worldly supporters of the congregation, it is easy to see what havoc he might make of the sheep. If it is said that the remedy is in the presbytery, without which body no man can be installed as pastor in a Presbyterian church, we answer, very true; but prevention is better and easier than cure.

Again, the ruling function of the pastor's office is that in which, on many accounts, the people are more concerned than in any other. It is this which gives him authority. It is this which places the character and happiness of the church members, in a great measure, in his hands. Everybody knows what tremendous power an ungenerous, malicious man has to persecute, and yet to keep clear of exposing himself to prosecution for transcending the legal bounds of his authority, provided he be invested with the power of jurisdiction over any department of his victim's life. The history of the pastoral office is not free from such examples. We are astonished, therefore, that men can be found, cautious, prudent, men of sense, to argue that because by the charters of many of the city churches the pastor is, *ex officio*, a member of the board of trustees, none but electors of trustees have a right to vote for him! Surely, if there is any force in such an argument it would conclude, *a fortiori*, that because a pastor is a ruling elder none but communicating members should have a right to vote. The office of ruling elder is a divine office, in which all church members are deeply and permanently concerned; the office of trustee is an office of the state, in which the people are only slightly and occasionally concerned.

But the committee base the assertion of the "propriety"—they do not say *right*—of non-communicating supporters of the ministry voting for pastor upon the ground that they have an interest in him as a teacher.

Upon this argument we submit the following considerations:

(1), It is the relation of a pastor, and not the relation of a mere teacher, that is now in question. Nobody doubts that a minister of the gospel might be invited by a number of persons making no profession of religion to preach to them, to instruct them in the plan of salvation. Each regiment in the army of the United States, or each ship in the navy, might be allowed to select their own chaplain, instead of receiving him as they do now by the appointment of the government. But the chaplain has no authority; he is a mere witness for the truth as it is in Jesus. In a settled church state, the case is different; a pastor implies the existence of a flock; he is invested with the function of discipline *in order to* the more effectual exercise of the function of teaching. Christ, the chief Shepherd, has two staves, the one of beauty and the other of bands. "Blessed is the man, O Lord, whom thou *chastenest* and *teachest* out of thy law." These two functions are combined in all the institutions of God for the education of the race. The mere supporters of the ministry, therefore, refusing to submit to the jurisdiction of the pastor, as invested with the power of discipline, cannot be said to have sufficient interest in him, even as teacher, to entitle them to vote.

(2), It is generally conceded that church members only should vote for deacons; and our constitution is perfectly explicit upon this point. But non-communicating supporters of the church contribute to its funds, some of them very liberally. According to the argument of the committee, therefore, they ought to be allowed to vote for deacons. These same supporters are interested in the election of ruling elders because the session regulates the whole affair of the distribution of the funds, the office of the deacon being merely executive; therefore, according to the argument, the supporters should vote for ruling elders. But the committee say no.

(3), The committee have not said what is meant by "supporters of the pastor's ministry." It is not every man who hears him preach. Is it every man who contributes to his salary? What, then, shall we say of those, of whom there are very many, who pay their pew-rent or their annual subscription, and yet seldom or never attend church? And is the elective franchise in the church of God, then, a thing to be bought with money, and capable of being expanded and contracted at the caprice or by the ambition of wicked men? Upon this view of the subject we do not see that the franchise has any limits. A property-holder in the neighborhood of a city church is interested in the teaching of the minister, and by the payment of a trifling sum may exercise the privilege of voting on the same footing with a church member, albeit he never comes inside of the meeting-house! He is not subject to the session; he cannot be disciplined for non-attendance. He has paid his money, and that is all that can be exacted. The conclusion seems to us to be monstrous.

(4), Again, if we understand the doctrine of the committee, baptized persons who are neither communicating members nor contributors have no right to vote for church officers of any sort, and yet they are subject to the jurisdiction of the session, and have an interest in the pastor as teacher. Then we have here a discrimination made in favor of a class of non-communicating persons who refuse to submit to the government of the pastor and session, against another class of non-communicating persons who do submit to that government, both classes having an equal interest in the pastor as teacher! This, also, to us, is a monstrous conclusion.

(5), Once more we deny that such a privilege should be allowed to unbelievers, for the reason that all power ecclesiastical, whether that which is exercised in office, or that of electing and setting apart to office, is "ministerial and declarative"; that is to say, is merely the power of servants to declare and obey the will of their master, Christ. The only rule in which this will is expressed is the word of Scripture; the only effectual source of the knowledge of this will is the Holy Spirit of God. The natural man receiveth not the things of the Spirit, for they are foolishness unto him; neither can he know them, because they are spiritually discerned. Now, in the election of all church officers the process is a spiritual process, regulated by the law laid down in the word of God. The qualifications of officers are described in the word; their existence in certain persons is an indication of the will of Christ that those persons should exercise the functions of such offices; their existence in said persons must be discerned by the church, rulers and people, through the operation of the same Spirit who bestowed them upon the possessors of them, and then acknowledged by a formal choice and formal ordination. But whether in the people who elect, or the man who accepts, or the court which ordains, the whole process is one of simple obedience to Christ, making known his will by his word and spirit. Now, since by the terms of the supposition non-professing supporters of the ministry are "natural" men, "not having the Spirit," have never acknowledged the authority of Christ and subjected themselves to his law, they are incapable of taking any part in this business, they are incapable of judging of a pastor's qualifications as a teacher in general, or of the suitableness of his ministry to a particular congregation. We do not see how these principles can be denied without making the church a human institute, or, at least, the calling of her officers a human calling.

In the last place, the constitution of the church, as it appears to us, takes it for granted that the members of the church only have a right to vote for pastor. We have seen that, although the terms "congregation" and "church" are both used in the chapter (XII.) on the election of elders and deacons, they yet mean the same thing, "*members of the church.*" The chapter on the election of bishops or pastors (XV.) uses the term "congregation" in all cases in which the people electing are referred to, but evidently in the same sense. To say nothing of the clause in section 4, which is confessedly ambiguous, the language of the call in Section 6, and the questions propounded to the people at the installation, are conclusive against the view of the committee.

The people in their call say, "being *well satisfied of the ministerial qualifications* of you, and having good hopes, from our past experience of your labors, that your ministrations in the gospel will be profitable to our spiritual interests, do earnestly call and desire you to undertake the pastoral office in said congregation, promising you, in the discharge of your duty, all proper support, encouragement, and *obedience in the Lord*." Now let it be remembered, that in the case of a licentiate this judgment of the congregation as to his ministerial qualifications is an important element in the evidence that God has called him, an evidence without which, in ordinary cases, the presbytery is not allowed to ordain him; and that it is important evidence, because regarded as the testimony of the Spirit in the people concurring with the testimony of the Spirit in the presbytery licensing him, and the testimony of the same Spirit in the man's own conscience, moving him to seek an opportunity to preach; and we cannot avoid the conclusion that the "congregation" of the call is the congregation of believers. This is confirmed by the fact that they promise him "*obedience* in the Lord," which none but believers could properly do.

Then, at the installation, the "congregation" calling are required to answer questions which none but believers can honestly answer in the affirmative. The second question especially shows that the people answering are members of the church: "Do you promise to receive the word of truth from his mouth with meekness and love, and to *submit to him in the due exercise of discipline?*" In the next chapter, on the translation of ministers from one charge to another, the terms "church" and "congregation" are again used interchangeably. "Instalment" is defined to be "constituting the pastoral relation between the minister and the people of the particular church" over which he is to be installed.[1]

Upon the whole, then, while there might be no impropriety, in certain cases, in mere "supporters" of a church sending up an expression of their judgment about a minister, in the way of memorial or petition to the Presbytery, they certainly are not entitled to vote in the election. And we think that consistency, as well as truth, required the Committee on Bills and Overtures to say so. The true statement of the case is, that inasmuch as the pastor sustains the relation of teacher to the non-communicating supporters of his ministry, their judgment ought to have some weight with the congregation, with the voters, in choosing a man for that office, and with the presbytery in putting the call into his hands.

3. The last proposition of their report is, that baptized persons not professing faith in Christ are minors in the church, and, as such, are not entitled to the full enjoyment of its privileges, though subject to its jurisdiction and protecting care.

This we believe to be a true statement of the relation of

---

[1] For a summary of the historical argument upon this subject the reader is referred to the article in the July number of the *Critic* for 1855, entitled, "Church Elections—Who Shall Vote for Pastor?" We have confined our remarks to the principles involved in this question; but if we chose to rest it upon considerations of expediency, the facts are unhappily abundant to show that to allow the claim set up for non-professing persons would be a fatal policy. And in this connection, as the question came before the Assembly by overture from a New England presbytery, it is appropriate to refer to the fact that Unitarianism was mainly indebted for its rapid progress in that region to the old theocratic system under which multitudes of persons making no credible profession of religion were allowed to vote for church officers. It is very true that the same thing would not have taken place so speedily if the government had been Presbyterian instead of Congregational; but that even a Presbyterian government, with such abuses, is no effectual bar against corruption, the history of moderatism in the Church of Scotland, and of Socinianism in the Church of Ireland, bears melancholy testimony.

baptized children to the church. (See *Critic*, Vol. I., p. 128.) And we think, although some disposition to dispute it was shown in the Assembly, that when the terms are understood it will be so acknowledged. Its bearing upon the subject of church elections will, of course, be variously determined, according to the various judgments of individuals upon that question. Our Confession (chap. XXV.) makes the children of believers constituent elements of the church visible and catholic; and the special privileges of this church are defined to be (*Larger Catechism*, Quest. 63)—"the privilege of being under God's special care and government; of being protected and preserved in all ages, notwithstanding the opposition of all enemies; and of enjoying the communion of saints, the ordinary means of salvation, and offers of grace by Christ, to all members of it, in the ministry of the gospel, testifying that whosoever believes in him shall be saved, and excluding none that will come to him." But in the actual participation of these privileges, the Presbyterian Church has always drawn a broad line between those members who make a credible profession of faith and those who do not. See *Directory for Worship*, Chap. IX., Sec. 1, which lays down, very distinctly, the true doctrine; and the *Book of Discipline*, Chap. I., Sec. 6, which is in entire harmony with it. Baptized non-professing persons are entitled to all the privileges of the other members of the church, except those which presuppose the existence of faith, or, what amounts to the same thing as before the church, a credible profession of it. It is this faith, or credible profession of it, that constitutes adultship, that makes a person a full citizen in the Christian commonwealth; and, according to the principles already illustrated, none but such adults have a right to vote for church officers.

It will be observed that, in the whole foregoing discussion, we regard as believers those who make a credible profession of faith, whether they have it or not. It is the prerogative of God alone to judge the heart; and in every question of right or privilege to be decided by men, the decision must be made upon what *appears*, and not what *is*. We doubt not that there are many unbelievers in the church, and some true believers out of it. The latter are better qualified, morally, to vote for church officers than the former. But this is not for us to judge.

SYSTEMATIC BENEVOLENCE.

The report of the standing committee upon the subject was, to those who have felt a special interest in the action of the Assemblies of 1854 and 1855, a very discouraging document. 1. In the first place, it appeared that the great majority of the presbyteries had paid no attention at all to the injunctions of the above-named Assemblies in the premises; at least, they reported no action. It is scarcely to be supposed that these delinquent bodies have declined to take action because they object to the doctrine of systematic benevolence, or to that aspect of it in which it is presented by those Assemblies; and we are driven to the conclusion either that they do not know what the highest court in the church has enjoined, or that they feel at liberty to disregard and set aside its injunctions. Upon either supposition, it is a very bad showing for a church which has always been distinguished for its intelligence and its respect for law and order. We speak only of those presbyteries which have taken no action; some of them have, doubtless, obeyed the direction of the Assembly, but, for some cause, have failed to report. It would be well for these last to bear in mind that they are directed to report as well as to act. 2. In the second place, the report of the committee was discouraging, because it gave no evidence that they themselves fully comprehended the action of the last two Assemblies, or entered into its spirit. They insisted upon the duty of giving, and giving systematically; but did not present the duty in the relation of an act of worship or an ordinance of the church. The habit of thinking too much of *measures*, and too little of *principles*, is a great enemy of real progress; and its mischievous operation is seen in the speeches and acts of all our deliberative assemblies, in church and state. One of the most painful features of the debates in the Assembly, for the most part, was the absence of appeal to great principles, and the prominence given to considerations of expediency, and that, too, a temporary expediency. The subject of systematic benevolence was taken up too late for discussion; but the mind of many in the house was indicated by two things, the report of itself and the opposition which was made to certain amendments, the design of which was to make the report reaffirm the action of the two preceding Assemblies. The house, by a small majority, agreed to the first, which was to insert the words "as an ordinance of worship"; but they rejected the second, which was designed to give an imperative form to the "request" sent down to the churches; thus practically abandoning the doctrine that contribution is an ordinance, the observance of which is to be enforced in every organized church, in the same manner as the ordinance of prayer, or of singing, or of preaching.

A great deal of prejudice against this doctrine has arisen from misconception of its true bearings. We have heard some intelligent ministers speak of it as if it were designed to bring down the censure of the church courts upon every church member who does not give something to the general cause of religion; and they asked, how can the church session know whether any member gives "as God hath prospered him," or whether he is able to give anything at all? This is a very pertinent question, in their view of the doctrine; but it has nothing to do with the Assembly's view of it. Suppose that praying, as an ordinance of public worship, was as much neglected among our three thousand churches as giving is, and the Assembly were to adopt resolutions precisely like those of 1854–'55 upon the subject of giving, saying to the churches that praying was an ordinance, and enjoining upon presbyteries and sessions the regular observance of it, would it be pertinent to object that prayer is a matter between the soul and God, that God alone can know whether any soul really prays, and that he has commanded us, when we pray, to do it in secret, and not before men; and, therefore, that the Assembly and the lower courts were transcending their authority in issuing such an injunction? Certainly not. Such an objection would be, in the highest degree, impertinent. Obviously, it is not secret prayer in the closet, it is not the fervor or sincerity of heart of any individual ostensibly engaged in the public prayer of the congregation, to which the action of the Assembly would be construed to refer, but the ordinance of prayer as a part of public worship, and as one form in which the fellowship of the saints is made visible. The meaning would be, that every church session is bound to give the people stated opportunities of joining in prayer with each other, and leave the question as to the real value and the true character of their worship to be settled between their own consciences and God. Is it not evident that this is precisely the action of the Assemblies of 1854 and 1855 in regard to giving? The first two resolutions of 1854 are as follows:

"1. *Resolved*, That this Assembly hereby enjoin upon the pastors of our churches to give greater prominence, in the ministration of the word, to the doctrine of the Scripture, as interpreted and set forth in our standards (more particularly in Chapter XXVI., Section 2, of the *Confession of Faith;* in Question 141 of the *Larger Catechism;* in Chapter VII. of the *Form of Government*, and in Chapter IV., Section 5, of the *Directory for Worship*), viz.: that 'saints, by profession, are bound to maintain a holy fellowship and communion in relieving each other in outward things, according to their several abilities and necessities, which communion, as God offereth opportunity, is to be extended unto all those who in every place call upon the Lord Jesus,' 'giving and lending freely according to their abilities'; and, in conformity to this doctrine, recognizing as one of the ordinances established by Christ, in connection with the sermon, prayer, and praise, 'a collection raised for the poor and other purposes of the church.'

"2. *Resolved*, That the presbyteries which have not anticipated the provisions of this action of the Assembly are most earnestly and affectionately enjoined, *First*, At their meetings following the rising of this Assembly to take order that the ministers and church sessions in their bounds shall be directed to adopt some practicable method by which an *opportunity shall be afforded*, and *an invitation given*, to all the members of their congregations to contribute regularly to the objects of Christian benevolence recognized by the Assembly in the organization of the boards of the church, and to such other institutions as to them may seem right. *Second*, And at every spring meeting to institute a proper inquiry into the diligence of ministers and church sessions in executing the provisions of such method."

The Assembly of the next year re-affirmed this action, by adopting the clear and able report of its Committee on Systematic Benevolence. We earnestly commend these papers (Minutes for 1854, pp. 37, 38; and Minutes for 1855, pp. 294, 296) to the careful study of the members of the committee of the Assembly of 1856, and to all who were opposed to amending their report.

A motion was made, in the last Assembly, to invite Mr. Cather, of England, to address the house, when the subject of systematic benevolence should come up. We confess we felt inclined to protest against the Assembly of the Presbyterian Church in the United States listening to the instructions of an English Wesleyan upon any subject, and especially upon a subject whose principles they understood, probably, far more thoroughly than he. The gentleman, however, did not make his speech.

There is one thing more to which we may refer, as at once an evidence of awakened interest in this subject, and of a very inadequate conception of the true doctrine concerning it; that is, the formation of a "Systematic Beneficence Society" in Philadelphia. We cannot, at this moment, lay our hands upon the circular we received, stating the objects and organization of this queer association; but we understood it to be a society for the diffusion of knowledge in reference to the duty of systematic giving. Surely, this is voluntary associationism "run into the ground." In the name of common sense, where will this rage for societies end? Where is the use of the church of the living God, with its divinely-appointed means and ordinances of *instruction*, and its divinely-appointed agencies for *doing* the will of its glorious Head? Are we to have a society for every commandment, for every promise, for every warning, in the Bible? a prayer society? a singing society? a preaching society? a baptism society? a Lord's-supper society? a justification-by-faith society? an efficacious-grace society? and so on endlessly? And are the agents of all these to go round and instruct the ignorant pastors and flocks, each in his own department, at the church's expense? We ask again, where is this folly to end? It is somewhat discouraging that, at the very time when the Presbyterian Church, moving in that path in which the great events of 1837 gave her such an impetus, is striving to disencumber herself of the burden of voluntaryism, and to reach the platform of her constitution and the Bible, by giving up extraordinary and extra-ecclesiastical agencies and measures, and doing God's work in God's way, this odd quiddity should arise to oppose and pervert her testimony. The very existence of this society is a protest against the doctrine of our Assembly; and we earnestly hope that no member of our church will be seduced and entrapped into the support of it.

We are far from believing that the persons who originated this movement meant to oppose the Assembly's action; we only repeat what we said before, that the rage for measures prevents even good men from looking at principles. They do evil that good may come, without knowing it. "In God's name," says the proverb, "all mischief begins."

We are constrained to believe that the failure of so many churches to contribute to the general "schemes" of benevolence, commended by the Assembly to their liberality, is due, in a great measure, to causes which we have already indicated in our remarks upon the inadequate support of the ministry. It will usually be found that a liberal support of the ordinances of religion in any particular congregation will be associated with liberal contributions to the general cause, provided the necessary instruction as to their duty has been given from the pulpit. The grace of God in the hearts of his people is the primary and fundamental condition in the whole business of giving; for liberality is a *fruit* of the Spirit. When the pulse of life beats feebly in the church every good work *must languish;* there can be no substitute for *life* devised by man. "That which is born of the *flesh* is *flesh,*" and can never be anything higher or better. Nature cannot rise above itself. That alone is *spirit* which is born of *the Spirit.* Oh! that we were able to honor more the Spirit of life in Christ Jesus!

1. Let the pure gospel of the Son of God be clearly, fully, earnestly, and tenderly preached; the unsearchable riches of Christ, the free and powerful grace of the Holy Comforter, and, through these, boldness of access to the Father in the holiest of all. Let this gospel be preached with unceasing prayer to him who sends forth his seraphim to touch the lips of whom he pleases, that his word may dwell richly in his children; that they may be rooted, grounded, established, and abounding therein with thanksgiving; that they may know what is the hope of their calling, and recognize

the great truth of their consecration to God; that they have been made a royal *priesthood*, and that, like as Christ, their great High Priest, came not into the world to be ministered unto, but to minister, and to give his life a ransom for many, so, also, they ought, if need be, to lay down their lives for the brethren, and offer themselves a sacrifice for their sakes; that they are a *royal* priesthood, and that, like as Christ entered into his glory through suffering, was exalted because he abased himself, conquered death by dying, was made a king through his sacrifice as a priest, so, also, they, the members of his body, must suffer if they would reign with him, must conquer the world by self-denial and self-sacrifice. If it be said that such a condition of the church as this is not to be expected, we answer, "Is anything too hard for the Lord?" "Can these bones live?" "Ah! Lord God, thou knowest!" "Why should it be thought a thing incredible with you that *God* should raise the dead?" We are not straitened in him; we are straitened in ourselves. May he give us his Spirit, that we may know the things that are freely given unto us!

2. Let the people be instructed as to what God has done, is doing, and has promised to do. Let history and prophecy stand together in the ministrations of the pulpit, as they do in the word of God, that his people may trust, with unshaken faith, in him who is the same yesterday, to-day, and forever. Let them be taught that God has condescended to make them co-workers with himself in reaching the glorious consummation for which they and the whole creation are travailing in agony; that, "though needing nothing at their hands, he has condescended, for the purpose of uniting their hearts to him in profounder sympathy, to assume a position in which he appeals to them as really and tenderly as if he needed all things; that, though their alms and their righteousness extend not directly to him, yet the Saviour is comforted and refreshed with the humblest ministrations to his saints upon the earth; that it is Christ whom they honor in

the interests of his kingdom, or, rather, that it is Christ *who honors them in thus permitting them to honor him*"; that it is not God or his ministers who are "*beggars*" when contributions are solicited, but that "he is the beggar who *solicits the favor of having his* gifts accepted, and he feels it to be a distinction that he can glorify God with the fruits of his substance; that, having given himself to the Lord, all that he possesses is equally devoted, and *what he uses for himself is rather by permission than by right of property.*"

Let the pastor and the church session go before the people with a firm conviction of these truths; let them feel, when they ask for a contribution, that they are really *conferring a favor* upon those from whom it is asked; and where is there any room for "delicacy"? Is this thing an ordinance established by the Saviour's wisdom and love for the *good* of his blood-bought people? Is it a privilege to give, as it is a privilege to pray or give thanks, because it brings us nearer to him who is our life, and likens us to him? Why, then, should there be any shrinking from this duty? Instead of presenting the matter timidly, and almost promising the people that we will not do it again, we ought to tell them boldly that the Lord will deign to receive their offerings, and that in proportion to his blessing upon the work in answer to their prayers will the demands upon their liberality increase; that they must expect to give more and more. Casting ourselves thus upon the faith and love of God's children, we shall be surprised, perhaps, at the cordiality and promptness with which they will respond to our appeals; and, as it is the property of the "treasure of the heart," whether good or evil, to grow by all the drafts which are made upon it, or, in other words, as habit, which strengthens by exercise, is the great controlling law of human nature, it will be found that the more they give, the more they will give. If our ministers, who are inadequately supported, and who, on that account, decline to ask for general contributions, will give their people an idea of the vast communion of saints by such general collections, they will reap the advantage of a larger measure of liberality at home. It is not to people who never have given at all that we go when we want money; it is to those who have been in the habit of giving freely. We say, therefore, to all, try it! try it! try it! We could mention more than one instance in which pastors have resolutely, amid the most dismal croaking and the most confident vaticinations as to the consequences, begun the work; and their faithfulness has been rewarded by the most gratifying results. But we forbear.

3. Let the people be shown, further—for we would have nothing done without appealing to their *convictions* and *faith*—that God has provided for the distribution of the funds thus consecrated to himself by appointing certain officers, elected by the people, for this very purpose; that the church is fully furnished for her whole work, and that no extra-constitutional agencies are needed; and that the expensive apparatus now commonly employed for this end is not of God's devising, but of man's.

We offer no apology for the length of these remarks. The fact that, notwithstanding all the efforts which have been made to bring the church up to her duty, less than one-half of our congregations are reported as having contributed anything to the most popular of all our causes, that of foreign missions, during the last year, is a very significant fact. The only reason we can imagine for this failure is, that Presbyterian people will not do anything in the dark, and that they are still in the dark, to a considerable extent, in regard to the great privilege and duty of giving. Let us have more light.

JUDICIAL CASE FROM THE SYNOD OF PHILADELPHIA—DOES THE PRESENCE OF A RULING ELDER, NOT REGULARLY INSTALLED, IN A CHURCH SESSION INVALIDATE THE COURT?

The Assembly was very fortunate in its Judicial Committee, of which Dr. Campbell, of Albany, was chairman. These gentlemen deserve the thanks of the whole body, which was spared the expense of a great deal of time and patience by their firmness and prudence. Some knotty cases were settled by themselves, with the consent of the parties in litigation; and in none of the cases which they reported for the adjudication of the house was it necessary to go into the "merits."

The only case of any great importance was that named in the caption of this part of our review; and the Assembly's decision was so extraordinary as to require some special notice. It appears that a Mr. Petrikin was arraigned before the session of the church of Muncy, in the Presbytery of Northumberland, upon three charges, two of which the session, on account of being personally concerned therein, referred to the presbytery for adjudication, and the other of which was issued by themselves. The accused protested against the court acting at all, upon the ground that one of the two elders sitting, though previously ordained and installed in another church, and re-elected in the Muncy church, had not been installed in the latter, and, therefore, had no right to sit. The Presbytery of Northumberland took up the case upon the reference, and rendered judgment against the accused, suspending him from the communion of the church. The suspended man then appealed to the Synod of Philadelphia, and the history of the case in that body is thus summed up in their own minute (synod's printed Minutes, 1855, p. 16): "The appeal of William A. Petrikin from the decision of the Presbytery of Northumberland was taken up, and after some progress had been made in reading the documents, it appeared that the session in which the case originated was not a competent court, because one of the elders of which it was composed had not been installed over the church of Muncy; whereupon it was

"*Resolved*, That the proceedings of the session in this case are null and void, *ab initio*, and the acts of the Presbytery of Northumberland, based upon those of the session, are also null and void, and that the appeal be dismissed."

After stating that an appeal of John Smalley, covering the same or similar ground, was likewise dismissed, the minute proceeds:

"In this decision synod does not intend to imply that there may not be a legal session when there is but one elder; but simply decides that the fact that one of the two persons acting as elders in a judicial capacity for the trial of character and church position, not having been a competent member of the court, destroyed the legality of the court and vitiated its adjudication of this case."

"The following resolution, supplementary to the above," the record proceeds, "was then offered by the Rev. H. S. Clark, and adopted:

"*Resolved*, That synod dismiss this appeal not only for the reasons already assigned, but also because both elders were personally interested in the issue, as appears from documents presented to synod."

It appears, further, from page 20 of the synod's Minutes, that Mr. Waller offered the following preamble and resolution, which the synod refused to consider, viz.: "Whereas, this synod has decided that the action of a church court is void, *ab initio*, by reason of the non-installation of one of the elders, while there was a session without the said elder; and whereas, the said elder is found by the record to have been a member of the Presbytery of Northumberland, and that by undisputed assertion other elders in a like situation were also members of the same presbytery, at the same sessions; and whereas, the Rev. William Life was ordained by that presbytery at said sessions; and whereas, the action of the synod has been thought to bring in question the validity of said ordination, therefore,

"*Resolved*, That synod declare the ordination of the Rev. William Life to be unquestionably valid."

Now, not to be tedious, the action of synod was complained against to the Assembly; and the Assembly sustained the synod by the following vote: Sustain the complaint, 50; not sustain, 100; sustain *in part*, 14. So the highest court in the church has decided by a majority of nearly two-thirds that the presence of one incompetent elder in a church session vitiates the whole court, and makes all its proceedings null and void from the beginning; and, by parity of reason, the presence of an incompetent elder in *any* of the courts makes all the proceedings of such courts null and void; and by the same inexorable logic, that venerable body which has so decided is no court, and all its proceedings which we have taken the trouble to discuss are null and void! This is no caricature. More than one elder in this Assembly, Judge Leavitt among them, confessed that they had never been regularly installed in the churches in which they were then exercising the office.

This difficulty was suggested in the Assembly, as it had been in synod, in the above-cited paper of Mr. Waller, and, therefore, in order not to make general havoc of the lower courts, to say nothing of *felo de se*, a committee was appointed to prepare a minute explanatory of the Assembly's judgment. The minute, so far as it bears upon the decision, is as follows:

"1. That any ruling elder regularly ordained or installed in one church, and subsequently elected to that sacred office in another church, and who has heretofore, pursuant to such election, served as a ruling elder in such other church *without objection*, shall be presumed to have been duly installed therein, and his right to act shall not now be questioned.

"2. That when a ruling elder shall hereafter be elected to the same office in a church other than that in which he has been ordained, the minister and session are hereby enjoined formally to install him."

It was suggested, that the first of these resolutions came in direct conflict with the decision of the Assembly upon the case; but Dr. Humphrey, who was of the committee which framed it, explained that "in the case decided, the elder's non-installation was objected to at the outset; whereas the first resolution provides that he shall have served without objection." Dr. Humphrey, however, we ought to state, voted with the minority, and was not at all responsible for the inconsistency in the rendering of the court. That this inconsistency exists, no man can doubt who listened to the papers, arguments and opinions presented to the house, or who will read the records of the synod. The lower court decided that the session was no session, not because an uninstalled elder was objected to by an accused person; not because one elder in a *vacant* church is not an *assembly*, and, therefore, according to the fundamental principle of Presbyterian government, not a constitutional court; but because the fact of non-installation makes the elder incompetent, and his incompetency destroys the validity of the court. For all that appears, the synod would have decided the case in the same way if the Muncy session had consisted of five elders instead of two. If not, why did they refuse to consider the cruelly pertinent paper of Mr. Waller? Were they afraid to look their own decision in the face? They do, indeed, say in their minute, that they did "not intend to imply that there may not be a legal session where there is but one elder"; but simply decided, "that the fact that one of the two persons acting as elders in a judicial capacity for the trial of character and church position, not having been a competent member of the court, destroyed the legality of the court, and vitiated its adjudication of the case." If they mean that the session ought not to have issued any part of the case, but referred the whole to the presbytery, it is an awkward way of expressing it, to say nothing of the injustice of censuring the presbytery for deciding the points which were referred to them. If the obvious meaning of the words is to be taken as the true meaning, the explanation contradicts their whole action. They declare a court legal and illegal in the same breath. As to the distinction about "judicial capacity for the trial of character and church position," it will not do. For this very session had already *admitted* certain persons to the Lord's table on *examination* and profession of their faith. Moreover, the decision of the synod is, that there was not session enough even to make a "*reference*."

We do not wish, by anything we have said, to be understood as sanctioning the practice of elders sitting in sessions without installation. We did not know, till this case came up, that it was ever allowed, much less that it was so frequent. But we object to making a single session a scapegoat for the sins of all others, *in pari delicto;* and especially to doing it upon such grounds.

This case furnishes additional proof of the truth of what was said in the review of the Assembly of 1855, in the *Critic*, as to the adaptation of the Assembly to judicial purposes. And we may add one more remark in this connection, which is, that there is scarcely any case of appeal or complaint before the Assembly which will admit of being righteously decided, simply "sustain," or "not sustain." At least, there is always danger of misapprehension in such a decision, unless a minute is drawn in which the judgment of the court is carefully expressed. And such a minute should always begin with a short but clear history of the case. Otherwise, the true effect of the judgment cannot be generally understood.

But we must conclude. If any of our readers have had the patience to follow us thus far, from the beginning, we tender them our thanks. We hope that they have not altogether been disappointed. If it has been our misfortune to give them nothing for their pains, we are truly sorry for it, and beg them to forgive us.

THE ACTION OF THE ASSEMBLY OF 1879 ON WORLDLY AMUSEMENTS, OR THE POWERS OF OUR SEVERAL CHURCH COURTS.[1]

Overture No. 5—From the Presbytery of Atlanta, asking the Assembly for definite instructions upon the following points, to-wit:

I. Are the deliverances of 1865, 1869, and 1877 on the subject of worldly amusements to be accepted and enforced as law by judicial process?

II. Are all the offences named in them to be so dealt with, or are exceptions to be made?

III. Are the deliverances of all our church courts of the same nature and authority, so far as the bounds of these respective courts extend?

In answer to these questions the committee recommend the adoption of the following minute:

I. This Assembly would answer the first question in the negative, upon the following grounds:

1. That these deliverances do not require judicial prosecution expressly, and could not require it, without violating the spirit of our law.

2. That none of these deliverances were made by the Assembly in a strictly judicial capacity, but were all deliverances *in thesi*, and, therefore, can be considered as only didactic, advisory, and monitory.

3. That the Assembly has no power to issue orders to institute process, except according to the provisions of *Book of Discipline*, Chapter VII. in the old, and Chapter XIII., Section 1, in the revised book; and all these provisions imply that the court of remote jurisdiction is dealing with a particular court of original jurisdiction, and not with such courts in general. The injunctions, therefore, upon the sessions to exercise discipline in the matter of worldly amusements are to be understood only as utterances of the solemn testimony of these Assemblies against a great and growing evil in the church. The power to utter such a testimony will not be disputed, since it is so expressly given to the Assemblies in the *Form of Government*, Chapter XII., Section 5, of the old, and in revised *Book of Church Order*, *Form of Government*, Chapter V., Section 6, Article VI.; and this testimony this Assembly does hereby most solemnly and affectionately reiterate.

In thus defining the meaning and intent of the action of former Assem-

[1] This article appeared in the April number of the *Southern Presbyterian Review*, 1880.

blies, this General Assembly does not mean, in the slightest degree, to interfere with the power of discipline, in any of its forms, which is given to the courts below by the constitution of the church; or to intimate that discipline in its sternest form may not be necessary, in some cases, in order to arrest the evils in question. The occasion, the mode, the degree, and the kind of discipline, must be left to the courts of original jurisdiction, under the checks and restraints of the constitution. All that is designed is, to deny the power of the Assembly to make law for the church in the matter of "offences," or to give to its deliverances *in thesi* the force of judicial decisions.

II. The second question, which is, "Are all the offences named in the deliverances of 1865, 1869, and 1877 to be dealt with in the way of judicial process, or are exceptions to be made?" needs no answer after what has been said in answer to the first.

III. In answer to the third question, relative to the nature and authority of our different church courts, this Assembly would say that the nature and authority of all our church courts are the same so far as the bounds of these respective courts extend, subject, of course, to the provisions for the review and control of the lower courts by the higher. The power of the whole is in every part, but the power of the whole is over the power of every part.

The perplexity about the nature of the deliverances in question has arisen from confounding two senses in which the word discipline is used in our constitution. One is that of "judicial process," the other is that of inspection, inquest, remonstrance, rebuke, and "private admonition." (*Form of Government*, Chapter IV., Section 3, Article IV.) The one is strictly judicial or forensic; the other is that general oversight of the flock which belongs to the officers of the church, as charged by the Holy Ghost with the duty of watching for souls. The one cannot be administered at all except by a court of the church; the other, while it is a function of that charity which all the members of the church are bound to possess and cherish for each other, is yet the special and official function of the rulers, to be exercised with authority toward those who are committed to their care. In the judgment of this Assembly, great harm is done by the custom of identifying, in popular speech, these two forms of discipline, or, rather, by forgetting that there is some other discipline than that of judicial process. Many an erring sheep might be restored to a place of safety within the fold by kind and tender, yet firm and faithful, efforts in private, who might be driven farther away by the immediate resort to discipline in its sterner and more terrifying forms. The distinction here asserted is recognized in the word of God, and in our constitution, for substance at least, in the directions given for the conduct of church members in the case of personal and private injuries. (See Chapter II., Article III., of the old *Book of*

Discipline, and Chapter I., Paragraph 4, of the revised; also Matt. xviii. 15, 16.) If scandal can be removed or prevented in such cases, more effectually, oftentimes, by faithful dealing in private with offenders than by judicial process, it does not appear why similar good results may not follow from the like dealing in the matter of worldly amusements. (*Minutes General Assembly*, 1879, pp. 23-25.)

THIS action was before the church for more than seven months before any serious assault was made upon it. The paper reported by the Committee on Bills and Overtures was read deliberately and distinctly twice, and the last paragraph three times, before the vote was taken, and then, after a slight verbal amendment, the whole paper was *unanimously* adopted.[1] The chairman and other members of the committee were amongst the most determined opponents of worldly amusements, and of the same complexion were many of the most intelligent members of the Assembly, men of nerve as well as of conscience, who had never been known to shrink from bearing their testimony and giving their vote for what they believed to be right.

Yet, from the tone of some criticisms that have recently appeared, the impression would be gotten that the Assembly was a trimming, time-serving body, which betrayed the interests of truth, set itself against the current of the teaching of the acts of previous Assemblies, and dishonored the Saviour before the world. We propose to show that the Assembly did no such thing.

It is not our purpose to follow the critics through all their discussions. They quote largely from authors, in Latin as well as in English, to prove what no Presbyterian denies, if the passages cited be taken in the sense of their authors. They spend a great deal of time in showing the evil of *dancing*, which the Assembly, indeed, says not one word about specifically, but yet condemns by implication, by "solemnly and affectionately reiterating" the testimonies of

[1] See printed Minutes, p. 23.

previous Assemblies. They insist upon the duty of obedience to the Assembly on the part of the lower courts, without attempting to define the conditions and limits of that obedience, except in the most general terms. Their statements tend to produce the impression, whether they intended it or not, that the Assembly discountenanced the exercise of discipline in the matter of worldly amusements, though, in this very paper, it cautions the church against such a misconstruction, and intimates that discipline, "in its sternest form," may be necessary in some cases in order to arrest the evils in question.

What, then, is the question, and the only question in fact, which the Assembly was asked to make a deliverance about? It was not one touching the evil of worldly amusements, or the duty of applying to them the discipline of the church. It was not one concerning what action the Scriptures required, or what the principles and rules of the Church of Holland, as expounded by Voetius, demanded, or what the principles and rules of the Kirk of Scotland, as expounded by Principal Cunningham, made necessary. None of these, but simply a question of law in our own church, "the Presbyterian Church in the United States," the question whether the Assembly has the power "to make law for the church in the matter of 'offences,' or to give to its deliverances *in thesi* the force of judicial decisions." It had been contended by some that the deliverances of the Assemblies of 1865, 1869, and 1877 *obliged* the courts of original jurisdiction to discipline for dancing, that is, to exclude every church member convicted of dancing from the privileges of the church; that these courts had no discretion; that they were not allowed to interpret the law of the church for themselves, but must accept the interpretation of the Assembly, albeit that interpretation had not been given in the investigation of a judicial case regularly brought up (that is, *in hypothesi*), but as an abstract and general proceeding (*in thesi*). It was contended by others that the above-named "deliverances" did *not* oblige the lower courts; that these courts have a power of judgment, both as to law and fact, given them in the constitution, with which the Assembly cannot directly interfere; that the power of the whole church is in every part, session, presbytery, etc.; and that, therefore, the judgment of the part is, constructively, the judgment of the whole, and is valid as such until constitutionally set aside; that, therefore, the authority of all our church courts is the same, so far as their bounds respectively extend, or within the sphere of their jurisdiction; and, lastly, that, while the higher courts are invested by the constitution with the power of "review and control" over the lower, this power is not a power *directly* over the part, but over *the power* of the part; that is to say, the power of judgment in the part can only be overruled and set aside by a *judicial decision* of the higher court upon a cause regularly (legally, constitutionally) brought up from a lower; and that, until such a judicial decision has been constitutionally rendered, the power of judgment in the courts of original jurisdiction, both as to law and fact, remains intact. These are the principles contained in the answer to the third question of the overture from the Presbytery of Atlanta.[1]

The reader will observe that the overture has reference only to matters of "offences" and discipline; and the Assembly's answer confines itself to those points. The question is one which concerns the administration of *law* by our courts, and not the making of *regulations* in matters of detail; it is a question belonging to the *diacritic*, or *judicial*, or *disciplinary* power of the church, not to its *diatactic*, or *arranging* power.

Before proceeding to vindicate the action of the Assembly, we beg leave to remind our readers that the principle here involved is one of immense importance. It lies at the root of all the struggles between the advocates of a constitutional

---

[1] Assembly's Minutes, page 24.

government and the advocates of an "absolutism." The forms of constitutional government and of absolutism, both in church and in state, have varied indefinitely; but the essence of the struggle has always been the same. Abstracted from its accidental forms, the question has always been, whether the power of the whole is over every part, or only over the power of the part; whether the whole is simply a great wheel, of which the parts are only spokes, or whether it be a wheel of which the parts are *also* wheels, each having a sphere and movement of its own, yet moving in subordination to the movement of the great wheel. It was the question between the Ultramontanes and the French in the Middle Ages, as to the relation of the Bishop of Rome to all the other bishops; the man of Rome contending that, as he represented the whole church and was the supreme bishop, all the inferior bishops derived all their authority from him, and were to be governed absolutely by him; that they had no rights which he was bound to respect, because none which he had not given, and which he, in his sovereign pleasure, could not take away; the bishops contending that their office was created by Christ, and its rights and duties defined by him; that they were subordinate to the man of Rome only in the way of appellate jurisdiction, or of general review and control. It was the question between the bishops and the rectors in parts of the Episcopal Church of the United States some years ago, the bishop asserting that by virtue of his being the highest officer in the church he contained in himself all the rights and functions of the rector of a parish; and that when the bishop was "visiting" a church the rector might be suspended from his office for the time, if it so pleased the superior. It was the question between the Northern Assembly of 1866 at St. Louis, and the Louisville Presbytery, as to the famous (or infamous) *ipso facto* order concerning the "Declaration and Testimony" ministers of that presbytery, the Assembly maintaining virtually the power to lay down the law on the subject, and to execute it, because the presbytery was a "smaller part," and the Assembly was the whole; the presbytery maintaining that, as small a part as it might be, it was a part with the power guaranteed to it by the constitution of "judging ministers," both as to the law and the facts; and, therefore, that the Assembly had been guilty of an usurpation of power. It was the question between the Federal or Consolidation party on the one side, and the States Rights party on the other, in the ante-bellum politics of the United States, the States Rights party contending for the power of the parts (in this case, the States), and resisting the attempt on the part of the Federal government to override that power without regard to the provisions of the Constitution. The great question in the convention that framed that Constitution was essentially the same, how to strengthen the whole, and at the same time so to preserve the power of the parts, and to such an extent, that the liberty of the people might be safe. Hence, the distribution of the powers of government; hence, the distribution of the power of legislation, a Senate and a House of Representatives, the one founded on the principle of a *numerical* majority, the other on the principle of a *concurrent* majority; the one acknowledging the power of the whole, the other protecting the power of the parts.

This is the principle of the Assembly's paper: that the courts of original jurisdiction cannot be directly interfered with by the General Assembly in their power of judgment as to law or fact; that to these courts "must be left the occasion, the mode, the degree, and the kind of discipline under the checks and restraints of the constitution."

We have thus endeavored to state clearly the real and only issue between the advocates and the opponents of the Assembly's action. A great many side issues have been introduced by its assailants. Hence, we must repeat "the state of the question" once more: Does the same force belong to the deliverances *in thesi* of the higher courts as to their judicial decisions? Do the two classes of decisions regulate and determine the administration of discipline in the same way and to the same extent? Or, to express the same thing in other words, does the interpretation of a law by an apellate court—the interpretation being given *in thesi*—bind a court of original jurisdiction in such a sense as to deprive it of its power of judgment as to the meaning of said law, and compel it to accept and act upon the interpretation of the appellate court as the law of the church? If we understand the assailants of the Assembly, they would answer positively and emphatically in the *affirmative* to this question. The General Assembly of 1879 answers it clearly and *unanimously* in the *negative;* and, we think, truly and righteously, for the following reasons:

1. The constitution of the church, by the very fact that it is a constitution, creates a presumption in favor of the Assembly's answer. There was a time in the history of our church when it had no written constitution. The first presbytery (the "General Presbytery") had none, and there seems to have been none until the "Adopting Act" in 1729, when "the synod" had been in existence for twelve years. Even after the Adopting Act had become the law of the church, and the standards of the Westminster Assembly had been accepted as its constitution, a wide difference was acknowledged as to the binding force of the doctrinal standards and the standards of government and discipline. "The synod," in 1729, simply pronounce "the Directory for Worship, Discipline and Government of the Church, commonly annexed to the *Westminster Confession*, to be agreeable in substance to the word of God, and founded thereupon, and therefore do earnestly *recommend* the same to all their members, to be by them observed as near as circumstances will allow and Christian prudence direct."[1] According to the

[1] Baird's *Digest*, p. 6.

same authority, this state of things continued down to 1788, when the "Synod of New York and Philadelphia," in preparation for the formation of the "General Assembly," formally adopted, after amendment, the standards of government and discipline. Up to this date, therefore, the highest court ("the presbytery," "the synod," "the Synod of New York and Philadelphia") seems to have been practically omnipotent, or practically impotent, according to the temper of ministers, elders, or congregations. Such a condition became, of course, intolerable, and it was felt to be necessary to have a constitution, an instrument which should *constitute*, should put together, the parts in some definite relations, should define and distribute the various powers and establish the checks and balances. It was necessary to have some more definite rule than vague references "to Stewart of Pardovan, and the acts of synod," to regulate discipline and the form of process in the church courts.[1] This was done in 1788.

Now, our position is, that all this creates a presumption in favor of the Assembly of 1879, and against its assailants. For, according to the Assembly, the courts of original jurisdiction *have* an original jurisdiction guaranteed to them by the same constitution under which the Assembly itself acts; while, according to the opposite side, the Assemblies of preceding years intended to stretch their hand over synod and presbyteries, and annihilate the original jurisdiction of the sessions, at least as to the interpretation of the law; exactly as we might suppose "the synod" of 1721 to have done, if the sessions of that day were willing to have their original jurisdiction annihilated. Our fathers of 1721 might have argued that all courts of the church were presbyteries, and therefore that each was entitled to exercise all the functions

[1] See Minutes of the Synod of New York and Philadelphia for 1786, cited in Hodge's *History of the Presbyterian Church in the United States*, Part I., p. 214.

of a scriptural presbytery; but that the unity of the church required the submission of the parts to the judgment of the whole, absolutely and without limitation, saving only the alienable rights of conscience. And we see not how such a conclusion could be resisted in the absence of a constitution, by which certain rights should be guaranteed to the parts. Accordingly, we find "the synod" exercising the powers of a classical presbytery.[1] This leads us to observe,

2. That such a distribution of powers to the parts, and definition of the relation of the whole to the parts, we find actually made for us in our constitution; and our second position is that no original jurisdiction is given to the General Assembly or the synod in the matter of discipline by our constitution. The courts of original jurisdiction are the presbytery and the session; and in the case of the presbytery, this jurisdiction is restricted to a particular class of objects—ministers of the gospel. All other members of the church are under the jurisdiction of the session. It is asserted, indeed, that the Assembly has some original jurisdiction in the matter of discipline, and the *Form of Government*, Chap. V., Sec. 6, Art. VI., is quoted in proof of it, which contains these words: "The General Assembly shall have power . . . to *decide* in all controversies respecting doctrine and discipline." According to the critics, "decide" means (and must mean) bring to an issue or conclusion in any way the General Assembly may see fit; for example, by deliverances *in thesi*. The General Assembly has only to fulminate its decree, when it is informed of any controversy going on in any part of the church, and the business is done, the controversy is *decided*. This is obliged to be their interpretation of the clause; for if they concede that the decision must be made only in certain ways, or according to certain rules, then the inquiry immediately arises, "in *what* ways?"

[1] See Hodge's *History of the Presbyterian Church in the United States*, Part I., pp. 229–230.

or "according to *what* rules?" And the only possible answer to this inquiry is, the ways and rules prescribed in the constitution. (See *Form of Government*, Chap. V., Sec. 2, Art. IV.: "The jurisdiction of these courts is limited by the express provisions of the constitution.") This necessary limitation is expressed in a subsequent clause of the same article, in connection with "schismatical contentions," etc. It was necessary there no more than here. We were present in the Committee of Revision when the limitation was put in, and have a very distinct recollection that it was proposed because that clause in the old book was without the limitation (expressed) and had been made the pretext of the infamous "*ipso facto*" order of the Assembly of the Northern Church in 1866, by which the original jurisdiction of the Louisville Presbytery over its ministers had been overridden and annihilated. But, whether expressed or not, it must be understood. If it is not understood, our book is either a mass of nonsense or an instrument of intolerable tyranny. If the clause means what the brethren on the other side assert, then the Assembly may decide a judicial case, if it choose, by a deliverance *in thesi.*

It is evident, however, that the meaning of the clause is simply this: that the Assembly is the court of *last resort.* The presbytery is a court of appeals, but it cannot *decide* a controversy, because an appeal may be taken to the synod; and the synod cannot *decide* it, because an appeal may be taken to the General Assembly; but the General Assembly *decides,* because there is no higher tribunal. That this is the true interpretation will be evident to any one who will compare *Form of Government* (of the *old* book), Chapter X., Article VIII., and Chapter XI. Article IV., with Chapter XII., Articles IV., V. The doctrine of that book is that the three courts of the church which have appellate jurisdiction are the presbytery, the synod, and the General Assembly; but that the difference between the General Assembly and the other two is that it has the power to "decide" all controversies judicially, so that these controversies "can no further go." And if this is the meaning of the clause in the old book, we suppose its meaning will be conceded to be the same in the new.

Further, the "controversies" of this clause are not mere debates or discussions between *any* parties in the church, but legal or forensic controversies, carried on, according to the forms prescribed, in the courts of the church by "parties" in the technical sense. Otherwise, it would be absurd to speak of any court *deciding* a controversy. A debate in the church will go on until the disputants are satisfied or tired out. But a controversy before the courts cannot go further than the Assembly; it must be decided there. The debate may still go on as before, but the legal controversy must stop, unless the lower courts venture to arraign the Assembly, and complain to that court of its own acts.

Another provision relied on by our opponents in this question is that of Chapter XIII., Section I, of the *Rules of Discipline*, "General Review and Control." In reference to this the act of the Assembly of 1879 very justly says that the provisions of this section "imply that the court of remote jurisdiction is dealing with a *particular* court of original jurisdiction, and not with such courts in general"; and, therefore, a general order from the Assembly to the presbyteries or sessions to institute process would not be constitutional. The Assembly might have added, (1), That the heading of the whole chapter ("Of the modes in which a *cause* may be carried from a lower to a higher court") shows that a judicial process and a judicial act are the things spoken of, not deliverances *in thesi;* and, (2), That the provisions of Section I. provide for the appellate court only in its action on the court *next* below.[1] The General Assembly has no power, in any case, to order a session to institute pro-

[1] See sub-sections 1, 5.

cess. It may order a synod, and, since the presbyteries are the constituent bodies of the Assembly, it might, by straining the constitution a little, order the presbyteries to institute process; but there is no color of pretext in the constitution for the exercise of such power over the session, except in deciding a cause judicially. Can any instance be produced from the records, or digest of the General Assembly, of an *injunction*, in the matter of discipline, addressed to a session, or to the sessions in general, before 1869? If it can, let it be produced.

We repeat, then, that the Assembly has no original jurisdiction in the matter of discipline. Now, what is the "jurisdiction" of a court? The very word means a declaration of law, according to its etymology (*jus dicere*), and suggests that to declare the law is one of the functions, the prime function, of a court. To deprive a court of this function, then, is to deprive it of jurisdiction; and in denying to the General Assembly original jurisdiction in the matter of discipline, the constitution *eo ipso* denies to it the *original* power of declaring the law in an authoritative manner, in the sense of jurisdiction. Such an authoritative declaration, such jurisdiction, belongs to it only as a court of appeals, or of last resort. On the other hand, if the Assembly assumes the power which is claimed for it, the courts of original jurisdiction are converted into mere commissions for taking testimony; for the functions of declaring the law and of fixing the penalty have been assumed by the Assembly, and the only function left is that of finding the facts.

3. Once more, the principle of the Assembly's paper is clearly sanctioned by sound reason. The court which is trying a case, which has all the circumstances before it which modify the act or acts charged in the indictment, is in a better condition for understanding the law than a court which is not trying the case, but is looking at the law in an abstract way. And, most assuredly, the court first named is in

a far better condition to graduate the censure according to the degree of criminality than the other. What is a judicial interpretation of a law but an interpretation in connection with a given case? Does the law against "lascivious" dancing apply to *this* case? Is *this* a case of "lascivious" dancing? This is the question that the court has to decide; and no court has a right to say that *all* dancing is lascivious any more than it has a right to pronounce all stage-plays lascivious. The church, indeed, might, in her fundamental law, have forbidden—whether she had the right before God and his word to do so is not now the question—the square and the round dance as equally lascivious, as she might have forbidden the reading of the stage-plays of Addison and those of Congreve, Wycherly, and Farquhar as equally lascivious; and she might have pronounced *any* act of dancing, or the reading of *any* of these plays, to be a sufficient reason for the exclusion of any of her members from her privileges. In such a case there would be no occasion to exercise the art of interpretation. But when she has used the words (*Larger Catechism*, Question 139) "lascivious songs, books, pictures, dancings, stage-plays," it is as certainly implied that there may be *some* dancings and stage-plays that are not lascivious as that there are some books and pictures that are not. Now, what are and what are not, the courts of original jurisdiction are better judges, when pronouncing judgment in actual process, than any court can be which is sitting in judgment upon the abstract question. So our constitution virtually says, and so the General Assembly of 1879 virtually says.

We confess to a great astonishment that brethren should insist that deliverances *in thesi* have the same force as judicial decisions. The two classes of acts are reached by processes wholly different. A deliverance *in thesi* may concern a subject which has never been before the church or any of its courts; may be "sprung" upon the Assembly by some ardent and eloquent member, and be carried by his personal influence and eloquence. A judicial decision by that court necessarily implies discussion in at least *two* of the lower courts—in a cause originating in the session it is implied that the matter has been discussed in *three*—before it is called to decide. The cause is represented on both sides by counsel, who are fully heard; and the members of the court next below are heard, etc., etc.; all circumstances which give assurance that the matter has been fully discussed by those most competent to do it. Further, the deliverance *in thesi* is apt to be sweeping and general. The judicial decision is upon a case, is interpreted by it, and is applicable only to similar cases. The responsibility in delivering a judgment in a judicial case will be more sensibly felt by the members of the court, because they are not only interpreting the law, but are judging a brother, and are determining his ecclesiastical status—perhaps even the complexion of his eternal destiny. It is to remind the members of the court of this very solemn responsibility that the provision is made in the *Rules of Discipline*, Chapter VI., Article XII. Why this emphatic discrimination between the judgment in a judicial case and a deliverance *in thesi*, if the two are of the same force and effect? And why, again, is the appellate court forbidden to reverse the judgment of an inferior court, even upon a formal review of its records, if it be *only* a "review," and not a judgment of the appellate court upon appeal or complaint?[1] And yet brethren contend that the Assembly may, by a sweeping deliverance *in thesi*, virtually do what the constitution says that it shall not do even on a deliberate "review," even in a single case, unless that case come before the court in the way of appeal or complaint.

It will be a dark day for our church when it shall decide that an accidental majority in a General Assembly may make law for the lower courts in a deliverance *in thesi*. The

[1] *Rules of Discipline*, Chapter XIII., Section 1, Article IV.

General Assembly of 1834 was a New Scnool body; that of 1835 was Old School; that of 1836 was New School; and that of 1837 was Old School again. How know we that such a very pleasant alternation may not occur again? We know it may be said that all this might happen even in judicial decisions, and that, in point of fact, one of these Assemblies *did* decide the same judicial case in contradictory ways at the same sessions. It has been also alleged that the Assembly of 1879 decided one way by its paper on "Worldly Amusements," and another way by its approval of the records of the Synod of Georgia. Granting this for the sake of argument (we think it a mistake), what do this and the other instances prove? They prove that the Assembly is in any case a fallible body; and this again is a reason for giving it all the aids above enumerated as belonging to a judicial process to help it in coming to a decision. In other words, a fallible body is less likely to fail (where the interpretation of the law is in question) in a judicial decision than in a deliverance *in thesi*.

Now, it may be said that if this new view be just, then the judgment of the court of original jurisdiction ought to be final as being more likely to be just than even in the judicial decisions of the appellate court. The answer is, that if the government is to embrace more than one congregation; if the idea of the unity of the church is to be realized on any larger scale than that of a single *coetus fidelium*, there must be appellate jurisdiction, and a power given to some higher court to "*decide*" all controversies. This is the reason why a "judicial decision" of the General Assembly becomes law and continues to be law until a contrary decision is rendered by the same court—law, in the sense of a regulator of the exercise of discipline in the courts below.

This is a sufficient answer to the objection. A fuller answer would be found in a general exposition of our theory of government and of the usefulness of our system of courts;

but for such an exposition a volume would be required. None of our readers are unreasonable enough to expect such an exposition here.

4. The principle of the Assembly's paper is also sanctioned by the practice of the civil courts. We are aware that prejudice exists against analogies from this source; and we acknowledge that harm has been done by not taking into account the differences between the nature and ends of the civil government and those of the ecclesiastical. But there are some principles and methods which all governments must recognize if they would secure justice and liberty. A single glance over the old *Book of Discipline* is sufficient to convince anybody that our fathers borrowed largely from the forms of process in the civil courts; and a careful comparison of the new book with the old will show that in the new there has been a greater approximation to those forms than in the old. Whether this feature of the new book be an improvement or not, is a question about which brethren will differ in opinion; but the fact is certain, and might be copiously illustrated if we had the time.

Now, what is the practice of the civil courts? Is a court below bound by an interpretation of a law which has been given *in thesi* by the Supreme Court? Does the Supreme Court give any such interpretation? Is any decision of that court, as to the meaning of the law not given in judgment upon a case, binding upon the courts below?

But it is said the analogy will not hold. The courts of the state are *only* courts, while the courts of the church are invested with legislative powers. If by legislative power is meant the power to make laws as distinct from *diatactic* regulations, we deny such a power altogether, even to the church as a whole, much more to any of her courts. Christ is the only lawgiver, and the power of the church is only "ministerial and declarative." If diatactic regulations are meant, then our answer is, as we said before, that we have nothing to do with that kind of power in this discussion, except so far as the constitution itself is in great part a result of the exercise of that power. Besides, all courts, civil and ecclesiastical, exercise a power of this sort. We see not, therefore what the objection means, or why the courts civil and the courts ecclesiastical are not in exactly the same predicament as to the matter in question. In both the law is behind the courts, both are acting under the law, and in both systems the courts of original jurisdiction have the right to interpret the law for themselves, until a judicial decision of the highest court shall *decide* the matter.

5. Lastly, the Assembly of 1879 is sustained by its predecessor of 1877. Being asked by the Presbytery of Atlanta to interpret "the law of the church concerning worldly amusements, as set forth in the deliverances of the Assemblies of 1865 and 1869," the Assembly gives the following as a part of its answer: "The extent of the mischief done depends largely upon circumstances. *The church session, therefore, is the only court competent to judge what remedy to apply.*"[1] Now, why should the Assembly of 1879 be censured for doing exactly what its predecessor had done? We know of no Assembly, indeed, which has gone beyond exhortation and admonition to the presbyteries and sessions on this subject, except that of 1869.

Since we began to write, our attention has been called to the action of the Synod of South Carolina on this subject, from which it appears that "many have understood the action of the General Assembly as favoring indulgence by church members in worldly amusements." This ought to surprise nobody who has any experience of the weakness of mankind. The Assembly does, indeed, "solemnly reiterate the testimonies" of its predecessors against indulgence in these amusements; but this goes for nothing with extremists, who meet in the conclusion that the Assembly, though pre-

[1] Minutes, p. 411.

tending to utter or to reiterate solemn testimonies, is really in favor of the thing testified against. This conclusion is derived by both extremes from the fact that the Assembly condemns a particular method of dealing with the subject. One extreme considers dancing and other worldly amusements so firmly lodged in the practice of church members that nothing but the weight of the Assembly's mandate compelling the sessions to suspend and excommunicate offenders can dislodge it. The other extreme, the offenders themselves, agree with the first in this view, and both conclude that, as the Assembly has refused to issue any such mandate, and refused upon the ground of the want of power, indulgence is granted. This is not the first time that church courts have been subject to misconstruction. They have been charged with favoring indulgence in strong drink, because they refused to say that all use of liquor as a beverage was a sin, and that all who retail liquor are unworthy of a place in the church. Perhaps the time will come when the Assembly will be asked to decree the moral obligation to the tithe, and that all church members who shall be convicted of paying less shall be turned out of the church. If it should refuse, then the tithe men may unite with the men who give nothing in asserting that it is "favoring indulgence" in the luxury of giving nothing to the cause of God.

We hope our brethren will not be frightened into taking unconstitutional ground by such clamors. The sessions who are unfaithful to their duty on this subject, can find no comfort in the act of the Assembly; for that act leaves their responsibility intact, leaves it where it was before, leaves it where the constitution has put it; that act refuses to relieve the sessions of their responsibility by transferring their responsibility to the Assembly. The sessions who are unfaithful will find in the Assembly's act no cover for their unfaithfulness in a cloud of dust such as would certainly be raised if the Assembly were to embody the views of its critics in a deliverance. They are brought face to face with their responsibility, and are given to understand that there must be no shirking or dodging. At the same time, the Assembly's deliverances *in thesi* have given all the *moral* support to the sessions that could be reasonably demanded.

We have said enough, we think, in the way of explanation and of positive argument, to vindicate the wisdom and righteousness of the Assembly's act. We propose now to consider an argument upon which the brethren on the other side seem to rely with great confidence for sustaining their position concerning the powers of the General Assembly. This argument is drawn from the acts of "the Council of Jerusalem," as recorded in the 15th chapter of the Acts of the Apostles.

The argument seems to be this: The council of Jerusalem issued a decree, an authoritative direction, an injunction, to the believers among the Gentiles to abstain for a time, through motives of charity towards their Jewish brethren, from the use of their Christian liberty in certain matters. *Ergo*, the General Assembly of the Presbyterian Church of the United States has the power to pronounce *in thesi* all dancing between the sexes to be "lascivious and therefore sinful," and to require that this deliverance be accepted and enforced by the courts of original jurisdiction in the way of judicial process, not for a time, but always. Now, the connection between these two propositions is not very obvious. One cannot help thinking that the last of the two is the conclusion of an extended *sorites*, of which there are many links missing. We confess we are too obtuse to find out what these missing links are. Meantime, while we are waiting for them to be pointed out, we shall attempt to show that there is no legitimate connection whatever between the acts of the council of Jerusalem and the special power claimed for the General Assembly of the Presbyterian Church of the United States by those who are opposed to the act of 1879.

We shall take no advantage from the opinion held by

many learned men, that the decree of the council of Jerusalem was given by inspiration of the Holy Ghost. (Acts xv. 28.)

This was the opinion of Dr. Thornwell, as we heard from his own lips; so, also, Dr. Addison Alexander: "'To the Holy Ghost and to us,' the natural and obvious construction is that the apostles and those joining with them in this act, claim for their own decision a divine authority, as having been suggested or inspired by the Holy Ghost. Nothing can, therefore, be inferred from this phrase, with respect to the authority of councils and their canons, except so far as they are known to be under the same guidance and control."[1]

This interpretation would make short work of the debate; for we suppose the most extreme champions of the Assembly's authority are not prepared to assert that its decrees are inspired in the high sense of being the rule of faith and practice. We give the brethren on the other side the advantage of the assumption that that ancient council, although consisting in part of apostles, had no other guidance of the Holy Spirit (at least in kind) than is enjoyed by our General Assembly; that in both the most ancient and the most recent of Assemblies the conclusion is reached under this guidance by arguments drawn from Scripture and providence, from what God has said and from what he has done. Supposing this to be so—

1. Our first remark is that the council of Jerusalem can furnish no warrant or model for our General Assembly, for the simple reason that it was not a General Assembly; that it was not a body of representatives from the whole church. Indeed, there is not a particle of evidence that there was any "church" in the apostolic age, in the sense of "the Presbyterian *Church* in the United States." The word *church* is never used in the New Testament, in the singular number, of an organized visible body of professed believers

[1] *Commentary on the Acts*, xv. 29.

more extensive than such a body within the limits of a single city. The passage in Acts ix. 31, even according to the oldest MSS. and the modern editions, does not necessarily mean anything more than the mass of the followers of Christ. The word in that place may have the same sense as in the phrase "visible church catholic," in our *Confession of Faith*, Chapter XXV., Article 2, which had been in Article 1 defined as consisting of "all throughout the world that profess the true religion." In the place in Acts it is a part only of this visible church which is described, those who professed the true religion "throughout Judea, Galilee, and Samaria." The reader will please observe we have only said that such a church as ours *did* not exist, not that it could not have existed. The principle (*ratio*) of such a church existed, and was exemplified or realized on the scale of a single city, say Jerusalem; but the time had not yet come when its exemplification on the scale of a province or nation was demanded. Now, if no such church existed, of course there was no General Assembly of such a church, and the council of Jerusalem was no such body. Accordingly, there is no evidence that any body of Christians beyond the city of Jerusalem was represented in the council. Paul and Barnabas were present, indeed, and gave an account of what the Lord had done by them among the Gentiles; but they do not seem to have taken any part in the debates. It would have been unwise in them to have done so; for it was *their* work which gave rise to the question before the council; and the very reason why Paul did not decide the question by his apostolic authority, and why a *Jewish* council was called to decide it, was, that it was a question which concerned the liberty of the Gentiles from the Levitical yoke. If this liberty could be recognized by the church at Jerusalem, the headquarters of Judaism, and by a council consisting exclusively of Jewish Christians, then the peace of the Gentile churches was secured against Judaizing impostors who pleaded authority from the church at Jerusalem. There ought not to have been, therefore, (as there were not) any Gentile element in the council. Even Paul and Barnabas, though Jews, had become too much identified by their work with the Gentile churches to admit of their taking part in the proceedings of the council without imminent danger of impairing the moral influence and effect of its decisions. They could not ' represent" the church of Antioch, since their special relation to that church had ceased, after they became missionaries. If Antioch was represented at all, it was by the "certain others" (Acts xv. 2) who went up with Paul and Barnabas; but, for the reasons above given, it is almost certain that it was not represented, and that the council was purely Jewish.

The case in the fifteenth of Acts was not analogous, therefore, to a case of "reference," in our own church, by a lower court to higher. The church of Antioch (session or presbytery) sustained no such constitutional relation to the church in Jerusalem as the session of the Central church in Atlanta, or the Presbytery of Atlanta, sustains to the General Assembly. And this leads us to observe—

2. In the second place, that the church of that age had no written constitution at all like that of the Presbyterian Church in the United States. Hence, we cannot argue from the one to the other, when treating a question of constitutional law in our own church. The question with us is not what powers a General Assembly might have had where there was no constitution; or what powers might have been conferred upon it by *a* constitution; but what powers belong to it by virtue of *the* constitution of the Presbyterian Church in the United States. It will not do to argue merely from the scriptural powers of a church court, of a presbytery, of this presbytery at Jerusalem. All the courts of our church are presbyteries ("congregational," "classical," "synodical," and "general"), and are all of equal powers and the same powers, until a distri-

bution of powers is made by a constitution. Hence, if we argue direct from the court of Jerusalem to the General Assembly of our own church, upon the ground of the scriptural powers of a presbytery, we can argue direct to *any* of our courts, and make the decrees of all equally authoritative. But the moment you bring in the fact of a constitution, in which the powers are distributed, the whole state of the question is changed. Hence, we cannot argue from the powers of a body not acting under a constitution, to the powers of a body acting under one; nor from the powers of a General Assembly of the Kirk of Scotland to the powers of our own Assembly.

It may be asked, why did the cities of Derbe, Lystra, Iconium, and others, as well as the "brethren of the Gentiles in Antioch, and Syria, and Cilicia," to whom the decree of the council at Jerusalem was addressed, submit to that decree? The answer is easy for those who hold that decree to have been inspired and to have been acknowledged to be such. For those who hold that the decree was uninspired, that the assembly at Jerusalem was simply the presbytery of that city, with the addition of the apostles sitting merely as presbyters, the answer would be more difficult. It would probably be either that the decree had received a subsequent apostolic sanction (of Paul or some other), or that it was submitted to by voluntary consent. In the case of Antioch, there would be an implied consent in the very act of sending the question up to Jerusalem to be decided. On either supposition, the brethren on the other side of the question which is concerned in the present discussion will receive little aid or comfort. On the first, the difficulty is that we have no apostles. On the second, their cause is given up, because the authority of the Assembly is made to rest on consent. If it should be said that the consent of the lower courts is implied in accepting the constitution, then the whole difficulty returns. The very question we are discussing is, whether the part, because it is a part, is subject to the whole, because it is a whole; or whether the power of the part is subject to the whole under conditions clearly defined in the constitution. The other side cannot be allowed to beg the question.

3. Once more, conceding, for the sake of argument, that the decree of the council at Jerusalem was accepted as binding, though uninspired, by all the Gentile believers, still we contend that the claim set up for the General Assembly to lay down the law *in thesi*, and to enforce it by judicial process, is unsupported by the doings of that council. The claim set up for the Assembly is in regard to "offences," and the power asserted for it is the power to make law for offences, or, at least, to interpret the law so authoritatively in regard to them as to compel the courts of original jurisdiction to institute judicial process.

Now, this is a power of *discipline*, the power of declaring the law of Christ, and of inflicting the censures which he has ordained for sin. No such power was exercised by the presbytery at Jerusalem. It exercised the *dogmatic* power in declaring the will of Christ in regard to the liberty of the Gentiles, and the *diatactic* power in regard to the use of their Christian liberty in certain things; but they exercised no *diacritic* or disciplinary power. Turretin, indeed, represents them as so doing in denouncing the Judaizers as "subverters of souls." But this denunciation is simply a corollary from the dogmatic decision, and the decree itself is a direction in regard to indifferent matters, with one exception. This exception has been a source of perplexity to interpreters of every grade and class, save those of the Greek Church. That church has held the decree to be of perpetual obligation. The papal body and the Reformed churches have held that it was temporary and provisional, with the exception before named.

Now, this is one of the characteristics of the objects of the diatactic power, that they are liable to change. The moral law is unchangeable, and the infraction of it is always sin; and sin is the proper object of discipline. But the diatactic power is exercised about "circumstances" which are variable, about modes of doing things, about restraints upon Christian liberty, etc. Hence, Turretin, in the passage referred to, gives as an example of this kind of power the decree of the council of Jerusalem touching the eating of blood, etc.

In order, therefore, to make this decree parallel with the deliverances *in thesi* of the General Assembly these last should be interpreted as referring to matters of Christian liberty, and as temporary restraints upon it. Are the brethren with whom it is our unhappiness to differ willing to take that view of them? Of course not. Why, then, ring the changes upon the council of Jerusalem?

But it may be asked, May not church members be disciplined for violations of diatactic regulations? We answer, Never *directly*. The disregard of such regulations may occasion so much scandal as to make the disorderly person liable to the censures of the church. (See *Confession of Faith*, Chapter XX., entitled "Of Christian Liberty and Liberty of Conscience," specially Article IV., where our faith on this subject is laid down.) The discipline is administered for the scandal rather than for the violation of the rule itself. The session of a church appoints the hour of 11 o'clock Sunday morning for public worship. One of the members of the church refuses to attend church, upon the pretext that there is no divine authority for holding service at that hour; that 9 A. M., 12 M., and 3 P. M., and, perhaps, "candle lighting" (Acts xx. 8) are the only hours that have the warrant of Scripture example for public worship. Such a member would, no doubt, be disciplined; but it would be for despising the divine ordinance of public worship. So it is easy to imagine the practice of dancing or of liquor-selling to be attended with such scandal as to require the session, in faithfulness, to subject the actors to discipline. We add our conviction that there are such scandals, and that there are sessions which are delinquent in their duty in regard to them. We earnestly hope that our defence of the independent jurisdiction which belongs to them will not be construed into an approval of their unfaithfulness.

The exposition which has been given of the nature of diatactic regulations will serve to show the irrelevancy of a great deal that has been said and quoted on the other side. Nobody denies that the General Assembly has original jurisdiction in certain matters; that it may issue "injunctions" which the courts below are bound to obey. For example, it has the power "to institute and superintend the agencies necessary in the general work of evangelization." This implies some system in collecting the revenue by which the work is to be maintained; and the Assembly has a right to regulate the details of the collecting and disbursing of the needful funds, and to issue "injunctions" in regard to them. We are far enough from denying to the Assembly the exercise of authority. We only deny that it has a certain kind of authority; and to refuse steadily to recognize any authority which has not been given to it in the constitution is the most effectual way to strengthen the authority which *has* been given to it. They are the real enemies of the Assembly's authority who would make its power absolute. If the Assembly assumes the powers of the sessions, then one of two things will almost certainly occur: either the sessions will rebel, in defence of their constitutional powers; or, they will consent to become ciphers, and their work will not be done at all. It is as certain as anything can be that the Assembly cannot discharge the judicial functions of the session. Why, then, attempt them? We believe the act of 1879 was a wise, just, and wholesome act, and earnestly hope it will not be reversed.

Before concluding this article we propose to notice some

of the arguments, or methods of argument, used on the other side of this question. And,

1. The argument *ad invidiam.* The position taken by the Assembly of 1879 is stigmatized as virtual independency. "If the authority of the Assembly," it is said, "be confined to judicial cases, then this is the only wall that separates us from independency. Throw down that narrow partition, and we are all at once embraced in a common fold." Upon this singular statement we remark—

(*a*), We are not aware that any defender of the Assembly's act has said that its "authority is confined to judicial cases." We have asserted its diatactic power as laid down in the constitution. We have not denied its dogmatic power. This power is asserted in the constitution, as is the last named, for *all* the courts, and of course for the highest also. So, also, the power of exercising discipline is claimed in a general way for all the courts. (See *Form of Government*, Chap. V., Sec. 2, Art. II., first sentence.) The ground upon which all these powers are claimed for all the courts is then stated in Article III. But now the difficulty arises, that if all the courts have the same original powers, how is confusion to be prevented? This question is answered in Article IV., and admirably answered. We wish we had the space to quote the whole of it. We must quote a sentence or two: "It is necessary that the sphere of action of each court should be distinctly defined." "The jurisdiction of these courts is limited by the express provisions of the constitution." "Although each court exercises exclusive original jurisdiction over all matters specially belonging to it, the lower courts are subject to the review and control of the higher courts, in regular gradation. Hence these courts are not separate and independent tribunals; but they have a mutual relation, and every act of jurisdiction is the act of the whole church, performed by it through the appropriate organ." If this is independency, then the act of the Assembly is independency, for it is exactly in the line of these sections and articles of the constitution.

(*b*), The statement that the power of ultimately deciding in judicial cases, according to *Rules of Discipline*, Chapter XIII., is "a narrow partition, and that, when thrown down, we and the independents are all at once embraced in a common fold," is both amazing and amusing. It is very much like saying that the narrow partition of rationality is the only thing that separates us from the brutes, and if this was thrown down, we all, men and brutes, should at once be embraced in a common fold. Abolish the specific difference in any case, and the species is of course "embraced in the same fold" with the genus. Now, in the matter of discipline, the acknowledgment of appellate jurisdiction in a court higher than the church sessions is precisely the specific difference by which Presbyterianism is distinguished from independency as expounded by John Owen.

(*c*), It is very easy to bandy epithets. We might charge the assailants of the General Assembly with popery with as much justice as they charge us with independency. What is popery but making the pope the *fountain* of all law, without regard to the rights and powers of the lower bishops, assembled in council or otherwise. If the Assembly is made the *fountain* of all law, without regard to the rights and powers of the courts of original jurisdiction, have we not a polyheaded pope?

2. It is argued that, if the doctrine of the Assembly of 1879 be sound, it is useless to overture it on any subject. "Of what value," is asked, "the answers to the hundreds of overtures sent up to the Assembly," if they have no binding authority? The answer is, If these overtures refer to matters over which the Assembly has original jurisdiction, the answers *have* binding authority; and, in regard to other matters, is it nothing to have the judgment of the Assembly as to the meaning of a law, in the way of instruction, as a guide and help to the lower courts? Does not everybody know that it was common in the Reformation era for the church of

one country to ask the judgment and advice of the churches and learned doctors and universities of other countries? If the "advice and instruction" of the Assembly are of no account, why does the constitution take the trouble expressly to provide for such "advice and instruction"? (See *Form of Government*, Chap. V., Sec. 6, Art. VI.) It seems we have a higher opinion of the Assembly's moral weight than the brethren who are set for the exaltation of its authority. We heartily wish that the sessions would heed its instructions and warnings in reference to worldly amusements, and administer discipline, both private and public, as circumstances may demand.

Brethren must be content to leave this matter of discipline, as to original jurisdiction, where the constitution has placed it, with the presbyteries and sessions. What more vital to the purity and prosperity of the church than the admission of men to the ministry and of members to the church? These are matters belonging to the presbyteries and sessions, and in one sense—since it is easier to keep unworthy people out of the ministry and the church than to get them out after they are in—more important than the discipline of exclusion. Indeed, a great deal of the discipline, in the sense of exclusion, is occasioned by the facility with which persons are admitted to the church and the ministry. Many pastors and sessions are now employed in turning out members who were brought in by the drag-net and machinery of itinerant "revivalists." Now, does anybody believe that the General Assembly could manage this evil by laying down, authoritatively, the terms of communion? Pass what "laws" it may, the character of the pastors and elders, after all, will determine the character of the church; and the character of the pastors and elders will be determined by the habitual training to which they have been subject, not by the acts of Assembly; by the continual dropping, not by the occasional deluge.

THORNWELL'S WRITINGS.[1]

THESE elegant and portly volumes have been several years before the public, as the dates upon the title pages will show; and yet, full as they are of the deepest and most inspiring thought of one of the greatest thinkers of the age, expressed in a style of the clearest and purest English, they have not, so far as we know, been commended to the attention of theologians and scholars in an extended review. Perhaps their extraordinary merit has been the cause of this apparent neglect. It might seem to indicate some audacity of enterprise, or, at least, some want of modesty, in an ordinary man to make such an attempt. The men who are best qualified for the task were prevented from undertaking it by their connection with the lamented author, either as his editors or as his biographers; and other men have, no doubt, been deterred by their consciousness of a want of ability to do justice to such a work, who would else have been glad to lay their tribute upon the tomb of one from whom they have received so much instruction and so much confirmation in "the glorious gospel of the blessed God." Those who are familiar with the history of *The Southern Presbyterian Review* may be especially excused for a feeling of surprise that no extended notice of these writings has appeared in this journal. They are aware that Dr. Thornwell was its main pillar; that the ablest articles that adorned its pages were the production of his pen; that he, it may be said without invidiousness, did more to give it reputation than any other regular contributor, or, possibly, than all other contributors combined. But does not this very fact, combined with the

[1] Appeared in *The Southern Presbyterian Review*, July, 1878.

fact that a large portion of these "collected writings" first appeared in the shape of articles in this *Review*, constitute a sufficient apology for the seeming neglect? We think it does.

But now, having said thus much, our readers are no doubt asking what apology can the present writer offer for his presumption? Our answer is, we have no apology but that of *love.* We are among the number of those who acknowledge a debt of gratitude to Dr. Thornwell which they feel can never be repaid. If we know anything of Christ's salvation; if we have any comfort of love or any fellowship of the Spirit; if we have any stability of faith in the midst of the temptations of the world, the flesh, and the devil; and joy in hope of glory, honor, and immortality; we owe it more to him, under God, than to any other human being, with the exception, perhaps, of her who bore us. Without the smallest affectation of modesty, we acknowledge our inability to do him justice. With but slender pretensions to theology or philosophy, we undertake to serve the purpose only of a finger-board to direct the attention of our readers who have not procured these volumes, or have not read them, to the treasures of theology and philosophy they contain.

We do not profess to be very familiar with the literature of South Carolina, but we know only three of the many distinguished men whose names adorn her annals, whose writings have been collected and published—Calhoun, Legaré, and Thornwell. It is a little remarkable that in the case of all these, the largest part (in the case of Mr. Legaré, the whole) of their literary remains consists of monographs, chiefly in the form of contributions to quarterly reviews, or in the form of discourses. In the works of Mr. Calhoun, there are two treatises only, both published after his death for the first time: One a "Dissertation on Government," and the other a "Dissertation on the Constitution of the United States." These occupy the first volume. The remaining volumes are composed, if our memory serves us, of speeches. It is greatly to be regretted that the lessons of statesmanship and of political philosophy which these speeches contain were not collected and digested by the master himself, and thus handed down to posterity. We are free to confess to a regret still deeper, that a similar thing was not done by Mr. Legaré. No more splendid man has this country produced. He was familiar with the whole range of Greek and Roman literature, a learned and accomplished lawyer, a profound and judicious thinker, a noble orator, a fascinating writer, and there was little within the compass of the human faculties which his genius could not have achieved. We think that the subject of this present notice was greater than either Calhoun or Legaré. With natural endowments equally great, he had that strength which was derived from the dedication of his endowments to God who gave them, and from the discipline of all his faculties in the bracing atmosphere of revealed truth. We hazard nothing in predicting that his writings will be studied long after those of the other two illustrious men we have named shall have been forgotten.

The comparison may be extended a little further. Dr. Thornwell has been more favored in his editors. The works of Calhoun and Legaré were edited by Virginians, and, in the case of the last named, very poorly edited. Dr. Thornwell's editors were "to the manner born," if we may judge by their success; and they have done their work *con amore*, both as fellow-countrymen and as devoted friends. He was a man of refined and exquisite taste, and we do not doubt that he would have been perfectly satisfied with these volumes in every respect, with the exception, perhaps, of the binding.[1] He loved sumptuously bound books.

[1] We do not mean to disparage the binding in its kind. It is excellent of its kind; but the kind is not the best. Would it not have been better to issue the work (after the manner of the French) in unbound volumes, and let the buyers have them bound to order

The first volume, according to the arrangement of the editors, contains Dr. Thornwell's "Theological" writings; the second, "Theological and Ethical"; the third, "Theological and Controversial"; the fourth, "Ecclesiastical." We shall attempt, in this article, to give our readers some idea of the author in each of these departments, and that, either by quotations, or, where this is impracticable, by a summary statement of his views in our own words.

I. His fame as a theologian must rest ultimately, of course, upon his writings. The tradition of his extraordinary ability in handling the great doctrines of revelation, which is now kept alive by the gratitude and enthusiasm of his pupils is doomed to fade, as they pass, one after another, from the world. We are thankful for what remains, but nothing can reconcile us to the loss of what has perished but the fact that it was all ordered by the wisdom of the great Head of the church, who makes no mistakes. We have, in truth, not much more than the foot of Hercules, and from this we may judge what the giant in his full proportions must have been.

The most valuable part of this first volume consists of sixteen lectures prepared by the author for his classes in the seminary. They were all written twice over, but were never prepared for the press. This accounts for the somewhat fragmentary appearance exhibited at the closing parts of one or two of them. The author proposed to divide theology into three parts: the *first*, treating of God and of moral government in its essential principles; the *second*, of moral government as modified by the covenant of works; and the *third*, of the same, as modified by the covenant of grace. These lectures cover with tolerable completeness the ground of the first two parts. They are occupied, therefore, with *theology* (in the narrower sense) and *anthropology*. The most elaborate and the most striking discussions in this last department are those on man and on the covenant of works, on the breach of the covenant, the fall of man, on sin, its nature, its pollution, and guilt, and on degrees of guilt. It would be difficult to exaggerate the ability with which these great subjects are handled. Let us tarry a moment on one or two points.

And *first*, as to the nature and purpose of the covenant of works, the great merit of our author, it appears to us, is the clearness with which he brings out the precise points of difference between the dispensation which goes under this name, and the dispensation under which man was by the mere fact of his creation; or, in other words, the difference between moral government absolutely considered and the same as modified by the covenant. The Westminster Standards throw no light on this question. They say nothing, in describing man's condition under the covenant of works, from which we can gather the import of the promise of life, or determine why such a promise could not have belonged to a dispensation of *mere* moral government. They make the condition of the covenant to be "perfect and personal obedience,"[1] or "perfect, personal, and perpetual obedience."[2] This is all. Now, what does "perpetual" mean? If it means throughout his whole career as an immortal being, then it is impossible to see how man's covenant condition differed from "the estate wherein he was created"; since his probation, in either case, must have been endless. The promise of *eternal* life would have no meaning. And how, in this case, could the condition of *all* his posterity be determined by his acts? Suppose he had sinned in his one thousandth year, after he had begotten a multitude of children! The promise of life, if it means anything more than that he should live so long as he continued to obey—or, in other words, that he should not die until he sinned—is left without any explanation by the statements of our Confession and Catechisms. Dr. Hodge says:[3] "The question whether

[1] *Confession of Faith*, VII., 2. [2] *Larger Catechism*, Question 20.
[3] *Systematic Theology*, II., 119.

perpetual as well as perfect obedience was the condition of the covenant made with Adam is probably to be answered in the negative. It seems to be reasonable in itself, and plainly implied in the Scriptures, that all rational creatures have a definite period of probation." This hesitating statement does not give us much relief, as it seems to make the limitation of the probation not so much an act of God's favor as an act of justice which reason might demand. This view of Dr. Hodge's meaning is confirmed by his explanation, on the preceding page, of the promise, which might all be said if there had been no covenant at all. "As the Scriptures everywhere represent God as a judge or moral ruler, it follows, of necessity, from that representation, that his rational creatures will be dealt with according to the principles of justice. If there be no transgression, there will be no punishment. And those who continue holy thereby continue in the favor and fellowship of him whose favor is life." Plainly, if this be all that is in the promise, it needed not to have been made. It is impossible for God to frown, it is impossible for him not to smile, on a holy creature. The promise is not one of a life which, in point of fact, shall be eternal in its duration if the man shall continue obedient forever, but of a life which is in its own nature inalienable, indestructible, eternal. It is exactly the promise, as Dr. Hodge goes on to state (inconsistently, we think), which Christ has secured for his people; and this is a life eternal, which every believer *now* has, is in actual possession of, though he be still compassed about with a body of death.

If the probation of the first man was limited in point of time, there could be the promise of such a life. At the close of the period of probation, Adam, if still faithful in his allegiance to his Maker, would have been put in possession of it. This life implied two things: *first*, that he should be justified and adopted, that he should pass from the precarious condition of a servant into the permanent condition of a son;

and *second*, that his will should be immutadly determined to good ("*felix necessitas boni*"), that the "*posse peccare*" and the "*posse non peccare*" should be changed into a "*non posse peccare*." How this immutability of the will would have been produced, it is, of course, impossible to say. We are very well assured that it would not have been the result of *habit*, as some theologians think. It would have been a part of the promise of life; not acquired at all, except in the sense that the condition of the covenant having been performed, a title to the whole life promised was acquired.[1]

This view of the covenant, as involving the ends of justification and adoption, enables the author, as he thinks, to unify the two forms of religion, that of nature (or of man in a state of innocence), and that of grace (or of man a sinner and yet a prisoner of hope). Cocceius and the "federal" theologians of Holland unified with the idea of a covenant only. Our author unifies with the idea of justification, which is common to both the covenants. (See the Inaugural Discourse at the end of the first volume.)

The *second* matter we propose to notice is the discussion towards the end of the thirteenth lecture. The subject of this lecture is "Original Sin," and the author grapples with the question, How the verdict of conscience, which pronounces us guilty on account of our native turpitude, can be justified? It is purely a speculative question. It may not be possible to find a satisfactory answer. It is not necessary to find one. The fundamental "deliverance" of conscience must stand, whether we be able or not to apprehend

---

[1] A *caveat* ought to be entered here against an unguarded statement on page 278 of Volume I., in which the author seems to teach that Adam had no positive holy character, but only the possibility of it, or tendencies to it; and that the positive character would have resulted from the deliberate determination of his will with reference to the forbidden fruit. That this is not his meaning is abundantly evident from the whole of the discussion, and especially from such formal and elaborate statements as that on page 231, in the lecture on "Man."

the grounds of its truth. Our author's solution, proposed with great modesty and not without some hesitation, is as follows:

"The human race is not an aggregate of separate and independent atoms, but constitutes an organic whole, with a common life springing from a common ground. There is an unity in the whole species; there is a point in which all the individuals meet, and through which they are all modified and conditioned. Society exerts even a more powerful influence upon the individual than the individual upon society, and every community impresses its own peculiar type upon the individuals who are born into it. This is the secret of the peculiarities of national character. There was one type among the Greeks, another among the Asiatics, and still another among the Romans. The Englishman is easily distinguished from the Frenchman, the Chinese from the European, and the Negro from all. In the same way there is a type of life, common to the entire race, in which a deeper ground of unity is recognized than that which attaches to national associations, or the narrower ties of kindred and blood. There is in a man what we may call a common nature. The common nature is not a mere generalization of logic, but a substantive reality. It is the ground of all individual existence, and conditions the type of its development. The parental relation expresses, but does not constitute it; propagates, but does not create it. In birth, there is the manifestation of the individual from a nature-basis which existed before. Birth, consequently, does not absolutely begin, but only individualizes humanity. As, then, descent from Adam is the exponent of a potential existence in him, as it is the revelation of a fact in relation to the nature which is individualized in a given case, it constitutes lawful and just ground for federal representation. God can deal with the natural as a covenant head, because the natural relation proceeds upon an union which justifies the moral." (II., pp. 349, 350.)

This passage has perplexed our author's friends. Some have gone so far as to say that he teaches the very realism which, in his review of the *Elohim Revealed* (see pp. 515–568 of this volume), he has censured Dr. Baird for teaching; that he holds to a "numerical identity of nature between Adam and his posterity." As even "Homer nodded," it is of course not impossible that Dr. Thornwell may have done the same. But those who are at all acquainted with the working of his mind, and with his habits of thought, will admit that the presumption against his having fallen into such a gross inconsistency is very strong; so strong, indeed, as to require the plainest proof to overthrow it. Whether his solution is any more satisfactory than Dr. Baird's, or whether it is even intelligible at all, is not here the question; but whether it is the same solution as Dr. Baird's. On this question let the reader consider the following suggestions which have been sent to us by one of Dr. Thornwell's intimate friends:

1. The review of Baird was written in 1860, and at that time these lectures were already written. The two compositions may therefore be considered as contemporaneous. If there is any inconsistency, Dr. Thornwell was not conscious of it.

2. In the two papers he uses two distinct phrases with such uniformity and consistency as to evince design, and to show that he did not consider them as identical. In the lecture he speaks of "a generic unity of man"; in the *Review* he combats Baird's notion of "a numerical identity of nature between Adam and his posterity.

3. In the *Review* he seems to affirm the view of the lecture in contrast with that of Baird. (See pp. 552 and 563.) The first of these passages is so conclusive that we quote it entire:

"The connection by blood betwixt Adam and his descendants constitutes a basis of unity by which, though numerically different as individuals, they may be treated as one collective whole. There is a close and intimate union, though not an identity, among the members of the human family. They are one race, one blood, one body—an unity, not like that of the Realists, growing out of the participation of a common objective reality, answering to the definition of a genus and species, but an unity founded in the relations of individual beings. It is this unity, and not the fancied identity of Dr. Baird, that distinguishes the family, the state, the church, the world. That the human race is not an aggregate of separate and independent atoms, but constitutes something analogous to an organic whole, with a common life springing from the intimate connection between the parts, is obvious from the very organization of society. There is one unity of nations, in consequence of which national character becomes as obtrusively marked as the peculiarities of individuals. There was one type among the Greeks, another among the Asiatics, still another among the Romans. The Englishman is in no danger of ever being mistaken for a Frenchman, and the Frenchman is not more distinguished from his continental neighbors by his language than by his habits, his sentiments, his modes of thought. These facts show that there is a bond among men, a fundamental basis of unity, which embraces the whole race. What it is we may be unable to define; we know, however, that it is connected with blood. The basis is that which justifies, but does not necessitate, God's dealing with the race in one man as a whole. So that Adam's federal headship is the immediate ground of our interest in his sin, and his natural headship is the ground of the representative economy."

Let the reader now compare this passage with that quoted from the lecture, and say whether the author did not, at least, *intend* to set his view in contrast with Dr. Baird's. He employs in both the same illustration of "the unity of nations" to set forth his idea of "generic unity" in opposition to the realistic notion of a "numerical identity." In the other passage of the *Review* (p. 563), he says:

"We are guilty; conscience testifies that we are guilty, that our native corruption is sin. But as we did not sin personally, as we did not sin naturally, we must have sinned vicariously. The only alternative is: In ourselves or in another. Ourselves are out of the question. Therefore we sinned in Adam, and our history truly began before our birth. Our appearance in time was not an absolute commencement, but moral relations preceded and determined it."

Here, again, he seems to intimate the doctrine of the lecture as different from that of Dr. Baird.

One of the most striking and delightful features of these lectures is the "unction" that pervades them from the beginning to the end. With the most relentless rigor of argument, a rigor which might satisfy any Doctor Irrefragabilis, or "*moulin raisonnant*," of a mediæval cloister or university, there is combined a fervor and sometimes an ecstasy of emotion which might satisfy a Doctor Seraphicus of the mystic school. The author was not of the opinion that because theology was a science it ought to be treated as an affair of the intellect only. He did not think it unseemly to express those powerful emotions which the truth of God is suited to excite, because he was in the professor's chair and not in the pulpit. When he is analyzing sin, he feels that he is handling a poison which has corrupted his own nature; and while his clear and subtle mind looks down into the depths, his own soul recoils with horror and disgust from what he sees there. When he is treating of God, his soul adores while his intellect explores. He holds religion to be "the spiritual knowledge of God," and, therefore, "not a single energy, intellectual, moral, or emotional, nor a state of mind in which each energy succeeds the other so rapidly as to make the impression that it is composed of them all as separate and separable elements." It is the whole energy of our being carried up to the highest unity; the concentration of our entire spiritual nature into one form of life; a condition in which intellect, conscience, and heart are blended into perfect union. "Spiritual cognition," according to him, "includes the perception of the beautiful and the good. The same energy which knows God unto salvation knows him in the unity of his being as the perfection of truth, beauty, and holiness. The perception of his glory is the effulgence of this unity." The author is "himself the great sublime he draws." God is contemplated by him as "the True, the Beautiful, and the Good"; and his whole being is poured out in these lectures in a stream of mingled love, thought, and adoration. All who have sighed, from Spencer down, for an edifying method of treating the science of theology, for a method which should stir the heart and purify and elevate the affections while it informed and strengthened the mind, might find their ideal realized here. Students of theology cannot make themselves too familiar with such a model. Private Christians, who are unable to rise to the height of this great argument, may yet imbibe something of the *tone* of these discussions. There is here a bracing, invigorating, spiritual atmosphere which no one can breathe without advantage to his soul's health.

II. We come now to notice his labors as a moral philosopher. The results of his thinking in this department, so far as this collection is concerned, are contained in the "Discourses on Truth," in the second volume.[1] These discourses were delivered as sermons to the students of the South Carolina College, in the regular course of his ministry as the chaplain of the college. They were published by the author himself; and this volume, indeed, was the only *treatise*, with the exception of the collection of *Letters on the Apocrypha*, which he ever published. He speaks of it, with characteristic modesty, as "an unpretending little volume." But in this case, as in many others, the merit is in inverse proportion to the pretension. It is, nominally, a series of discourses preached in the ordinary routine of his ministrations as chaplain in a college; it is, really, a series of profound discussions touching the very foundations of truth and duty; discussions so profound and searching, displaying such extraordinary subtlety and thoroughness of analysis, as to make it impossible that they should have been adequately understood, at the time of their delivery, by any other audience than one accustomed to listen to the more detailed expositions of the lecture-room. But they are not mere discussions. They are sermons, full of earnest exhortation, of pungent appeals to the conscience, of zealous remonstrances against all that is false, low, and dishonorable in human impulses and human conduct, and pervaded by a lofty and generous enthusiasm in the cause of truth and righteousness, which shows that

---

[1] We remember to have read a very thorough and masterly discussion of Paley's *System of Morals* from the pen of Dr. Thornwell in one of the quarterly reviews (*The Southern Review*, probably, during the short time that he was the editor of it). We trust that this article may appear in some future additional volume of his writings. For an account of this review (not *The Southern Presbyterian Review*) and Dr. Thornwell's connection with it, see Dr. Palmer's *Biography*, pp. 397 *et seq.*

the preacher is not contending for barren generalities of the schools, but for living principles which have moulded and controlled his own character and life. He speaks and writes in what the ancient masters of rhetoric called the "agonistic," or "wrestling," style; and there are few of his hearers or readers so athletic in stupidity or in wickedness as not to feel the force of his reasoning, and yield to the influence of his intense enthusiasm. We find no far-fetched fancies, no coruscation of brilliant images, introduced for the sake of coruscation, no effort to produce a "sensation," no chasing of tropical butterflies for the amusement of an auditory; but a solemn simplicity of purpose and a unity of design such as befits an ambassador of God rushing in between the living and the dead. Nothing can divert his eye, or relax the vigor of his arm, as he wrestles with dying men for their salvation. Happy or wretched are the young men who listen to such preaching! Supremely happy, if they give heed; supremely wretched, if they do not! Would that the lessons of these sermons might awaken the dull, cold ear of an age of sophists, economists, and calculators![1]

Before we pass from the sermons of Dr. Thornwell we cannot refrain from calling attention specially to the one entitled "The sacrifice of Christ, the type and model of missionary effort." We were in the Assembly in New York, in

---

[1] Among the papers of Dr. Thornwell the editor discovered the following note from Sir William Hamilton, which does honor to both these illustrious men:

"EDINBURGH, 23d *July*, 1855.

"*Rev. Dr. Thornwell:*

"SIR: I beg leave to return my warmest acknowledgments for your *Discourses on Truth.* I have read them with great interest and no less admiration. I was particularly pleased with the justice with which, it seems to me, you have spoken of the comparative merits of Aristotle as a moralist, and I cordially coincide with your judgment upon Paley and other modern ethical writers. I need hardly say that I feel much flattered by the way in which you have been pleased to make reference to myself; and I remain, sir, your most obedient servant, W. HAMILTON."

1856, before which this great sermon was preached, and shall never forget the impression it produced. Those who heard it seemed to be filled with awe produced by the greatness of the preacher; not only or chiefly by the greatness of his intellect, but by the greatness of his heart, filled and expanded as it was by the truth and by the mighty working of the Holy Ghost. It was of this sermon that Dr. Addison Alexander is reported to have said, "that it was as fine a specimen of Demosthenian eloquence as he had ever heard from the pulpit, and that it realized his idea of what preaching should be."

III. We come next, in this rapid and imperfect review, to notice the contents of the third volume, which, according to the arrangement and classification of the editors, contains the author's "controversial" writings. The contents are distributed under the heads of "rationalist controversy" and "papal controversy." The first embraces three essays: one on the "standard and nature of religion," the second on "the office of reason in regard to revelation," and the third on "miracles," their nature, their apologetic worth, and their credibility. A few words on each of these.

The paper on "the standard and nature of religion" was not so entitled by the author, but by the editors. It appeared in sections in *The Southern Presbyterian Review*, as a criticism upon Morell's *Philosophy of Religion*. This book of Morell's was doing great mischief. It was applauded not only by fools and sciolists, but even by good and sensible men, who had been deceived by its pious, hypocritical cant. We have a very distinct recollection of hearing a pastor of a large Presbyterian congregation in a large city say that he considered it one of the most edifying books he had ever read. He was astounded when he discovered that its pious phrases were a disguise for the most radical species of infidelity, an infidelity which was not satisfied with denying that the Bible was authenticated as a divine message by sufficient evidence, but asserted and attempted to prove, by reforming psychology, that any external revelation was an impossibility. In short, the infidelity of the *Philosophy of Religion* was almost identical with that which Henry Rogers so relentlessly demolishes and so mercilessly ridicules in the *Eclipse of Faith* and the *Defence of the Eclipse of Faith.* It is, indeed, no new phase of infidelity. It is as old, at least, as Ammonius Saccas; and Mosheim's account of the neo-platonic doctrines reads, in some parts, as if it were intended to describe the modern form of the error. The ancient and the modern sprang from a similar source, pantheism; and we find in both the same idea of an "absolute" religion, and the same hypocritical use of a phraseology which had been consecrated by the use of Christians to the expression of thoughts and emotions utterly different. None knew better than these deceivers "the fatal force and imposture of words," and they have practiced the imposture, from Ammonius down to Morell, with fatal success. Give us anything to contend with but a pious devil.

The criticism on Morell is divided into two parts. In the *first*, his book is considered as an argument, and the question discussed is: Granting his premises (the truth of his psychology), does the conclusion follow which he seeks to draw? In the *second*, the question is: Is his psychology sound? The *first* is a question of logic; the *second* is a question of philosophy. This whole discussion reveals the author's powers as a reasoner and a thinker more strikingly, perhaps, than any other of his productions, with the exception, perhaps, as to his power as a reasoner, of the work on the Apocrypha, to be afterwards noticed. The first part is a complete and overwhelming logical discomfiture of Morell. He has not left him an inch of ground to stand on. In the second part, if we do not find anything absolutely new, we find at least a very thorough-going explanation and defence of "the philosophy of common sense" against the German philosophy of the absolute, and against the scheme attempted by Cousin, of conciliation of the German philosophy with the Scotch philosophy of common sense. Here Dr. Thornwell shows himself a profound philosopher, as in the preceding part he had shown himself a masterly logician.

We quote a paragraph or two as a specimen of his manner:

"The philosophy with which Mr. Morell is impregnated is essentially arrogant; and it is more to it than to him that we ascribe the pretending tone of his work. The pervading consciousness of the weakness and ignorance of men, the diffidence of themselves, the profound impression of the boundlessness of nature and of the limitless range of inquiry which lies beyond the present grasp of our faculties, the humility, modesty, and caution which characterize the writings of the great English masters, will in vain be sought among the leading philosophers of modern Germany and France. Aspiring to penetrate to the very essence of things, to know them in themselves as well as in the laws which regulate their changes and vicissitudes, they advance to the discussion of the sublimest problems of God, the soul, and the universe, with an audacity of enterprise in which it is hard to say whether presumption or folly is most conspicuous. They seem to think that the human faculties are competent to all things; that whatever reaches beyond their compass is mere vanity and emptiness; that omniscience, by the due use of their favorite organon, may become the attainment of man as it is the prerogative of God, and that, in the very structure of the mind, the seeds are deposited from which may be developed the true system of the universe.

"Within the limits of legitimate inquiry we would lay no restrictions upon freedom of thought. All truly great men are conscious of their powers; and the confidence which they have in themselves inspires the strength, intensity, and enthusiasm which enable them to conceive and to execute purposes worthy of their gifts. To the timid and distrustful, their excursions may often seem bold and presumptuous; but in the most daring adventures of their genius they are restrained, as if by an instinct, from the visionary projects and chimerical speculations which transcend the sphere of their capacities, as the eagle, in his loftiest flights, never soars beyond the strength of his pinion. Confidence adjusted to the measure of power never degenerates in arrogance. It is the soul of courage, perseverance, and heroic achievement; it supports its possessor amid discouragements and obstacles; it represses the melancholy, languor and fits of despondency to which the choicest spirits are subject; it gives steadiness to effort, patience to industry, and sublimity to hope. But when men forget that their capacities are finite, that there are boundaries to human investigation and research, that there are questions which, from the very nature of the mind and the necessary conditions of human knowledge, never can be solved in this sublunary state—when they are determined to make their understandings the sole and adequate standard of all truth, and presumptuously assume that the end of their line is the bottom of the ocean—this is intolerable arrogance, the very spirit of Moloch,

> Whose trust was with the Eternal to be deemed
> Equal in strength; and rather than be less,
> Cared not to be at all.'"—Vol. III., pp. 11, 12.

The next paper, under the head of "Rationalistic Controversy," is entitled "The Office of Reason in Regard to Revelation." It was published in June, 1847, as the first article of the first volume of the *Southern Presbyterian Review*. The question which he considers here is not the office of reason in relation to doctrines *known* to be a revelation from God—where, of course, the understanding is simply to believe—but the office of reason where the reality of the revelation remains to be proved and the interpretation of the doctrine to be settled. The general principle is maintained, that the competency of reason to judge in any case is the measure of its right. And—a distinction being made in the contents of Scripture betwixt the supernatural or what is strictly revealed, and the natural or what is confirmed but not made known by the divine testimony—it is argued that the office of reason in the supernatural department of revelation may be *positive* but never can be *negative*, while in the natural it is negative, but to a very limited extent, if at all, positive. In other words, in the supernatural, reason may prove but cannot refute; in the natural, she may refute but cannot establish.

It is not to be supposed that this view of the office of reason would satisfy the infidel. In the first place, a difficulty would be made about the "supernatural" altogether. A professed revelation which contains supernatural elements is self-condemned. But in the second place, granting the supernatural, how shall we draw the line between it and the natural? The death of Jesus of Nazareth, for example, belongs to the natural in so far as it is an event in history capable of being established by the same sort of proof as the death of Cæsar or of Brutus. It is supernatural so far as its *meaning* is concerned, its relations to the government of God and to the salvation of men. So we say, and so the Bible teaches. We cannot know who this Jesus is, nor for what end he died, except by a revelation from God. But the infidel and Socinian think that all can be explained upon the principles of human nature and the principles of moral government. In the third place, the natural must not only be consistent with itself and with other natural knowledge, but has a right to demand that the supernatural shall show itself consistent with the natural. Here is the tug of war. It is perfectly plain that the Bible as a *revelation*, as that by which the supernatural contents of a divine message can alone be made known, must show itself to be such to the unbeliever by some external evidence which is palpable to the senses. The testimony of Jesus concerning himself is perfectly conclusive to those who are likeminded with himself. Their souls respond to his testimony readily and joyfully. "Though I bear witness of myself, my testimony is true." Amen! say all his people. But those who are not his people say: "Thou bearest witness of thyself; thy witness is not true" (not valid, not sufficient). The Saviour seems to concede the justness of the demand: "If I bear witness of myself, my witness is not true. There is another that beareth witness of me, . . . the works which the Father hath given me to finish, the same works that I do bear witness of me, that the Father hath sent me." The evidence of miracles, therefore, is that which he presents to unbelievers.

This brings us to the *third* paper, under the head of "Rationalist Controversy," the paper on miracles, their nature, apologetic worth, and credibility. It was first published in the *Southern Review* in July, 1857. Its peculiar value lies in the thorough analysis of the nature of testimony and of the conditions of its credibility. The possibility of an event is the sole limit to the credibility of testimony, and the possibility of the miracle is simply the question of the existence of a personal God. The author furnishes a complete polemic against rationalism as a method. He extracts it from our Saviour's reply to the Sadducees' question concerning the woman who had seven husbands. The Sadducees argued from *analogy*, from the principle that the unknown must be *like* the known (likelihood, probability); that if there was to be a resurrection state, it must be like the present, must have relations similar to the present, must have the marriage relation among others; and, therefore, it would be difficult to determine, in the case presented, whose wife of the seven the woman should be. The Saviour's answer exposes the fallacy of the method: "Ye do err, not knowing the Scriptures, nor the power of God." Ye err in supposing that you are dependent upon analogy for a knowledge of the resurrection state. You have an altogether different source of information: that of testimony, and the testimony of him alone who knows anything at all about the matter, God. This testimony is contained in the Scriptures which you, Sadducees, profess to receive as the word of God. Testimony does not depend for its validity upon the likelihood of its matter, but upon the competency and credibility of the witness. There is no limit to its credibility but possibility. And if you doubt the possibility of a state in which there shall be no marrying or giving in marriage, but human beings shall be like the angels—consider "the power of God." This power is a sufficient answer to all objections drawn from the antecedent improbability, unlikelihood of such a state.[1]

The principles here laid down by the Saviour are exceed-

[1] The illustrations of Dr. Thornwell's views here employed are taken mainly from his discussion of the same subject in a baccalaureate sermon on Matt. xxii. 29, published in this journal in April, 1851.

ingly fruitful in their applications. All arguments from analogy are subject to correction by authentic testimony. All the theories of geologists are subject to correction by the testimony of the Scriptures, if the Scriptures bear any testimony in reference to the matter, and the true meaning of that tesmony can be ascertained. Whether *this* application of the principle be allowed or not, the principle itself no sane man will dispute. Nothing can be idler than a controversy about this or that theory devised to account for certain facts, if credible testimony can be had as to the real historical origin of the phenomena.

Under the head of "'The Papal Controversy," we find two discussions, the first on the "Validity of Roman Baptism," and the other on the "Romanist Arguments for the Apocrypha." Our author, like every other man who loves the gospel and knows what Romanism is, judged that system to be the greatest and most dangerous enemy which the gospel has to encounter in this world. He was an ardent patriot, and fully concurred in the opinion of LaFayette that the liberties of this country were in danger from the machinations of papal priests. The "syllabus" had not then appered in which Rome declares herself the enemy of all modern civilization; but her whole history had shown that no part of the human race would be tolerated which did not acknowledge its subjection to her authority, and was not willing to subserve her schemes of avarice and ambition. Hence, he detested Rome with his whole soul, and was prompt to use his great talents in resisting her.

The treatise on the "Validity of Roman Baptism" originated in a speech made by him in the General Assembly at Cincinnati, in 1845, against the validity. The decision of the Assembly in accordance with his views was, no doubt, due to his great speech; and when the decision was attacked by *The Princeton Review*, he felt bound to appear in its defence. The speech and the defence at once gave him great reputation throughout the church; and Princeton gained nothing in reputation either for ability or learning in the contest with the young Timothy.

The paper adopted by the Assembly is a sort of brief of this article of our author. The principal ground on which the validity of papal baptism is denied is, that the sacraments belong to the visible church, and are its ordinances; where there is no church there is no baptism; but the papal body is no church, *ergo*, its baptism is no baptism. The General Assembly, in pronouncing Rome to be no church of Christ, simply followed in the track of the Reformers. But in deducing the conclusion from this position, that Roman baptism was not valid, they went further than the Reformers, and, we may add, were more logically consistent. We are constrained to admit that our author does not make out his case as against Princeton upon this particular point. Turretin, we apprehend, expressed the common view when he said that in Rome the sacrament of baptism was preserved "*integer quoad substantiam.*" (*Lib.* XVIII., Quest. 14, Par. 3.) So, also, in *Liber* XIX., Question 18, he decides that the true doctrine concerning baptism remains in that body, as to its essence, and that, therefore, baptism administered in Rome is to be considered valid, and not to be repeated.[1] This, indeed, was the counterpart of the Roman doctrine itself from the time of Stephen, in the third century, down; and the position of his great antagonist, Cyprian, who denied the validity of heretical baptism, was given up by the North-African church in Augustine's time. As before intimated, however, we think the position of our own church more consistent, a posi-

[1] Turretin, in the fourteenth paragraph of this question, gives three reasons why the baptism of the papists is not to be "iterated": 1. That the essence of the sacrament remains among them. 2. That its efficacy does not depend on the heretical administrator, but on Christ. 3. Because there are still some remains of a church in the papacy; now, baptism belongs to the church, etc. He seems to feel that the papacy must be in some sense acknowledged to be a church, or its baptism must be pronounced invalid.

tion it had assumed as early as 1835,as to the question whether the papal body is a church, and precisely analogous to the position it assumed in 1814 as to the Unitarian body and its ordinances. Within the last few years it has taken a similar attitude as to the Campbellite body. The church, in pronouncing this judgment, is, of course, not to be understood as denying that any members of these communions are saved. It simply affirms that they are destitute of the notes or marks of a visible church.

This treatise of Dr. Thornwell is well worthy of attentive study, not only in its bearings upon the question of the validity of Roman baptism, but as a masterly discussion of justification and sanctification, the water and the blood. The denial of these by Rome furnishes the most terrible indictment against her. She has abolished the gospel; and those who are saved within her pale are saved in spite of her.

The history of the origin of the other treatise needs not to be recounted here. Its beginning was "accidental," as the beginning of many great works has been, or has been called. It is sufficient to say that a controversy begun in Baltimore, was taken up in South Carolina by Bishop Lynch (then plain Mr. Lynch) of the papal body. Pugnacity is a trait not unexampled among the priests in that State. We remember a famous instance of a controversy there, concerning the existence and authority of the "Tax Book of the Roman Chancery," an infamous production of popery, in which all imaginable and unimaginable sins are set down, with the prices in money opposite, at which they may be committed. Bishop England was the champion on one side, and the late Dr. Fuller, of the Baptist Church, on the other. This controversy was transferred to Baltimore, or rather was *settled* there by Dr. R. J. Breckinridge, in a single article against Bishop England, which he never, so far as we know, attempted to answer. Both these priests were a little unfortunate in having adversaries who were not only too much for them, but were perhaps the ablest men in the American church. Certain it is, that the work of demolition performed by Breckinridge and Thornwell was complete.

The work on the Apocrypha was published in 1844, before the author had completed his thirty-second year. Critics who were not specially friendly to him acknowledged their amazement at the learning displayed. The first and only separate edition was full of errata. The author was at a great distance from the press, and the proofs were badly read, though read by one of the most learned men in the city of New York. The errors, however, were chiefly in the Greek and Latin notes, and have, no doubt, been corrected by the painstaking editors of the collection now before us. The title, *Romanist Arguments for the Apocrypha Discussed*, is a very modest one, and conveys a very inadequate idea of the range and completeness of the discussion. The author's mind was of such a cast that he could not be satisfied, like most controversialists, with merely answering the arguments or refuting the positions of his antagonists. He could never be content with merely "Thornwell *vs.* A. P. F." He must go to the bottom of the subject, and produce a work which should have a permanent value, independent altogether of the occasion which gave rise to it, and which determined its force. He who reads this work will find that it is not only a discussion of Romanist arguments for the Apocrypha, but an able treatise on the canon, and a crushing refutation of popery.

IV. We come now to consider the "ecclesiastical" writings of our author, as contained in the fourth volume of this collection. His influence as an ecclesiastic upon the church at large was more direct than his influence as a theologian. As a theologian, he could scarcely have been said to have any peculiar views, any views in which he did not have the sympathy of the great mass of the church. It was not so with his views of the nature, polity, mission of the church. The organs of a very large and respectable party pronounced many of his positions to be mere "whimsies," and the same section continues to act upon the views he opposed as unscriptural and dangerous, as hampering and limiting the liberty which Christ had bought for his people, as compelling them to walk by rules, like Jews, when it was their privilege to act upon "general principles," like freemen. We proceed to notice some features of his ecclesiasticism.

1. He insisted upon the rigorous observance and application of the great principle of the sufficiency of the Scriptures as a rule of faith and practice. He believed thoroughly the doctrine laid down in the first chapter of the Westminster *Confession*, that "the whole counsel of God concerning all things necessary for his own glory, man's salvation, faith, and life, is either expressly set down in Scripture, or by good and necessary consequence may be deduced from Scripture," while he admitted fully, what the *Confession* also admits, that "there are some circumstances concerning the worship of God and the government of the church, common to human actions and societies, which are to be ordered by the light of nature and Christian prudence, according to the general rules of the word, which are always to be observed." He urged that the liberty of the people of God was not a license to walk in the light of their own eyes, restrained only by the prohibitions of the word, but that it consisted in being governed by the word only, and in being "free from the commandments of men"; that the discretionary power contended for by the other side was a power to enslave the Lord's freemen, it being a power to make laws which the people were bound to obey; that this had been the history of the exercise of such a power, especially on a grand scale, in the papacy and in the Church of England; and that the martyrs had contended against it even unto blood.

It may seem strange that we should seem, by implication at least, to charge eminent ministers in our own church, who have solemnly adopted the *Confession of Faith*, with denying its doctrine on so fundamental a point. We do not mean to assert that they intend to deny it. We do not impeach their integrity. But we all know that even great men may hold doctrines unconsciously which cannot be reconciled. There have been few greater minds than that of Augustine, and few teachers have controlled the thinking of the church as he has done. Yet Augustine held two sets of views, which were utterly at variance with each other; his views of grace on the one hand, and his views of the church and the sacraments on the other. There was no conflict in his own mind. But the legacy he bequeathed to the church in his writings contained both, and the conflict was obliged to come. It did come. The history of the Middle Age is, in great part, a history of this conflict. The Thomists represented the one set, and the Scotists the other set, of doctrines. After the Reformation, which was itself a triumph of Augustine's doctrine of grace over Augustine's doctrine of the church, we find the conflict revived in the sixteenth century between the Dominicans and the Jesuits, and again in the seventeenth, between the Jansenists and the Jesuits. It does not follow, therefore, that because a great and good man holds the truth in the main, he may not hold serious error, which may be all the more pernicious by virtue of the reputation he has acquired in the exposition and defence of the truth.

We only mean to assert, therefore, in the case before us, that the brethren on the other side give such a latitude of meaning to the word "circumstances" in the *Confession*, as virtually to deny the sufficiency of the Scriptures as a rule, and to invest the church with a discretionary power, limited only by the prohibitions of the word. The "general principles" by which they contend that the church is to be governed in matters of polity and worship seem to be "regulative" only, principles which define only ends to be aimed at, or conditions to be observed; while the other side contends that the general principles are "constitutive" also, determining the concrete forms in which those ends are to be realized. The Scriptures, for example, not only lay down the regulative principle of the parity of the ministry, but they give us also the constitutive principle, that the jurisdiction of the ministers is to be exercised jointly with elders who are not ministers, in courts called presbyteries. Again, according to one view, the "circumstances" of the *Confession* are inseparable adjuncts of the action as such, and so surround it (*circum stant*) that they cannot be separated from it. According to the other view, circumstances are attending adjuncts which may be separated from it, but which need not be separated, if they are not forbidden in the word. Of circumstances in the first sense, we have an example in the appointment of time and place for the assemblies of the church, the use of moderators, committees, etc. *Every* assembly, sacred or civil, implies an agreement as to the time and place of meeting. Every *deliberative* assembly must have a chairman and committees, in order to accomplish its business with decorum and despatch. Of circumstances in the second sense, we have an example in a liturgy, or in instrumental music. Public prayer can be performed, and was performed for two centuries, at least, without a liturgy; the service of praise for nine centuries, at least, without an instrument of music.

This statement will remind our readers of the Puritan controversy in the Church of England. That was mainly a controversy about these very circumstances, in connection with the great principle of the sufficiency of the Scriptures as a rule. The "general principle" insisted on by the Puritan leaders was that nothing be added to the rule; that the Bible was the charter, the constitution, the statute-book of the kingdom of Christ; that all which was not granted was for this very reason to be deemed prohibited; that all additions to the word, if not explicitly prohibited, are, at least, implicitedly prohibited in the general command that "nothing be added." This was the ground upon which Dr. Thornwell took his stand in the controversy about "boards," denying that a board was a "circumstance," in the sense of our *Confession*, and asserting that it was an unauthorized addition to the law given to the church for doing its work.

We have dwelt the longer on this position of Dr. Thornwell on account of its fundamental importance considered in itself, and on account of its importance in his own ecclesiology and churchmanship. The intrinsic importance of the principle cannot be overrated. It is a question whether the church shall walk by faith in her great head, or in the light of her own wisdom; whether she shall depend for success in her work on a worldly policy, or on the ordinances of Christ, administered by the power of the Holy Ghost. There have always been "two manner of people" in the bowels of the church: a people who insist upon walking according to the rule given of God, "strict constructionists," and a people who insist on the right to make additions to the rule as exigencies may demand, "latitudinarians"; a people who testify that "our faith must not stand in the wisdom of man, but in the power of God," and a people who contend that our faith must stand in the wisdom of man as well as in the power of God. We believe "the Presbyterian Church in the United States" to be as pure as any other on earth; but even in *her* bowels these two manner of people are found. In how many of *her* congregations do the people humble themselves before God with fasting and prayer for the quickening power of the Holy Ghost, when the ordinances of Christ seem barren? In how many do they resort for help to inventions of their own? Is there no congregation in which the people trust more in the breath of a bellows than in the breath of the Spirit? None in which fairs and festivals are more relied upon for revenue than upon the grace of God in the hearts of his people? How many Presbyterians, not to say Protestants, act habitually on the principle that the Bible, and the

Bible alone, is their religion? We do not doubt that the hopes of final victory in this country and in England which inspire the papal hierarchy are built upon the fact that the most pronounced Protestants are to so great an extent conforming themselves to the principles and maxims which have made the papal communion what it is. Papal Rome was not built in a day. *Nemo repente fit turpissimus.* We are very far from being idolaters like the Romanists, a thousand voices will exclaim, and we do not intend to be. So, doubtless, the Church of Rome would have said at the close of the second century. But, behold it now! and ponder the wisdom of the maxim, "*Obsta principiis.*"

2. This principle of the Bible, and the Bible alone, led Dr. Thornwell to his position as to the nature and scope of the church's *mission.* An opinion or feeling existed to a considerable extent, if it might not be called a prevailing opinion, that every good thing, good in the sense of conducive to the welfare of man in this life as well as in the life to come, fell within the proper scope of the church's mission. She was to be a great philanthropist, as well as a witness for God and a preacher of salvation. She was to patronize every association which had for its object the relief of human distress, or the promotion of human comfort. She was to patronize even the government of the civil commonwealth, direct it or correct it, if necessary or practicable, since the temporal welfare of men was so dependent upon the character of its administration. Hence, resolutions of the General Assembly commending temperance societies, colonization societies, and what not. Hence, resolutions condemning the institution of slavery. Hence, at last, resolutions asserting Federalism to be the true theory of the Constitution, and condemning the theory of "States' rights."

Now, Dr. Thornwell did not deny that some of these things might be good things. Much less did he deny that the mission of the church was a philanthropic mission; that the results of a faithful fulfilment of it would promote in the highest degree the temporal welfare of men. He was a philanthropist of the highest style and of the most ardent sort; not a *humanitarian* philanthropist, but a *divine*. He held that the highest welfare of men was subordinate to the glory of God; subordinate, not hostile or opposed; subordinate, yet in harmony with it, moving in the same plane with it. The church's *sole* function was to be a witness for God, to be an expounder and administrator of his revealed will, both law and gospel. She had no vocation to interfere with any human institution directly, but to declare the law for all moral relations, and to condemn all immoral. She had no vocation to manage benevolent societies, but to leaven the whole community with the principles of the gospel, which, while they are "glory to God," are also "good will to men." She had no commission to direct or to correct the political administration, but so to saturate the community with the Spirit of Jesus Christ that magistrates would rule with justice, truth, and moderation, and the people would obey the laws with cheerfulness and for conscience sake. He held that this legitimate influence of the church was the more powerful for being *indirect;* that history would confirm this view; that in the so-called theocracies (New England, for example), where the church was made τὸ πᾶν, the church became corrupt by handling matters which were secular and did not belong to her; and, having become corrupt, lost her influence upon the community for good, and exerted an influence for evil.

It required no small nerve to maintain this view of the church's mission. He would, of course, be charged with being unfriendly to colonization, or temperance, and so on. But he had the sublime courage which the possession of God's truth, and the conviction that it *is* his truth, impart. He testified, whether men heard or forbore. If these principles had been acted on by the church, how much sin and misery would have been prevented! But most men seem to be incapable of comprehending principles. Statesmen like Edmund Burke, and ecclesiastics like Thornwell, who, by the constitution of their minds and their intellectual training, are "seers," do not frequently appear. The vast majority must wait to see how a principle works, must wait for results, in order to make up their minds. The process of reasoning in the minds of enthusiastic managers of societies is something like this: Whoever is opposed to *this* way of doing the good thing is opposed to the good thing itself. You are opposed to *this* way of doing, etc. *Ergo, etc.* Others who are not managers, and who have no interest, or very little, in the object or the means, take some credit to themselves for voting to recommend it, and put on an air of pious surprise that any people professing to be good should oppose so benevolent an institution. Human nature is a bundle of contradictions; but in any large body of men, we may generally count, with a considerable degree of certainty, upon their showing more indignation when the wisdom of their own inventions is questioned than when the ordinances of God are violated, provided these ordinances have not a *very* obvious bearing for good upon their temporal welfare.

3. Another position of Dr. Thornwell intimately connected with the foregoing, but a position not at all peculiar to himself, was one which concerned the relation of the civil to the ecclesiastical power, or of the state to the church. The true doctrine was expounded very clearly by him in "the letter of the General Assembly of the Confederate States of 1861 to the churches of Christ throughout the world." We do not propose to dwell upon it here, as there is no difference of judgment about it theoretically in this country; certainly none in our own church, and, we believe, none in any other. The papal body, of course, abhors the American doctrine, and is plotting to subjugate the civil power to itself. This it has recently itself proclaimed in "the syllabus"; and the

syllabus is simply a reiteration of the principles avowed by Rome since the days of Hildebrand, and before. We do not recognize that body as a church at all, but as a political empire, like the Roman, which preceded it; with this difference only, that the old pagan maintained its authority and extended its dominion by the iron hand only; the papal by ghostly means always, and by the iron hand when possible.

4. It is only in connection with another position of Dr. Thornwell, that we have noticed at all his view of the relations of church and state. The position referred to is contained in a "memorial" presented to the first General Assembly of our church, held in Augusta, Georgia, in the year 1861. It may be found in the fourth volume of his writings, pages 549 *et seq.* From the doctrine and purpose of this memorial, we are obliged to enter our decided and emphatic dissent. If our readers have had the patience to read this article thus far, they will find no difficulty in believing us when we say that we record our dissent with the greatest reluctance. Yet it was in *his* school that we learned to call no man master. To him, if to any man, the line of Horace might be applied—

> "Nullius addictus jurare in verba magistri,"

and the independence which he exercised himself he inculcated on others. In expressing the different views which we hold, we are not conscious of doing anything inconsistent with the profound veneration we feel for his memory. Indeed, we have a strong impression that we are not dissenting from a view of Dr. Thornwell's which he had long and carefully considered, but from one taken up and presented under the impulse of a glowing patriotism. Next to the interests of the church, that which lay nearest to his heart was the interests of the infant Confederacy. He longed to have it baptized with the name of Christ and dedicated to his service. If he were now alive, and could see who they are in the Northern States who are advocating his doctrine, we believe he would at least give the subject a thorough reconsideration.

But this is more than enough of apology, even if any at all were called for.

The amendment he proposed to be made in the Constitution of the Confederate States (to the section providing for liberty of conscience) was in these words: "Nevertheless, we, the people of these Confederate States, distinctly acknowledge our responsibility to God, and the supremacy of his Son, Jesus Christ, as King of kings and Lord of lords; and hereby ordain that no law shall be passed by the Congress of these Confederate States inconsistent with the will of God as revealed in the Holy Scriptures."

It is impossible for us to go into an argument here to show that such an amendment to the Constitution would be utterly inconsistent with the theory of the relation of church and state, as held in the United States and held by Dr. Thornwell himself; that it is a virtual confounding of the spheres of the two powers; and that its inevitable effect would be the infringement of the liberty of conscience. We content ourselves with simply recording our dissent and protest. The reader who wishes to see some of the grounds on which such an amendment would be resisted may consult the article on "Church and State" in this journal for October, 1863.[1] The views of that article have been immensely strengthened by events which have occurred since it was written; events which, we are firmly persuaded, would have lead Dr. Thornwell to recoil from his position, or at least to give it a careful reconsideration.

5. We pass from this, the only unpleasant part of our task, to consider next his views of Presbyterianism. These are contained in the papers which his editors have published under the heads of "Church Officers" and "Church Operations" in the fourth volume. We must be brief in our notices of them, as the space allotted to us is almost exhausted.

And *first*, as to the relation of all church officers to the

[1] Vol. XVI., No. 2.

church itself, he held that they were *representatives;* that the rulers were representatives as to rule, and the deacons representatives as to their functions, the custody and distribution of the revenues. This view is opposed to the view, on the one hand, of papists and high church prelatists, and, on on the other, to the view of Congregationalism as distinct from Independency.[1]

The papists hold that all power, both as to its being and its exercise (in the language of the schools, both in "the first act" and "the second act"), is lodged in the clergy alone. The Congregationalists lodge it, in both acts, in the brotherhood alone. Hence, their sameness of views as to the nature of the privilege of election of officers—both holding that election belongs to the power of government. But they draw very different conclusions from the doctrine that election belongs to the power of government. The argument of the papist, as stated by Bellarmine, is: "The power of election belongs to government. It belongs not to the people to govern. *Ergo,* it belongs not to the people to elect." The argument of the Congregationalist is: "The power of election belongs to government. The power of election belongs to the people. *Ergo,* the power of government belongs to the people." The Presbyterian of Dr. Thornwell's school denies

[1] The terms Congregationalism and Independency are often used interchangeably. But when distinguished, the former has reference to the *subject* (*materia in qua*) of church power, the Congregationalists holding that the power, both as to its *being* and in its *exercise*, is lodged in "the brotherhood"; the latter having reference to the nature of the unity of the church, the Independents holding that every congregation statedly worshipping in one place is a *complete* church, and therefore denying the authority of synods, or of all courts, above that which governs a single congregation. All Congregationalists are Independents, but all Independents are not Congregationalists. Independency is the genus, Congregationalism a species or variety. The Independents of Savoy (in London) were not Congregationalists; at least their leader, John Owen, was not, as anybody may see by consulting his "True Nature of a Gospel Church." The Independents were strong in the Westminster Assembly, the Congregationalists were weak.

the principle which is common to both syllogisms, and asserts that election belongs only to the process by which the government is constituted: "*Pertineat ad gubernationem et regimen constituendum, non tamen est actus regiminis aut gubernationis.*" According to the view of popery, the ministry is a *caste*, having no life in common with the people. According to the Congregational view, the ministry is simply the *proxy* of the people. According to Presbyterianism, the ministry is the *representative* of the people. The difference between a proxy and a representative is, that the former merely obeys the people and carries out their wishes, while it is the duty of the latter to consult the interests of the people, whether in accordance with their wishes or not. The eye sees *for* the body, while it is the body that sees *by* the eye.

The occasion for bringing forward the representative character of church officers was twofold. It was asserted, or strongly insinuated, as to the minister of the word, that he was not a representative of the people; that he was a member of a sort of caste, holding his place in the higher courts by a tenure independent of the people. It was asserted, or strongly insinuated, that the ruling elder was a representative of the people only in the sense of appearing for them as a proxy where it was inconvenient for them to appear *in propria persona.* In other words, it seemed to be attempted, in theory at least, to convert our government into a mixture of prelacy and democracy. In opposition to this mongrel government our author and the brethren on his side contended that Presbyterian government was a government by assemblies, consisting of presbyters, chosen rulers of the church; and these of two sorts, teaching and ruling presbyters, equal in rank or order, but differing in function; both representatives of the people, the one class more directly (like the members of the lower House of Congress), the other class indirectly (like the senators of the upper House).

According to this view, the ruling elder is called "the representative of the people" in our book, not as asserting that he is the only representative (to the exclusion of the minister), but for the same reason that the members of the lower House of Congress are called "representatives"—because that term is an adequate description of their office. The members of the lower House are representatives of the people as to law-making, and nothing more. The Senate consists of chosen rulers, who are representatives of the people as to law-making, and something more, to-wit, as to certain "executive" functions.

2. This brings us to another question between the same parties: "What is the meaning of *presbyter* in the New Testament?" Is it synonymous with preacher or minister of the word? Dr. Thornwell denied, the brethren of the other part affirmed. The importance of the question is very obvious. If presbyter means preacher and nothing else, then there are no elders but preachers; then the officer known as "the ruling elder" is not entitled to the name; he is no presbyter or elder, has no proper place in a presbytery, which is a college of presbyters; he is a mere proxy or deputy of the people, to make known to the presbyters (preachers) in presbytery assembled what the humble wishes of the people may be. His *jus divinum* is clean gone. He has no rights given him of God as ruling elder which the church is bound to respect. It was held that a presbytery might be legally constituted without his presence; and that for him to assume the right to lay on his hands in the ordination of a minister, because the Bible and our book said a minister should be ordained by the laying on of the hands of the presbytery, was sheer audacity. He had no such right on another account: "*Nemo dare potest quod non habet*"; "Like begets like."[1] Any number of wise saws might be

[1] Why not quote also, Dr. Thornwell suggests, from the parody of Johnson, "Who drives fat oxen must himself be fat"?

quoted to show that a man who is not a preacher cannot make, or help make, a preacher; much less can a ruling elder, who is not even a presbyter or proper member of a presbytery, help in such a work. All these plausibilities were blown to atoms by the arguments of Breckinridge and Thornwell. It was established beyond contradiction that the meaning of presbyter was not "preacher," but "ruler"; that preachers are called presbyters, not because they preach, but because they rule; and, therefore, that there may be presbyters who do not preach. It was further shown that in accordance with these views of the meaning of the term, the apostolic church had rulers who did not preach, and that this feature of the apostolic polity lingered in parts of the church (North Africa, for instance) as late, at least, as the middle of the third century.[1] The right divine of the ruling elder having been established, it was very easy to show that his hands would not profane a minister's head in the ceremony of ordination, or interrupt the current of spiritual electricity as it was passing from the hands of the ministers, by showing that the elders of the whole congregation ordained of old the tribe of Levi, and that there was no current of spiritual electricity to flow or to be interrupted.

These discussions revealed the fact that no small amount of prelatical error still lingered even in the Presbyterian Church. This fact was specially manifest in the denial of the right of the ruling elder to lay on hands in the ordination of a minister. Ordination was practically treated as a sacrament. The administration of it, therefore, belonged, like that of other sacraments, to the minister of the word, and "a layman," like the ruling elder, could take no part in

[1] Calvin says in his commentary on 1 Timothy v. 17, after noticing that the passage implies that there were then two kinds of presbyters, and that all were not ordained to preach, "Ambrose (Bishop of Milan, †397) laments that this custom had become obsolete by the negligence of the teachers, or rather, by their pride, because they wished to be eminent alone."

it. Dr. Thornwell did great service to the church in recalling its attention to the true nature of ordination as simply a formal recognition and publication of the fact that God, in the judgment of the church, expressed by one of its courts, had called the ordained man to the office. There was nothing in the ceremony of ordination, therefore, which made it improper for the ruling elder to take part in it. Ordination does not make a man a minister, as the prelatical doctrine affirms. It is an act of a *court*, sitting under the law of Christ, which prescribes the qualifications of a minister, and finding a verdict according to the law and the evidence. It is an act precisely analogous to that of a court admitting a person to the communion of the church. The law of Christ prescribes the qualifications of a church member. The court inquires whether A B has these qualifications; and if it finds that he has, the verdict is that God gives him a right to communion. The session does not make him a member, or give him a right to communion. It simply recognizes the fact that the right has been given him of God.

3. Thus far, two distinctive features of Presbyterian polity have been noticed: *first*, its governing by parliamentary assemblies of representatives; *secondly*, its representatives being all presbyters, but of two sorts—teaching presbyters and presbyters who rule without teaching. One more feature remains to complete the view, and that is the mode in which it realizes the idea of the unity of the church. The idea of the unity is realized by the elasticity of the representative system. Its method is opposed to that of Rome, which also attempts to realize the unity, as the principle itself of the unity is opposed to Independency. As against Independency, Presbyterianism holds that two or more congregations may be united under one government. This is the principle. The extent of its application, or exemplification, is "a circumstance" common to human societies, which is to be regulated "by the light of nature and Christian prudence, according to

the general rules of the word." If there was but one congregation of saints in the world, the presbytery governing that congregation would be the parliament of the whole church. Let the congregations be increased a hundred or a thousand fold, the unity of the whole would be represented by a parliament composed of presbyters from the parts. On the other hand, the *method* of realizing the unity differs as widely from the method adopted by Rome as the principle differs from the principle of Independency. Rome realizes the unity by a *graded* hierarchy composed of officers of different ranks and orders, the pyramid being capped by a supreme pontiff at Rome, who embraces within himself all powers and rights, and delegates, as he pleases, powers and rights to be exercised by all the officers below him. Presbyterianism realizes the unity by a series of courts composed, all of them, of exactly the same officers, the highest court being, of course, the representative of the unity of the whole. These courts are the organs through which the one body acts. The life is in the whole and in every part; the life of the whole is in every part; and the life of the whole controls the life of every part. The judges of the lower courts, in some of the States of this Union, constitute "in bank" a court of appeals; but the same commonwealth appears in all the courts, confronting the criminal by the indictment, as an offender against its majesty, alike in the court of original jurisdiction and in the court of last resort. But let it be well observed, the General Assembly and the session are composed of the same elements. Every ruling elder who sits in the Assembly belongs to some church session. "Of such a council as this," says Milton, "every parochial consistory is a right homogeneous and constituting part; being in itself a little synod, and towards a general assembly, moving upon her own basis in an even and firm progression, as those smaller squares in battle unite in one great cube, the main phalanx, an emblem of truth and steadfastness." ("Reason of Church Government urged against Prelaty," Chap. VI.) The Presbyterian method of realizing the unity of the church protects the rights of its private members; the Roman method destroys them. Rome is a great iron wheel of which individuals and tribunals are only spokes. Presbyterianism is a wheel which contains within it a multitude of wheels, each having a life and movement of its own, yet all instinct with the spirit of the living creature, which is in the wheel.

We are now prepared for Dr. Thornwell's definition of Presbyterianism—the only satisfactory definition we have ever met with: "Presbyterianism is the government of the church by parliamentary assemblies, composed of two classes of presbyters, and of presbyters only, and so arranged as to realize the visible unity of the whole church."

Here we make an end. It has been a great delight to us to follow the track of the illustrious thinker whose writings we have been reviewing. We trust we have not failed to impress the reader, who has followed us to the end, with the conviction that there are treasures of thought in Dr. Thornwell's works which will amply repay the most assiduous study. Our exhortation to all, and especially to all students of theology, may be summed up in the line of Horace in reference to the Greek authors,—

> "Nocturna versate manu, versate diurna."

INDEX OF SCRIPTURES

REFERRED TO IN THE PRECEDING PAPERS.

NOTE.—This Index is *approximately* complete—ED.